pg. 133 - Christian church
142
206
209
210 - windows - 1820
212
215
220
224
321
339
355

Hanna's TOWN

W. WILLIAM WIMBERLY II

Indiana Historical Society Press | Indianapolis 2010

Printed in the United States of America

This book is a publication of the
Indiana Historical Society Press
Eugene and Marilyn Glick Indiana History Center
450 West Ohio Street
Indianapolis, Indiana 46202-3269 USA
www.indianahistory.org
Telephone orders 1-800-447-1830
Fax orders 1-317-234-0562
Online orders @ http://shop.indianahistory.org

The paper in this publication meets the minimum requirements of American National Standard for Information Sciences—Permanence of Paper for Printed Library Materials, ANSI Z39. 48–1984

Library of Congress Cataloging-in-Publication Data

Wimberly, W. William.
Hanna's town : a little world we have lost / W. William Wimberly II.
p. cm.
Includes bibliographical references and index.
ISBN 978-0-87195-289-9 (cloth : alk. paper) 1. Wabash (Ind.)—History. 2. Wabash (Ind.)—Social life and customs. 3. Community life—Indiana—Wabash—History. 4. Social change—Indiana—Wabash—History. 5. Wabash (Ind.)—Social life and customs. 6. Wabash (Ind.)—Biography. 7. Hanna, Hugh, 1799-1869. I. Title.
F534.W2W56 2010
977.2'83—dc22

2010017859

Publication of this book was made possible by the generous support of the following donors: Community Foundation of Wabash County, Ford Meter Box Foundation, Charley Creek Foundation, and Richard E. Ford.

To my wife Tracy Temple Wimberly;

to our parents: Ware W. Wimberly, Isabel Connelly Wimberly,
Howard Rex Temple, and Julia Ann Smallwood Temple;

to Tracy's and my offspring: Ware III, Maggie, Amira,
Alexander, Kiran, Eva, and Amos;

to our closest living kin: Jane, Izzy Lou, Tony, B B., Johnny Bill;

to the rest of this expanding family, all of it,
both the Quick and the Dead;

and to all who have called Wabash, Indiana, home.

Contents

Acknowledgments

In my pursuit of the present work, *Hanna's Town*, the person who heads a long list of those to whom I am indebted is Tracy Temple Wimberly, herself a product of Wabash County pioneer stock. She has been a strong-minded critic of style, language usage, and punctuation; and she is also the strong-hearted wife whom I love and whose marital calling seems to be to approve of me and of my works despite manifest deficiencies therein. Others in my immediate family—Ware III, Alexander, Kiran, Jane, Izzy, and Bob—maintained high levels of encouragement during the long research and writing stages; several of them read *Hanna's Town* in manuscript form and offered helpful suggestions.

A great many others have also contributed to the completion of *Hanna's Town*. I am indebted to Wabash County Historian, Ronald L. Woodward, who has been supportive since a day in 2004 when I walked into the county museum to ask him for information about Hugh Hanna. Since then he has answered many questions, guided me in many directions and, in the end, vetted the manuscript I produced. Pete Jones, another historian, answered scores of questions about nineteenth-century Wabash and sent me numerous references about people, places, and events from his own vast files. He also vetted the manuscript, as did his wife, Susie. Pete's journalist brother, Steve, likewise answered questions and shared aspects of his own research.

I am especially grateful for the staff of the Wabash County Historical Museum, an institution that has been wonderfully rejuvenated and reinvented into a showcase of local antiquity, so very different from the musty "Civic Attic" in Memorial Hall that I frequented as a boy. The staff of the present museum gave me free access to its archival holdings, including the hard copies of newspapers dating back to 1847; I did not have to read newspapers on microfilm but could handle the originals at will, which was a huge advantage in completing my research. The museum's archivist, Heather Allen, has become a good friend over the many months of my research as she and I asked each other questions about Wabash's past and then tried to dig up the answers in the archive's considerable collection. In addition to Heather, the museum's director Tracy Stewart and her associates Judy Bayshore, Bill Barnes, Art Conner, Brian Haupert, Lisa Iverson, Lois Knecht, Jennifer McSpadden, Marion Meek, Emily Perkins, Jane Purdy, Judy Randas, Jim Ridenhour, and John Rockwell were ever hospitable and helpful.

Many others have offered their encouragement and specialized points of view: friends or classmates such as Sharon Beauchamp, Richard Bird, Virginia Ford, Martha Biggerstaff Jones, John Koenig, Jane Shroyer Skeans, Frank and Betty Stewart, Graden and Shirley Walter; John Wardlaw; school superintendent Celia Shand; businessmen Jack Francis, Kent Henderson, and Tom Kelch; local historian and genealogist Susan Neff; canal historian Tom Castaldi; geologist Jack Sunderman; Phi Gamma Delta executive William Martin; the staff of the Wabash Carnegie Public Library; homeowners Robert and Laurie Kiefaber, Loren Watkins, and Susan Winger; attorney Donn Alspaugh and his wife Kathleen; and various acquaintances such as Judy Cheatham, Ken Crace, Trula Cramer, Joe Eddingfield, David Ericsson, Linda Gable, Gladys Dove Harvey, Posey Jasen, Mary Kramer, Christopher Lee, Carrie Makin, Beth Stein, Gaynel and Jim Vickery, and Cathy Wright, all of whom shared tidbits of information or clues about the past.

The Charley Creek Foundation of Wabash, the Community Foundation of Wabash County, and the Ford Meter Box Foundation of Wabash have graciously contributed to technical and monetary aspects of publication. I am especially grateful to boyhood chum, classmate, philanthropist, and Sagamore of Charley Creek, Richard Edwin Ford, for his support of this project.

Any profits from sales of the book will be donated to charitable causes within Wabash County.

Although I probably inherited a natural interest in history from my father, it was Professor L. C. Rudolph, formerly of Indiana University's Lilly Library, who kindly guided my first efforts at professional research. Much later, Indiana University professor James Madison encouraged me to pursue publication of *Hanna's Town.* More recently I have become indebted to my editor Paula Corpuz for helping me craft the final version. Assisted by Kathy Breen, Paula has patiently led me through the maze of editing and the tangle of footnotes and never complained about my unsophisticated relationship with computer technology. I feel fortunate that *Hanna's Town* qualified to be one of the last projects prior to her retirement from the Indiana Historical Society Press, which she has served so honorably for many years.

I apologize to any whom I have failed to thank. I apologize also for factual errors readers might find in *Hanna's Town*; they are all mine and no one else's.

I have been daily mindful of how much fun it has been to do my research as a resident of Wabash again (after a forty-seven-year absence). I found answers to a great many of my questions about Wabash's past simply by being able to jump in a car on the spur of the moment to go in search of a clue or a fact that existed "in situ" at a cemetery, along a downtown street, or in residential areas. Those frequent jaunts through town have confirmed for me that Wabash is a wonderful little city with an enviable past, and, I trust, a promising future.

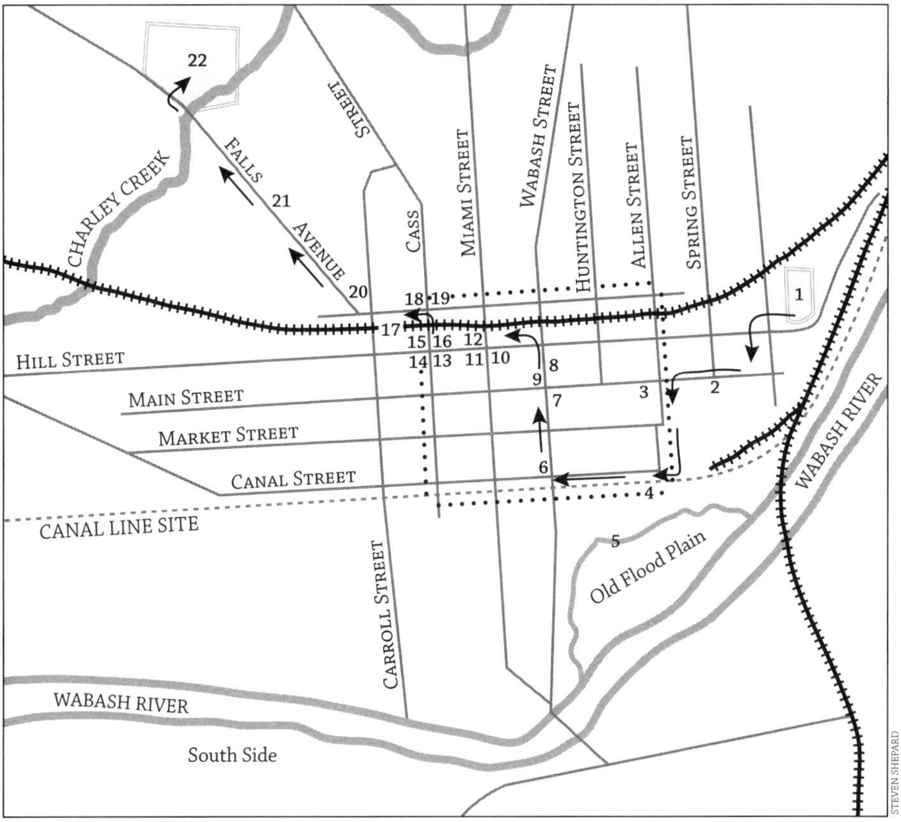

Map indicating the route of the 1902 funeral cortege described in the prologue.

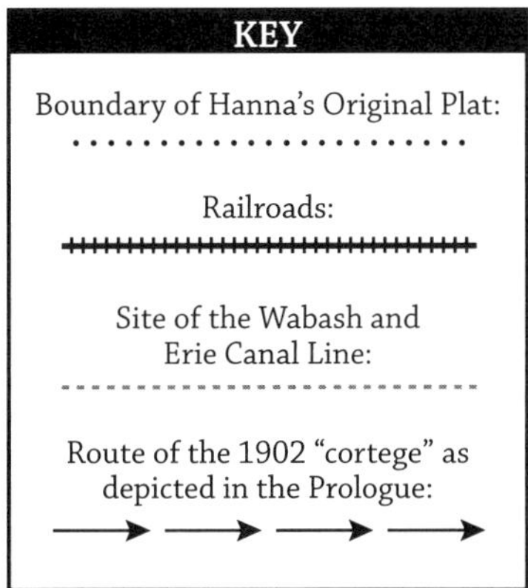

The forty to sixty foot high bluff which cuts east and west through Wabash lies roughly between Market and Hill streets.

1. Hanna (Old) Cemetery
2. Hanna's House
3. J. D. Conner's house
4. Site of Hanna's slaughterhouse
5. Site of Hanna's millrace and mill
6. Hanna's Corner
7. Masons' Hanna Lodge
8. Site of First Presbyterian Church
9. Site of Hanna's courthouse
10. Memorial Hall
11. Presbyterian Church
12. Christian Church
13. James Ford house
14. High School site
15. Thomas McNamee house
16. Site of future public library
17. Wabash Railroad
18. Methodist Church
19. Roman Catholic Church
20. Rodef Shalom Jewish Synagogue
21. George King house
22. Falls (New) Cemetery

Prologue: A Translation of Bones[1]

In late autumn 1902 a macabre scene unfolded at the original burial ground of Wabash, Indiana, which had been called both the Old Cemetery and Hanna's Cemetery. It lay at the eastern extremity of the town, five blocks from the county courthouse. Although picturesquely sited on a gentle, shaded knoll high above a bend in the Wabash River three hundred yards distant, the graveyard had fallen into disrepair, weeds grew unheeded, briars grabbed at visitors' clothing, many graves were unmarked or untended, and the fence around the cemetery was disintegrating. The cemetery's dereliction had long been an object of public shame and complaint. In the past cattle had roamed freely in the area; hogs had rooted about the graves and from time to time human skeletal parts had been exposed when new interments were attempted in the overcrowded grounds. On probably November 18 or 19, 1902, Judge J. D. Conner met in the cemetery with workmen from Clark Brothers, a local monument firm. Conner was an aging patrician of the town, a slender, bony man with a carefully trimmed white beard.

The task at hand was the disinterment of four bodies, all of whom were relatives of Conner's wife, Julia Hanna Conner. The newest of the four graves held whatever might be left of the corpse of Colonel Hugh Hanna, Julia's father, who had died in January 1869. The cortege that had followed his coffin to the Old Cemetery that distant winter was then the largest ever gathered in Wabash County. Hanna's grave was clearly marked, despite the weeds. Its stone was a tall obelisk of white marble rising from stepped marble blocks. The remains of Hanna's wife, daughter, and mother-in-law shared the family plot, with the names of the four carved into the four sides of the obelisk.

Digging began. It must have taken several hours, longer surely than might be required for graves with their contents still intact, where an exhumation would be mostly a matter of raising a whole casket to the surface. This disinterment was a bits-and-pieces affair, requiring a careful sifting of detritus and soil, for after three-plus decades little survived of the cadavers beyond a medley of bones. Local newspapers reported the grim inventory in some detail, though not in enough detail to satisfy gratuitous curiosity. The caskets had dissolved, and the bones "were not consumed." Found also was a paucity of artifacts: Hanna's shoes; the hair and hair comb of Julia Everly, Hanna's mother-in-law; and silver casket plates and sets of silver coffin handles, those from Hanna's casket bearing Masonic emblems. "Particles of clothing" were intact; these latter were of interest because since 1869 shrouds had become preferred burial garb. Everything was scooped up, placed in new coffins, and carted off. The Old Cemetery would be completely abandoned in a few years, its area much too confined for a growing community. In the previous decade, Julia Hanna Conner had been buried on a hilltop in the New Cemetery. Therefore, it made sense to transfer her family there. Eventually, Hanna Cemetery became Hanna Park, a small green spot in the east end.

The Hanna reinterment was unheralded, "quiet but not secret," and not at all like the public participation in Hanna's original burial in 1869, and that of his wife, Elizabeth, in 1863, when crowds of neighbors and other citizens followed their remains to interments in the Old Cemetery. In 1902 there was no procession, no solemn pageantry, no reported religious service, and no known family gathering. The four new caskets, bearing what was left of the bodies, were escorted by Clark Brothers and by Conner to high ground in Wabash's New Cemetery, renamed Falls Cemetery. And there, again on a knoll, this time overlooking Chief Charley's creek and the top of Charley Creek Falls, the remains were gently and respectfully laid to rest, now in company with Julia and other Conner kinfolk.

Had Hugh had a say about all this, he might have preferred to remain in the Old Cemetery, the one he established, the one located closer to his original town. So far as that town's first plat is concerned, Hanna and his partner, David Burr, had once possessed the whole kit and caboodle. East to west from Allen Street to Cass Street, south to north from the projected path of the Wabash and Erie Canal to Sinclair Street, all 118 acres of it were theirs in 1835. And when Burr left the next year, Hanna was sole proprietor.

In 1902 it might have been appropriate to have made the translation of Hanna bones something other than a private, unheralded digging project. If Conner or other citizens had possessed a deeper appreciation of their own history, of that self-interested but irrepressible urge toward community development that Hanna represented—or if they could have foreseen with what blows the emerging twentieth century would hammer Wabash and similar small cities—they might have organized a public procession to mark the reinterment of Hanna, who, more than any other single citizen, was the founding father and civic icon of a prospering, rather stunning little city called Wabash—Hanna's town.

With that kind of sensitivity molding the decisions of Conner and others of his ilk in 1902, the route of such a grand procession from Old Cemetery to

New Cemetery could itself have served to highlight Hanna's career and, more importantly, to pass in review of a nineteenth-century, midwestern town that was at the very pinnacle of its development, beauty, and civic success.

One could imagine what such a procession might have entailed:

Four black, ostrich-plumed, horse-drawn hearses move slowly, solemnly, out of the Old Cemetery onto East Street, going west. A procession of town leaders, family members, and ordinary citizens follow, some on horseback, some in carriages, and many on foot. Within a few yards the procession turns south on East Street for a block, then west again on East Main so that it can pass the Hanna homestead, a two-story, deep-roofed frame house sporting a classic bay window at one end. It stands as Hanna had intended, on a height overlooking the Treaty Ground where Wabash had begun. There the persisting flow of Paradise Spring (Hanna's Spring) created a woodland setting where Native Americans and whites had powwowed in 1826, dividing up broad sweeps of northern Indiana.

The cortege reaches Allen Street and turns south. Participants notice on their right the frame, classic mansion of J. D. Conner, a house like his father-in-law's in the sense that its backside looks out over the bluff onto the town below. The procession moves down Allen Street, a forty-foot descent to Market Street in a single, short block. It continues on level ground one block farther to the east end of Canal Street. On the left, off toward the river's bend, sprawl the shops and tracks of the Big Four Railroad yard. A new, elegant depot rises at the foot of the bluff. Any sign of the ancient Treaty Ground, other than the spring, is buried in cinders and fill. Dead ahead, just beyond the turn west onto Canal Street, is the site of Hanna's slaughterhouse, and beyond it the remnants of his millrace. In the near distance, perhaps a hundred yards away to the southwest, are the ruins of Hanna's sawmill.

The somber parade enters Canal Street, passing sites of canal-side warehouses. It turns north at Wabash Street, a corner occupying ground just a few feet higher than the river's bottom land close by. In Hanna's lifetime this intersection was the hub of business, the early center of commercial and manufacturing enterprises, and the place from which the town's agora spread along the base of the steep bluff. Shops, eateries, groceries, banks, hotels, newspapers, gathering spots, saloons, and whorehouses developed north, west, and east of it. Just south of this corner, the Wabash and Erie Canal had its main loading dock and earliest bridge. This corner was the town's economic womb because soon after plating Wabash, Hanna erected the first business building on its northwest point—Hanna's Corner. It was a two-story brick, suitable for his dry goods store, with rental space for lawyers and merchants; there was also room for community social events.

The hearse-drawing horses plod north, cross Market Street, and begin the ascent of Wabash Street hill. It is no easy climb. Although the bluff was cut down in places decades ago to accommodate traffic, it is still steep in 1902, still an undertaking for horse teams as they climb approximately fifty feet in the space of two blocks to reach Hill Street. The hearses pass the Masonic Lodge, Hanna Lodge, Number 61. As they near the top they come to the site of First Presbyterian Church (New School) that Hanna joined in 1848. West, across from the church site, rises the county courthouse, a neo-classical structure, with a domed clock tower and sporting corner minarets. The cortege pauses between church site and courthouse near the heights of Hill Street. The procession has left the valley and now enters the town's lofty acropolis, a generous space for courts, churches, library, schools, civic memorials, steeples, turrets, towers, lawns, and stately homes along shade-lined streets.

A pause here before the east façade of the courthouse is a reminder of Hanna's vision. By locating a courthouse where he did, above the business district, Hanna took full advantage of the town's natural splendor. Most other county seats in the upper Wabash valley—Huntington, Peru, Logansport, Lafayette—failed to appropriate so definitively their hills and bluffs. Wabash did it in spades. Not only did its hall of justice rise serenely above the daily bustle of commerce, so, in time, did most religious, educational, cultural, and domestic entities, all seeming to collect naturally along the heights. Hanna, with one or two swift donations, drew the future map of nineteenth-century Wabash.

After pausing at the courthouse, the procession turns left (west) on Hill Street, passing the magnificently massive Memorial Hall, honoring Civil War combatants. It crosses Miami Street. To the south rises the 1880 Presbyterian Church sanctuary, a neatly executed American Gothic edifice with large rose window and slender, soaring spire. Next to it is the Queen Anne–styled manse, the home of Doctor Charles Little, the town's prestigious, perennial clergyman, now in the thirtieth of his fifty years of service. Opposite the manse stands the older Christian Church building, a charming mix of gothic and classical. Farther west is the residence of Doctor James Ford, an early settler and architect of the Christian Church. Just beyond Ford's, to the west of Cass Street, rise the limestone turrets, arches, and lofty, gargoyle-encrusted tower of a high school, a Richardsonian Romanesque masterpiece. Facing it, across Hill Street, is businessman Thomas McNamee's mansard-towered mansion. As the procession turns right (north) onto Cass Street, it passes a corner house recently owned by one of the Herffs and soon to be the site of a new city library, financed in part by the Carnegie foundation.

The final leg of the procession crosses the tracks of the Wabash Railroad (formerly another investment of the Hanna family) to Sinclair—sometimes St. Clair—Street. A block and a half to the west on Sinclair, the hearses head northwest, up "the Avenue," Falls Avenue, then across Charley Creek to Falls Cemetery. The burial site is one of the highest points of the cemetery, prominent enough to honor the remains of the town's founder and first major investor in its promise. Hanna's grave is surrounded by scores of others, commemorating his colleagues, men and women, rich and poor, black and white, who collectively seemed determined to build a town out of virtually nothing, who were often ruggedly optimistic about their ability to do so and who were born in the right century to get it done.

This imagined reinterment of Hanna bones from Old to New Cemetery in 1902 has served to review briefly the nineteenth-century settlement that Hanna and many others developed into a city.

The creation of the Carnegie Library (1903), at Hill and Cass streets, seemed to mark the beginning of a new era, which is illustrated by the town's architecture in general. Gone is the high Victorian élan of previous decades. The Eagles Theater, built in 1906, looks as if it belonged to the previous century, although it was exceedingly bulky and lacked the more ornamental presence of the Tremont Hotel, the First National Bank, and J. P. Ross's insurance building to the east. It is also true that just as the stately new post office, built in 1912, would be underwritten by federal funds and not by local enterprise, so the elegance of the library owed more to a Carnegie grant from the East than to local money. Carnegie's generosity was keenly sought by community leaders, perhaps illustrating that if they sensed newly restricted limits on local resources they still had the moxie to mine a larger world.

However that may be, locally financed, large and elegantly designed structures such as Memorial Hall and the high school had become projects of the past. When the high school was replaced in 1926, the newer building was nobly situated on high ground. It was, however, a rather timidly executed art deco affair, was smaller than originally planned because of funds shortages, and was constructed too far away from the acropolis of the old town to contribute to that area's ambiance. Certainly it was not in the same expensively aesthetic league as its predecessor at Hill and Cass streets. Indeed an objective comparison of the new high school with its predecessor (1894), if such a measurement could be scientifically achieved, might register a considerable drop in community panache and/or willful extravagance by the later date. The same downshift of flair in the new century could also be measured in the turn of domestic architecture from high Victorian styles to more restrained, more modest dwellings, even for the rich. Few twentieth-century homes would rival the fanciful opulence of the Atkinson, Bigler, Busick, Cowgill, Eagle, King, McCrea, and Shively mansions (to name a few), no matter how wealthy the occupants.

It might be argued, then, that the disinterment of Hanna in 1902, inadvertently but not inappropriately, marked high water in an outpouring of visible progress, cultural energy, and palpable optimism that his town had experienced during the preceding sixty-seven years. Those years ought not to be evaluated nostalgically, however. History emphatically records that Wabash was neither an ideal society by 1902 nor even outstandingly progressive for its time. Indeed, it continued to display rustic and seedy aspects of its unpolished past. It was still home to racism, gender inequity, crime, prostitution, pollution, and wide (possibly widening) divisions between rich and poor, drunk and sober, labor and management, and educated and uneducated. By contrast, in the new century, cultural advances, industrial growth, myriad technological breakthroughs, and the triumphant progress of justice and social causes—such as Social Security, civil rights, women's rights, and advances against poverty—enriched life for Wabash and the nation. It could never be asserted, then, that the nineteenth century was somehow superior to its successors in the achievements of civilization.

One might assert, however, that the twentieth century would leach from towns such as Wabash what had once loomed large with them: a sense of communal significance and a frontier-bred, can-do confidence. The opportunity to create a community out of the virtual tabula rasa of a forest wilderness would be gone. One could no longer simply lay out a plat on uninhabited land, start building infrastructure, and hope to keep up with the demand of those rushing in to live there. It must have been a heady thought, if folks thought about it at all, to be engaged mostly in building anew and in adding to, rather than in replacing or restoring, what others had left behind. The new century inevitably overwhelmed some of the spirit of the old century: two world wars, the Great Depression, the urbanization of America, the spread of suburbs, the sprawl of malls, and the growth of industry would reshape the nation. The coming ubiquity of the automobile was part of a travel and communication revolution that tied large regions of the nation together around urban centers. Folks in communities far from city suburbs, as in Wabash, began to believe they were again in the hinterlands of progress rather than the very engine of it, as their nineteenth-century counterparts so often were.

By 1902, before the complications of the new century washed over them, Wabash citizens had reasons to stand tall and proud. A sincere local boosterism was all but a religion. The wilderness had been subdued. In its place was a city of almost palpable optimism, boasting a bustling economy, a sense of community, civic pride, broad economic connections, architectural achievements, and various other cultural pretensions, all of which more than fulfilled any visionary hopes early settlers may have cherished. Many streets at last were paved. By the time its founder was reburied in 1902, the town had achieved a kind of apotheosis: progressive, confident, quite possibly gorgeous—Hanna's town.

WABASH COUNTY HISTORICAL MUSEUM

INDIANA HISTORICAL SOCIETY

Portraits of four participants in the 1826 treaty. ***Above:*** *James B. Ray, governor of Indiana* ***Left:*** *Jean Baptiste Richardville, Miami chief.* ***Opposite:*** *Lewis Cass, governor of Michigan.* ***Inset:*** *John Tipton, U.S. Indian agent.*

WABASH COUNTY HISTORICAL MUSEUM

WABASH COUNTY HISTORICAL MUSEUM

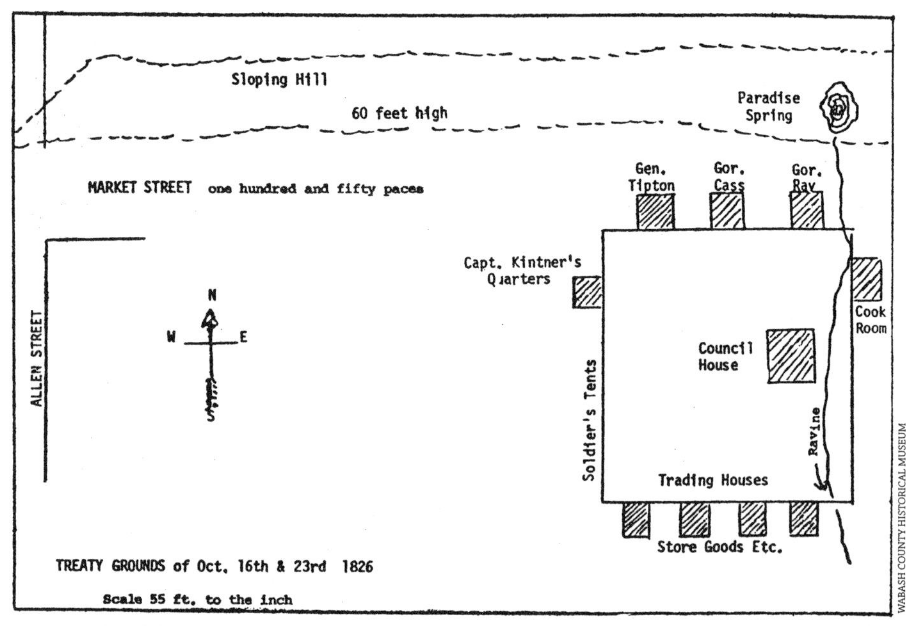

A facsimile of Elijah Hackleman's map of Treaty Ground.

WABASH COUNTY HISTORICAL MUSEUM

Facsimile of the original plat of Wabash, 1834.

Samuel Hanna family, 1843. (Horace Rockwell [American 1811–1877]. Oil on canvas, 68" x 63". Gift of the Hanna Family Heirs, 1937.02. Fort Wayne Museum of Art. Indiana.) Samuel was Hugh Hanna's older brother and the founder of Fort Wayne.

WABASH COUNTY HISTORICAL MUSEUM

WABASH COUNTY HISTORICAL MUSEUM

Clockwise from top: *Julia, Josephine, and Hugh Hanna, 1850s; Hugh Hanna as an elderly gentleman, mid-1860s; An early-twentieth-century photograph of Hugh Hanna's house on the bluff above the Treaty Ground.*

WABASH COUNTY HISTORICAL MUSEUM

ALL PHOTOGRAPHS BY W. WILLIAM WIMBERLY II

Clockwise from top: *Three grave sites: Rodef Shalom, the Jewish cemetery; reburial site of Hanna Cemetery graves in Falls Cemetery, beginning 1902; Hugh Hanna's grave in Falls Cemetery.*

WABASH COUNTY HISTORICAL MUSEUM

James Ford, a pioneer physician, late in life.

PHI GAMMA DELTA HEADQUARTERS, LOUISVILLE

Left: *Naaman Fletcher, newspaper publisher and editor.* ***Below:*** *Union School, ca. 1860s, with homes typical of the period along Maple Street (foreground) and Miami Street.*

WABASH COUNTY HISTORICAL MUSEUM

WABASH COUNTY HISTORICAL MUSEUM

CLARKSON WEESNER, *A HISTORY OF WABASH COUNTY*, 2 VOLS. (CHICAGO: LEWIS PUBLISHING COMPANY, 1914), 2:478

Above: *Charles S. Parrish, circa 1861–65, a Wabash Civil War officer and future mayor.* ***Left:*** *Catherine (Mrs. Archibald) Stitt was a home-front leader during the Civil War.*

1

A Rivulet Ran through It . . . and a Man Danced Naked

If there could be a definable beginning, this would be as good as any: Wabash began in water. Four hundred million years ago, give or take a dozen millennia, the Silurian Sea covered the land. It was relatively shallow, quiet, and eternally boring as seas go. From the sea's nutrients, its plant and fish life, its trilobites and crustaceans, there sifted downward layer by layer of sediment to form the Wabash Reef and Hanging Rock as well as the massive foundation of limestone and dolomite that underpins the present-day town and bluffs of Wabash. This watery blanket of the Silurian Sea covered everything for seventy million years or more and then slowly leached away, leaving swamps in its wake where vegetation sprang up. Two hundred million years later glaciers (*frozen* water this time) crawled south, plowing the land and scraping the tops of reefs and rocks. These moving ice mountains dominated the landscape until intermittent warming spells forced their slow, halting retreat. As the ice hills pulled back going north, their melting flanks dropped debris that had been scooped up on the way south, debris called "end moraine" or "till," a "chaotic deposit of all sizes of sediments."[1] In other words, retreating glaciers flung down rocks, gravel, and boulders indiscriminately and often in heaps. These spewed sediments exist now as the forested and cultivated surface topography around Wabash.

As glaciers melted, increasing volumes of water merged with ground-level streams to form rivers that carved out valleys. The Wabash valley, for example, was a child of the so-called Huron-Erie ice lobe, a glacial field that also spawned two great lakes as it retreated northeast out of the future site of Indiana. The flow ate away at the soil, the hills, and the rock until a defined waterway emerged, arching northwest out of the future state of Ohio, turning southwest about where Huntington, Indiana, now sits, then plunging south at Lafayette's site until the Ohio River swallowed it whole. It was not long before the banks and bluffs along this waterway were shaded in a spreading, luxuriant forest, fed by major and minor streams and by abundant rainfall.

Meanwhile, at some point in these elongated periods of geological time, another abundant water source developed, one that would gladden the hearts of nineteenth-century Americans. Deep below the surface there were (and are) vast aquifers: enormous, seemingly endless supplies of mineral-rich "aqua pura" that have percolated through enough sand and gravel to reach a high standard of clarity and tastiness. In the nineteenth century Wabash citizens tapped this water by artesian wells drilled sixty feet into the ground just south of the river. An artesian well is powered primarily by gravity, in that the underground well's end receives its water from sources above it, the pressure of which forces a firm—sometimes volatile—flow up the well toward the surface. These artesian water sources should not be confused with the River Teays, which was once thought to be an enormous underground aquifer flowing out of the Appalachians, under Ohio, Indiana, and Illinois to empty into the Mississippi River. Generations of midwesterners sank wells thinking they were tapping into the ever-flowing Teays, but geologists now teach that the Teays is "a valley, not a flowing river."[2] That valley is filled with glacially deposited sediments that trap enormous quantities of groundwater. Thus, there has long been a bountiful supply of underground water available beneath the Wabash River valley, much of it waiting to be tapped by humans, but some of it springing out of the ground of its own volition.

It was water of the latter type, a natural spring, that most directly affected the birth of Wabash. In the 1820s this spring gushed as it had for ages from a bluff that rises just north of the Wabash River between the sites of present-day Hill and Market streets. Originally the spring surfaced part way up the bluff and cut a gully south to the river; but as civilization in the area intruded, its outlet was piped to a lower level, perhaps for convenience, perhaps because part of the bluff collapsed in the nineteenth century. More likely, however, the spring had to be rerouted after 1896, when the Big Four Railroad Company dynamited away much of the bluff in order to improve train access through the area. Paradise Spring may even have disappeared from sight for a time because of this destruction, but in the twenty-first century it gushes still, with cold, clear water.[3]

The Miami Indians had long enjoyed this spring. They called it Kin-com-a-ong (King-com-e-ong, etc.), which in English is "Paradise." It lay across the river from the mouth of an attractive stream, later named Treaty Creek, which entered the Wabash River just above a convenient ford, a relatively shallow, rock-strewn breadth of river that was easily crossed on foot or horseback when floods were not on the move. The Miami called the river Wah-bah-shi-ki (sometimes Wah-ah-shik-ki), roughly meaning "clear bright water over pure white rocks." Indeed, there are still shoals of bright, white (perhaps not *pure white*) rocks in this vicinity, especially when the sun shines fully on certain banks and shallows; conversely, the water is rarely "clear bright" in the twenty-first century. The juxtaposition of river, spring, creek, and ford, together with relatively open bottomland on the north side of the river, created at Paradise Spring an attractive wooded setting for tribal gatherings. The Miami also had a name for the area adjacent to the spring. They called it Tah-king-gah-me-con-gi, which meant "Running water place," an obvious reference to the spring.

The area was also graced with an imposing extension of the Wabash Reef sedimentation, later called "Limestone Hill" (and largely dynamited away in 1896), which jutted south from the bluff toward the river's bend. Elijah Hackleman remembered it as a "cliff that once stood out in such bold relief, like a promontory jutting down to the water's edge."[4] Speculation says such a promontory, if it were relatively free of forest growth, would have been commonly known to Miami as a convenient lookout. Although subsequent legend suggested that Wabash's Old Cemetery, located further back on the bluff, had originally been a Miami burial ground, one local historian argues cogently that such an idea "entirely disregards known Indian burial customs in pre-pioneer Indiana."[5]

Nonetheless, it seems safe to assume that, so far as human habitation is concerned, the site of Wabash was first of all a Native American commons of sorts, a place where the Miami gathered for the fun of it or to collect water, as often as to meet for more serious business. Paradise Spring was popular with the Miami before the landmark Treaty of 1826. In that year, when Miami chieftains and white American leaders needed a place to negotiate, Kin-com-a-ong must have seemed suitable for both convivial intercourse and serious negotiations. It proved to be so. The area of Paradise Spring became Treaty Ground.

The Miami were not the first humans to roam the valley. There is some limited evidence of human habitation in the Indiana area as early as 11,000 BCE, roughly about the time the glaciers were receding. These inhabitants lived almost exclusively by hunting wild animals, including some that later became extinct. There followed a succession of cultures, each lasting hundreds or even thousands of years, some more nomadic than others. Archaeologists categorize each influx according to the sophistication and type of artifacts left behind. The last of these groups included the mound builders, whose engineering wonders are concentrated mostly in the middle and southern parts of the state. These people disappeared by 1600 CE. Those now called Native Americans, or Indians, who were largely nomadic in the early years, arrived in the eighteenth century; many were already experienced with the rising European tide: the French, the English, and the more recently hatched Americans, former English colonists.[6]

Various tribes had probably moved in and out of the upper Wabash valley during these years. At one point many had abandoned the area because of an invasion of fierce Iroquois. In the long run, most of those who returned and settled were the Miami and Potawatomi. The latter dominated in northern Indiana, scattering villages around the tip of Lake Michigan and as far south as the Eel River, which flows through northern Wabash County. Branches of the Miami established bases along most of the length of the Wabash River. The so-called Detroit band of the Miami concentrated in the upper Wabash and Maumee valleys, with their most important village at Kekionga (later Fort Wayne). Representatives of these Miami established villages of huts and wigwams in the future Wabash County. In comparison to tribes such as the Iroquois, noted for warlike ways, the Miami had a reputation as gentle, settled, agrarian types. Although some of their villages were impermanent affairs, they had largely put away a nomadic existence and were not automatically disdainful of American innovations. Chiefs LeGros (at Lagro), Black Raccoon (on the bluff south of the Wabash River), and Little Charley (north of the river) maintained villages in the area near the future site of Wabash and enjoyed good relations with white pioneers. As early as the Treaty of 1818, Miami living a few miles southwest of Kin-com-a-ong had accepted a government-built mill on Mill Creek near the Richvalley prairie. Although government representatives then warned that the stream was a "wet weather creek," too seasonal in its water flow for a reliable mill, the Miami insisted on the site, and the mill was erected by 1820.[7] In the long run it was not successful.

Similarly, the government attempted at times to provide modern housing for influential Miami. Soon after 1826, in conformity to the treaty of that year, Moses Scott constructed a brick residence on what became Lot 126 in downtown Lagro for the prominent chieftain, Le Gros (Legro, Lagrow, Le Gris, etc.), for whom the place would be named. Although the house was a two-story brick with parlor, dining room, kitchen, and bedrooms, a traveler who happened upon the house late at night reported that the chief, his wives, and their papooses were sleeping in the yard while the chief's ponies occupied the interior. A pioneer described a similar house as having become the "abode of serpents and retreat of toads."[8] Le Gros's house later became an inn, then a store, and Roman Catholics also worshipped there on occasion. These accounts illustrate some of the frustration of white American and Native American interaction in the Wabash area. Both sides seemed to have wanted to get along with each other and showed signs of mutual respect, though, of course, the Americans' insatiable appetite for more and more land worked against any equitable coexistence.[9]

The legendary saga of Frances Slocum, an American girl stolen by Native Americans in Pennsylvania and raised as a Miami just west of southern Wabash County, indicates that assimilation was not impossible. When, as an aging adult, Frances was reunited with her original family, she chose to maintain her Miami identity and residence. Certainly isolated white traders, besides the French, occasionally took Native American brides. It is also true that individual Miami, such as Chief Charley, seemed to have no trouble being neighborly with the pioneers. Indeed, Charley was an American hero of sorts, honored for his loyalty to the U.S. government and a close friend and ally of Lewis Cass. However, generally speaking, the cultural divide made for awkward relationships, so that wholesale absorption of the Miami into the rising complexity of the white settlement never materialized and was never seriously attempted. As government payment for Miami lands became a regular event, providing warriors with ready cash and serving as a substitute for their diminishing livelihood in fur trading, a more lethal problem arose—alcohol dependence. Unscrupulous white whiskey vendors eagerly preyed on those Miami who would not drink moderately or could not metabolize whiskey safely.

Such was the situation as white incursion into northern Indiana became more substantial in the 1820s and 1830s. For decades the policy of the U.S. government was to make treaties that would assure that additional tribal land became available to American pioneers. Nothing ever stood in the way of that policy for long. Slowly but inexorably, beginning in 1783 and continuing through 1840, treaty after treaty pushed Native Americans out of land ownership in the Old Northwest, something natives did not fully value in the way white pioneers did. In 1840 any charade of peaceful coexistence in Indiana collapsed completely as Miami tribal remnants and others were sent west to Kansas, following the Potawatomi who began their "Trail of Death" in 1838. In these years of great land grabs, many Miami families remained behind, cosseted by generous grants called a "reserve" or a "section," the latter being 640 acres or 1/36 of a township. One was the enormous Thirty Mile Reserve on the south side of the Wabash River that temporarily curtailed white settlement in those areas of Wabash and Miami counties.

Just west of Paradise Spring lay a section that the 1826 treaty confirmed as belonging to Chief Charley's family. Charley was the chief of the Eel River Miami and had a collection of tribal and American names: Charlow Constant, Kitunga, Sha-mes-kun-nee-sa, the Soldier, She-moc-e-nish, Captain Charley, Little Charley. The section's defining feature was Charley's Creek (Charley Creek), which ran diagonally through its center. Charley maintained a residence on the west bank of the creek, where a railroad bridge now cuts through City Park. Farther up the creek, near the falls, he maintained a wigwam or tepee and was remembered sitting cross-legged in front of it, smoking a pipe. Charley's section included much of what became the western end of the town of Wabash.[10]

Although twenty-first century Wabash citizens share with their Miami forebears the general topography of the place, the forested nature of its hills, and the indelible fact of its river, it is difficult for them to fathom the utter, intractable wildness that American pioneers experienced or to envision how traders, soldiers, and politicians actually pushed through the landscape to reach the Treaty Ground in 1826. The first two great obstacles in such travel were always the density of forests and the want of roads.

Forests rose thick and high above tangles of unruly underbrush composed of nettles, milkweed, vines, wild flowers, and other vegetation, at times "higher than a horse's back."[11] Later in the nineteenth century Wabash residents began to reflect on how much their community building had cost in terms of forest loss. There was still plenty of forest on the hills and along the river, but vast acres in the country had been leveled for farming, plank roads, construction lumber, and other uses. Wabash's furniture, barrel, lathe, stave, and spoke industries consumed enormous amounts of nearby timber. Most of the individual giants of the woods had fallen in the first two or three decades of settlement. A newspaper reporter in 1878 marveled that an oak tree near Lagro had just sold for $112.45 and would be marketed in the East for $53.75 per one thousand board feet. Its felled trunk measured fifty-six feet; its average thickness was five feet. More marvelous and saddening was the wholesale harvest in 1899 of a seventy-five acre tract of virgin timber near the Mississinewa River that had survived earlier onslaughts because it was part of the Miami Reserve. Sixty-five massive walnut trees were cut that year, none less than four feet in diameter and ranging to nine and a half feet. Some grew upward for sixty-five feet before branching, with a single branch as long as thirty-three feet and three feet thick. There were also enormous oaks, six to eight feet in diameter and limbless for sixty or seventy feet. The trunks were straight. Shellbark hickories could send up straight trunks as high as seventy-five feet. After being harvested the acreage looked as if vandals had attacked it. Entrepreneurs in the East, who paid $60,000 for the lot, shipped the walnut to the European market. In the twenty-first century the finished timber from a single walnut tree the size of those described in 1899 could fetch millions of dollars in the woodworking market.[12]

The fact is the woodlands had long been under attack, beginning with the arrival of the first pioneer farmers, who viewed forests as enemies of agriculture. This attitude was somewhat contradictory in the sense that they also believed the presence of forest, in contrast to unforested land, indicated fertile soil. It would have been far easier to cultivate the open prairies that were, in many cases, just as fertile as wooded land. Once a settler had chopped down enough trees to build a log cabin, he became intent on bringing direct sunlight to an acre or two of land in the fastest, least labor-intensive way. Depending on the type of trees he could either "girdle" them, chopping into the bark around the circumference so that they died of malnutrition, or he could light brushfires at the base of trees, burning them to death. He might stock any extra brush from the forest floor and from dying trees in elongated piles for temporary fencing around cabin and fields. With the trees moribund and leafless, plowing and planting began. Only later might a farmer go to the trouble of felling dead trees and using ox teams to pull up stumps. The deadening of forests became increasingly common as the pioneer population rose, marring the landscape but gladdening the hearts of farmers who hated to "go into the green" in search of farmland. Deadening allowed them to move agricultural production fairly quickly past subsistence levels toward a surplus that could be marketed.[13]

Before the forests began to fall, however, it was simply maddening trying to get anywhere in such terrain. The only transportation offering a modicum of speed was a boat on the Wabash River: some kind of primitive canoe to paddle, or a pirogue, a raft, a keelboat, or perhaps a flat-bottomed pole boat to push along. Early explorers had traveled this way long before there was thought of permanent white settlements. Near the site of Wabash they may have made use of the so-called Hospital near Shanty Falls. It was a cave in the south bluff of the river that is supposed to have served as a shelter for travelers. They were guided to it by a large boulder called the "moon rock," which was a "glacial erratic" high on the north bank of the river. In times of drought or flood, traveling the river could be nearly impossible, and in the best of times it was hazardous. In 1831 sixteen-year-old James Coppock accompanied his father on a sojourn from Dayton, Ohio, to the upper Wabash River. The objective was to deliver $20,000 in silver to Logansport, where it would be paid out to Native Americans for their land forfeitures. Weighing 1,300 pounds and packed in kegs, the silver had traveled from Washington, D.C., to Cincinnati, and finally to Dayton where the two Coppocks and a few guards took charge. They set out with four wagons and four horses. There being no trail in the desired direction, they pushed through trackless forest. Occasionally they were favored with a corduroy road, logs thrown down across marsh or bog. They soon learned to double the number of horses on a single wagon in order to drag the vehicle through deep, viscous, sucking mud. In this way, stop and start, they covered eight miles in one or two days. A potentially disastrous situation developed, however, as they began to use the Mississinewa River. They transferred their heavy, precious cargo to a "tree boat," a pirogue, which ran aground on a sandbar almost as soon as it was launched. There the group stayed for the night, a guard posted at each end of the pirogue, armed with rifles. Next day they divided the silver between two pirogues and successfully completed the journey to Logansport.

The Coppocks with their silver were going downstream, a relatively easy undertaking despite their cargo. Upstream travel, on the other hand, was slow and arduous. After pushing up the Maumee in a pole boat to Fort Wayne in 1834, Wabash sojourner John Brooks gave up on water travel and hired an ox team to finish the trek to Wabash County over very primitive roads. Brooks's entire trip from Cleveland took a month. Once in Wabash, Brooks discovered that the closest gristmill was at Marion, a three-day trip, and the only place to acquire a cow was Logansport, thirty-five miles down river. Water passage to the former place was unavailable, and driving a cow from the latter was highly problematic.[14]

When Brooks rode his ox team from Fort Wayne to Wabash County he was almost certainly using remnants of the most venerable track in the area, the northeastern end of what was called the Old French Traders Road. It mostly meandered across bottomland as it followed the Wabash River upstream from Vincennes; eventually long stretches of it would be eradicated as the Wabash and Erie Canal plowed through the same ground. Native Americans had used the route long before the French. At the 1795 Treaty of Greenville, General Anthony Wayne stipulated that whites were guaranteed free access to the road. It was up this rude trail that a fiery Frenchman, with the incongruous name of LaBalme (Augustin Mottin de LaBalme), once marched several dozen Creole recruits toward Detroit in an effort to dislodge the British and Indian alliance in the area, including at Kekionga (Fort Wayne) in 1780. LaBalme had come to America with the Marquis de Lafayette to serve in the army of the new American republic. He soon left that service to pursue a more private war against British interests in the Old Northwest. He proved not only inept but also unnecessarily cruel and destructive in his treatment of natives, paying with his life when Chief Little Turtle's Miami braves ambushed him near the upper Eel River.

LaBalme's march along the French road toward his demise was, however, the first event of a broader historical connection to occur on ground that became Wabash fifty-five years later. The only certain trace of LaBalme's route locally is believed to be the now-asphalt drive that rises in front of the Lincoln memorial log cabin in City Park. Probably this stretch of the French Traders Road had been following the north bank of the river after crossing from the south bank near Richvalley. It then turned inland near the mouth of Charley Creek and followed that stream for a few hundred feet before turning southeast to achieve high ground where West Hill and West Main streets subsequently materialized. Assuming that the route continued to follow the river, then in all likelihood LaBalme's little army marched through future Wabash property, perhaps along the crest of the bluff as now defined by Hill and Main streets. Another possibility is that the route dropped toward the floodplain along the site of the future business district and passed near Kin-com-a-ong. This lower route gains some confirmation in the fact that Samuel McClure, an early settler in 1828, worked to mark an established "highway" from Logansport to the mouth of the Salamonie River along a route later followed, east of Wabash, by the canal. This would put the established "highway" near the river rather than on the bluff. Reportedly McClure's labors were relatively easy in that he needed only to straighten out the curves of the old French Traders Road. Whatever the exact pathway—high ground or low ground—Wabash is sited along a primary, but utterly crude, eighteenth-century highway.[15]

There were other primitive "roads" in the area at this time, but none so extensive as the French route. They were variously called buffalo traces, horse and panther roads, and Indian traces. At best they were well-worn bridle paths. At worst they were too narrow or too obscured by brush to accommodate more than slow, single-file passage, so that a wagon team attempting the same route had to widen the track by the wagon's brute force and the application of axe or hatchet. Pioneers helped each other by hacking marks on trees to indicate negotiable paths. A fairly popular route zigzagged across the landscape in the fashion of a "worm fence" because, it was learned later, the woodsman doing the marking was badly intoxicated. An important, much used path, which was marked as early as 1827, began in northern Grant County at Conner's Mill on the Mississinewa River and led northeast through dense woods toward Lagro, passing a half mile east of the site of America (now extinct) and a mile west of where Lincolnville would rise. Another trail originated in the same place but aimed for Fort Wayne. It was an especially difficult route because after tunneling through almost impenetrable woods under lofty leaf canopies (which blocked sunlight but nonetheless allowed the nettles to flourish), it wound blindly around the perimeters of malarial swamps and bogs.

The same was true north of Paradise Spring. Once pioneers had negotiated woodlands on the bluff there, they ran into flat uplands that were annoyingly wet. In trying to push through these "marshy prairies" to the far-distant village of Goshen, the Reverend George Abbott devised "a kind of swinging bridge" for use over wetlands. He mowed huge quantities of wild grasses, threw them together, and laid them over the boggy ground. This was part of the first road to the Goshen region, or so Abbott claimed in 1890. His contemporary, Fred Haupert, referred to part of the area, from Wabash to the Eel River, as "one continuous swamp."[16]

Greater distances meant greater hardship in travel, of course. In 1834 John Russell carried fifteen pounds of clover seed on his back from Indianapolis to Wabash while driving a cow and calf over ice-bound terrain. At one point the cow stopped before a frozen stream, refusing to cross. When prodded forward it fell down, so that Russell had to slide the prone animal over the ice on its side; the calf crossed in the same manner. Significantly, no matter what other material improvements graced life in the last seventy years of the nineteenth century, and there were many, the quality of roadways was a perennial frustration for local governments and the general populace. The development of Wabash is, in part, the story of citizens trying to master their streets and roads.[17]

Where there was wilderness there were wild animals. Squirrels were almost too ubiquitous to mention. A popular pioneer tale, however, is of the great squirrel stampede of 1834. Suddenly, unbidden and unexplained, thousands of squirrels scampered in a rapid, seemingly crazed, migration across the landscape, halting for nothing in their path. They swarmed through woods, leaped from limb to limb, broke down branches by their weight, scurried across open areas, and swam the Wabash in hordes. Sometimes they created chains with their bodies so that other squirrels could cross from branch to branch. The infestation lasted for nearly two weeks, keeping boys with clubs and men with guns busy. Contemporary accounts of this are scarce, but the event was branded as gospel by early settlers and seems in retrospect too absurd to have been invented. Certainly local historians took it seriously. Stampeding or not, squirrels were a ready source of food, a staple in the diet of both pioneers and settlers. Indeed they never entirely disappeared from the dining table throughout the century and were sometimes served up for old-time's sake. Aging settlers fondly remembered the camaraderie of "pik-niks" that featured grilled squirrel by the score. A monumental hunt near Ashland (later, Wolf Trap and LaFontaine) bagged fourteen hundred of the critters and inspired daylong festivities for participants from across the country. It was said that Hugh Hanna consumed more squirrels at one sitting than anyone else present. His meal that day also included a generous helping of venison.[18]

Squirrels were among the least challenging wildlife. If asked to name the most prevalent creatures, a pioneer might reply bear, deer, wolves, turkeys, raccoons, rattlesnakes, pheasants, quail, and fish; others would quickly add honeybees, wild hogs, frogs, and mosquitoes. In order to sleep in the open, travelers sometimes stretched sheets between four stakes in the ground and built a smoky fire nearby to ward off the bugs. Meanwhile the noise of owls and wolves was "hideous" all night long, and the gobble of wild turkeys broke the dawn. Wolves were hated and feared not only in the days of endless forest but also after Wabash became a viable village. A settler who built one of the earliest houses on the bluff moved into his new abode and that same night shot a wolf from his front door. More frightening was the experience of Robert Amber, probably in 1837. He and a neighbor from north of town had enjoyed a successful day fishing in the river at Wabash, so successful that they tarried at the sport until dusk when they began carrying home strings of fish over their backs, as many as they could carry. It grew darker as they made their way up the bluff. By the time they had reached the vicinity of the future intersection of Wabash Street with Walnut Street—described as eighty rods from town—they had become grimly aware of a gathering of wolves around them, attracted by the smell of fish. As the wolves moved in, the men were compelled to retreat. They fled back south to Canal Street where Hanna or one of his employees loaned them lanterns and torches, which, held aloft, kept the wolves at bay as the men retraced their steps.

The two were in unusual circumstances in that they were unarmed, especially at night. Because of wolves, abundant game, the occasional bear, and the possibility of a violent human being, nearly all males and some females either packed firearms or kept them handy and expected to use them. John Russell's boast in 1895, that he had shot two thousand deer in his lifetime is credible. Deer were omnipresent and killed for food. Hunters might float down a stream at night carrying a lamp to spot the deer; the carcass could be sunk in the stream and claimed later. Russell's other boast that he eventually killed the last deer in Indiana may be suspect, but it indicates that pioneers and settlers cleared the area of a lot of wildlife during the nineteenth century. Rattlesnakes, for example, were numerous and universally feared in the 1830s. Great nests of them along the river were shot, hacked, burned, and sometimes eradicated by the hundreds in specially planned campaigns. One trick was to build a pen around a "snake cave" entrance; when snakes crawled out in the spring they were confined by the pen long enough to be slaughtered. By the end of the century rattlesnakes were rarely referred to except in reminiscences. The same might be said of a great many other wild species, except, of course, mice and rats.

Certainly the Wabash River fish of yesteryear seem nearly incredible to twenty-first-century Hoosiers who have experienced decades of river pollution and relatively meager fish life in the Wabash. Yet, dependable records indicate that the river once teemed with desirable fish. Major Meredith Kidd, who arrived in the area in 1837, recalls the clear, silvery waters of the Wabash that were filled with "the finest fish imaginable."[19] Likewise, local historian Elijah Hackleman and his brother, Doctor James Hackleman, could take a wheelbarrow to the river and fill it with bass and other species. It was not unusual in a dry season when the river "pooled," trapping still water among dry rocks, for citizens to pluck out sizable fish with their hands. As late as 1878 a local paper reported that pike weighing seven and eight pounds were being taken out of the river.[20]

Such was the lay of the land, as well as the encumbrances and joys of pioneer life, when Wabash emerged in 1826 at Kin-com-a-ong. The principals in its conception were the Miami who lived mostly along the south side of the river; the Potawatomi, from north of the Eel River; John Tipton, Indian agent for the United States; Tipton's superior in Indian matters, General Lewis Cass, governor of Michigan and veteran of the Indian Treaty of Greenville in 1795; and Governor James B. Ray of Indiana. There were also a few interpreters and a secretary for the white delegation in the person of James M. Ray, thought by some to have been the governor's nephew, though the two were apparently unrelated. A state military captain, Fred R. Kintner, commanded seventeen other men to secure the treaty grounds. There were three officers, including Kintner, who were paid thirty-five dollars for forty days' service. The rest earned fifty cents to one dollar plus a gill of whiskey per day and other provisions. The soldiers had taken oaths of sobriety before embarking on their service. Somewhat in the shadows because of his own reticence was Miami chief Jean Baptiste Richardville, a man who exceeded all his tribal comrades in adopting American standards of living. Richardville eventually owned a string of commodious, even elegant, houses between Fort Wayne and Peru. In a letter to Tipton in June 1826 Hugh B. McKeen observed that "Richardville carries the Key" in any negotiation.[21]

Because Tipton was centrally located at Fort Wayne with the Indian agency, it fell to him to recommend a site and make arrangements. The pure, abundant water of Kin-com-a-ong, which "spouted out a few feet up the side of the hill," was a main attraction for Tipton.[22] By the end of July Tipton verified to Cass the selection as a place twelve miles above the mouth of the "mississinaway river." This communication resulted in the subsequent negotiations mistakenly being named the "Treaty of the Mississinewa" in some records, though Paradise Spring is not very near that river. At the same time he reported on his order for 40,000 pounds of fresh beef, 10,000 pounds of pork, 250 barrels of flour, and 50 muskets with bayonets. Wagon roads from both Anderson and Huntington had to be hacked through the wilderness in order to have the goods delivered. Two years earlier Tipton had estimated the population of Potawatomi and Miami tribes under his jurisdiction to be 2,441 Indians; he may have had no idea how many natives would attend the negotiations. Eventually the count of Indian attendees was 944 Potawatomi and 1,090 Miami. In August Tipton began to construct the log buildings that housed the Americans.[23]

These buildings later constituted the nucleus of a settlement that became Wabash. According to Hackleman's hand-drawn map (ca. 1860), they consisted of nine structures on the perimeter of a square of land, roughly 150 feet on a side; a tenth building in the center area served as a council house or meeting room. Kintner's cabin was on the west side, flanked by soldiers' tents. Three cabins for Tipton, Cass, and Ray defined the north side. A flagstaff with stars and stripes rose near the governor's cabin. A cookhouse sat on the eastern perimeter. Four of the ten structures lined the south side of the square to serve as trading houses. If Hackleman applied his map's overall scale of forty-five feet to the inch to the cabins (and Hackleman was practiced in the precision of land surveying), then five cabins were each approximately twenty-two feet square, with the cookhouse being larger.

There may have been more structures than Hackleman depicts. It is known, for example, that the Reverend Isaac McCoy occupied a dwelling, probably on the north side near Governor Ray's cabin. There he housed several Indian scholars from his Baptist mission in lower Michigan. In addition, there may have been rudimentary supply structures south of Kintner's cabin near the troops' tents. Presumably the Potawatomi occupied much of the remaining ground between bluff and river. Miami who lived on the near south bank might not have spent many nights at the treaty grounds, except when festivities ran high. At this time Miami chief Black Raccoon maintained a Miami village of bark huts and wigwams high on the south bluff, west of Treaty Creek, and overlooking the Wabash River. The village housed at least fifty braves and their families at this time; many of the treaty participants came from that village.[24]

On his map Hackleman locates the camp's main square as being 150 paces east of modern Allen Street. He clearly draws Paradise Spring burbling out of a sixty-foot bluff to the north, about a third of the way up. From the spring a "little rivulet" ran through the camp toward the river, passing just east of the council house. One cannot be certain how dramatic the erosion of this rivulet was. Information accompanying Hackleman's map twice refers to "the Ravine" as if it were a major component of the landscape; it may have cut a considerable gash through the bottomland. There is no trace of a ravine in the twenty-first century, the flow from the spring having been routed underground. Indeed, after 1872, when the "Old Treaty Ground" began to succumb to the construction of railroad shops and the laying of tracks, the ground level was surely raised several feet, leveled, and reconfigured with cinders and other fill. Two decades later, in order to improve access to the shops, the railroad company destroyed part of the Wabash Reef, "Limestone Hill," thus further altering the original topography.[25]

Pioneers and soldiers of the time were wonderfully adept in the construction of wilderness dwellings, so the camp at Paradise Spring was surely ready well in advance of the arrival of the principal players. Tipton apparently approached the area from Fort Wayne by way of the Salamonie River where, on September 18, he authorized credit to Chief LaGros for farming expenses. Tipton and Ray were settled in at the spring by September 20. Cass did not arrive until October 2. It is safe to say that the treaty-making process lasted about five weeks. A document was eventually signed with the Potawatomi on October 16, and another with the Miami on October 23, the official closing date for the meetings. Ray writes of several weeks of powwow. Hackleman indicates that there was a long period of time preceding the serious discussions, so it seems likely that parties began drifting in through late September, spent a number of weeks in socializing, getting acquainted, and entertainment, and then got down to business in mid-October. The exact sequence of events is less clear, though the highlights are discernible. Having a prelude of socializing was doubtless necessary, especially because the Potawatomi and the Miami were not necessarily on good terms. Each tribe was jealous of the potential value of the other's land. Some few members of the Wea and Ottawa tribes were also in this mix and may have shared in the jealousy, but records are not specific about them. The Americans, of course, were united.

They wanted the remaining tribal land in Indiana, were willing to pay for it, and expected to buy off the Native American chiefs' opposition with personal reservation grants as necessary.[26]

James Brown Ray (1794–1848) was a Kentuckian by birth who had settled in Brookville, Indiana, and launched into politics as a relatively young man in 1821. In the fall of 1826 he approached Kin-com-a-ong from Indianapolis through Logansport, where he connected with the venerable French Traders Road. Once at the treaty grounds he may have served as an unofficial host of the gathering, for the flagstaff was at his cabin, and he was governor of the state. A tall man with a full head of hair pulled back in a ponytail, he was considered to be handsome but also egotistical, and, later in life, eccentric. His political rise had been meteoric. As state senate president pro tempore, not an especially powerful position, Ray had assumed the governorship in 1825, when Governor William Hendricks was elected to the U.S. Senate and Lieutenant Governor Ratliff Boon resigned to run for Congress. It was a controversial elevation, but he was subsequently elected governor in his own right and reelected in 1828. Initially his appeal with voters had been his steady independence from political factionalism, steering a course between Andrew Jackson Democrats and John Quincy Adams Jeffersonian Republicans. By 1828, however, politics had become so volatile he had to overcome a Jacksonian exodus from his ranks in order to win re-election.

Lacking seasoned political savvy and managerial experience, Ray enjoyed little peace in the governor's office. In May 1826, however, he did win appointment from the secretary of war to the commission charged with ending Native American occupation in Indiana. The state legislature protested Ray's appointment, charging that it was illegal because Indiana's constitution forbade a governor from simultaneously holding office in the federal government. In a close vote the legislature chose not to remove Ray. After the Paradise Spring treaty (Treaty of Mississinewa) was concluded, he faced another barrage of charges from the state's treasurer who believed Ray had spent public funds too freely, among other offenses. Ray wrote Tipton asking the latter to comment honestly on Ray's performance at the treaty meetings. Although his response was supportive of the governor, it was not especially fervid. On the positive side, like many frontier politicians, the governor was a steadfast advocate of internal improvements. During his second term plans for the Wabash and Erie Canal progressed steadily, and the future of that canal would depend rather heavily on the success of the Paradise Spring treaty. One of Ray's visions, which never completely materialized, was construction of a series of turnpikes radiating to all sections of the state from the new capital, Indianapolis.[27]

A formal, midlife portrait of Lewis Cass (1782–1866) shows him to have had dark hair, a deeply receding hairline, and rather jowly features. In 1826 he traveled south from his home in Detroit through Flint Springs (Huntington) to reach the treaty ground. Of the three American commissioners none was to have the exalted career of this man. Cass was already a monumental figure in the Old Northwest and was a national political power until the Civil War. Raised and educated in the East, he sought his career in Ohio where he studied law and then entered that state's legislature at age twenty-four. The War of 1812 launched his military career. He served under William Henry Harrison and thereafter rose quickly through the ranks to become a brigadier general in the national army. His appointment in 1813 as territorial governor of Michigan placed him in control of Indian affairs in that region for eighteen years, and his natural bent seemed to be against the tribes and in favor of trading companies. President Jackson appointed him secretary of war in 1831. From that office he directed the nation's involvement in the Black Hawk War and the Seminole War. Serving as America's ambassador to France from 1836 to 1842, he proved to be popular with politicians and the general public. While in France he was instrumental in keeping that country from ratifying a multinational treaty that would have allowed American vessels to be searched by European powers trying to suppress the slave trade. He later resigned his post because Britain, despite a new naval treaty with the United States, did not foreswear the right to search American vessels. Subsequently, for the better part of a decade, he was a U.S. senator from Michigan, a strong supporter of James Polk's manifest destiny policy, and a politician willing to compromise on issues touching slavery. The Democrats nominated him for president in 1848. He lost to Zachary Taylor in part because he could not hold the loyalty of the "free soil" faction of his party and was portrayed as pandering to southern slave interests. Over such issues he also lost his Senate seat in 1857. However, James Buchanan appointed him secretary of state, which allowed him finally to obtain a concession from Britain regarding its searches of American ships. Cass also published studies about Native Americans and about the government of France.[28]

John Tipton (1786–1839), the American government's Indian agent in Indiana, had undoubtedly visited the treaty site several times before the negotiations began, and he was the man charged with making arrangements. He lived in Fort Wayne and knew the general area well. Indeed, likely better than any other contemporary, Tipton knew the whole of Indiana. Born along the eastern Tennessee frontier, he lost his father to an Indian fight when he was a boy and subsequently moved with his mother to Harrison County, Indiana, on the Ohio River, where the white population was still exceedingly sparse. His education was scanty, being mostly of the self-taught variety. He read little and wrote in terse, to-the-point style. As a young man Tipton was variously a ferry boat operator on the Ohio River, a tavern keeper, a farmer, and, by 1816, sheriff of Harrison County at Corydon. He held strong and sometimes contradictory views. He was known to help Kentuckians retrieve escaped slaves, but he also opposed the annexation of Texas because he feared it would extend the institution of slavery. Later in his career, when he led Potawatomi west toward their exile in Kansas, a Roman Catholic priest, Benjamin Pettit, called Tipton "dictatorial" and accused him of making "free men slaves."[29]

Tipton probably would have been impervious to such criticism had he known of it. He seems not to have been easily intimidated and has been described as persuasive, rugged, fearless, shrewd, harsh, grasping, and aggressive; at the same time folks also credited him with being fair. A painting of him—probably from early middle-age—shows a slender man in gentleman's clothing, with dark hair, generous sideburns, and a fairly stern demeanor. Tipton's big break in public service came with the Indian wars. He served under Harrison at the Battle of Tippecanoe in 1811, which established his reputation as an Indian fighter and inspired him to become increasingly familiar with native society and its leaders. This, in turn, made him valuable to state and federal governments intent on wresting the remainder of Indiana from its natives. He served in a number of state and military posts and in 1820 became one of the commissioners charged with locating Indiana's new capital city. The same year he was elected to the state general assembly. A number of appointments and assignments followed, mostly having to do with land and Indian affairs.

Although Tipton's most exalted honor was to be twice elected to the U.S. Senate from Indiana (1831–1839), probably his most influential contribution came as a result of his position as U.S. Indian Agent for the region from

1823 to 1831. It was in that capacity that he was present at Kin-com-a-ong in 1826. Initially he was paid $1,200 a year as agent, a relatively princely sum. For this he labored peacefully but forcefully to free Indiana for white American settlement. It is clear that the title "Indian agent" was not meant to imply a bureaucrat advocating on behalf of Indians, though he did support generous distribution of annuities to the natives for their peaceful surrender of land. By 1826 Tipton was both experienced and gifted in Indian relations. At the Paradise Spring negotiations he knew that the natives were already so "softened" by increased annuities, whiskey, and other white man's goods as to pose no real resistance to further alienation of their land.[30]

The fourth principal player in the Treaty of 1826 was Richardville (ca. 1761–1841), high chief of the Miami. Richardville was living proof that whereas British and Americans did not easily assimilate with Native Americans, and vice versa, the same had not held true with the French. French explorers and *couriers de bois*, being mostly single men, had readily wooed Indian women and, by acquiescing in tribal courting and marriage customs, were normally welcomed into the women's families. Undoubtedly there were also tragic stories of sexual abuse during this time, but an avenue of conciliation and assimilation existed for those who used it. The Richardville genealogy exemplified the tradition. Richardville's father was Antoine-Joseph Drouet de Richerville, an eighteenth-century French trader at Kekionga (Fort Wayne). His mother was a sister of Miami chief Pacanne, whose village was nearby. Jean Baptiste also wed a Miami. One of their daughters, Catherine, married a Miami chief with a French name, Francois La Fontaine. An upshot of this permutation of races is that Jean Baptiste easily crossed cultural boundaries and was, in fact, fluent in Miami, English, and French. However, the man was not naturally assertive or gregarious. It had fallen to his mother, the strong-willed Marie-Louise Pacanne Richardville (Tacumwah), to raise him to be a disciple of her powerful brother. In this she succeeded, for when Pacanne died, Richardville took his place without difficulty and held it until his death.

Chief Richardville may never have completely overcome a certain public shyness and a reticence about speaking in councils. This may explain his inconsistent attendance at the 1826 treaty meetings and his preference for private conferences. He may also have been worried lest a treaty curtail his own material ambitions, which were manifest. He was known to be a grasping, manipulative, even duplicitous, and successful negotiator. The government built a substantial brick house for him in Fort Wayne and at least two more of his area residences were also in the style of American housing. The American secretary, James M. Ray, noted the chief's apparent disdain for open meetings and believed that the real progress in treaty making depended on Richardville's sidebar conferences with the commissioners and lesser chiefs. Richardville lived to be eighty, dying in 1841 and leaving $200,000 in cash, several trading posts, and thousands of acres of land. As he grew older he tended to dress and speak more as a Miami than as a white man.[31]

While considering major players in the treaty-making process, it is important to remember the white traders. The fact that four of the ten buildings Tipton erected at Kin-com-a-ong were trading houses underscores an essential element in the process of treaty making—the exchange of money and goods. Chief Richardville's considerable estate shows that treaties resulted in the distribution of wealth in the interior, generating hikes in commerce and speculation. As the U.S. government had appropriated more and more Native American land, it established "annuity payments" on designated dates when enormous sums of money in payment for native turf were distributed to chiefs and braves at specified locations. Fort Wayne was such a location in northern Indiana until 1828, when it was replaced by the new town of Logansport. Whites and Native Americans poured in at the proper time, anticipating another influx of silver. The Indians came to receive what the government owed them for their land. The traders arrived to barter and fleece the natives out of it. Had the whites simply set up shops for selling goods such as food, equipment, or clothing, the trade could have been respectable enough and enriching enough for both sides. It was rarely that benign because of whiskey, which the traders imported in abundance and which many Native Americans craved while not being able to control the craving.

While reform-minded missionaries and some churches fought the practice of combining annuity payments with whiskey sales, government representatives did little to discourage the practice. Traders got richer while Indians lost enormous sums of money to acquire both colossal hangovers and further deterioration of the quality of their lives. Although traders attending the 1826 powwow are now mostly nameless, they were there in force with an agenda—wanting reimbursement for their expenses, the opportunity to buy land cheap, collection of Indian debts guaranteed by the government, and, most of all, open access to the Indians' thirst for goods and whiskey. In this agenda they were unofficially allied with Richardville, for he also had become wealthy through Indian treaties. The American leaders then, needing to please Richardville, had also to please the traders in order to negotiate a treaty. It would not take much of a cynic to conclude that treaties of the period seemed to be, at base, unholy alliances of white economic/political forces and some Native Americans against an increasingly vulnerable and dispirited native population. The Treaty of 1826, which made Wabash possible, was not any nobler in intention than that.[32]

In his preface to *The Tipton Papers*, Paul Wallace Gates offers a procedure for treaties that had become "fairly stereotyped" by 1826:

> The Indians were gathered together by agents who made liberal promises of good things to come. At the meeting place preparations were made for feeding great numbers of people; droves of cattle and hogs were purchased for butchering; traders were instructed to attend with attractive selections of goods; barrels of whisky were imported; and every precaution was taken to satisfy the appetites and desires of the Indians. At the proper time the agent in charge assembled the braves, to whom he read a stilted and pompous message from the Great White Father in which the Indians were upbraided for their depredations, drunkenness, and other misconduct, and reminded of the forbearance, generosity and friendliness of the whites. At this point the Indians were asked what lands they would surrender and if they would remove to an area farther west. Then the braves would withdraw to consult among themselves.[33]

Negotiations at Paradise Spring may very well have begun in just that fashion, though the culminating talks followed nearly a month of less formal interaction. Few accounts of the Treaty of 1826 are so detailed as that of the secretary, Ray. Years later he offered his own eyewitness rendition of some of the activities. He seemed especially fascinated with the socializing that erupted intermittently during negotiations. Early on, according to Ray, the three commissioners met with Potawatomi chiefs around a council fire. Introductions were made and previous encounters recalled. On learning that the governor's name was Ray, the Indians shook their heads, perplexed. The name made no sense to them. William Conner, one of the interpreters, dreamed up the explanation that the governor had been named for "the first dawn of morning." Satisfied with that answer the chiefs conferred briefly, then bestowed on Ray the title "Waw-sa-augh" and pulled out a peace pipe to share; everyone present took a puff, a positive beginning. Although liquor consumption was an expected part of social intercourse, the commissioners tried to keep its consumption under control through daily rationing. This ploy failed when several Indians tore a stick chimney off a supply cabin one night, commandeered whiskey barrels, passed them around camp, and, as Secretary Ray insensitively described it, got "heap drunk." They grabbed tomahawks and clubs and began yelling and shouting for more liquor. They banged on Governor Ray's cabin door, shouting "Waw-sa-augh whisk, whisk." The melee lasted nearly until daylight. It took the armed authority of the interpreters and other whites to restore order. Next morning the commissioners ordered the remaining barrels destroyed. As the Americans executed this order on the hillside, Indians ran to the spot to scoop up the liquor from the ground with their hands.

On a subsequent night the natives entertained the camp with an elaborate dance. They had carefully cleared a "park" across the Wabash River and marked a circular path on it with leaves soft enough for dancing in moccasins. Tree limbs in the area were festooned with lighted candles borrowed from the commissioners. A brightly painted brave led the dancing. Other painted braves joined in, each of whom would try to inspire Indian girls to follow him. It became a contest to see which brave was most popular. Shouts of approval broke out with each choice a girl made, and jeering greeted the brave who was left to dance alone. It took place with "the best of humor," and it lasted past midnight, though the commissioners turned in before that. Another dance on another evening was more warlike. Braves painted their bodies for battle, boasted loudly of their collection of scalps, yelled and ran wildly, and hurled tomahawks into a tree trunk. As an encore a single brave performed "the beggar dance." He suddenly burst into the assembly, screaming and stark naked, except that he had covered himself head to toe in fresh river mud, so thick his eyelids were pasted shut.[34]

Such entertainment greased the rougher edges of the cultural divide as whites and natives prepared for the serious work before them. Some events were less dramatic than the drinking and the dancing, yet, illustrated how Indians at times responded to white culture. While general socializing had proceeded, the Reverend McCoy was busy teaching Miami children in his cabin. Apparently he had brought his students to the treaty meeting as a way of demonstrating the benefits of the Christian faith and American education, benefits he pursued at his Indian mission school on the Saint Joseph River. Some of the braves—perhaps the younger ones—found this school too tempting a target to ignore. As the students inside tried to concentrate on their studies, the Indians outside taunted them, yelling, grinning, and laughing at them through cracks in the cabin wall. Secretary Ray reports that McCoy's students were not deterred in the least by these shenanigans (which might have occurred repeatedly) and that his school won grudging respect from the natives. McCoy's school acquired a valuable grant through the treaty with the Miami, as would another Indian school in Kentucky.[35]

Eventually it came time to finalize the issues. Richardville was still mostly absent but the lesser chiefs were ready to barter. In the long run they had little choice but to confirm what the Americans wanted. Gifts and whiskey and the prospect of higher annuities had no doubt done their work, though it cannot be said the natives capitulated without some hard bargaining: "It was only after vast quantities of food had been gorged, barrels of fiery whisky consumed, and brilliantly colored cloth and blankets and glittering ornaments to the value of $61,588 distributed that the stolid savages showed signs of weakening."[36] Having no desire to abandon their homeland, the Miami and Potawatomi slowly surrendered to the pressure and made counterproposals along the way. Indicative of the vigor of their bargaining is the fact that at this treaty's conclusion there was no provision for the mass removal of Native Americans farther west; Americans did not accomplish that injustice until a few years later. Tipton's reputation suggests that he would have insisted on a resolution that was reasonably fair to the Indians, at least by the standards of the day. He was certainly willing to defend the granting of generous reserves; and it was probably he who first recognized that an insistence on Native American removal would jeopardize the whole treaty.

With regard to the Potawatomi, the Americans secured a mile-wide swath through northern Indiana from Logansport to Lake Michigan in order to build a pike along that route. The government covered Potawatomi debts and increased annuities. Settlement with the Miami was far more expensive. The whites had dreamed of building what became the Wabash and Erie Canal linking Lake Erie with the Ohio River. Generous cessions north of the Wabash River were necessary for that project to go forward. Because of Richardville's stature and because of his common interests with Indian traders, both he and the traders had to be satisfied before the Americans could realize their objectives. A great many cash and in-kind elements went into the final agreement, including government assumption of debts totaling in excess of $17,000 Indians owed traders, distribution of more than $40,000 worth of goods over two years to the Miami, funds for the education of Indian children, gifts of large numbers of hogs and cattle, a gristmill, and appointment of skilled craftsmen and laborers in the remaining Indian reserves.

Although the Americans secured huge tracts of land for settlers and internal improvements, there were so many private reservations created that in the case of the Miami, at least, large numbers were never forced to relocate. Many of them and their descendants continued to be neighbors to the white settlers and eventually to intermarry into that society. Nevertheless, in the end the two treaties, one with the Potawatomi and one with the Miami, changed the status of a lot of land. The Potawatomi ceded 276,000 acres of northern Indiana. Both tribes surrendered jointly held land immediately north of the Wabash River totaling about 700,000 acres. However, in their final report the commissioners noted that former maps of the area were inaccurate in that the Eel River was much farther north than shown. This meant, they wrote, that "the whole extent of the cession is not less than 2,000,000 of acres, and perhaps amounts to 3,000,000."[37] Despite the facts that enormous acreage was ceded and that both the Michigan Road to the lake and the Wabash and Erie Canal became guaranteed rights-of-way, the treaty was not especially popular in the white community. Too much money and too many goods had been bartered away for too little land, especially in light of the approximately 95,000 acres that had been distributed in various Indian reservations.[38]

After October 23, 1826, Native Americans, commissioners, soldiers, traders, and hangers-on began to depart Kin-com-a-ong. Ray, Cass, and Tipton were probably the most illustrious group of Americans ever to assemble in the history of Wabash, albeit a prenatal history.

Crucial for the birthing of Wabash, when this illustrious trio departed it left the camp's buildings behind intact. The prospect of new lands opening up, coupled with plans for a canal through the region, meant that soon settlements materialized along the north bank of the Wabash River, but not necessarily at Kin-com-a-ong. In recording his earlier travels through the region, McCoy made no mention of Kin-com-a-ong or its immediate environs, though he was acquainted with Chief Charley whose compound was nearby; with Americans Kin-com-a-ong simply had no importance previous to 1826. Furthermore, the bluff was steep enough and close enough to the river and its floodplain to have discouraged speculators, who might logically have decided there was too little dry, level ground on which a settlement might grow and prosper. The availability of ready housing, then, may have made all the difference in attracting immigrants. Here was a settlement laid out in a clearing, for the taking. The names for the area, Kin-com-a-ong and its English translation, Paradise Spring, began to fall into misuse and were increasingly replaced by "Treaty Ground." The abandoned camp at Treaty Ground was not long without some kind of occupancy by traders, hunters, or pioneers looking for a place to settle temporarily. David Burr, rising canal commissioner and Hugh Hanna's future partner, had begun trading with the Miami from a Treaty Ground building before the end of 1826, perhaps immediately after the treaty was completed, although he seems not to have taken up permanent residence until the next year. Members of the Kintner and McClure families resided there through much of 1827, before settling in other parts of the county.

Burr and these other newcomers quickly appropriated the commissioners' quarters, the trading houses, the council house, and cookhouse for lodging, storage, or business. Tipton and the Indian agency also continued to make use of the compound as a logical place to deliver promised largesse to the Miami. In October 1827 Hanna helped deliver $25,000 in silver, $10,000 in goods, and a thousand barrels of salt to complete that year's obligation. This was in addition to a payment two months earlier of more than $26,000 worth of goods. Given these developments and the continuing importance of Treaty Ground, it is safe to postulate that Wabash as a viable settlement is older by nearly a decade than its formal founding in 1835 indicates. For nine years (1826 to 1835) Treaty Ground served as a gathering place in the wilderness and as a kind of incubation station for the village that would be platted on its west flank. When folks did not use "Treaty Ground" as the name of the place, they sometimes called it "Headquarters for New Comers." It would have a few other names before everyone settled on "Wabash."[39]

2

One Cent and a Stale Chew of Tobacco: The Proprietor

The early settlers' nickname for the place, "Headquarters for Newcomers," was too cumbersome a moniker for any town and did not stick, descriptive though it was. Also unwieldy but accurate would have been a name based on Judge William H. Coombs's remembrance of the 1835 town: "Little Clearing Below the Bluffs." The first names that were not mouthfuls were variously Treaty Springs, and as noted, Treaty Ground, both of which could be shortened to Treaty. During 1827 and 1828, the name was officially Treaty Ground, Miami Nation, with Robert Horse, possibly a local Miami, as postmaster. When David Burr assumed that position in 1829, the place's designation changed to Treaty Ground, Indiana. The same year the state incorporated the place into Cass County as the seat of Wabash Township, the easternmost of three townships. The separate creation of Wabash County came in 1832. Burr, who had appropriated one of the log cabins almost before the embers grew cold on John Tipton's campfire, took up residence there in early 1827. By the time he and Hugh Hanna got serious about imposing a town plat on the adjacent landscape in 1834, folks had started referring to the place as Wabashtown and then, more succinctly, as Wabash, reflecting the township name. It served well also for the obvious reason of the settlement's location on the river and, just possibly, because the Miami had it right; it was indeed a place where clear, bright water flowed over white rocks—Wah-bah-shi-ki, which the French had transposed as *Quabache*. Elijah Hackleman, among other newcomers, waxed lyrical over the fecund beauty of the stream: "I . . . took a survey of its water," he wrote, "and found [it] to be litteraly [*sic*] teeming with the finest Fish I had ever seen."[1]

Because of his early residence, plus his appointment as postmaster, Burr would most likely have been the person remembered as the town's founder. Naming the place "Burrsburg," "Burrston," "Burrsopolis," or something similar, would have been plausible. Burr did not receive that honor because he was not a "persister," meaning that he did not stay around very long. He does not appear in the 1840 U.S. Census of the county, and he left no family behind. In fact, this erstwhile founder not only had other fish to fry at the time of Wabash's formation, but in terms of accurate historical information, he also is a scantily understood figure. A Wabash County historian tracked Burr down to a sparse biographical outline. He was a native of Connecticut, birth date unknown. Between 1817 and 1821, he was postmaster at Salem in Washington County, Indiana, and he lived in Brownstown for a spell. Burr, Samuel Hanna of Fort Wayne, and Tipton worked together and knew each other well. Soon after the Paradise Spring treaty, Burr surfaced as an Indian trader at Treaty Ground. His inn/tavern-cum-post office at Wabash, circa 1827 to 1836, which may have been located in the old cookhouse or the former council house, was a successful enterprise and an important civilizing agent in the woodland frontier. In 1835 Burr was instrumental in bringing a potentially violent confrontation between canal workers to a peaceful conclusion. It is known that Burr's wife, Phebe, was with him in Wabash in 1836, when their names appear on a court record in connection with the sale of more than three hundred acres of land to the state, land he had purchased in 1830. The fact that their acreage lay just north and east of Treaty Ground, and on both sides of the river, strongly suggests that they had intended to take advantage of the canal's promise and to put down roots in the area.

The Indiana General Assembly appointed Burr to be one of three canal commissioners, along with Samuel Hanna (Hugh Hanna's brother) and Robert John in 1828, the year after Burr settled on the Wabash. Samuel's biographer calls Burr "a scholarly gentleman of ability and influence."[2] Appointment as a canal commissioner complicated Burr's plans. Any speculation along the canal route by a commissioner could be suspect, smelling of inside information and unfair advantage. In 1836, scarcely two years after he had partnered with Hugh, Burr pulled out, selling both county and town holdings, the latter to Hugh for four thousand dollars. In a letter to Tipton in 1836, Lagro's Elias Murray stated that Burr had recently realized a total of ten thousand dollars for various properties, and that he had sold out because his position as commissioner made his role as an investor awkward. Murray's testimony might support an idea that Burr was an incorruptible man, or at least one who did not want his reputation sullied. However, it should be noted that

Samuel Hanna was also a commissioner who invested concurrently in community development along the canal, especially in Fort Wayne. Samuel might simply have been more tenaciously self-interested in such matters than Burr. However, Burr was already tainted. He had previously been investigated for improprieties. By January 1837 Calvin Fletcher of Indianapolis pronounced him to be a corrupt man who was in default of $21,000 as commissioner. He may also have become deranged because of his problems. Although as late as 1845 Hugh sold Burr a lot on West Sinclair Street in Wabash, Burr otherwise recedes into obscurity. There are no place names honoring this founder of Wabash, unless Burr Creek, east of the city, was named for him.[3]

The Burrs were scarcely alone at Treaty Ground between 1827 and 1832, the latter date being the year he and Hugh joined forces. Tipton, for example, reclaimed use of his cabin briefly in August 1827, when he met Miami representatives to deliver more than $26,000 worth of goods in accordance with the treaty. He also took that opportunity to lecture the natives on the necessity of their pursuing farming more deliberately and of avoiding the consumption of whiskey. Tipton offered a reward of a horse and a gun to the first brave who reported any white man selling liquor to Indians. Others who did not have Tipton's ties to the place had nevertheless heard of the treaty or of plans for a canal, and, realizing what fresh opportunities loomed in the area, pushed through the wilderness until they lighted upon the ready-made convenience of the treaty buildings. Probably there was a fairly steady stream of traders, hunters, and would-be settlers who availed themselves of Burr's inn and tavern and then moved on, unimpressed, but nonetheless grateful for the morsel of civilization Burr's outpost provided.

Whether pioneers stayed or not, word of the place spread. In her work on the treaty, Mary C. O'Hair speculates reasonably that some of the newcomers who joined Burr at Wabash had been present at the time of the treaty negotiations, liked what they saw in the environs, and returned with their families. She cites as a case in point the Samuel McClure family, originally from North Carolina. Samuel McClure Jr., scarcely twenty years old, was already experienced in Indian trading with the Ewing family of Fort Wayne. Samuel Jr. and his father traveled from Ohio with a load of apples to sell at the treaty. They returned with their family to settle down soon after the treaty was concluded, in January 1827, beating Burr's move there by a few weeks. The family lived in one of the extant cabins while it selected a site for a permanent homestead. As spring approached, the McClures built a cabin at or near the treaty site, plowed fifteen acres of bottomland a short distance west, and planted corn. Samuel Jr. and his brother, Robert, hacked out roads, which were probably crude affairs. Such roads might have stumps left standing just low enough to allow a wagon to pass over, or they might consist mostly of axe marks that led travelers around bogs and through woods. An especially important McClure road wound from Wabash to the Eel River. When the family discovered that its farmland west of the treaty cabins was on Chief Charley's section, the McClures pulled up stakes and left Wabash, homesteading three miles downstream. While in Wabash the McClures had trouble with Tipton, who twice wrote the McClures (probably specifically Samuel Jr.), remonstrating with them about selling liquor. In August 1827 he wrote, "I want to see you in camp there is a number of Drunk Indians in the neighborhood and I . . . believe the liquor was obtained from [your] house."[4] A month later, he ordered them to stop vending whiskey for five days while he distributed goods to the natives. Interestingly there is no record of Tipton opposing Burr's tavern. The difference may be that Burr did not sell liquor to natives. Local historian Clarkson Weesner, writing in 1914, credits the McClures with being the county's first permanent residents. The term "permanent" is suspect in this case, however, for Samuel Sr. died in 1838, and Samuel Jr. and Robert do not appear as residents in the 1840 census. By that time they had moved to Grant County.[5]

Others, such as the Jonathan Keller family, are worthy of a comment though they did not settle in Wabash proper. Keller operated the Indian mill on Mill Creek Pike, a few miles southwest of Wabash where the pike crosses the creek just above the Richvalley prairie. They moved there in 1829. Keller is credited with having discovered or established a "cow ford" over the river four miles downstream from Treaty Ground, facilitating cattle drives back and forth; the crossing was probably where the ancient Indian and French traders' road passed over the river. Keller fathered enough healthy offspring that in 1879 Alanson P. Ferry wrote that his descendants "are still among us," making the Kellers classic county "persisters."[6] When Elizabeth Keller wed Joseph McClure in 1832, it was the first recorded marriage of settlers in the county. In fact, the family is locally noteworthy most of all because Jonathan Keller Jr. was the first white child born in Wabash County. Some challenged that claim, saying that John Miller, son of the mill's blacksmith, was first. Ferry asserted, however, that Mrs. Keller carried her son in her arms to visit the newborn Miller boy.

The examples of the McClures and the Kellers illustrate that early settlers were highly aware of each others' presence even if they lived miles apart, and that those homesteading in the country were often well known in the infant town of Wabash. One of these was Isaac Fowler who, with his son Newton, farmed a couple of miles north of town, west of the junction of modern routes numbered 24 and 13. Both father and son frequently traveled to Wabash, although in the early years there was no direct road between farm and town. Isaac was a former teacher, a surveyor, and a staunch Presbyterian. In May 1836 he and his wife comprised more than a fourth of the founding membership in Wabash's first organized congregation. Although Isaac did not live long, Newton's personal diary shows that he carried on the tradition of being deeply involved in the communal life of Wabash while continuing to live in the country.[7]

Hugh Hanna had also been in and about the treaty site before he moved there, doing some odd jobs for Tipton, building coffins for Chief La Gros's family, and overseeing projects that fulfilled the government's obligations to other Miami. He had once earned Tipton's anger for being a laggard in reporting on certain assignments. But Hanna sprang from a slightly different background than that which most of the earliest Wabash settlers had known, different even from Tipton's heritage, for Hugh had a very successful, very powerful, and very wealthy older brother in Fort Wayne. One writer noted that "Sam Hanna made, perhaps, more significant and lasting contributions to the growth and prosperity of Fort Wayne and the area of northeastern Indiana than any other man of his time."[8] He virtually founded Fort Wayne and made his fortune helping it develop from a Miami village (Kekionga), and a decaying frontier fort, into a promising canal and railroad city. Hugh and his younger brother Joseph Hanna always worked in Samuel's shadow. Both emulated, but never equaled, Samuel's success, Hugh at Wabash and Joseph at Lafayette. Wabash, in some spiritual sense at least, is as much an extension of Samuel's entrepreneurial passion as it is the result of Hugh's energy and investments.[9]

To understand Hugh's drive toward community development, and toward prospering in the process, it is helpful to examine his family's heritage. The Hanna boys were sons of James Hanna, a farmer in Kentucky, then Ohio; a workman skilled in tanning, weaving, and woodcraft; a champion of education; a Presbyterian elder; an advocate of the Sunday School movement of the early nineteenth century; and scion of a Scots-Irish line for whom land hunger and business enterprise were seemingly in the blood. The line rose up in Scotland during the twelfth century in the southwestern peninsula of Wigtownshire, a remote lowland county. Its ancestral seat still stands; it is a rather modest castle or fortified manor, Sorbie Tower, now a roofless, four-story mass of stone staircases, garderobes (privies), generous hearths, and empty window groins rising out of scarcely penetrable woods two miles south of the village of Sorbie. During Elizabethan times young bloods of the family who were economically oppressed, hungry for land, and encouraged by Her Majesty's government, had immigrated to Ireland, settling in County Monagham where the English had seized vast tracts from the natives. For several generations the primitive village of Ballybay was the Irish center for Hannas. There they became Scots-Irish.

Then, in the eighteenth century, Irish immigrated en masse to America, sometimes crossing the sea together as whole congregations. In 1771 Hanna, age one year, moved with his parents, Alexander and Martha, to Pennsylvania. He sprang from yeoman stock: farmers who were staunchly Protestant, often Presbyterian, rabid for personal independence, eager for material success, open to taking risks, not afraid of hard work or of stringent morality, and often supportive of education as an invention of the Almighty. Having lived in closely knit congregations around Ballybay, Hannas quickly discovered that their welfare in the New World might also be inseparably linked to community development. In any case, the next generation of Hannas demonstrated an alliance of individual ambition with the American frontier's need for viable community life.[10]

James's eldest son, Samuel, was a man of moderate build, thick dark hair, and large ears. He wore a beard at times, but he was clean shaven in 1843 when he, his wife Eliza Taylor Hanna, and their eight sons sat for a family portrait. The portrait shows a well-groomed, quintessentially successful Victorian family. Two adulatory biographies have been produced about Samuel. The first of these appeared soon after his death and virtually canonizes the man. The more reliable comes from the staff of the Fort Wayne and Allen County Public Library, compiled in 1953. Both accounts illustrate Samuel's integrity and self-discipline with the same two stories. One concerns the nineteen-year-old working as a clerk in a Piqua, Ohio, store. He and an equally inexperienced partner bought out the store's proprietor with personal notes. The enterprise went belly-up, leaving the partners with a three thousand-dollar debt. Pleading "infancy," Samuel's partner fled responsibility. Samuel, however, accepted the burden and paid off the debt, principal and interest, though it is not explained exactly how he did this. He had been a long-distance mail carrier for a time and had also taught a country school where he earned a reputation as a "vigorous" disciplinarian. Probably most of his income in these early years came from trade. He and another brother, Thomas, had been sutlers (purveyors) who provided food for men and beasts at the Treaty of Saint Marys in 1818, importing goods by ox team from Troy, Ohio. Samuel was clearly exhibiting unsinkable characteristics at an early age.

A second story focuses on Samuel's midlife career in Fort Wayne, some time after 1819, the year he settled there at age twenty-two. He was respected locally as a man of rigid economy, industry, and sagacity. These principles were so ingrained in his character that he reputedly refused to spend even one dollar on personal pleasure or luxury until he was worth $50,000 ($1.25 million in present-day currency). When he did decide to spend some of his wealth on nonessentials, part went into splendid conspicuous consumption. His mansion east of downtown Fort Wayne was pillared with high porches. Legend says he built it on a rise in such a way that from the basement ballroom guests could gaze upon the rising skyline of antebellum Fort Wayne as the sun set behind the western horizon. He became deeply involved in two major railroads and oversaw construction of huge railroad repair shops in Fort Wayne. Other interests included banking and partnerships in foundries, woolen mills, and the spoke-and-bending industry. After his death in 1866, more than $54,000 worth of furnishings was sold. When outstanding debts of $151,000 had been paid, Samuel's estate amounted to more than $260,000, equaling more than $3.5 million in twenty-first-century currency. The breadth of his wealth is illustrated by the observation that by 1843 "he could go to Indianapolis by way of Lafayette, return by way of Anderson, and feed his horse at his own corn crib [on a farm he owned] every night during his journey."[11]

Samuel built the first significant commercial building in Fort Wayne. It was a log-cabin warehouse that rose before streets existed, where Columbia and Barr streets would one day cross, just west of the juncture of Saint Marys and Saint Joseph rivers. The original Hanna residence also occupied this ground. Goods were shipped in from Ohio by means of flatboats and pirogues on the Saint Marys or from New York by way of Lake Erie and the Maumee River. The limitations of such transport doubtless helped make Samuel and other visionaries passionate for road construction and any other internal improvements that might accelerate their prosperity. A story-and-a-half frame building soon replaced Samuel's original cabin, only to be superseded by a brick block of business houses. Samuel offered Fort Wayne a variety of desirable trade goods, space for cabinet making (which Hugh pursued), and probably rentals for lawyers and other professionals. Hanna's block became the focus of the town's emerging business complex. All of this initial enterprise in the village was prelude to the outpouring of Samuel's ample business genius, which by the early 1830s had targeted canal building, a monumental undertaking that transformed the area's economy. After several years' experience and success with the canal, he launched an even more prominent career as northern Indiana's entrepreneurial railroad prince. His funeral in 1866 was an enormous public display of Fort Wayne's communal sense of the loss of one who, more than any other, had brought the town out of its pioneer status, making it an economic success.[12]

Biographers are quick to credit Samuel with intense social consciousness, calling him a "planter and builder" and implying that his drive for success was not merely a matter of self-interest.[13] It would be more accurate to say that the Hannas' rather passionate and obvious self-interest easily endorsed religious, moral, and cultural progress. They not only were motivated by sincere religious convictions but also by the knowledge that a stable, progressive community generates and protects wealth. Thus, Samuel was an early advocate of the Sabbath School movement, which offered a substitute for nonexistent public education in many frontier communities. His father set up a school in Samuel's business block in 1826 or 1827. Samuel is also credited with being a founder of the First Presbyterian Church of Fort Wayne, a congregation that initially met at his warehouse and was notable for supporting various social reforms. Although Samuel did not join the church he helped found until 1843, twelve years after its creation, he was quickly elected an elder of the church, a lifetime position.

The man may also have been quite well read and a local bulwark of secular cultural attainment. Such a view is supported somewhat by an inventory of a library that Samuel's son, Hugh T. Hanna, owned. There were approximately 450 titles in the collection, covering a broad range of interests, from books of sermons to fiction, philosophy, poetry, and the sciences. It is likely that Hugh T. had inherited at least part of such a large library from his father, whose executor he was. Additionally, Samuel eventually stood firmly for temperance reform, though it is quite possible he had postponed formally joining First

Presbyterian because its minister, James Chute, was too rigidly a teetotal (abstinence) reformer. It had been of some concern to his fellow bank directors that on one occasion Samuel and a son had to be carried home, having consumed too much champagne after the 1836 political campaign. The war on liquor was at its height in the 1840s and 1850s, with prohibition laws rising in legislatures across the nation. Frontier Presbyterians, in particular, had adopted the movement as an essential tenet of congregational discipline. They were foremost in the temperance fight in Fort Wayne, though there and elsewhere their support of that cause seemed sometimes to have had less to do with personal moral purity than with the desire to promote a salutary sobriety in rough-and-tumble settlements.[14]

Lastly, it should be noted that although Samuel held such exalted positions as associate judge of the circuit court, he had a reputation for fighting for the little guy. Already known locally as one who easily extended credit and was lenient with debtors in hard times, he won the undying gratitude of less-fortunate folks when, in the late 1850s, he successfully sought to preserve railroad jobs locally. In the next decade, when his funeral cortege led the mass of mourners through Fort Wayne toward his tomb, it passed at least one Hanna-owned factory that flew a banner reading, "Samuel Hanna, the Working Man's Friend." There is reason to believe it was a sincere sentiment.[15]

Hugh Hanna of Wabash probably strived to be a carbon copy of his elder brother. Anatomically speaking, he nearly succeeded. In a formal mid-1850s photograph of Hugh, seated with his wife, Elizabeth Everly Hanna, and daughter Josephine (Josephena), he appears to have the same body structure as his brother, the same full head of hair (though grayer), and similar facial features. They were both so-called Black Irishman who tended toward middle-aged portliness. As a young man, Hugh had been described as standing five feet, ten inches tall and having a dark complexion with dark hair and blue eyes. While living in Fort Wayne, Hugh gained enormous practical experience in carpentry and cabinetry, helping build the first courthouse there. More important, however, Samuel's pattern of operations was a template for Hugh: start various businesses; buy and sell land; build mills, warehouses, and merchandising facilities; encourage trade and manufacturing; encourage church and reform societies; and invest in the canals, railroads, and roads. Hugh, by comparison, founded a church, joined the Masons, encouraged public education, supported temperance and civic improvements, focused on multiple businesses, and was involved in community governance without being overly political, endearing him to his fellow citizens. Both men succeeded, though on differing scales, in part because Fort Wayne was the grander stage, in part because Samuel gave the better performance. However, it is safe to assert that the role Samuel played for Fort Wayne, Hugh played for Wabash.[16]

Samuel's early interest in the canal almost certainly galvanized Hugh's, and it was Samuel's alliance with Burr in the canal project that provided Hugh with a partner in Wabash. In the mid-1820s Samuel and Burr began their correspondence with Congress, urging creation of a canal that would link Lake Erie to the interior of Indiana. In 1827 the United States donated large tracts of former Indian land to Indiana for support of its construction. Partly on the basis of these activities Samuel was elected to the state legislature, which soon authorized the surveying required to map a canal to Lafayette, where the Wabash River became dependably navigable. When both Samuel and Burr were appointed as canal commissioners it was probably a forgone conclusion that the waterway would follow a route beneficial to Fort Wayne and the upper Wabash valley. As it turned out the route eventually followed the river past Lafayette all the way to Terre Haute before turning "in-land" toward a point many miles east of the Wabash and then dropping south to the Ohio River.

Meanwhile, about the time of the 1826 treaty if not before, Samuel must have impressed on Burr and Hugh the wisdom of investing in land along the proposed canal and becoming proprietors of a town plat there, a proprietor commonly being the owner, developer, and realtor of a parcel of land. By this time both Hugh and Burr knew Treaty Ground well enough through their relationship with Tipton. If they were to buy land along the canal, this area in particular would have leapt quickly to their minds. Samuel encouraged this partnership by supporting it financially. He cosigned for Hugh's bank loans, and his name appears frequently as the owner of Wabash town lots. Quite probably, when Hugh ran short on cash he could always sell a few more lots to his brother.[17]

In February 1832 officials broke ground for the Wabash and Erie Canal in Fort Wayne. The same year Wabash County was established with somewhat impermanent boundaries, boundaries that were solidified in fairly short order. It would be three years before the new canal from Fort Wayne to Huntington was usable and two more years after that before it reached Treaty Ground. Meanwhile, early in 1832, Burr and Hugh had purchased 118.60 acres from the U.S. land office in Fort Wayne. Some land was still selling for

$1.25 an acre; if they got it at that price, the partners bought Wabash for about $150 and were ahead of inflated prices caused by canal speculations. The acreage lay immediately west and northwest of the treaty cabins and the spring. It did not include bottomland on the lower floodplain abutting the river. The southern boundary was the east-west line of the projected canal, scarcely above the lower floodplain, with the whole of the plat—just over four blocks square—extending north.

It was customary to plat a new town in rectilinear form, with parallel streets running fairly true north-south and east-west. Such platting reflected the nation's continuing romance with Jeffersonian economy and design, a kind of leftover deism that wanted to impose logical order upon a wild landscape. It also made surveying and land titles easier. A visit to many former frontier towns in the Midwest will reveal the pattern: the oldest sections of a place echo the original grid that had first appeared on paper and had then been transposed upon the landscape by surveyors. Such a grid made sense in places such as Fort Wayne, Huntington, and Peru where level, dry land slightly above a floodplain spread out wide enough to accommodate a sizable settlement. It made a lot less sense for Wabash. There the forty- to sixty-foot bluff ran through the center of the grid, east to west, a bluff so steep in places that horses and pedestrians struggled to mount it. Indeed, one of the original streets, Huntington, was platted but never completed between Main and Market streets, undoubtedly because the grade there was too precipitous. The same was true for the south half of Court Street. As the town grew, new streets such as Spring, Comstock, and Thorne abruptly ended at the bluff, it being pointless to build a street on a near perpendicular. A postmodern visionary would no doubt have wound and curved streets to the tune of the bluff's natural contours, taking advantage of its charm. That Hanna and Burr did not take such a tack probably issues from nineteenth-century expectations, from considerations of economy, and, possibly, from a stubborn lack of imagination. However that may be, a rectilinear, highly geometric, two-dimensional grid superimposed on Wabash's highly curvilinear, three-dimensional topography was, at base, an awkward beginning for a town.[18]

Having platted the place in April 1834, Hanna and Burr began selling lots as early as the next month. Through the 1830s, lots sold at prices ranging from twenty-two dollars to one hundred fifty each. The most expensive of these was located on the canal line. In 1835 Hugh moved permanently with his family from Fort Wayne to Wabash. Burr left the next year. Those three years before the partnership dissolved, 1834–36, represented a whirlwind of activity in the process of jump-starting Wabash. The partners had named the streets in a logical if unimaginative manner. North-south streets bear names of contiguous counties: Allen, Huntington, Wabash, Miami, and Cass; an exception is Court Street that was platted to connect Hill and Main next to a "Public Square." The names of most east-west streets describe their location or function: Canal, Market, Main, and on top of the bluff, Hill. The exception in this case is the northernmost street on the Original Plat, "St. Clair Street." Presumably named for General Arthur St. Clair, a former governor of the Northwest Territory, the street's name eventually morphed into "Sinclair." The fact that a street located three-quarters the way up the bluff and not easily accessible was named Main seems to indicate that the founders had in mind some important construction for the high ground. Here were soon located a jail, then a courthouse, and, not so incidentally, Hanna's residence.

For the short haul, however, Hanna did not worry that an irregular bluff cut through his town. He directed most of his early efforts toward developing infrastructure on the lower level to serve the future "downtown," an eight-block area defined by Canal, Market, South Allen, and South Cass streets. Initially settlers favored this area and built the first homes and commercial outlets along these streets. One of the very earliest lower-level projects was actually outside the town plat. It was a dam, possibly built of river rocks, that Hanna threw up across the Wabash River sometime before May 1836. It was just south of Treaty Ground and just west of the mouth of Treaty Creek and created a splendid bathing and fishing hole. William Combs bragged of catching ninety-three fish there in one day, but its main function was to serve as a reservoir for its related project, a millrace. The race began east of the dam, arched northwest through the southeast edge of the treaty area, and then—near the future corner of Huntington and Water streets—turned southwest. It emptied back into the river close to the site of later Wabash Street bridges.

Neither the construction of the dam nor the digging of the trench could have been a simple undertaking. The race had to have been at least a third of a mile long and deep enough to maintain a good current, cutting through timbered, possibly rocky, ground. It is known that Hanna owned or rented a team of oxen in 1835. This would be tantamount to controlling the heaviest machinery available and could account for a fairly quick execution of a dam and a race. Also, though Hanna was not above physical labor for himself, he frequently hired local settlers and sojourners to work on his various projects.

A millrace meant a sawmill, of course, and one soon rose as the first building to occupy the floodplain. Hackleman remembered it rising halfway between the canal line and the site of the first river bridge. Warren Hanna, Hugh's son, put it halfway from Hanna's Corner to the river. A map, hand drawn in pencil by one of Hugh's associates, probably in the 1850s, locates a "mill lot," number 14, east of Wabash Street, south of Water Street, and on the north bank of the "old mill race." This is likely the site of Hugh's original mill. Given the fact that settlers who brought grain with them had to process it by hand, a little at a time, Hanna quickly added flour-milling capability to the structure, what Warren called his father's "corn cracker." But considering how impatient the man was to create infrastructure for his town, it is clear he built the mill mainly to process timber, turning logs into the planks, joists, posts, siding, and lathe that Hugh soon needed for his own house and that he could sell to settlers. Until such a mill was up and running, lumber had to be floated on rafts from a mill on the Mississinewa River, down that rocky river, and then up the Wabash River, an inconvenient, seasonal, and labor-intensive transport. Hugh was an inventive and versatile creature, and his first mill would produce both lumber and grain.[19]

Early accounts credit Hugh with building the first brick commercial building in town in 1835 on the northwest corner of Wabash and Canal streets, lot number 29 on the original plat. Folks called it Hanna's Corner. However, in 1915 Warren, who was born in 1838, reported that his birth took place at an earlier brick structure, which housed his family at the time. Hanna's Corner, he recalled, came a little later. Although the Hannas probably housed themselves first at Treaty Ground, as many newcomers did, they must have moved into Warren's birthplace shortly after their arrival. By this account, then, Hanna's Corner would probably not have been occupied in 1835, though construction might have been under way. For its foundation, rock quarried south of the river was dragged by ox team to the site. At one point in this process Hanna felt obliged to tip the stoneworkers a dollar after the oxen had stalled in the middle of the river, forcing their drivers to wade waist deep in ice-cold water to move the team. The new building stood directly and conveniently across Canal Street from an area Hugh had reserved to be a principal dock for the canal that was still two years away from reality. Hanna's Corner became the magnet and anchor for Wabash's earliest business district and shopping area. The two-story structure there was multipurpose: dry goods, commercial space, professional offices, and room for social events.

Somewhere in the process of his practical training, Hanna had become a self-taught hydrologist. Not only had he managed to dam the Wabash River and to create a water-powered mill, he now set out to install Wabash's first—and for decades, only—indoor plumbing. His creativity in this regard would be completely lost to history if Johnny Ivory, scion of a family of laborers, had not been employed in 1896 to repair a sewer on Wabash Street at its juncture with the east/west alley between Canal and Market streets. He dug up a log, five feet under the surface, and threw it up to the top of his trench as a nuisance to be discarded. Hanna's son-in-law, J. D. Conner, and Thomas McNamee, both major community icons, spotted the log and immediately identified it as part of Hanna's water system. At their behest, Ivory inspected the item more closely and realized that he could insert his arm into the log lengthwise because it had been hollowed out from end to end. The wood was well preserved, with parts of the bark still adhering. Conner and McNamee affirmed that Hanna had buried a line of such logs, end to end, stretching from the spring at Treaty Ground to Hanna's Corner, where it provided fresh, running water. This kind of wooden plumbing, in which water flow was controlled by driving a sliding metal plate crosswise through a wooden pipe, had been used sparingly elsewhere since about 1800. It is not known if Hanna's system had control mechanisms.

His experimentation with hydrology continued after he built a permanent home on the bluff above the spring, which still spouted from a point part way up the steep incline. Hanna was then using some of the north-to-south treaty cabins for stabling livestock. Just below the spring, he built a small shack over running water where his wife, Elizabeth, cooled milk and butter. Below the shack he constructed a trough for watering animals and made it available to the general public. His pièce de résistance, however, was a contraption that allowed the family and their neighbors to draw fresh water up the bluff to the Main Street level. Hanna rigged a water bucket at the end of a wire that was threaded through a pulley system anchored to an overhanging sycamore limb at the top of the bluff and then to a windlass near the ground. Apparently it worked. In any case it was about this time that folks began to refer to Paradise Spring, Kin-com-a-ong, as Hanna's Spring.[20]

The Hanna family must have moved to the bluff after Warren was born in 1838, though their house there was under construction in 1837. By the latter date Hugh's mill had been in operation nearly two years, presumably churning out the necessary timbers, siding, and lathe. One of the first settlers, carpenter Jesse Myers, built the house. By 1856 it was already being described, lightheartedly, as "that antiquated dwelling" and "an antique cottage," which stood "On, or rather in, the hillside."[21] While the house was scarcely in the same league as Samuel's Fort Wayne mansion, in a rough frontier settlement it qualified as a showplace. Early maps depict it distinctly as a long structure occupying the center of three lots on the south side of Main Street near its intersection with Spring Street. Like Hanna's Corner, the foundation was stone quarried from the surrounding landscape. Good limestone was as abundant as water, and throughout the nineteenth century citizens used it for foundations and often for entire buildings.

A single photograph of Hanna's homestead survives. Although taken in the early twentieth century after the house had become derelict, it shows the basic shape and style of the place. It was a two-story structure, but the bedroom level was so entirely defined by a steep roof and jutting double gables that headroom had to have been at a premium on that floor. The house's exterior is distinguished by a gracefully executed bay of five windows looking west, presumably from the main parlor. The bay may have faced Hugh's orchard that occupied part of the bluff top. Some upper gable windows appear to be tall and narrow, like French doors. First-floor windows are also large, originally holding many small squares of glass. Although there is no evidence of the usual decorative gimcrack, the house seems to be a rough version of the Gothic Revival style. Victorian cottage is another possible description. In twenty-first-century Wabash at least two houses survive to represent these styles. One is the pleasantly restored Carr-Durnbaugh House at Cass and Maple streets, built in 1857, which displays the same deep roofline and long, narrow upper windows. A second, at 29 East Sinclair Street, is probably less than half the size of Hanna's house, but it closely mimics the west end of it, including a dramatic bay window. Doubtless the Hanna building sported a front porch of some kind, but it was long gone by the time of the photograph. The ground sloped sharply from the front of the house toward the bluff's edge, allowing for habitable basement space, at least on the south side. The house was a very ample home for its place and period, easily evocative of a town's founding father and a strong statement of Hanna's place in the local scheme of things.

It is somewhat inexplicable that the man did not build his permanent residence of brick. Brick had been available since 1835, as Hanna's Corner and at least two residences of the time testify. A kiln turning out this material was two blocks away at the bottom of the bluff on the south side of East Market, east of Huntington Street. Pioneer settlers Alphaeus Blackman and Hannibal Parcell built the kiln and started selling bricks shortly after Blackman's arrival in 1835. Indeed, at one point Hanna himself may have had an interest in an early kiln. At this juncture, however, a frame home may simply have been more economically attractive because he operated a sawmill. Then, too, he was a carpenter by trade, and his home in Fort Wayne had also been a large frame.[22]

In this house on the bluff Hugh and Elizabeth added to their family every two to six years until there were six children, two boys and four girls. The great loss was Josephine, who died at age twelve in 1858. Isophena married a local boy, A. L. Tyer, in 1861 and lived next door to her father's house. Ada married Will Miles, son of one of Hanna's erstwhile business partners, and the couple eventually moved into Hanna's house on the bluff. Julia married the future Judge James Dicken Conner. Conner was a lawyer with ambitions that more than matched his father-in-law's, so that Julia lived a high-profile life in Wabash until her death in 1898. Their offspring presided with strength through most of the twentieth century. The older boy, Hugh W., was born in Fort Wayne in 1834. J. Warren, born in 1838, had once been alleged to be the first white child born in Wabash town, an idea that questions couples' fecundity if no births occurred between 1835 and 1838. In fact the first white child was probably the offspring of George Shepherd who arrived in 1835. In time both of Hugh's sons became involved with their father in various partnerships; but in the end both sought their fortunes elsewhere, Hugh in Chicago, Warren in Warsaw.

In his advanced years Hugh W. fondly remembered the family home that gave his father daily visual connection with the old spring and the treaty cabins below. By all available accounts, Hanna family life had been normal for the times, displaying a healthy balance of serious purpose and good humor. The death of the youngest surviving child, Josephine, the only child to sit with her parents for an extant formal portrait, must have been excruciating. Elizabeth's death in 1863 cast Hugh in the role of a widower in charge of a large house devoid of other family inhabitants. He did not retreat into loneliness, however. He remained dutifully in touch with his town and with his various responsibilities in it. In 1868 he married Mary Scott, the widow of his pioneer acquaintance, Moses Scott. Hugh died soon afterwards.[23]

On February 29, 1856, when times were still good in the house on the bluff, a great many "gleesome girls of Wabash" invaded the Hanna homestead to celebrate Leap Year Day. They dragged along, willingly and unwillingly, a cross-section of unmarried males from the community, some of the professional class, some not, and one or two bachelors who were already long in the tooth. Eighteen-year-old Warren's generation of teenagers may have instigated the party. The event seemed to have been an unannounced celebration of a tradition that Leap Year Day granted young spinsters permission to express openly their interest in single males. For the occasion an unidentified guest concocted a very long poem in the style of Henry Wadsworth Longfellow's "Hiawatha." A few of its opening stanzas are enough to illustrate that Hugh, at age fifty-seven, had attained status as a respected, jovial, popular first citizen. By this time he had been wearing the honorary title Colonel for a number of years and living in rather conspicuous dignity in his home on the bluff.

I've a story worth the telling
Were my telling worth the story.
If I tell it will you listen?
Will you hear it, if I'll tell you?
You <u>will</u> hear it,

Near the eastern
Bounds of Wabash; near the Big Ditch
Which the State dug; by the Big Spring
Where the Red man made a treaty;
Made a treaty with the Pale face;
By a treaty sold his birthright;
Sold it for a mess of pottage:
On, or rather in, the hill-side,
Overlooking the said Big Spring,
Stands an antique cottage building,
Home of the "good humored Colonel,"
'Bove the Big Spring, in the hill-side,
Stands that antiquated dwelling.

On a day that may be nameless,
Since the name don't suit my measure,
To the Colonel's hill-side cottage,
Came the gleesome girls of Wabash;

From the country some there came too;
From the well-known Grove of Locusts,
And the regions farther westward,
Came the lithesome, youthful maidens;
Came the maidens, gay and joyous,
Greeting Wabash's winsome daughters
At the hearth-stone of the Colonel;
"Our good humored friend, the Colonel."[24]

Hanna would not have attained material success, recognition of his historic status in town, or a high degree of popularity without his continued personal involvement. Although he never became enormously rich and died intestate, "he left a large amount of property," according to official records.[25] For more than thirty years he kept selling Wabash lots, acquiring debt, paying off debts (sometimes late), and developing the town's economic and cultural base. An appraisal of his activities during those decades not only illustrates Hanna's entrepreneurial intrepidity and civic-mindedness, but it also indicates the kinds of activities many of his fellow citizens commonly pursued, often with the same gusto Hanna exhibited, often with greater financial return.

Before Burr left town in 1836, he and Hanna had built a warehouse on the south side of Canal Street, west of Allen Street, abutting the line of the anticipated canal. They called their company Hanna and Burr. Without being absolutely certain one can reasonably speculate that they built it to store grain, lumber, and pork because a decade and a half later the second floor of the building collapsed under the weight of two thousand pounds of corn that tumbled down to burst off the siding, spewing "a jumble of corn, boards, timber [and] pork" about the place.[26] Grain, lumber, and pork were vital commodities in a new settlement, and Hanna was involved in producing, selling, and storing all of them.

He located a pork-rendering plant south of the intersection of Allen and Canal streets, but it was not a felicitous placement for such work. Lacking a creek and too far from the millrace, it offered no way to sluice off the offal, the inevitable by-products of slaughtering. On Christmas Day 1848 Hanna began slaughtering three thousand hogs and dumped the offal onto Canal Street, a quick and easy solution. But this was 1849, not 1835, and there were statutes on the books and a local government in place to deal with such primitive behavior. A grand jury indicted him in wonderfully descriptive language: "the excrement, blood, entrails, offals and other filth coming from said hogs . . . [were left in Canal Street], whereby divers fetid noisome, obnoxious offensive and unwholesome smells, did then and there arise and ascend from the said excrements, blood, entrails, offals and other filth, and the air thereby, and thereabouts became corrupted, contaminated and infected, and the said dwelling houses, of the said citizens were rendered very unwholesome, offensive, unfit and improper for habitation."[27] That a grand jury could confront the man who was the county seat's founding father is not only a study in grassroots democracy, but it is also a good indication that Wabash had developed from a mere frontier settlement with few rules to something resembling a bona fide town.

Warehouse followed warehouse, business begat business, as Hanna's ambition planted new capital on the ground. Hugh Hanna and Company (H. H. & Co.) specialized in lumber, solicited logs from county landowners, and boasted of a new steam saw that could produce lumber "inferior to none in the west."[28] Another sawmill, or a newer version of H. H. & Co. in 1860, was Hanna and Brothers, probably a partnership of Hugh with his sons. The *Wabash Plain Dealer* reported that its saw ripped timbers into lathes "in quicker time than it takes to read this," producing material of uniform width and thickness, "better than found in Toledo."[29] Just below the canal bridge, a half block south of Hanna's Corner, was Hanna's Storage, Forwarding and Commission Business that handled flour, fish, salt, ash, linseed oil, grindstones, and wrapping paper. This property later housed the Hanna and Bruner Hub and Spoke Works, one of several businesses Hanna's sons engaged in, if somewhat inconsistently. The Hanna and Smiley warehouse experimented with a new invention, "sugar evaporators," which processed sorghum into a cooking syrup. The partner was Sam Smiley with whom Hanna also shared a forwarding and commissioning business that collected and shipped grains.

These various enterprises—warehousing, milling, slaughtering, evaporating, transporting, plus his original dry goods store and the selling of town lots—Hanna pursued in addition to the two most prominent business concerns, the Wabash and Erie Canal, which he helped bring to Wabash in 1837, and the Toledo, Wabash and Saint Louis Railroad, which arrived in the mid-1850s. Although his personal investments in canal and railroad may not have been large, his name was linked with his older brother, Samuel, as one of the principal movers and shakers. Another of Hugh's concerns is worthy of mention, even though it failed to materialize in ways he dreamed it might.

After he had Wabash up and running, albeit in a rudimentary way, Hanna partnered with a couple of other citizens to lay out the town of Laketon, located fifteen miles north on the Eel River. The place had no canal and no river traffic and when a railroad at last came through, it did so on the south side of the river, not the town side. An additional drawback was the development of North Manchester as the dominant town in the northern part of the county.[30]

Examples of Hanna's nonbusiness activities between 1835 and his death in 1869 suffice to illustrate that his interests were broader than merely those of creating raw, private capital. Just as he never dominated Wabash economically, neither did he dominate it politically, socially, or culturally. He was, however, an active, if sporadic, player in every realm.

There were, of course, those quasi-legal, quasi-political dealings that were prerequisites for birthing a town. In 1834 and 1835 Treaty Ground, once the seat of Wabash Township, Cass County, functioned—unofficially—as the seat of the new county of Wabash. Burr's tavern/inn at the treaty site was the virtual county courthouse, although business was also conducted at Duffy's tavern, at Murphy's tavern, and possibly at McKibben's store and other taverns, which were located farther west in the new town plat. It was at Burr's, on May 4, 1834, that Hanna, Burr, and others had met to finalize plans for the canal, which was already approaching Huntington from the east. According to Ferry, a newspaper editor and early local historian, it was also there that commissioners chose an official county seat twelve months later. All the commissioners on that occasion were from other counties so that their selection of Wabash was presumably without undue local influence.

Other versions, however, point out that, in practical terms, the choice depended on donations of land or on the commissioners' ability to purchase suitable land for a seat of government. On May 18, 1835, Burr's and Hanna's offer to such an end was accepted. They proposed to donate suitable town lots for a public square, to construct a courthouse worth at least three thousand dollars, to guarantee three hundred dollars for library purposes, and to supply acreage for a cemetery, two seminaries, and two churches. A courthouse was to be completed by November 1839, excluding plastering. It would be a two-story brick, forty feet square, well furnished, having a bench and bar and a steeple with bell and spire.

When, in 1838, nothing resembling a courthouse had materialized in any form, the county board reviewed the contract. Burr had sold out three years earlier, having received $4,000 from Hanna for his share of the town. Hanna was then solely responsible for the full expense of the courthouse, which may account for his foot dragging. At this point the county board became more detailed in its specifications. The new specifications included thickness of foundations, type of rock used, height of the walls, types of sills, transoms, joists, pillars, chimneys, and shingles, and a dozen other items, as well as the fact that there were to be twenty-one windows of twenty-five panes, each pane ten inches by twelve inches, bathing the interior with natural light. Hanna must have regretted not having built the thing in 1835. Nothing happened until January 1840, when the county board cited him for neglect of contract and the sheriff served him a summons: another case of the founding father being held responsible in the coils of decent democratic process. He was getting by with nothing.

After some adjustments of dimensions and details, the work on the courthouse began that spring. It was not the end of officialdom's specifications, however. In March 1841 the county board weighed in on matters such as the width of the stairs, the quality of washboards, and the appearance of roof and steeple. Specification piled on top of specification, detail on top of detail, as if officials were fearful of being short-changed by Hanna. His involvement extended at least through 1843 when he paid fifty dollars for a decorative cornice. The upstairs courtroom had been finished with walnut floors, white walls, and stately décor for judge and jury seats. Outside, the brick was painted Venetian red with white penciling, the window trim and steeple were white, except for the Venetian blinds (louvers) on the steeple, which were green. There must have been a privy and a well at this time but, if so, their locations were not specified. County officials very quickly rented the two western rooms downstairs for a dollar a month to teachers who wished to gather classes there. Soon after construction was complete, the state mandated counties to store records in fireproof space, which the new courthouse lacked. To comply, commissioners built a long, single-story, brick annex of three rooms north of the courthouse. It housed a fire-resistant vault, and its attic was rigged with a layer of sand eight inches deep that was kept moist as protection against roof fire. That last device would prove its worth in 1870. The construction of the annex was not, however, charged to Hanna.[31]

Hanna and Burr's donation of a public square and offer to build a courthouse was, in the end, the most precious gift they gave Wabash. It guaranteed, first, that Wabash would have the honor of being the county seat, and second, but more important, that it would attract settlers interested in county government and legal matters, in particular attorneys, printers, clerks, journalists, and those who might have a yen for the local political game. It is true that advocates of Lagro, including Tipton, tried to wrestle the seat of justice away from Wabash. Lagro residents raised subscriptions worth $1,600, to be added to Tipton's donation. Nevertheless, the Lagro offer seemed somewhat indefinite, whereas the Hanna-Burr proposal was specific. Moreover, Elias Murray believed that Wabash citizens were galvanized by a fear that Tipton, who already had interests in Lagro and Huntington, was trying to extend his influence down river. In any case, the matter was never really in question because of the Hanna-Burr donation.

Lagro's real competition with Wabash in these years was economic. It was a bustling little settlement of great promise when Wabash was not much more than Hanna's rectilinear grid. When a young Wabash blade, William Ross, needed a new suit of clothes for his approaching wedding he traveled to Lagro to find such an item. (Even there the pickings were slim. Although Ross was not a tall man, he had to make do with trousers much too short and tight and the rest of the outfit was made up of scraps of cloth.) Just then Lagro was enjoying a boomlet in shops, taverns, inns, a mill, a ferry, and new housing and looking more progressive than the downstream settlement at Wabash. Such an economic edge was doomed in the long run, however, by the courthouse magnet that attracted those professionals who helped make the place seem important, which, in turn, attracted businessmen and entrepreneurs, who, in turn, attracted the laborers, shop keepers, domestics, and others who kept the wheels turning and the bread baking. Capturing the courthouse was a huge economic victory for a frontier town.[32]

The more intriguing question about the Hanna-Burr donation of a public square is whether its location, which was their choice, reflected some larger vision of the town they were creating. Did they understand in 1834 that the sixty-foot-high bluff that bent their two-dimensional grid skyward in a two-block stretch was not a liability at all, but a remarkable, inspiring asset to be used advantageously? Did they envision the possibility that business and industry would be circumscribed and largely contained between canal and bluff, or perhaps between river and bluff, while churches, schools, courts, and residential areas would gradually take over the bluff top and provide the town with a soaring skyline of steeples, towers, and turrets, as so clearly happened?

There are small, though inconclusive, hints that this was their vision: agora beneath, acropolis above. One hint is that the ground they set aside for cemetery, school, and churches were likely all on top, along Hill and Sinclair streets. Lot #157 on East Hill Street, designated for public school use, was on top of the bluff. The first permanent schoolhouse, which Hanna had a hand in building, sat in the same vicinity, on top of the bluff. Lot #184, on West Sinclair just east of Miami Street, was designated as a "church lot," on top of the bluff. The cemetery—Hanna Cemetery or the Old Cemetery—was on the bluff. That churches, schools, and courts should rise on the heights may reflect the founders' ideas. Certainly the first bona fide church building, First Presbyterian, was high up the Wabash Street hill. Even though a school or church lot could be sold and the money used to build elsewhere, an upper-level location for these pursuits seems to have been inspired by Hanna and Burr. Another hint is the location of Hanna's home, on the bluff, forty or fifty feet above the downtown level. He may simply have been one of those men who found the uneven, steep terrain of the place attractive and wanted to make the most of it, eyeing the bluff top as better suited for domestic life than for business. He might have sensed what his fellow townsman, Doctor James Ford, would later teach, that the air on higher ground was likely healthier than that of the miasmic floodplain. Hanna could not have known at that time, however, that the railroad, when it came, would also take the high ground, belching smoke through the most desirable residential areas and drowning out preachers' sermons with its racket.

What should one make of the specific location of the 1840s courthouse, described as being on the southeast corner of the public square, where Main and Wabash streets meet? Had Hanna wanted to dramatize the bluff, making an indelible statement of its presence, would he not have placed the hall of justice as high as possible on the public square, on its north side nearer Hill Street, where the 1880 courthouse stands? That question assumes that in 1835 the south side of the square was considerably lower than the north side, as it subsequently has been. In fact, the square's southeast side, where Hanna built the first courthouse, may have risen bullishly above the downtown in 1840. In the 1860s the city fathers went to great lengths to facilitate hillside traffic by cutting down the grade of Wabash Street at least as far north as Maple Street, an operation that may have included some serious earth removal all along the square's eastern border. The earliest extant photograph of Wabash, taken in 1866, before Wabash Street grading was completed, shows the 1840 courthouse rising high above Market and Canal streets, giving the appearance that the building's foundation is on the same level as Hill Street. It would not be completely beyond the pale of sound reason to credit the founding fathers with having both an eye for the dramatic use of topography and a strategy that went beyond merely superimposing a grid, willy-nilly, on the wild landscape.[33]

After 1835, while citizens anticipated the eventual erection of a courthouse, the county's government convened semiregularly at Burr's place near the spring, at Jacob Cassatt's house, at Henry Dixon's tavern (these latter two places probably were on Canal Street), and, most often, at Patrick Duffy's log house and saloon on the northeast corner of Market and Huntington streets. Although Hanna was far more interested in business than in politics or governance, he was elected the county's first treasurer, perhaps on the notion that he knew money better than most and assuredly on the notion that he had more at stake financially than most. Conceivably the job was a headache for him, though it did come with a stipend. He served as Wabash's third postmaster—a position that not only had a salary but also put him in personal touch with a wide range of settlers—and as the county's "agent," a position later called "auditor."

Despite his official public service, Hanna preferred lending his name and influence to cultural, religious, and fraternal causes that, along with the growth of business, enhanced the tone and promise of his town. Thus, for example, he provided space at Hanna and Sons for a Bible Society depository, from which Bibles and tracts could be distributed. Bible societies, such as Sabbath Schools and temperance organizations, were not always the sectarian propaganda machines that later Americans knew. In many instances they were highly respectable agencies of cultural enlightenment supported by mainstream, prosperous, and progressive Americans. They were certainly favorite devices of Hanna's fellow Presbyterians for taming and elevating frontier life; through his family and his church affiliation, Hugh had been familiar with them all his adult life. If there was no tax-supported public education in town—and there would not be for years—there could at least be private Sabbath Schools, plus Bible and tract distributions, promoting basic literacy along with biblical lore. Hanna was thus supporting a movement that represented a serious assault on cultural deprivation. There was a Presbyterian church of seven members up and running in Wabash by late May 1836. It was the first organized church in town, though preachers of other denominations had been around since the Baptist, Isaac McCoy, occupied space at the 1826 treaty deliberations. Hanna was not one of First Presbyterian's seven original members. He joined in 1848 and before that may have remained technically a member of First Presbyterian, Fort Wayne.

Although there is no evidence that Hugh drank heavily, it is reasonable to guess that his tardiness in officially joining a church was akin to his brother's. On the frontier alcohol was a common, accepted beverage among all classes, and excessive drinking was easily tolerated. Hugh hosted the first community dance in Wabash in his new brick building in 1835. It would have been unusual if liquor had not flowed freely at that party and on many other occasions in early Wabash. It is also true that Hanna was a founding member and first Worshipful Master of the local Masonic Lodge, specifically Hanna Lodge Number 61. It is unlikely that the fraternity disavowed the consumption of liquor in practice. After the more radical principle of teetotalism (total abstinence) took root among many temperance reformers in the 1830s and 1840s, however, it would have been difficult, though not impossible, to be both a known imbiber and a Presbyterian in high standing. First Presbyterian of Wabash was of the New School persuasion, which meant, in part, that its members would be particularly reform minded. In 1844, for example, the Reverend James Thomson of the Wabash church boasted that not only had all his members signed a temperance pledge but also that most citizens in town took the pledge. Although the first claim rings true, the second is questionable. Hanna's nonmembership for so many years does not spell a lack of church support. Quite the contrary—he would have seen his brand of Presbyterianism as an important civilizing agent. Undoubtedly he regularly worshipped at First Church, and it is known that Presbyterian missionaries coming to the village were encouraged by the discovery that the town's "proprietor" was New School Presbyterian and an active congregant. As time passed, Hugh, like his brother Samuel, became recognized as an avid temperance man. Whether that meant he was a teetotaler is less certain.[34]

In the last decades of his life Hanna lent his influence and labor to several other public causes. In the early 1850s, just as public schools in the state were finally being organized in a comprehensive manner, he served as treasurer for the Northern Indiana Teachers Institute, which promoted graded, consolidated ("union") schools and encouraged programs of faculty support and training. When state officials elected to build a northern prison at Michigan City rather than at Wabash, Hanna was named a director of that institution. Though in the beginning his appointment seemed like a sop to a disappointed community, the local press noted Hanna's reputation for honesty, the renewals of his appointment, and his intimacy with prison operations. At Fourth of July celebrations, as long parades wound through town toward the fairgrounds or other gathering spots, Hanna, likely as not, was the grand marshal. When the agricultural fair board invited the county at large to gather annually in Wabash for livestock, produce, and floral shows, or for speeches, contests, and horse races, Hanna might not always have an official title for the event but he was the recognized, unofficial host. He had been, after all, the county's first agricultural agent, charged with encouraging farming improvements. As the Civil War approached, Hanna's politics and his nationalism became more apparent. He attended the Republican convention in Chicago to see Abraham Lincoln nominated for president, and about this time he flew a Lincoln banner at Hanna's Corner.

During the war, Wabash men over forty-five, whose service was not crucial on the field of battle, organized their own company and elected their own officers. They offered Hanna the rank of captain, but he remarked "in a jocular way" that he did not feel like sacrificing his honorary title of colonel for a mere captaincy.[35] The war brought Hanna two important duties on the home front, both toward the end of the conflict when its duration and carnage had long since robbed the nation, North and South, of its original bravado. He was appointed to be the state's solicitor for support of the "sanitation" cause in Wabash County. This cause grew out of awareness of the appalling health conditions on the front. He was praised for being tireless in the effort to raise funds to provide bandages, medicines, and other equipment that might save soldiers from disease. At one juncture he personally operated two stands, one at the fairgrounds and one at a Democratic rally, selling oysters, candies, cigars, cakes, cider, apples, nuts, cheese, and sardines to raise the necessary funds. Wabash County chalked up an admirable record in support of the sanitation cause. It was about this same time that Hanna accepted chairmanship of the county's Union Party. The Union Party was created by Republicans and Democrats of the North who were united in the presidential campaign of 1864 to reelect Lincoln, and thus, it was hoped, to reunite the country after the war. Like most Wabash voters, Hanna was a Republican, but he was never rabidly partisan and was, therefore, a logical choice to pull Republicans and Democrats together for the Union.[36]

In the interests of historical accuracy it is not helpful to canonize such a man as Hanna. A balanced understanding of him has been somewhat crippled by newspapers and other sources that accentuate his virtues and minimize, even ignore, his vices. As a young carpenter apprentice, aged nineteen, Hanna ran away from his employer who cared enough to advertise for his return but offered as reward only "one cent, and a stale chew of tobacco."[37] The advertisement further advised that expenses incurred in returning the culprit could be paid by any person who has money to throw away. It should be remembered also that Tipton had once chastised Hanna for tardiness in communicating about assigned projects. Did the man have a lazy streak, problems dealing with those in authority, or did he lack focus, drifting from one project to another, as his many businesses might imply? What might be said about his disregard of fellow citizens when he used Canal Street as an entrails dump for his slaughterhouse? Was there an above-the-law arrogance about him? And what about the county government's need to prosecute him, virtually for fraud, when he failed to deliver on the courthouse proposal? Was he simply short of funds because he had just bought out Burr, was Hanna a poor money manager, or did he have a dishonest streak? What of his tardiness in joining First Presbyterian? Was that a matter of his not wanting to be hypocritical about a drinking habit, or was he a man of serious religious doubt—doubts he did not resolve until the late 1840s?

In 1837 Hanna ran afoul of the law when a court, meeting at Patrick Duffy's tavern, fined him twenty-five dollars for illegally taking timber off state land. In 1839 the state took Hanna to court again, this time for failing to deliver an accounting for his role as county treasurer. Sheriff William Steele physically took him into custody, and Hanna confessed to owing the county fifty dollars. In 1844 he was again indicted for mishandling tax money as county treasurer. As late as 1857 Hanna began a letter to his brother, Samuel, with these words, "Dear Brother, if it were within my power to send the amount I would be glad to do so."[38] Hugh had a long history of trouble with his brother over finances. In *Samuel Hanna vs. Hugh Hanna*, a bill of complaint filed in Chancery of the Circuit Court of Wabash in 1842, Samuel took Hugh to task for owing him $2,150.60 in unpaid debts, principal, and interest. The complaint stipulated that Hugh also owed the state bank more than $5,000 on several notes cosigned by Samuel. To cover these debts Hugh was ordered to sell over eighty lots in Wabash, representing roughly a third of the original town plat. Since it is known that Samuel's name was attached to dozens of Wabash lots in the 1840s, it is possible that the older brother helped assuage Hugh's legal problems by accepting lots as payment, keeping the property in family hands. Thus the legal proceedings may not have indicated deep personal rancor between the brothers, especially in light of the fact that Samuel's legal representative in the complaint was Hugh's friend and future son-in-law J. D. Conner.

However, the topic of Hanna's immense debts indicates a serious flaw in the man. Although at his death he was described as owning a lot of property, Hanna clearly did not achieve his full potential in terms of material prosperity. An accurate understanding of the man would have to take into account all the questions of character that can be raised by some of his known actions, and leave to wonderment what flaws may have been present of which there is no record at all. At least one of his contemporaries believed Hanna was autocratic, and other negative opinions of him may simply be lost in the mists of time. Little is known of his marriage, his family life, or his personal habits beyond a general, positive impression, and, therefore, we have to give him the benefit of the doubt in such areas. On balance Hanna surely deserved the esteem in which he was held, even though, as with humans generally, he was manifestly tainted in some ways and not a likely candidate for sainthood.[39]

Whatever Hugh Hanna's legal and financial woes, whatever his flaws, most Wabash citizens revered their colonel and proprietor and, in the end, praised him as much for his personableness as for his accomplishments. He continued to lead parades and preside at public festivals well into the 1860s, and as he aged he may have achieved higher degrees of lovableness in the eyes of the public. In 1859 the *Indianapolis Sentinel* published a column titled "Wabash" that was reprinted in the *Intelligencer.* In the piece a reporter noted that brothers Samuel of Fort Wayne, Joseph of Lafayette, and Hugh of Wabash—"these three Hannas"—were all self-made men who were honored far beyond their home turf.[40]

So there was broad respect for the man and his heritage, but locally it may have been more important that during the Civil War, at a Sanitary Fair, the town's proprietor was seen holding a three-year-old child above the crowd so it could see what was happening. Such small, neighborly gestures from him were deemed noteworthy. In 1864 the *Intelligencer* reported about a practical joke Hanna played on a politician in Indianapolis, telling the man he had lost an election that he had actually won; the reporter marveled at Hanna's acting agility in pulling this off. Even though the report noted how Hanna appeared "as active as a young man of twenty," it seems rather more true that by this time he was metamorphosing into a kind of unofficial town "uncle": sage, approachable, and benevolent.[41]

Perhaps the most endearing remembrance of him concerned Colonel Hanna's "convenient horse." The horse in question was not Hanna's "Black Jim," also a celebrated steed, who lived to be thirty-one, "the oldest horse in Indiana," and was still good for minor buggy work when he died in 1867.[42] Rather, the "convenient horse" was Black Jim's stablemate and successor who pulled Hanna in his buggy around town on a daily basis. Thad Butler, a journalist, remembered Hanna at this time as a "kindly old gentleman" who habitually visited friends in downtown businesses. He would tie up his horse and buggy, enter a shop or office, swap tales with friends there, and frequently take a nap. Meanwhile, out on the street, young bloods, knowing the Hanna habit, made free with his horse and buggy. It became almost a daily occurrence, offering teenage males an opportunity to impress girl friends with a buggy ride. Hanna attempted a correction by taking the reins with him to his nap, but the horse was docile and the young men simply substituted strings for reins and took their "joy rides . . . whether the Colonel visited or napped." No one seemed especially outraged by this commission of lese majesty, least of all the proprietor.[43]

3

Canal Burg

In 1915 J. Warren Hanna, Hugh Hanna's son and a man then in his seventy-seventh year, explained to fellow Old Settlers of Wabash why his elder brother, Hugh W. Hanna, had a yellowish, dark complexion. It was the result, Warren said, of his family's move to Wabash in 1835, an especially wet year. Hugh W., less than a year old at the time, had been bundled in a horse-drawn "burrough" for the trip, accompanied by his older sister, Julia Ann Hanna, his mother, Elizabeth Hanna, and father. The passage from Fort Wayne was predictably tiresome because of all-too-normal conditions. Roads frequently seemed more liquid than solid, inspiring some pioneers to refer to land travel as "navigation." Others spoke of "bottomless turnpikes."[1] In his prize-winning history of the Old Northwest, R. Carlyle Buley records the frontier tale about a traveler who spied a beaver hat in the middle of a mud puddle. He waded out to it, only to discover a man beneath it. He called for help, but the man under the hat protested, saying, "Leave me alone, stranger; I've got a good horse under me, and have just found bottom."[2] This was a joke, of course, but the fact was that horses and vehicles were often sucked down while in transit. Buley cites one case of a team drowning in mud and another of a family having to hitch eight oxen to a single wagon to pull it through the bad places. Mindful of such conditions, Warren recalled that on his family's move to Wabash its vehicle upset in mud, and baby Hugh was nowhere to be seen. It took his parents a while before they spotted his head poking out of the ooze. Warren claimed the incident accounted for Hugh W.'s muddy complexion.[3]

The story also indicates something of the primitive nature of precanal Wabash (1835 to 1837). Hugh Hanna and David Burr had designed their plat in 1834, registering lots 1 through 152 in Huntington County that year. In

1837 Hanna completed an amended registration in Wabash County of all 234 lots for what is called the O.P. (Original Plat). No surveyor's "monument," no stake, boulder, or tree has been identified as the proprietors' starting point but undoubtedly they used the canal line, surveyed in the 1820s, as their southern plat line. Using the canal line meant that the plat fails to be on a true north-south axis by a few degrees: all north-south streets lean a little to the west. Probably all that existed of the town in the very beginning was a series of tall sticks in the mud indicating where streets were expected to cross one another. Between those would be smaller sticks staking out lots. The lowest numbered lots, and the most valuable, ran west to east along the south side of Canal Street between Cass and Allen streets. Most of the highest numbered lots, and the cheaper ones, ran along Sinclair Street, four-plus blocks from the proposed canal route. Presumably the founders cleared timber from the primary downtown street sites, where they expected to sell lots first. Perhaps they dragged logs down some of those thoroughfares as a means of grading them in a preliminary fashion, but there were no ditches for drainage. Streets were sixty-six feet wide except for Market between Wabash and Huntington streets, which was twenty-four feet wider, suggesting that Hanna and Burr may have entertained some particular plan for that block. Most lots measured 66 by 132 feet, though there were smaller ones as well and a few larger. East-west alleys were sixteen feet wide, and north-south alleys were ten feet wide. Many lots remained indefinitely in their natural state, heavily wooded in places, rank with vegetation (nettles, milkweed, poison ivy, briars, shrubs, and trees), and waiting for new owners to clear them. A fairly dense woods extended from the plat south to the river and extended north, covering most of the town in that direction until well into the 1840s. Good water was readily available from springs and rain buckets.[4]

One potentially egregious impediment to Wabash's progress, and symptomatic of its primitive state, was a body of water on West Market Street. A pond of sorts stretched, west to east, for half a block from Miami Street, covering at least the south half of Market Street for that distance. At times it expanded to soak Market as far east as Huntington Street. Its depth is not known. Neither is the source of its water, whether from a spring or from run-off. What is known is that it seemed annoyingly permanent, or at least perennially recurrent. After Doctor James Ford moved to town in 1841, he began to beat the drum for improved community hygiene, citing the pond as an unwarranted disease factory, but it was several years before it was eradicated permanently. The pond had not posed an immediate barrier to town growth because most of the early merchants preferred to open their stores on Canal Street, which had easy access to canal workers and to anticipated canal transportation. Meanwhile, other settlers tended to build homes or businesses in the area of town immediately west of Treaty Ground at the east end of the Original Plat.[5]

Happily for Hanna and Burr, the staking of their plat was, as planned, contemporaneous with the land rush that the canal's advent had inspired. Even before the platting was complete in 1834, squatters had arrived in the area to take advantage of preemption laws that allowed them to claim up to 160 acres at $1.25 per acre if they would legally record their claim within a year or two. By 1835 shanties along the canal line housed great numbers of canal workers, and although there are no known complaints about squatters settling in Wabash proper, these shanties may have housed some folks who had not yet decided where to take up permanent residence. It did not take long for serious settlers with long-term intentions to arrive also, spurred in part by speculators who literally raced each other at times to record purchases at the land office in Logansport.[6]

Daniel R. Bearss, later a settler down river at Peru, was involved in a claims race when he was a teenage employee of the W. G. and G. W. Ewing concern in Fort Wayne. One day one of his bosses ordered young Bearss to get up early and ride as quickly as possible to reserve a claim at the Logansport land office, eighty miles distant. The Ewings intended to edge out their competitor, Frank Lasselle, who had already headed west that morning. A few hours later Bearss caught sight of Lasselle at a little settlement called Raccoon Village and passed him there by taking an alternate route around town. Twenty-seven miles east of Wabash, however, Bearss's pony gave out, and the youth had to continue on foot to maintain his lead. He claimed to have run all the way to Burr's Tavern at Treaty Ground, where he procured a second mount and succeeded in beating Lasselle to the land office. Such feats symbolize the passion for land that the canal was generating—a passion Hanna and Burr had counted on. Despite mud, drowned streets, and unimproved lots, the land boom indicated that Wabash could become a viable, permanent home for its founding generation.[7]

Estimates of Wabash's population in 1835, the first year of its official existence, are obtainable through the filter of aging pioneers' reminiscences, which were often recorded at annual reunions following the Civil War. Understandably, the veracity of some details in "Old Settler" stories can at times be challenged, but in general they are a rich and reliable source. William H. Coombs, for example, remembered the town's population at between one hundred and two hundred inhabitants in 1835, with a majority being canal hands. At first blush these numbers seem like an overestimate because the town was so new and the canal had not yet been completed that far west. Nevertheless, Coombs's memory is largely corroborated by the fact that tax records from 1835 reveal that sixty men were operating in town, largely, it is thought, to provide food, housing, tavern fare, and other commodities for canal laborers. It is further known that in July 1835, 300 to 350 laborers were living along the canal line as far downstream as Richvalley, five miles west. A great many of these had built shanties in what became downtown Wabash. In contrast to such estimates, sojourner Elijah Hackleman found "Wabashtown" in 1836 to consist of only a dozen families, many of whom had settled on the plat's southeasternmost square, bounded by Allen, Canal, Huntington, and Market streets. Hackleman was probably not counting the itinerant canal hands in their shanties.[8]

Precise population figures for 1835 are difficult to ascertain because no census exists for that year. The federal census for 1830 had been taken when the Wabash area was still a Cass County township and shows no figures for Treaty Ground specifically. Figures for the town are available from the 1840 census, but, naturally, those say nothing about Wabash at its founding five years earlier. The average household size in Cass County in 1830 was approximately six persons. The average in Wabash town in 1840 was five-plus persons, ranging from three single males in one home to Hanna's bulging household of twelve, which undoubtedly included indentured hands and/or employees whom he was housing. For 1840 the average household for Noble Township (surrounding Wabash) was about the same, just under five and a half. Given these three averages, it would be reasonable to multiply Hackleman's "dozen families" by five and a half in order to estimate that at least sixty-six people had taken up permanent residence in Wabash in 1835. The fact that Hackleman proved to be a stickler for details at times and that he was a keen observer of pioneer life in and around Wabash make his figure of a dozen families credible, so long as canal hands and shanty dwellers are not included.[9]

The 1840 census helps with estimates about gender and age distribution, too. It records that by then Wabash had seventy-nine males and sixty-three females. Many were very young. Transient canal workers had left by then, and the town was attracting permanent settlers. Five years earlier, in 1835, gender proportions and age distributions were probably about the same as in 1840, even if total population was much lower. One might have expected there to be more single men (former hunters or traders) living alone at the earlier date, but in all of Cass County in 1830 there were only eight single male heads of households out of 657 residents counted. Bachelors may have often lived alone when hunting or trading on a sparsely settled frontier (and not been counted), but in town they surely tended to board with a household until marriage or cohabitation. Based both on demographic figures and on pioneer observations, then, it is possible to estimate that the new town of Wabash in 1835 was home to considerably fewer than a hundred settled residents, of whom almost half would have been twenty years old or younger. Males outnumbered females by twenty or more. In addition to these settled residents, there were more than a hundred male canal laborers, many of them single, living quite impermanently up and down the canal ditch within the town plat or close to it.[10]

Although there were advantages to living in town as compared with living in the woods or on the open prairie, Wabash could be bleak and uncomfortable before the canal provided more generous tokens of civilization. The weather in 1835 and 1836 was severe, harshly cold in winter with heavy snow, drearily wet at other times. There were no bridges across river or streams, and no ferry. At times men waded in icy water four feet deep to reach Wabash from the south. Extended, bitter cold actually facilitated travel: the mud froze, making it passable. So did the river, to a depth of ice that easily supported wagon teams. The short trek across the flats from the river to the town was problematic in all but dry or frozen times.[11]

Some of the earliest dwellings in town were little more than temporary shelters, three-sided affairs thrown up in a hurry and heated by a fire kept blazing at the open end. Women normally slept in the sheds while the men bedded down in their wagons. These accommodations were replaced as quickly as possible with what one pioneer called "log mansions," a version of which might incorporate a good fireplace with a stick chimney plus a window or two to let light into the single room. Scaly barked hickory aflame in the fireplace helped make the place cozy, bright, and warm, relatively speaking, although starting a blaze with only flint and tinder required patience and experience. An exterior door was sometimes no more than blankets draped over an opening.

To let in light but keep out breezes, settlers glazed their windows with greased paper. Raccoon grease worked best, according to one experienced glazier, and raccoons were everywhere. The Reverend George Abbott, a North Manchester settler, believed he had stumbled onto a surefire way of snagging multiple raccoons when he cut down an oak tree containing seven of the critters plus one porcupine. The pelts helped pay his taxes. The grease may have graced his windows. If a cabin floor were dirt, which was common, then beds could be constructed by pounding large poles into the floor, attaching crossbeams to them, and topping the beams with a mattress made out of twisted bark. Undoubtedly neighbors in town mimicked the country custom of log rolling and house raising: several families joining together to build a dwelling for newcomers. Enough hands working together could raise a cabin in a day.[12]

Such unsophisticated housing, however, was expected to be temporary, even in the first year. Many soon strove for something more substantial, such as a larger log house with puncheon floor; hewn, squared logs rather than round ones; more windows; a sleeping loft; and a porch and a stone hearth and fireplace. A frame house would be next, or a brick structure if possible. Hanna, for example, bypassed the log cabin phase once he left Treaty Ground and, as noted earlier, immediately began to gather brick and stone for his business block, moving his family soon thereafter into its frame house above Treaty Ground. Certainly there was no shortage of timber in the area, though, as Hanna's first enterprise indicated, it needed to be milled. Other folks were also eager to quarry limestone for foundations and bake bricks for walls. Alphaeus Blackman and Hannibal Parsell operated a kiln on the south side of Market Street, west of Allen Street, in the very block where most Wabash residents settled that first year. By the end of the year at least one commercial building and probably two private homes were being built of brick.[13]

Near the kiln, on lot 62, lived George Shepherd and his wife in what may have been the very first house erected in Wabash. Their son was born shortly after their arrival and was the first white child born in town. Next door to the west lived Doctor James Hackleman, Elijah's brother. Another neighbor of the kiln was William Steele Sr., a lawyer and the first county clerk, who opened one of Wabash's earliest provision stores. Steele built his house on lot 22, the northeast corner of Canal and Huntington streets. Steele kept official county records in one room of his house. David Cassatt settled on the southeast corner of the same block. A full block away from the kiln to the west was Doctor Isaac Finley's one-story brick cottage on lot 54, just across the street from the location of the present-day county museum. One or two fearless settlers built on top of the bluff, an area known for its wolf population. In spite of considerable progress in domestic construction, the general impression left by witnesses is that log houses still dominated that first year and possibly for several years following.[14]

Based on the limited information available, it is possible to imagine something of what Wabash looked like at its earliest manifestation. From the top of the bluff, one would see a cluster of completed cabins on the east end of the village, just west of Allen Street; one or two more cabins are also under construction. A couple of frame houses are rising, plus a brick structure or two. There are not fewer than a dozen homes in all, and some of the newer ones are located a little farther west, toward Wabash Street, perhaps beyond. Well-developed lots might include sheds and fences. There is a tavern or rudimentary inn run by Patrick Duffy on the northeast corner of Market and Huntington streets. All these structures enjoy the shade of a variety of mature deciduous trees. In summer small gardens grow in patches of sunlight.

There are few wells. Although rain water and Hanna's Spring are still important sources of water, a fifty-foot-deep well may already exist on the south side of Market Street west of Wabash Street. It eventually was equipped with a wooden pump. Because of its water quality the well is a popular gathering spot even though it is a block west of most houses and close to the Market Street pond—possibly *in* the pond during wet seasons. Men, women, boys, and girls are out and about, pursuing chores, gathering buckets of water, or spending time in conversation and play. An open space at the northwest corner of Miami and Market streets—where Eagles Theater later stood—is a good place for ball games. No doubt, also, one soon notices evidence of Wabash's primitive sanitation system—the privies gracing many lots and crude chamber pots airing on stoops. Snaking west from Treaty Ground there is a line of disturbed earth that indicates where Hanna is beginning to lay down his wooden-pipe water system. Here and there, possibly staked or fenced, but just as possibly roaming free, are family cows. It is not unusual for citizens to bump unexpectedly into the side of a random cow as they walk through the village at night (citizens learn to carry lanterns). Not contained at all are the pigs that rut, eat garbage thrown from cabin doors, rummage for food in the woods, and wallow in the underlying ooze of the Market Street pond. Chickens are likely more ubiquitous and only slightly more restrained than the pigs. Dogs also have the run of the place, for there is hardly a home without one. They bark and growl and fight and mate at will when they are not out hunting with their masters. Perhaps they are tied up or kept indoors at night, the better to warn of intruders.[15]

Southwest of most of the earliest houses is Hanna's Corner, a work in progress. Men who are carrying bricks up ladders are earning twenty-five cents per diem. Visible along Canal Street are smaller, wooden structures that house taverns and various shops, blacksmiths being numerous among the latter. One of these enterprises, west of Miami Street, is Andrew Murphy's tavern, the first one in Wabash that he had established in the summer of 1834 to serve the early influx of canal hands. If it is true, as canal historian Thomas Castaldi states, that dozens of vendors serviced canal hands at this time, there may be a goodly number of small commercial structures in that part of town. Beyond them one spots a fringe of shanties—rude, log things—trailing off toward the west. Most of them house bachelors, itinerant laborers, and small, young families of laborers. One can see shanty dwellers moving up and down Canal Street.[16]

Glancing far to the south horizon, a viewer might see smoke rising from a Miami Indian village high on the bluff across the river, where Hanna sometimes visited a friend, Chief Sala (Al-lo-hah, Black Raccoon). Several hundred Miami still live south of the Wabash River and an undetermined number live west of Wabash on Chief Charley's section. Looking closer in, just south of Canal Street on or near the floodplain, one spots Hanna's first mill. Along Canal Street—depending on how far west the work has come—runs the naked swath of grubbed land waiting to receive the canal's ditch. The rest of the plat of Wabash—virtually everything west of Wabash Street and north of Market Street, and almost everything on the bluff—is empty of human habitation. True, by the end of the year a jail will rise on the public square, the highest building in town for a while. Otherwise, Wabash is still mostly forest, undergrowth, and the crisscross of downtown streets that often glisten with deep, wet mud and the waters of the Market Street pond. It is a humble but promising beginning.[17]

Elements of civilization continued to be minimal to 1837. The government was rudimentary and simple, composed of a few officials, mostly on the county level, who held court or conducted other essential business at one of the taverns. This elementary government, for example, issued its first marriage license on June 6, 1835, to Edward Tirney and Mary Hannah (who did not settle in Wabash). A month later it authorized construction of the jail, the first public building, which was completed in the following months. Its construction was surely inspired, in part, by concern over the rowdiness of canal workers that had heated up to the boiling point that summer. The jail was a two-story log structure with a hefty stone foundation erected on the west side of the public square. Its presence put teeth in a nascent penal system and had probably been sought by those few settlers trained in law. In any case the founding generation was not comprised of idealists; they expected crime and were soon ready for it. In 1837 no less a personage than the county clerk, Steele, was bound over for "official negligence" because of a fifty-dollar inconsistency in public records. At this time the county seat's part-time staff included a sheriff, a treasurer, a surveyor, a clerk, an agent, an assessor, a postmaster, and a judge. They were not overworked in these positions, and sometimes a court had to issue an "attachment for his body" order so that the judge would be forced to come to work and preside at a trial.[18]

Citizens had no newspapers, no dependable mail service, no reliable monetary system, and no unifying incentives beyond the unmeasurable ones of friendship, common sense, and a shared instinct to civilize the environs. Folks had to guess what national and world news might be, had to cross their fingers when mailing letters, and had to pay for things with chickens, butter, and hides. Being difficult to import, commodities were scarce. A lot of corn bread was consumed because regular flour was hard to come by. At times even corn was unavailable, though a lot of people kept their hominy mortars handy nonetheless. Other standard utensils were a good iron skillet, a Dutch oven, and a "spider" (a skillet with legs) that could be set over a fire. The common diet was heavy on bread, fat meat, and coffee. Merchants tried to bring some goods in by pole boats, long cumbersome craft that required two to six men to navigate and had minds of their own in the wrong kind of river current. Other merchants hauled salt overland from as far away as the Michigan border. That trip could take four weeks, there and back, but once in Wabash salt brought twelve dollars a barrel. John Holloway, a county resident living some eleven miles distant, often trekked to town with eggs for bartering. He recalled that originally a yard of calico cost him three or four dozen eggs, but that in later years he could buy two or three yards of calico for one dozen eggs. Men and boys hunted and fished for food and for fun, with deer, turkeys, and squirrels being easy prey. Standard wisdom was to get out and shoot one's food before breakfast.[19]

Citizens partied, danced, smoked, and drank on a fairly regular basis, especially the smoking and the drinking. Tobacco and whiskey made it to town when other commodities did not. The Reverend George Abbott, a Baptist, remembered that everyone drank and felt no disgrace about it. In winter men drank and gossiped around a hot potbelly stove, spitting tobacco juice at it. Horse racing and foot racing were popular pastimes. While serving on the first court jury in Wabash, Abbott used his breaks in court proceedings to run races against other jurors. The prize was a gallon of whiskey. Abbott won and unapologetically enjoyed his prize, though he also shared it with the entire court. For Abbott and for many others, whiskey consumption was a form of entertainment and an acceptable source of inner cheer against the harsher realities of life.[20]

Among those harsher realities were frequent visitations of raging diseases—cholera, malaria, dysentery, bilious fever, and ague—which were almost expected and against which medical aid remained pathetically feeble. Milk sickness could affect animals as well as humans, causing what some called the "slows," a dramatic decline in energy and fortitude. Charles Votaw complained that his dog could not keep up with the deer they hunted because of the "slows." Any illness, such as ague that did not kill a person outright might do so indirectly by rendering him vulnerable to the next lethal wave. Hanna's cemetery, high on the bluff, became a useful addition to the pioneer town. Deaths among young and old came so often as to steel the human spirit with something akin to acceptance. In commiserating with his son, Spear, on the death of Spear's daughter, John Tipton wrote (in his spelling):

> Parents should prepare their minds for such heart rending events. in this life nothing is certain but death, and it appears that the author of our existence fore ordained such afflictions as necessary to make life the less disereable, and to prepare us for death. to give up to gloom and despondency would betray weakness without relieving your feeling of

> blasted hopes. it is now your duties to yeald to the bereavement and console yourselves with the reflection that although the wound sinks deep in your hearts for your dear departed child it is perhaps best. she is removed from this world of troubles to be no more subjected to its cares or its evils.[21]

Oddly, at this very juncture in Wabash's story, when it was only a meager hatchling of an outpost on the margins of civilization and only halfway through its first year of existence, it hosted an event that regional historical studies intermittently alluded to during the following one hundred seventy years. It was significant enough at the time for the current governor of Indiana, Noah Noble, to report on the event in his annual address. Various histories of Indiana, accounts of the Wabash and Erie Canal, and studies of Irish Americans mention it, often as no more than a footnote, sometimes as a topic of serious ethnic analysis.

The event is called "The Irish War" (sometimes "The Irish Riot"), though in truth it turned out to be not much more than a brief, aborted sectarian melee between club-toting Irish canal hands. The contesting parties are normally identified as Corkonians and Fardowners, the former being Irish Roman Catholics with roots in the south of Ireland and the latter Irish Protestants from Ulster. The site of the pending confrontation was bottomland lying about a hundred yards west of Enyeart Creek in Lagro Township and about three miles east/northeast of the Wabash settlement. In 1835 this bottomland was being sliced by the new canal trench. The Irish War is sometimes identified by historians solely with Lagro, which is fair placement because the town lies fairly close to the battlefield, and Lagro citizens were involved. However, Wabash residents and people from west of Wabash—perhaps more than three hundred of them—were also engaged in the event, both as would-be combatants and as referees, their numbers roughly equal to those from the Lagro end of the line.

Similar to Colonel Augustin de LaBalme's march through Wabash eighty years earlier, the Irish War of 1835 directly connects the town to a larger historical event. In this case that event is the Battle of the Boyne of 1690, one hundred forty-five years earlier. In a very real sense the Irish War threatened to explode as one more skirmish of that seventeenth-century battle, albeit deep in the interior of a new continent. In 1690 Protestant troops led by William of Orange (William III of England) had defeated the Roman Catholic army of James II, the ousted king of England and William's father-in-law. This

English victory established, once again, British (and Protestant) suzerainty over what was a mostly Roman Catholic population, resulting in a bitterness that has continued in a variety of intensities to the twenty-first century, especially in British-ruled Northern Ireland. The Irish of America, both Roman Catholic and Protestant, being rabidly loyal to their respective traditions, had not left their mutual animosity in the Old World.

Fights among them had already disturbed canal projects in the East prior to 1835, so that when these same laborers were hired to work the Wabash and Erie Canal, their supervisors planned to keep the belligerents separated. In this instance they had assigned the Roman Catholic Irish to the upper portion of the canal, which in 1835 was in the Huntington-to-Lagro section of construction. Protestant Irish were housed downriver, as far as Richvalley but with at least one concentration of their shanties rising at Wabash. Simply stated, Lagro was to be Roman Catholic in its Irish labor population, Wabash was to be Protestant. The separation had not been altogether successful in that both sides complained of nighttime raids by their opposites. Fights between individuals and gang beatings had also occurred. Allegedly there had been murders. Although laborers who had small families, a wife and a child or two, felt especially vulnerable, tensions rose among all the Irish laborers as the summer of 1835 progressed.

July 12 is the anniversary of the Battle of the Boyne. Even in the twenty-first century it has been that day in Northern Ireland when Orangemen (Protestant) extremists march in celebration of victory and Roman Catholic extremists try to find ways to thwart the marches. As July 12, 1835, approached, it became apparent to canal overseers in general and to commissioner Burr in particular that their labor forces would not let the day pass without trying to settle past and recent grievances. It was also true that the Irish had a reputation for drunkenness, a factor calculated to fan flames of confrontation. Conflict was imminent by July 10. The canal workers' women and children had been hustled away from the shanties to seek refuge elsewhere; some hid in a riverside cave, others in the woods.

The battleground having been agreed to ahead of time, all began to converge on the same spot. To arm themselves men had scoured the woods for makeshift clubs, collected rocks, and brought tools from their work sites. It is not known if the clubs the Irish fashioned were of the short-handled shillelagh type, such as billy clubs that could protect the wrist of its owner while cracking a skull of an opponent. They might have been like clubs allegedly developed by Hoosiers that were longer and more lethal in that they could knock a man out without close engagement. Though some hands carried pistols, the canal administration had tried to enforce a rule against possessing guns, a merciful prohibition in the circumstance. The Roman Catholics of Lagro, however, had secured the use of a somewhat ineffectual cannon—possibly a ceremonial one—that they hauled from Huntington. Protestant Irish arrived from Wabash prepared to dig in, presumably planning to carve out protective ditches with dirt ramparts. Now, two days ahead of the Boyne anniversary date, hundreds of men—possibly seven hundred—brought their biases, prejudices, hatreds, grievances, and vigorous impatience to the site of showdown. The Corkonians' cannon, lacking real ammunition, may have burped a few rocks as a preliminary show of force. The Fardowners, digging in, may have hurled a few stones.

Then it was all over. Before it began. The hero of the day was that erstwhile and dimly understood cofounder of Wabash, David Burr, still a canal commissioner at the time. Riding out from Treaty Ground, he had intercepted both forces, first those from Wabash and the west, and then, riding ahead, those from Lagro and the east. He was pleased by the general sobriety and order of the combatants, but each side protested against his pleas for peace by insisting they needed to settle the matter in battle—permanently driving their enemies from the canal project—because their families and their shanties were no longer safe from attack.

Burr met with Father Simon Lalumiere, a Fort Wayne priest, who encouraged Burr's peacemaking efforts. Burr took the risk of bringing together representatives of both sides, asking them for a truce. He got only an agreement to postpone hostilities, but he made the most of it. He sent to Logansport for militia. On the Lagro side of the battle lines, concerned noncombatants also had time to call for troops from Fort Wayne and Huntington. Even Chief Charley, Wabash's benign neighbor, offered to send Miami warriors to act as peacekeepers. The arrival of troops, or the expectation of their arrival, discouraged further open hostilities. Several hundred workers were arrested and marched off to Wabash for a day. Their ringleaders were then sent to a secure jail in Indianapolis to await trial. The rest returned to their shanties. The Irish War ended as wars should end, by not starting.[22]

Although believed by many to be rough, rowdy, belligerent, often drunk, sometimes lewd, poorly educated, and probably unwashed to the point of odoriferous, canal hands faced daily backbreaking work for which, at the very least, they deserved their daily ladles of whiskey (despite occasional rules against such payment). Ralph Waldo Emerson had written, "The poor Irishman, the wheelbarrow is his country."[23] Canal hands seemed born for hard labor. In terms of such factors as repetitive chores, dismal living conditions, susceptibility to disease, and the expenditure of youthful muscular brawn—indeed, the expenditure of youth itself—digging a canal was a lavish investment of human resources. "The Song of the Canal" indicates the whimsical attitude the Irish could sometimes muster about their employment:

> We're digging the ditch through the mire,
> Through the mud and the slime and the mire, by heck!
> And the mud is our principal hire;
> Up our pants, in our shirts, down our neck, by heck![24]

Their work—mucking, grubbing, and ditching—was more than just digging, though the ditch was obviously the centerpiece of the project. All loose and porous dirt had to be moved aside. Then a right-of-way, through rock and forest as well as mud, was cleared. Regulations called for removal of all trees, saplings, bushes, roots, and other growth in a swath sixty feet wide, roughly the width of a town street; remaining stumps were to be no higher than one foot. This deforestation protected the canal from falling timbers that might block traffic or damage canal banks. Superintendents sometimes made exceptions, for the sixty-foot rule inevitably needed to bow to nature and to business. At Wabash, for example, the canal line had to edge between the river and the southern projection of the limestone bluff just east of Treaty Ground; in order to avoid low floodplain, the ditch may have hugged the bluff, leaving very little of the sixty feet on the swath's north edge. Additionally, in going through Wabash the canal abutted private business property that may have encroached on the swath.

The standard ditch (typically centered in the swath) was eventually to be at least thirty-nine feet wide at water top between its banks. These dimensions amended some early specifications that called for a canal sixty feet wide at the top of the waterline. In Indiana and elsewhere, however, there was not enough water available to maintain the required four-foot water level in a channel that wide. In general, the completed channel for the Wabash and Erie worked out to about forty feet wide at the top of the waterline and twenty-six feet wide at the bottom.

The ditch was dug at least fifty feet in advance of berms, which were to rise about two feet above water level on either side of it. In certain topography, a canal might be defined by banking alone, without the excavation of a ditch. Berms had to be substantial enough to hold canal water in and keep flood waters out. One of the two berms was to be at least ten feet across at the top so that it could accommodate the towpath. The use of felled timbers in berm construction was disallowed because it was feared that they would make the canal more susceptible to washout.[25]

Beside the swath, ditch, and berms, the canal required various supportive constructs: dams to retain water, feeders to sluice water into the canal from the river, channels to sluice out overflow, viaducts across creeks, and locks to adjust the canal to the change in sea level elevations. Some of these structures involved the quarrying and shaping of limestone blocks. For more specialized requirements, superintendents might hire locals, as in the case of Lagro farmer and erstwhile canal captain, David Watkins, who "burned lime" to be used in the mortar that sealed the walls of dams and locks. A sixty-eight-foot drop in elevation between Huntington and Wabash necessitated several locks. One of these was built at the foot of Cass Street in Wabash.[26]

For wages canal hands received between $10.00 and $13.00 a month. Depending on the liberality of management they were also issued up to three jiggers of whiskey (sometimes brandy) per workday, to be increased to six jiggers in wet weather. When one "jigger-boss" was asked whether his job meant that the hands were drunk on the job, he replied, "You wouldn't expect them to work on the canal if they were sober, would you?"[27] Jigger pay exacerbated excessive drinking habits, of course, so that canal hands were likely to spend off-hours drinking at local grogshops as well. There they were allowed to ring up debts against their next pay, a useful system of credit; however, it carried the risk of putting them at the mercy of unscrupulous tavern keepers who, keeping the tab, might cheat uneducated customers with impunity. Thus, a state of near poverty characterized life in a great many shanties, especially those where families lived.[28]

Add to that dismal prospect the universal susceptibility to disease and death among laborers and their wives and children. Ague—nonfatal but with recurrent, often debilitating, flu-like symptoms—was the bane of all Hoosier society. It caused the "Hoosier shakes" and was thought to be produced by the miasmic landscape of the frontier. It certainly would have been endemic along the canal. Far worse was malaria, brought on by summer's squadrons of mosquitoes. Cholera, snake bites, fights, and accidents took their toll. Quite possibly the most common illness was dysentery, of varying types and intensities, that physicians blamed on poor diet and sanitation. The death rate among children, wives, and workers was undoubtedly high, very probably higher than among the permanent settlers, because of their living conditions and even poorer medical aid. Quinine and calomel were common remedies for dysentery. Canal management provided these commodities, but they are now thought to have been virtually ineffectual. It is quite likely that a large number of Protestant canal workers were interred in Wabash's Old Cemetery. If they were interred without headstones they might conceivably have missed reinterment in the twentieth century, in which case their remains are still in Hanna Park.[29]

Doubtless, some citizens of Wabash, 1835 to 1837, were overly critical of those aspects of the Irish canal hands' characteristics, which later generations called "colorful": their fisticuffs, their inebriation, the traces of the old sod in their speech, their allegedly comical and "ape-like" facial features.[30] Many early settlers looked down upon these erstwhile neighbors as virtual outcasts, as lesser mortals, and as sojourners who were not invested in the enterprise of Wabash the way permanent settlers might be. In the unspoken hopes of residents, this Irish host would move on quickly with the westward progress of the canal. Beyond giving their business to Andrew Murphy's tavern and other establishments along Canal Street, they were not incorporated into Wabash society to any great extent.

It is known that Roman Catholic priests visiting Lagro worried about the spiritual state of the Irish laborers in that town, remonstrated with them about their waywardness, and worked to get them connected with the church by offering to celebrate mass with them before there was a formal parish. Priests tried to anticipate the day that canal hands and their families would take up permanent residence near Lagro. The same intentional pastoral care of Protestant Fardowners in Wabash cannot be proved. By mid-1836 the only organized congregation in Wabash was the small but viable Presbyterian Church with clergy support from Peru once a month. If the Protestant shanty dwellers had a dominant denominational preference, it would possibly have been Presbyterian because of that denomination's ubiquity in Northern Ireland. However, no records show that either congregation or clergy paid much heed to the concentration of Protestant Irish in their midst.

Presbyterians such as Hanna were of the same ethnic background as canal hands, though not of the same socioeconomic status. There is no reason to think Hanna would have snubbed the workers, for he was not that sort and seems to have had amiable relationships with his own hired help. Indeed, canal hands may well have attended the community dances he hosted. But there is not a clear indication of regular interaction between the churched and the canalers. None of the laborers is identified among the local church's founders or known early members. Some canal hands may have attended Sunday worship, for the number of congregants in a service was often much higher than the number of formal adherents listed on membership rolls. Given the laborers' reputation, temperance advocates of the church would have found them fertile ground to plow. However, temperance was still a feeble cause in Wabash. If Presbyterians or other citizens in Wabash reached out to laborers in other ways, or vice versa, the evidence for it is lost. In their correspondence, Presbyterian missionaries in the region were likely to mention the canal only for its potential to bring in new residents "of the right stamp" who might raise the tone of a place. In Fort Wayne, when the canal was new there, the Reverend James Chute, also a Presbyterian missionary, had opined that "The influence of a canal, especially in its incipient stages, is decidedly adverse to morality and religion." Like many other permanent settlers, Chute had looked askance when it came to the transient, rowdy Irish canalers. He agonized about their reputation for unwholesome lifestyles and worried about their effect on community development, but he probably did not invite them to worship.[31]

Labor relations notwithstanding, the advent of the Wabash and Erie Canal was eagerly anticipated for what it was—a colossal internal improvement project that transformed communities. Just its length was impressive, running for 468 miles, probably the second longest canal in the world, exceeded only by China's twelve hundred-mile Grand Canal. When canal boats reached Wabash in 1837, they actualized a dream more than four decades old. In 1794 Fort Wayne had been located strategically to control the confluence where the Saint Marys and the Saint Joseph rivers joined to spawn the Maumee River. However, an additional reason for the fort's location may have been the nine-mile portage between the Saint Marys River and the Little Wabash River that lay to the west. The fort's builder, General "Mad Anthony" Wayne, would likely have been aware that other national leaders, including George

Washington, had speculated on the possibility of facilitating trade from eastward flowing rivers, such as the Maumee, to those that would connect to the Ohio and Mississippi valleys. Although it represented a continental divide, the nine-mile portage was mostly level, marshy land that Miami and white traders had long used.

When canal fever struck Indiana early in the nineteenth century, it raged first far to the south at New Albany where a canal around the Ohio River falls was futilely attempted, only to be completed later by Kentucky on the south side of the river. The fever went dormant for a few years and then broke out again farther north in the 1820s and 1830s, spurred by the removal of Native American claims to northern Indiana, by the opening of the Erie Canal in New York state, and by the encouragement of politicians and investors who saw internal improvements as magic avenues toward prosperity. Some Hoosiers hoped that a northern canal linking Indiana by water to New York would bring in a stronger Yankee element, offsetting the state's dominant southern connections.

Because the natural waterway of the Little Wabash and Wabash valleys already connected the west end of the nine-mile portage to the Ohio River and was a dependable source of water, constructing a canal deep into the interior along that route loomed as common sense. Such a waterway would solve chronic problems of navigation on the Wabash: its dramatic, sometimes dangerous, variations in water levels, from raging floods to seasonal, rock-bottom lows. The canal would also be seasonal, of course, in that it would be closed for much of each winter, but most of the year its water would flow at a steady, calm, and manageable depth, with no rocks or rapids to trouble it.

Tipton and Governor James B. Ray, two of the stars of the 1826 treaty at Wabash, had used their considerable influence and manipulative powers to promote the surveying of the Maumee to Wabash route about the time of the treaty. The surveying went forward over the objections of citizens from downstate who had plans for a Whitewater valley canal. The fact that Tipton owned more than eight thousand acres of land in the area of the northern route, land that would increase in value once a canal was completed, did not seem to bother his conscience or anyone else's in the north. In 1827 the U.S. Congress granted more than 500,000 acres of former Indian land to the canal project; Indiana accepted this gift at the next meeting of the general assembly. The survey that Tipton and Ray had sought was completed about the same time, showing that in the first 128 miles from the Maumee River the land dropped only 220 feet, which meant that the canal would not require an unusual number of locks. For budget reasons this was encouraging. In 1828 the state legislature formally launched the northern canal project. In light of the fact that thirty years later the canals began to lose out to railroad competition, it is interesting to note that final approval of the Wabash and Erie Canal was momentarily jeopardized by Ray, who suddenly injected his favorite hobby horse, railroads, into the debate, suggesting that railroads might prove to be a more efficient form of transportation. Ray's prescience here was fairly quickly overridden by a legislature heavily weighted with canal advocates who were angered by the governor's apparent defection. Although Ray was often eccentric and controversial, had his ideas been more patiently received in this case the state might have avoided enormous financial crises generated by the canal's eventual failure.[32]

The ditch at Wabash was ready for water in 1836 but was not filled until about three weeks before opening exercises on July 4, 1837. Completion of the ditch meant a sudden drop in the town's population and a dramatic change in its ethnic demography, for at least a hundred Irish shanty households moved on to new construction sites. Though it had never been expected that they would be permanent residents, their exodus meant at least a 50 percent drop in the local population. Meanwhile, during the ten months the completed ditch was dry, its level surface invited quick trips to Lagro and back by horse and sometimes inspired horse racing on its smooth, sunken track. Just before water was let in at Lagro, citizens had gathered in the dry canal bed and then walked to Wabash ahead of the tide rising slowly behind them.

At some point prior to July Fourth, Hanna, David Cassatt, and Steele put their heads together for a little fun. They dragged Cassatt's large maple sap trough across Canal Street to the still-virgin waters of the new canal. Cassatt normally used the trough in making maple sugar, but on this day it was expected to make history. Steele brought his old mare with him and a long, tough grapevine he had cut from the woods, attaching the mare to the trough with the vine. Hanna and Cassatt christened the trough *The Davy Crockett*, shoved it into the canal, and climbed aboard. Steele and his mare pulled *The Davy Crockett* to Lagro and back to Wabash, thus making a used sap trough the first canal boat to reach Wabash. There are two things wrong with this claim. First, the sap trough did not meet the required specifications for a canal boat, and second, another version of the event says it was not a sap trough at all, but a log, launched by the same three friends. In the latter case, however, a log in the canal was contrary to regulations and would not have qualified as a canal boat either.[33]

It took the real canal boats about an hour to cruise from Lagro to Wabash for the grand opening. The speed limit was four miles an hour, a speed that protected the berms from wake wash. Although Wabash's celebration mimicked exercises that had been used previously in towns farther up the line, a couple of misadventures made the day special. There were the usual firings of guns, cheers of the crowd, and speeches. As previously arranged, one of the heroes of the event was supposed to be Dana Columbia, master of the packet *Indiana*, who was scheduled to guide his vessel to the Wabash Street bridge and dock and there be cheered as captain of the first canal boat to arrive in the village. The *Indiana* had been newly painted for the occasion. It carried dignitaries from Fort Wayne and Huntington, plus a German band playing unmelodious music, perhaps of the oom-pah, oom-pah variety. Somewhere, not far out of Lagro, the apparently more cunning or more dextrous captain of the *Prairie Hen*, Ed Patchen (some accounts say Will Dale), maneuvered his inelegant packet around Columbia's and sailed victoriously into Wabash several rods ahead of the *Indiana*. Half the *Prairie Hen*'s passengers were Miami who were reportedly excited about both a boat ride and the possibility that firewater was among its cargo.

Folks waiting at the Wabash Street landing yelled, shouted, and shot off muskets, pistols, and rifles in celebration. Their welcome of passengers from upstream may have been especially heartfelt because the presence of those visitors indicated how the canal could bring pioneer folks more easily together. Meanwhile, wanting to add a bit of roar to the cheering and the gunshot, saddle maker and trader James Kintner prepared to fire off a ceremonial cannon. He miscalculated something, however, and ignited a stack of gunpowder instead. The blast flung Kintner skyward, a flight from which he walked away virtually unharmed. Festivities resumed.[34]

At some point celebrants moved in procession to Treaty Ground. There settlers and guests satisfied hunger with a picnic-like feast near the old cabins that had birthed the town. Years later William H. Coombs, by then a Fort Wayne judge, remembered having been one of the speakers that day. He had arrived in Wabash in 1835, just after the Irish War, when scores of prisoners were still in town waiting for disposition of their case. The substance of his speech in 1837 is not recorded, though it may have been Coombs who had rehearsed his speech aloud in the forest the previous day and in so doing stirred up a nest of rattlesnakes. The speaker most remembered was Elijah Hackleman, a frequent visitor to the area, who became Wabash's premier resident historian of the nineteenth century. His later addresses suggest that on this occasion Hackleman would have reviewed a lot of American history that, in his opinion, had culminated in the significant day at hand. His erudition would have been a weave of unassailable facts flavored with hearty patriotism.

Formalities having been completed at Treaty Ground, Hanna opened the upstairs of his brick building for a more impromptu celebration. It was the least he could do; for Hanna and for others the canal's epiphany dramatically improved their chances for prosperity. Indeed, it is doubtful if Hanna would have platted Wabash at all had it not been for anticipation of this day. The gathering at Hanna's Corner turned into a ball of some kind, probably to the accompaniment of fiddles, and then into something else. Another local historian, Alanson P. Ferry, reported that the drinking habits of the boatmen (and perhaps of any Irish laborers who were still around as well, not to mention stalwart Scots-Irish of Hanna's ilk) led to heightened joviality. Ferry suspected that drinks had been spiked. In fact, many celebrants were doubtlessly taking their whiskey straight.[35]

Wabash had become a canal burg.

4

A Little Town Called Wabash . . . One of the Most Beautiful

A passenger named Charles H. Titus eyeballed Wabash as he was riding past on a packet boat in 1843. In his journal he said this about it:

> About noon on Friday, passed a little town called Wabash—one of the most beautiful I had seen since I left home. It is the only one, so far, that is situated on high, rolling land. The town is north of the canal. Between the canal & the Wabash river, south of the town, is a beautiful tract of bottom land, of exceeding fertility. The land on the north of the canal, being high and hilly, renders the town very wealthy, and gives to it something of the appearance of a New England village.[1]

Interestingly, eighty years later, on the eve of the First World War, county historian Clarkson Weesner opened his chapter on Wabash with an appraisal that echoes Titus's:

> Its site on the Wabash River is striking from the viewpoint of picturesqueness, and favorable to the best hygienic conditions. . . . The business and manufacturing districts stretch away on comparatively level ground from the river and canal, while toward both the north and the south the resident sections cover bold and healthful highlands. The rise is especially abrupt and striking north of the Wabash, which embraces the main portion of the city.[2]

Something of a romantic view of the place seems to have survived intact for eight decades.

Titus's observation in 1843 is not only felicitous, it is rare. Although his delight in the town's appearance may have been shared generally by other travelers of the time and by Wabash residents as well, there is little extant evidence of it. Indeed, while there are some bare bones to the town's story at this juncture, there is not much by way of flesh and blood. Between the excitement of the canal's grand opening in 1837 and the establishment, ten years later, of a local newspaper, the *Upper Wabash Argus* in 1847, the record of life in Wabash is comparatively thin and dry. Sources such as deeds, mortgages, and other official detritus, plus lists of who held what office when, dominate but do not elucidate. The two great histories of the county, T. B. Helm's 1884 tome and Weesner's 1914 work, reduce this period for Wabash to brief paragraphs. The recorded memories of old settlers are extremely valuable, but they tend to focus on those heady seminal years when Wabash was a wide spot in the forest striving to become a bona fide canal town, and not the mundane years that followed the canal opening. The old settlers did not wax poetic about, for example, working in the pork industry, or shopping on Canal Street, or what homes and home life were like, and much less about tavern brawls, common crimes, or moral indiscretions.

The arrival of local journalism eventually saved local history from this dearth of colorful information. Meanwhile the present chapter in Wabash's story will be strung together on the witness of seven men: a census taker (George R. Cooke); three professional gentlemen (James Dicken Conner Jr., Joseph Mackey, and Doctor James Ford); four temporary missionaries to the town (Samuel Newbury, Asa Johnson, James Thomson, and Samuel Smith); and one merchant (Elmer Hersey Cox). Sketchy though these available accounts are, they serve to portray something of Wabash in its youthful adolescence, when it was just beginning to feel a little muscle along its frame.

Cooke, a Liberty Township settler, with a wife and possibly six offspring, was hired as a part-time federal employee to tally the Wabash County census for 1840. In 1980 county historian Ronald L. Woodward took Cooke's figure from microfilm and compiled a twenty-seven-page synopsis of the census to facilitate local archival use. This compilation reveals that five years after Wabash's creation, the town's population had more than doubled, from a roughly estimated sixty-six permanent settlers in 1835 to a somewhat more scientific figure of 142 in 1840. These 142 or so (populations change almost before they are recorded) lived in twenty-eight separate households, an average of five persons per household. There were seventy-nine males and sixty-three females. Of the twenty-eight heads of household, three (possibly four) were single men. Three or four were single fathers, no doubt indicating a high death rate among women of child-bearing age. One young couple had no child. Although there were two single mothers in Noble Township, none resided in Wabash. Eleven "free colored" citizens (African Americans) lived in the county, but none in Wabash at this date. There were no unnaturalized, foreign-born residents registered in the census, and no slaves. As noted earlier, Hugh Hanna's house on the bluff bulged with twelve occupants even though his immediate family numbered only seven (the extra five were possibly unmarried employees and household help). Sometimes a juvenile, orphaned or homeless, was indentured to an established citizen until adulthood. The indentured person might live as a foster child or serve as a hired hand. It is not known how many Wabash residents were indentured in 1840.

Approximately 47 percent of Wabash residents—sixty-eight individuals—were under twenty years of age. Of these, fewer than a dozen were in their upper teens, fifteen to nineteen years old. Roughly fifty-seven infants, toddlers, preteens, and young teens comprised the "kids" in the town and surely enlivened the place by playing games in the streets, letting the mud ooze between their toes, swimming the canal, fishing the river, fighting, hunting with their fathers or friends, and generally trying to avoid being civilized, if Mark Twain is to be believed. Amazingly the 1840 census reports no one in Wabash over the age of sixty, which may say something about the accuracy of census taking at the time or perhaps about the death rate. On the other hand, it may simply illustrate how youthful and vigorous the community was. Inasmuch as there were fewer than a dozen men and women over age forty, it is clear that folks still of child-bearing age (late teens through the thirties) represented a dominant statistic, a fact that promised growth through childbirth in addition to immigration. Interestingly, however, of the twenty-eight heads of households listed in the 1840 census, only sixteen or seventeen became "persisters," that is, appearing as residents in the 1850 census. Thus, about 41 percent of the earliest settlers vanished from the local scene over ten years. The surnames of the twenty-eight heads of household indicate that Wabash in 1840 was overwhelmingly of the British Isles in its lineage; only two or three names could be associated with the European continent, and none reflect non-European roots.[3]

About the time Cooke was gathering his census data, Conner moved to town. He was to become a major player in the community and one of the best-known citizens outside Wabash County in the nineteenth century. Born near Connersville in 1819, he had grown up a poor Baptist "preacher's kid" whose early education was rudimentary at best, due to the incomplete nature of public education generally. He filled some of the gaps with personal study and, later, by attending a seminary (private school) in Connersville. After teaching for a couple of years, he read law at the office of Caleb B. Smith, a man destined to become Abraham Lincoln's secretary of the interior. In seeking endorsements for his admission to the Indiana Bar from senior jurors around the state, Conner happened to pass through Wabash in 1840. Something about the place attracted him, possibly the shortage of attorneys in town just then. He returned in October that same year to hang his shingle at an office near Hanna's Corner, an office he maintained without interruption for the next sixty-nine years.

By 1842 Conner had secured his connections in Wabash circles by marrying Julia Ann Hanna, Hugh's oldest daughter. In the 1850s the Conners built a home on the bluff in the block west of Hanna's house. Conner was enthusiastic for the new Republican Party, which replaced the moribund Whigs in 1856. He attended the national convention that year and in many subsequent presidential election years. He knew some of the national candidates on a personal basis, including Lincoln and William Howard Taft. Having experienced state politics as a legislator and senator, he topped his career in 1884 by being elected judge of the Wabash Circuit Court. He retired from the active practice of law after his one six-year term on the bench.[4]

It was through Conner, rather than through his sons, that Hugh's bloodlines were to persist in Wabash into the late twentieth century. Janet Jones Mahaney, Hugh's great-great-granddaughter, who died in 1988 and is buried near Hugh, was probably the last of the proprietor's direct descendants to have lived in Wabash through most of adulthood. Her grandfather was Hanna's grandson, J. D. Jr., the judge's son. J. D. Jr. was a man whose pursuit of Belgium draft horse husbandry led to his being knighted by the Belgian crown. The elevation tickled his Wabash chums, who delighted in calling him "Sir J. D."

Be that as it may, J. D. Jr. was heir not only to local bloodlines of note but also to whatever lore about early Wabash his father's (James D.) and grandfather's (Hanna) generations may have shared in casual storytelling. J. D. Jr. was to some degree a bona fide conduit of the oral history of early Wabash, specifically including those years, 1837 to 1847, when the record is spotty. It was he, for example, who has confirmed that the *Davey Crockett* his grandfather launched as the first canal boat was, indeed, a sap trough and not a mere log. For historical purposes, then, it is significant that in 1886, the Presbyterian Church, celebrating its fiftieth anniversary, invited J. D. Jr., a member of the church, to deliver a history of the town.[5]

That history, faithfully reported word for word in the *Wabash Courier*, is rich in anecdotes—the kind that must have enlivened family table talk and tavern chatter at the time and that gives something of the flavor of the period. There is, for example, Conner's story of Sal Slinker, a canal boat cook, a slinger of hash and other packet fare. Locals standing on the canal bridge liked to watch Slinker hit the upper deck, going completely prone, face down, when someone yelled "low bridge!" the universal canal boat warning. Later, Slinker turned to singing and became a minor prima donna in traveling musical shows. Two men in the audience of such a show fell to arguing over whether the soloist was the Sal Slinker they had known in Wabash. Said one, "I'll settle that. When she comes out to sing next, you just watch her." She came out. The man yelled, "Low bridge!" and the prima donna hit the stage floor, face down. Argument won.

Being a lawyer, Conner was especially mindful of political and court lore. In early years county and village offices tended to rotate among a half dozen or so men, and sometimes the duties were light enough for one man to wear two or more hats. In the late 1830s Colonel William Steele Sr., a respected but eccentric town father, served simultaneously as county clerk and county recorder. He was also postmaster about the same time. Conner observed that in Steele's hands these offices were entirely portable, in that the man kept current official papers in his hat. Where he went the offices went. This arrangement had the advantages of simplicity and accessibility, yet subjected official papers to unpredictable jeopardy. The property around Steele's small brick house on the northeastern corner of Canal and Huntington streets included a fenced vegetable garden. Inspecting his garden one day, Steele discovered that much of it had been uprooted by an old "elm peeler," one of Wabash's free-ranging hogs, which were known for chewing the bark of trees. This one had managed to get a long snout through the cracks in the fence and pick off turnips three rows in. Steele took after it with a club. The hog headed northwest, diagonally across Huntington Street, and into the Market Street pond, which, being in one of its expansive moods, had inundated town lots south of Market. Just as the animal reached the water's edge Steele lunged to give it a final blow, but tripped over his own feet, causing his hat and the offices of county clerk, county recorder, and the U.S. Post Office to take a dive.

The mail—a letter and a ginseng circular—was retrieved with little damage. Steele, however, had to work a day and a half to make copies of the soaked papers of the clerk and recorder offices. The Market Street pond remained a menace until 1855 when a "canal" was dug to drain at least a part of it.[6]

Before the county moved into Hanna's courthouse in the early 1840s, trials were normally held in cabins, most often Patrick Duffy's. Court cases constituted public entertainment, attracting virtually all citizens. If the weather was decent, court could adjourn to the woods where there was more space and fresher air. There the jury perched along a log, and the clerk signed indictments on his knee. Shoes were not required of participants, indoors or outdoors. Tobacco and whiskey were handy. One early settler reported his attendance at court by saying, "As I entered the court room, the Judge was sitting on a block paring his toe-nails, when the Sheriff entered out of breath and informed the Court that he had six jurors tied and his deputies were running down the others." Cases were frequently inconsequential in a legal or financial sense but provided high drama nonetheless. In one case a plaintiff accused a defendant of slander because the former charged the latter with stealing a goose. Plaintiff maintained that the goose was his. Defendant countered that the goose was plainly his because it was white, that he had owned its mother and grandmother, and that this particular line of geese took to water immediately on hatching. Testimony became opaque on the rather technical question of whether the goose was a pacer, perhaps as opposed to a trotter, but these distinctions seemed lost even on one of the lawyers. There was a break for dinner, after which the plaintiff's attorney called a rebuttal witness. It was then that the testimony of "a respectable old Irish lady of some 70 years" saved the day for the plaintiff, breaking a deadlocked situation. The woman testified before the packed courtroom that she had been acquainted with geese for sixty years and that the goose in question undoubtedly belonged to the plaintiff's wife. When asked how she knew such a fact, the woman answered in deep Irish brogue, "Faith, an' how do Oye know! Because she was a white goose and paced. Oye owned her mither and grandmother, who Oye brought from owld Ireland, an' they each paced, an' so did all that brade." One senses that the original trial might not have been any more entertaining than J. D. Jr.'s version of it in 1886.

According to J. D. Jr., the most immediately significant change wrought by the canal was to turn Wabash into a great grain emporium. Despite the primitive nature of all roads into town, the place became a magnet for those farmers who desperately needed an outlet for their produce, especially wheat. Because Wabash was located on the upper part of the Wabash River and Erie Canal, which had opened before downstate canals were completed, it drew in stores of grain from Delaware, Madison, Grant, Howard, Kosciusko, Whitley, Fulton, and Blackford counties. There were days during harvest when roads into town were packed with teams hauling produce. Before a bridge was erected at the foot of Wabash Street in 1845, a ferry transported goods across the river. It is known that C. L. Rice paid the county three dollars for a ferry license in 1841; he may have been the second ferryman at that location. Whether a ferry had the heft to carry the weight of grain-loaded wagon teams is an unanswered question. Just upriver, about where Huntington Street bridge later stood, there was the natural ford, which Miami and pioneers had used, a bumpy avenue of boulders, rocks, and gravel that was navigable at all but flood times.

By whatever passage a team took across the river, it had to enter town along South Wabash Street to the only bridge over the canal. On busy days, then, there was an enormous concentration of traffic at the bridge. Teams had to wait in line to unload at the new warehouses rising along the canal. Business in taverns, eateries, and other shops doubtless boomed. Meanwhile, cargo boats threatened to clog the canal. A basinlike wide place had been built into the canal west of town, where boats could moor, stay out of the traffic lane, or turn around. Long delays in loading and unloading were common annoyances in high season. When farmers found warehouses full, and too few boats to speed the process, they piled grain harum-scarum along streets or roads until it could be transported to Toledo and the eastern markets. Though J. D. Jr. does not give us a date for his figures, he speculated with considerable confidence that in those days when grain teams clogged Wabash streets, the town was exporting between a half million and a million bushels of wheat a year.[7]

J. D. Jr.'s lengthy address was followed by another from Mackey whose areas of interest for the occasion were early business and educational concerns. These were appropriate topics because the man had stellar careers in both disciplines. He had come to Wabash in 1860 as the assistant superintendent of the high school, rose to superintendent, studied law, opened a practice with J. M. Amoss, and then launched a high-profile and successful business career. According to eulogies delivered at two separate memorial services for him in 1887, Mackey was responsible for founding and helping to direct the Wabash School Furniture Company, the Wabash Novelty Works, and the Building and Loan Association, among other enterprises. He sat for twenty years on the Wabash School Board and was active on the town's council. When he died unexpectedly at age fifty-four, factories closed for half a day out of respect, and the Presbyterian Church was packed with the legal, business, and school officials of town as well as scores of employees. Mackey's impressive tombstone in Falls Cemetery was of such quality that it has aged remarkably well. It was the gift of "the laboring men of Wabash," a tribute to Mackey's personality and skills.[8]

Mackey's 1886 speech is mostly a rapid review of men and women who pioneered in business and education, but the very volume of information is impressive. Mackey begins by illustrating the vacuum in enterprise that existed prior to the surge that the canal created. He cites Albert Pauling (Pawling), an erstwhile Pleasant Township resident who subsequently settled in Wabash. Pauling bought a cow from Hanna, apparently with the idea of producing butter to offset the high cost of living: flour was fourteen dollars a barrel, salt was six cents a pound, and other commodities were correspondingly dear. Having acquired a cow, Pauling needed a churn. There were only two churns in town, neither adequate for his purposes even if he had borrowed them. Those two churns had been imported with the pioneers, and no one in Wabash had ever made a churn. Although Pauling lacked mechanical and carpentry skills, he, nevertheless, made a churn. With axe, pen knife, a borrowed plane, and a gauge of some kind, Pauling built a churn that turned out butter for years. The Pauling vignette illustrated Mackey's point that in terms of having the bare essentials of a civilized society on hand, Wabash, at this stage, had nowhere to go but up. The founding of businesses, however small, and of schools, however primitive, was to be essential for the town's future.

One reason Mackey's catalog of rising businesses is so important is his remembrance, by name, of individuals who were not necessarily movers and shakers in the sense that Hanna, Conner, and Mackey himself were. Rather, he names lesser-known craftsmen whose labors filled the entrepreneurial vacuum, multiplying the infrastructure of Wabash's economy. Perhaps the best way to appreciate Mackey's contribution to an understanding of that process is to recapitulate his list in an abbreviated fashion.

Mackey begins with David Cassatt, who established the first blacksmith shop on the north side of East Canal Street, probably on lot 26, half way between Wabash and Huntington streets. So essential was blacksmithing to a village that Cassatt was followed by several others, including John Woods, Jacob Vandergrift, John Shiles, Harry Wheeler, Mike Shanahan, John Donovan, Dan Morgan, and Johnny Fireburnd. Andy Lowman was Wabash's first tailor, followed by Timothy Craft and Malotha Reece. Reece also kept the county's post office in a small box at his second-story shop, charging eighteen cents for letters sent no farther than two hundred miles away and twenty-five cents for those going farther. William Tyner was the first saddler and harness maker. Tobias Beck took up the same business in 1844 and kept it for thirty years. William Iliff made shoes. William Luark established a wagon factory in a log house on the north side of Market Street. (He built a carriage for Hugh Hanna that was so big he had to saw out the front of his shop to extract the carriage for delivery.) Luark's business was the mother of a woodworking industry that was to boom in Wabash. Joseph A. Large, Richard Durbin, Henry Sayre, Allen Beroth, Joseph Faunce, and Cornelius Beroth all followed Luark in the trade, although some of these men did not arrive until the 1850s.

The town's first tinsmith was John Davis. By 1848 there would be two more, Thomas McNamee and Kirby Davis. F. E. Catlin and E. G. Sackett were silversmiths. A man named Holmes was the first gunsmith. Joshua Burson also made guns, probably on East Canal Street. Although many pioneers and settlers knew carpentry, the first professional in that trade was William Johnson, who had built William Steele's and Doctor Finley's brick houses. Johnson was also the county's first sheriff. Soon came the Myers brothers—James, George, and William—who, in addition to James H. Ray, specialized in cabinetry. Meanwhile, by the mid-1840s, grain milling had become big business. Hanna had already added a "corn cracker" to his lumber mill. Robert Cissna arrived in town to build the Lock Mill at the foot of Cass Street. The architect and contractor for that project was a man named Sanford Honeywell, who eventually owned some land just north of the Original Plat and regularly came to town with produce from his gardens. The Honeywell name was to become internationally recognizable in the twentieth century in connection with the Minneapolis Honeywell Corporation, a far-flung industry founded by Sanford's son, Mark. About the same time, N. D. Myers joined Hanna in the foundry business, located on or near the west side of Allen Street. Many services that Mackey lists—from blacksmithing to foundry, from carpentry to mill construction—grew and diversified through the 1840s and 1850s and then, after the Civil War, expanded dramatically into a powerful industrial base for the city.

Mackey's interest in local education also dominated a large portion of his speech. He credits Ira Burr with opening Wabash's first school in a log cabin and former storeroom that stood on the north side of the canal just east of Wabash Street. This was not the location of the first school mentioned by J. D. Jr. that same evening; apparently the two men had not compared notes. J. D.'s location was near the downtown in a "hollow" that is difficult to identify. Burr was a quiet man from Connecticut who was especially well read in history and science. He served as county auditor for a time, married Doctor James Hackleman's daughter, and later moved to Kansas. A second school opened in the one-room log cabin owned by Patrick Duffy on the northwest corner of Market and Huntington streets. Sarah Blackman was the teacher, but she left after a term to marry. A strict disciplinarian, Emma Swift, "took up the birch" at the same location, which was also used by the community as a church meeting room. Duffy's cabin was available because its owner was often traveling elsewhere. Later in life when he boarded a steamer to visit his homeland of Ireland, Duffy was asked if he wanted accommodation on deck or in cabin. He chose cabin, he later reported, because he had always lived in a cabin.

A frame house on the north side of Main Street was the third schoolhouse. Mrs. Daniel Richards, both a wife and a good scholar, taught there. She was succeeded at the same location by Nathan O. Ross, a future lawyer in Peru and Logansport. Next came David W. Lumaree, called "Doc" by fellow citizens. He began teaching in a log house on the lower level of town but soon moved the school to the upper level to a place in the woods. It may have been on the north side of East Sinclair Street. However, some records suggest that the first permanent schoolhouse was built by Hanna on the north side of East Hill Street between Wabash and Huntington streets. Other records place Hanna's school on a little hill near the intersection of Huntington and Maple streets. Lumaree was respected for his ability to keep older male scholars in line. Wherever it stood his schoolhouse served for eighteen years. Mackey states that it was the only school in town for those years, but he then contradicts himself, saying that a great many rooms and houses were used subsequently for educational purposes, several of them in the west part of town along Hill Street. The homes of the Reverend James Thomson and the Reverend Samuel D. Smith served classes at different times. Teachers also rented school space in the original courthouse. Teacher followed teacher in quick succession. According to Mackey's record, between the early efforts of Ira Burr and the year 1850, at least twenty teachers tried their hand at educating the youngsters of Wabash.

Just because a teacher offered a school did not mean students wanted to be there. Because even many older boys and girls had no prior experience with formal education, school must often have meant a tiresome curtailment of accustomed freedom. Attendance was not mandated by law. The fact is, young children were loose and on their own much of a day; their older brothers and sisters were less free if they were part of the workforce at home, in town, or on a farm. Owing tuition probably inspired parents to get their money's worth by making sure their students were in attendance. School terms were brief by later standards but never brief enough for reluctant scholars. J. D. Jr. cited Billy Wilson, a young student in the earliest Wabash school, who during recess one morning discovered that it would be more fun to chase Hanna's sheep than to return docilely to the schoolroom. The sheep were possibly pasturing near Hanna's Spring, not far from the schoolhouse. The boy reckoned without considering an ancient ram that was the leader of the flock. Its horns were especially intimidating, massive, and curled over its head. As young Wilson tried to make his escape he discovered himself sailing through the air, fifteen to twenty feet up, according to Conner. Billy hit the ground on the run, but the ram was right on target. Up Billy went. Down Billy came. Up again, down again, "Mr. Ram furnishing the motive power" each time. In the end the ram beat Billy back to school.

Teachers clearly endured a surfeit of unorthodox behavior. One favorite game among older boys was called "Locking the Teacher Out." They did just that, barred the schoolhouse door against the protesting teacher until he relented and granted them a boon: more recess or a treat or games instead of lessons. A strong, authoritative, and creative will was an essential trait in an effective teacher. As it is an established fact that much later in the town's educational development so-called flagellation of students was regularly applied as a disciplinary measure, it is reasonably certain that early teachers were also free to apply harsh physical punishment. One teacher may have overstepped the bounds when he disciplined the future Major M. H. Kidd by making him sit on a hot stove.[9]

Before township trustees waded into public education issues, these schools were private affairs, their quality wholly dependent on the knowledge, talents, and creativity of the teacher. There was no state system and no local school board to set policy, oversee operations, or pick up expenses. Teachers set the length of a term—often three months—bartered for rental costs, determined the tuition students paid, selected the curricula, and advertised as best they could for students. Teachers might rent a room in the courthouse for a dollar a week and charge students a few dollars for a three-month term, payable at the close of that term. In 1848 a Miss Hoopes charged $1.50 a term for primary subjects such as reading, writing, geography, and grammar, and $2.00 for more advanced subjects. Given the local economy at the time, some of that tuition undoubtedly materialized as produce. There were certainly community sponsors, men such as Hanna who erected a building at his own cost and others who might house a teacher or subsidize his or her expenses.[10]

A mature curricula that all serious educators desired was easy to define, but how close Wabash schools came to such standards in the 1830s and 1840s is less well documented. For previously uneducated students classroom time would have focused on basics—spelling, reading, writing, geography, and arithmetic. A second level might add history, grammar, composition, and even drawing or singing to the mix. It is doubtful that the first Wabash schools reached beyond this level, but there would be well-educated citizens, especially among the legal and ecclesiastical professions, who expected schools to move toward a high school equivalency. It is known from published academic schedules in private academies of the time that such expectations included instruction in rhetoric, physiology, biblical antiquities, ancient history, church history, algebra, meteorology, natural history, chemistry, geometry, philosophy, geology, botany, logic, and government.[11]

The primitive nature of education mirrors the primitive nature of Wabash society generally, not only in learning but also in manners, culture, and morality. Self-appointed, high-minded, and well-meaning social architects of the time were quite aware of this situation and sought to address it. Thomson was one of them. He is best remembered as one of the founders of Wabash

College at Crawfordsville, Indiana, where he was the minister of a local church and a close associate of the college faculty. Relative to its social setting, the college was a hotbed of liberal reform. It had been created by New Englanders who were not only determined to plant the right kind of education in the dark interior but also to plant a forward-looking, reform-minded version of the Christian gospel. It was a powerful combination. It demanded of the clergy far more than preaching, evangelism, and pastoral care. It expected them to use all their disciplines to change the social order around them, to be "voices crying in the wilderness" against what they perceived to be a pervasively ignorant, demoralized, and demoralizing culture.

By 1842 Thomson had tired of his work at Crawfordsville and was longing for fresh fields. He bundled his family and their possessions on a canal boat headed to that other Wabash, the town on the upper canal. The Thomsons arrived in early November, just as a severe winter set in early. The day after their arrival their docked canal boat, with all their possessions on board, sank. Efforts were made to salvage household furnishings and personal gear by dragging them onto the canal dock. The temperature plummeted that night. Their possessions, including Thomson's library, two-thirds of which got wet, froze. It was an ominous beginning for Thomson's five-year, not very happy, sojourn in Wabash.[12]

Thomson was not only connected to Wabash College, he was also aligned with an organization headquartered in New York City, the American Home Missionary Society, one of the fountainheads of social reclamation of the time. Founded in 1826, the AHMS was one of a series of national volunteer societies that sought various reforms. The American Education Society, the American Sunday School Union, the American Tract Society, the American Bible Society, the American Society for the Promotion of Temperance, the American Peace Society, and the American Antislavery Society sprang up in the same generation as the AHMS. These organizations were not officially affiliated with any religious denomination, but they drew their support from churches and from civic-minded individuals who were fearful of deteriorating social, domestic, and educational standards, especially in the emerging western states. Support collected specifically for the AHMS came largely from those who stood, religiously, in the Calvinist-Reformed theological tradition that Scots-Irish and English Presbyterians and Congregationalists had indelibly planted on American shores. Thus, the churches that AHMS missionaries were likely to found were Presbyterian or Congregationalist. Society men believed, often intensely, that the pursuit of community improvement was as morally incumbent upon them as the pursuit of righteous personal behavior—an orientation that sometimes set them apart from their Christian neighbors and classified them as troublemakers. It made perfect sense to them that a community could not excel culturally if many of its citizens were uneducated, profane, inebriated, and promiscuous. In their opinion Wabash qualified as needing their services. Unless change occurred, the growing importance of an uncivil West would soon overshadow the influence of the eastern establishment in matters of national values and politics. Systemic reform was essential, a task larger than just growing churches. The job of Thomson and other AHMS missionaries was to tame the West through preaching, teaching, and community building.[13]

Between 1836 and 1848, when local records are especially skimpy, the AHMS placed four missionaries in the area of Wabash: Newbury, Johnson, Thomson, and Smith. Although the AHMS expected its clergy to solicit local funding in cash or in kind for their support, it guaranteed its missionaries a total annual income worth up to three hundred dollars. The AHMS stipulated that its contributions were contingent on receipt of quarterly reports from the missionaries. Those reports were to reflect on the nature of the area served, the moral and cultural condition of citizens, and the progress of church growth in the field. The result of this stipulation is a massive collection of personal testimony about frontier and pioneer life from all parts of the United States.[14]

Newbury, Johnson, Thomson, and Smith wrote a total of sixty-six reports, many of which reflect on conditions in Wabash or its area. Understandably their letters are awash in missionary and ecclesiastical jargon, which means, in part, that they express judgmental and negative assessments of life on the edge of civilization, so different from their vision of what it should be. All of them, for example, exhibit strong anti-Catholic bias, especially because they were aware of "popery's" dominance in Lagro, fearing its spread down the canal. On other occasions they seem relatively hopeful about the area's spiritual potential. Their reports voice concerns about personal dangers and hardships, conditions that all Wabash citizens would have faced. Neither Newbury (1836–37) nor Johnson (1837–42) lived in Wabash. They operated out of Peru but preached in Wabash about once a month. In Newbury's short term he founded Wabash's first church in the spring of 1836. He was encouraged by the strong showing of easterners among immigrants, noting that many wealthy and enterprising men were among them.

Although the Presbyterians were first with an established congregation, they were by no means the only folks with religious intentions. The Methodists had heard itinerant preachers irregularly since 1835 and were meeting as a bona fide congregation in Patrick Duffy's house by the late 1830s. First Christian (Disciples of Christ) Church organized officially in 1842. By late 1841 or early 1842, a Baptist congregation was functioning. By the end of the decade there were probably three Jewish families in town. All of these religious groups, by their very presence and vitality, changed the tone of the community. None of their founding ministers, elders, or members, however, left known records to match, in volume and community purview, the reports of the AHMS missionaries.[15]

Johnson, from western New York, built on Newbury's foundation. His work schedule was typical of the calling, preaching twice a week, superintending Sabbath schools, distributing tracts, holding prayer meetings, organizing temperance groups, and visiting house to house. When no other means of transportation was available Johnson walked, sometimes forty miles at a stretch, to attend to his duties. For the most part Johnson was upbeat. Although he estimated that 90 percent of the people who died were dispatched without benefit of clergy or a religious funeral and that not one eighteen-year-old in fifty could repeat the Ten Commandments or the Lord's Prayer, he believed the valley was destined to be a very desirable part of the state. He was delighted and surprised to find the Sabbath well observed in Wabash, where in the spring of 1839 there were "several prosecutions for hunting & fishing & other servile labour on that day."[16] This was especially remarkable, he thought, because there had been little preaching in the place.

Johnson's Sabbath schools flourished and were the means by which he introduced literacy to the young. Students learned to read from the Bible by committing hundreds of verses to memory. "One little boy," Johnson bragged, "who a few months ago could not tell his letters has since learned to read in the Sabbath school. Last week he repeated 60 verses."[17] Likewise, news was good on the temperance front; the Wabash County group now numbered a hundred members. Johnson's perennial concern was keeping body and soul together. Hard cash was scarce, and the AHMS payments were often delayed. He and his wife were willing to live or die on the field, he wrote, but "[t]here is very little money to be had here. The times are very hard . . . if we are not able to furnish our table with meat, [we will] do it with milk; & if [we are] not able to keep house & over-coat & boots [we will] part with all & do without."[18]

Johnson's successor, Thomson, despite the deep freeze of his library in the canal the night of his arrival, seemed at first to be headed toward great success in Wabash. Initially he complained that he had to pay rent for a house that was much too small for his family of at least five persons, but within seven months he had built a log cabin a little west of the town, which meant it lay just beyond Carroll Street on the south side of Hill Street. At the same time his cabin was completed, he was able to report to the AHMS that thirty-nine members had been added to the Wabash church, a dramatic jump in membership, and hoped that one young man among them was headed for the ministry. By the following January, just a year after his arrival, the congregation needed more worship space and found it in a newly built house. The recent gift of a library from New York had improved the chance for his Sabbath school to meet expectations. Even more positive is Thomson's report in 1843 that "There has been a great advance in this field in relation to its moral and religious character." In addition, the population was booming, and there was ten times more building construction in Wabash than the previous year.[19]

Just then, when matters were well in hand, Thomson's prospects seemed to fall apart. Much of the negative tone of the remainder of his reports may be more a reflection of Thomson's mood rather than something caused by facts, but it is difficult to tell. Ominously, late in 1844, he reports, "there is a liability to fevers and agues etc. in all this western world."[20] This is followed by an insistence that his AHMS supplement be boosted from $150 to $200 because crop failure has made everyone poorer. Later he was still concerned about the crop failure but adds the more distressful news that intemperance has increased all along the canal. Except for some success in lecturing on church history and in the well-being of one of his Sabbath schools, 1845 did not produce much promise either. Immigration to Wabash was disappointing, in part because among those who did settle were representatives of the more conservative Old School Presbyterians, not New School as the Wabash church was, and this influx clearly threatened to divide Thomson's congregation. In September Thomson was incapacitated with bilious fever; a month later he was still so shaky he could scarcely write his report; and he did not fully recover until the following January. Meanwhile, in mid-1845, he began to confess failure. "It is my painful duty," he wrote, "to report to you another quarter of apparently unprofitable service."[21] The following year was as bad:

"It has become painful to me to be under the necessity of reiterating the same story of barrenness and dearth."[22]

By the end of 1846, the Old School Presbyterians had successfully subverted a third of Thomson's church members, plus two of his three elders. His remaining elder was excommunicated by the presbytery (a regional governing body) for making an adulterous proposal to a woman. After four years, Thomson returned to Crawfordsville to superintend a female academy. "I am troubled," he said in his final report from Wabash, "for the prospect of northern Indiana."[23] Despite this sense of failure and doom, Thomson left a good impression in Wabash. Three years later he returned for a second pastorate there and successfully inspired the flock to build a permanent church. Hardships aside, he does seem to have been a man of wry, self-skewering humor. After an especially soul-numbing trip riding sixty miles through flooded landscapes and mud to attend a church meeting, he reported on having mastered the "Hoosier method" of crossing a swollen stream: carry the horse's saddle across on a fallen log, force the horse to swim the stream, catch the horse, resaddle it, and ride on to the next stream. The man was perhaps more sanguine about travel than about missionary work.[24]

Smith followed Thomson. His years in Wabash extended beyond 1847, but his work reflects the concerns of the preceding missionaries. Temperance and education were high on his agenda. He could boast of a hundred members in the local Sons of Temperance, a national fraternity of men who had signed a temperance pledge and met regularly in mutual support of their commitment to sobriety. Not long after that accomplishment his focus shifted to educational matters because of a pending statewide vote on a free, common school proposal. Although that vote was favorable, a state school system did not actually materialize until the 1850s. Before the vote Smith preached twice in support of common schools. He wanted to make the congregation aware of "the blessings of intelligence especially when sweetened by piety," but he feared that most folks believed that knowledge led to "rascality" and that, therefore, ignorance was preferable to education.[25]

Despite the apparent progress toward public schools, Smith was troubled by the kinds of personal hardships that were potential encumbrances upon all Wabash citizens. Besides a "pinched" financial condition, there were prevalent illnesses and all too common tragedies. He spent unusual amounts of time visiting the sick and conducting funerals. He lost friends and supporters to death, including at least one church elder, a local physician, Doctor Loop.

"We have buried some of our most valuable citizens," Smith lamented.[26] Then, in April 1849, his wife, who was about eight months pregnant, fell ill, overcome by a "great feebleness."[27] He began breaking up housekeeping and trying to find foster homes for his children. In late summer the newborn died, the two older children fell ill, and so did Smith; for two weeks he could not sit up. He hung on at Wabash until the next year when Thomson returned. Near the close of 1849, Smith wrote, "The trials of the West are many and great. But I know of no where where I would rather spend my life in trying to do good. . . . I could say much more but I am so sick."[28] Smith did have one minor personal triumph about this time. It was during his tenure that Hugh Hanna finally made his relationship with the church official and joined other leading citizens to become a member.

One of Thomson's friends was a merchant named Cox. He and his wife, Livia, moved to town in 1839. Prior to that Cox had been a contractor working for the Central Canal in the middle of the state. One of his specialties there had been building shanties for the canal hands. In Wabash he opened a multipurpose store on Canal Street where he extended ready credit, took produce as payment, and generally catered to the broad merchandise needs of the community. Cox remained in Wabash until 1852 when he caught a touch of gold fever and left for California. As an asthma victim, he may also have been looking for a more amenable climate. In 1882 he died in Colfax, California, northeast of Sacramento. An obituary mentions his work as a superintendent of schools for a short stint and praises him for having been well known throughout California, but it does not reveal how he earned a living.[29]

While Cox's store was probably not unique in town, his "Day Book," which he left to posterity, is a valuable record of daily transactions, of who bought what, how much they paid, and who owed him what. The book is about three-quarters of an inch thick, hardbound, and measures twelve by eight inches. It rests in the archives of the Wabash County Historical Museum in the section on canal lore. The opening pages contain Cox's notes from his canal days when he kept a tally of laborers' work time and their pay schedule. There are personal memoranda also. He scrawled the date his sow conceived. He copied recipes for various treatments in man and beast, for bloody murrain and dry murrain in cows and for ague in humans. Cox's cure for ague seems designed to cover those symptoms with hangover: combine one ounce of aloes, one ounce of rhubarb, one dram of an indecipherable ingredient, and put all of this in a quart of whiskey, shake, and take every two hours.

In some sense the "Day Book" is a peek into the private lives of Wabash citizens. It reveals that John Koogle smoked, paying twenty-five cents for a pound of tobacco; that in October 1841 Hanna paid off a credit bill of $126.50 that covered a great many building supplies and, possibly, the rental of Cox's ox team; and that James Conner's family apparently liked butter because through April 1846 he spent fifty-three cents on more than seven pounds of it. Sarah Fowler, Isaac's widow, was a steady customer. She had a great use for coffee. She paid fifty cents for two-and-a-half pounds in July 1842 and was back in the next month to trade fifty pounds of flour for seven more pounds of coffee. At one point Mrs. Fowler paid off a $13.81 ¼ debt to Cox with 325 pounds of pork. Linsey-woolsey—coarse cloth made of wool and cotton or wool and linen—must have been the material of choice for homemade clothing. Cox sold a lot of it at 62 ½ cents a yard. Peter Everly, one of Hanna's in-laws who was probably still living in an old Treaty Ground cabin, was partial to "linsey." Cox's records also reveal him to have been a major donor to Thomson's work, extending the missionary credit and subscribing twenty dollars a year to his support, which represented more than 6 percent of the missionary's expected annual income. No one purchased liquor from Cox, doubtlessly because—being a Presbyterian elder—he was a serious, practicing temperance man, his cure for ague notwithstanding.

The "Day Book" is a primary source for prices and costs. In addition to those already noted, it reveals the following charges (among many others) in Cox's store: a washboard, $.75; potatoes, $.25 a bushel; flour $5.00 a barrel; corn, $.37 ½ a bushel; nails, $.10 a pound; a ball of candlewick, $.12 ½; gum overshoes, $1.37 ½; buckles and buttons, $.08 ¼; eggs, 45 for $.23; salt, $.02 a pound; dried peaches, $62 ½ for half a bushel; and a truckle bedstead, $3.00.

It is also clear that Cox was involved in more than just the retail business. He did a little farming on the side, contracting with laborers to do the time-consuming work. He taught school at one point, earning a dollar a day for a term of three months. He dabbled regularly in real estate, rented out property, and in some cases provided room and board for travelers and newcomers. By the end of the decade he was the proprietor of the Indiana House, a hotel conveniently located a few rods east of the canal bridge. He contracted with builders for a structure that could have been a warehouse or business block with upper rooms for rental purposes. He himself bought an ox team for $27.50 that he leased out on occasion and also used on his own projects.

Using his notes one could almost reconstruct one of his buildings, knowing the thickness and height of the basement walls and upper walls, the required doors and windows, and the plastering and painting. One also would be able to conjecture what Cox expected to pay for this building: approximately five hundred dollars, to be paid for in Indiana treasury notes. Terms were always clearly stated and the schedule of payments defined. The "Day Book" also shows that Cox's earlier experience of keeping track of canal hands' pay was not wasted in Wabash. In 1840 he kept a schedule of wages for six to ten workers who were being paid a dollar a day; it is not clear whether all those workers were in Cox's employ exclusively or whether he was keeping track for another employer as well.

In addition to the 1840 census, Conner's and Mackey's histories, the reports of missionaries, and Cox's "Day Book," there is at least one more credible witness to life in Wabash during those poorly documented years between the opening of the canal (1837) and the establishment of a newspaper (1847). In 1841 Ford moved to town and remained a resident until his death in 1899. Ford was born in Ohio and educated at Kenyon, at the Ohio Medical School in Cincinnati, and at Rush Hospital in Chicago. He was proficient in Greek and Latin. Among personal acquaintances were Salmon P. Chase and William T. Sherman, both of whom he knew in Ohio before they were nationally famous. In 1835 he opened a practice in Connersville, Indiana. While there he married America Holton and fathered their first child. After six years in Connersville, he brought wife and child north to Wabash, where he opened both a medical practice and a drugstore.[30]

Of his contribution to Wabash, more will be stated in due course. In the present context he is significant because in 1896 the *Wabash Daily Tribune* published Ford's reminiscence of the town as he found it in 1841. It is a succinct vignette, a tiny verbal photograph, of this largely undocumented period in Wabash's history. The Fords arrived when there was no available housing save for the old Treaty Ground cabins, by then showing their age. The snow was eight inches deep, it was a very cold February day, and the cabins had lost much of their chinking. The cabins' roofs leaned, their doors were hingeless, and they preserved much of the filth left from having served as stables and corn cribs. They were the only shelter available, however, so Ford requisitioned three of them for his family. When Benjamin Pawling and his family subsequently arrived from Pennsylvania to find no shelter at all, the Fords surrendered one of their cabins, believing that "misery loves company." Still later, an old friend of Ford's, General William Caldwell, and his large family arrived, and the third cabin went to Caldwell.

Ford remembered that at this time the new county jail rose on the bluff, noting that it was the only county jail "that rascals could never break out of." He does not mention Hanna's courthouse that also should have been completed about this time. Ford believed that the town's population "could not have exceeded one hundred and fifty souls," which roughly tallies with the 1840 census. Although Canal and Market streets were open from Allen Street to Cass Street, Miami and Wabash streets were "impassable," and forest covered the balance of the plat. He was especially scandalized by the Market Street pond, which he called a "Pandora's Box" of mosquitoes and ague that would "rattle the teeth and shake the bones" of those it infected. The setting may have seemed crude to him, but he was favorably impressed by the settlers, writing, "The first inhabitants were a brave people, a little coarse in the grain, perhaps, judged by present standards, yet they were the right people in the right place and right well, too, did they fill their mission. This community is now enjoying the fruits of their labor."

Ford seemed especially cognizant of the Miami who were still living in the area. They occupied the south bank of the river where few white people lived. Wabash residents had sometimes visited their village of rude cabins and bark wigwams high on the bluff, and relations between natives and newcomers were generally positive. Ford confirms that the Miami visited Wabash regularly. Braves and squaws came to town on Saturday to trade their raccoon skins for liquor, in particular, but probably for other goods as well. To Ford's mind they were a rambunctious sort, always looking for a reason to fight, whether brave or squaw. Ford cited two "dusky ladies, large and vigorous," who quarreled over the ownership of a dog. Whites and natives gathered to watch the showdown. One Miami woman seized the dog by the ears, another by the tail. The one holding the ears could not get to her knife. The other could and stabbed the dog behind its shoulder blade. The fight abruptly ended. "Someone in the crowd yelled 'Puck-a-chee!' (Clear out!)," and the Miami disappeared into the landscape.

Despite the limited sources available for the years 1837 to 1847, it is possible to speculate about the nature of Wabash in that decade. The fact that a bear was spotted within a couple of miles of town as late as 1841 indicates that the frontier had not retreated very far. The 1840 census and Ford's 1841 estimate of the population roughly agree that there were about 150 residents at that juncture, whereas five years earlier there had been about 66 settlers. It seems easy to conclude, then, that the canal's opening in 1837 had not resulted in an immediate population explosion and must have represented a serious disappointment at the time when one considers the anticipated potential of the new canal to deliver immigrants. Something more dramatic did happen, however, during the balance of the decade of the 1840s because the census of 1850 shows that roughly 800 more people had settled in town by then. Eight hundred more in nine years constitutes a respectable expansion. On average about seven new households a month were being established in those years. We know that housing was scarce in 1841. We know that Cox was busy selling building supplies, as well as many other commodities, and that he himself was engaged in having a house and one other building constructed at this time. Cox was probably not alone in such endeavors. Yet, where were *hundreds* of newcomers to live? We have to conclude that, like the Fords, folks were squeezing multiple families into those homes that already existed and that, concurrently, there was a building boom after 1841. Indeed, Ford did not reside for long in the former stables of the Treaty Ground cabins. He may have housed his family with friends or relatives for a time and then soon began to build on the three lots he had purchased at the southeast corner of Hill and Cass streets, on the bluff. Other newcomers would have been in a hurry to make similar moves.[31]

By 1847 some community sophistication was budding but scarcely blooming. Although at least four congregations were in the process of getting organized during this time, no bona fide church structure yet existed; the faithful were meeting in homes and in Patrick Duffy's cabin. Neither did schools have permanent housing and their existence was extraordinarily seasonal, shifting location and teachers every few months. Because it was a private-pay system, probably only a minority of school-age children were actually being educated. Undoubtedly, as in years past, the streets often swarmed with children of all ages. Occasionally these children joined their parents to watch a court case unfold, cheered on a couple of drunks having a fistfight, and stood on the Wabash Street canal bridge to welcome a packet into town or to count the wagons bringing grain in from the country.

It is tempting to assume that folks' moral behavior was generally far from exemplary, that they lived crudely in more ways than dress, housing, and language. However, the fact is that such a conclusion cannot be firmly substantiated for lack of evidence. If the one hundred Wabash males who joined the Sons of Temperance in the late 1840s were serious in their commitment, then the missionary vision was truly making in-roads into what Ford called the "coarse" nature of Wabash society. The precarious state of the missionaries' physical health, on the other hand, may be an accurate measurement of their neighbors' condition also, in which case many Wabash folks were under the weather often and for extended periods of time and death was common among all ages.

Perhaps the locus of the most visible progress in town would have been found in the business community. Cox's "Day Book" suggests steady merchandising, spurred by a location near the canal and by an economy that extended credit for the asking at no interest. In common commercial transactions, produce was almost as good as cash. Any paper money (canal scrip, personal note, bank, or state issue) that was recognizable as trustworthy probably worked. Given a population boom after 1841, a lot of new construction would have occurred along Canal Street as merchants, such as Cox, attempted to keep pace with an influx of customers. Upbeat economy or not, town streets were still raw earth with scarcely definable sidewalks. If one wanted to get to Cox's store—or any other—on a rainy day, one simply slogged through mud. In hot summer, one kicked up the dust of the streets on a similar journey.

The appearance of the Original Plat of Wabash at this time is very conjectural, much of it roughly suggested by Ford's brief comments, in particular his observation that the "balance of the town plat stood in timber." Though great swaths of wildness remained on the bluff, people were becoming more aware of that area. The jail and the courthouse poked sunward through the forest canopy, but the trees on high ground now began to give way to newcomers' houses. The streets on top of the bluff were even more primitive than the streets in the bottoms and the passage between top and bottom could be slickly treacherous. Thomson's decision to build a cabin "west of town," two blocks outside Hanna's plat, indicates that even at this early date Wabash was spawning "suburbs," homes of folks who might not appear on a census as Wabash residents but who were much involved in the town anyway. With so many people moving in, and so many enterprises starting up, there must have been an almost palpable energy to the place. Titus's romantic interpretation of Wabash in 1843 as "one of the most beautiful" towns he had seen may certainly merit some acceptance, so long as one can avert attention from those horrendous streets and remember that a still formidable forest surrounded the place.

5

Out of the Woods at Last

The week the Lake Erie, Wabash and Saint Louis Railroad Company finally sent a train into town for the first time, the editor of the *Wabash Weekly Gazette* declared in print:

> We are no longer in the woods . . . we bid a fond adieu to that miserable corduroy road from here to Huntington. Hurrah for the railroad.[1]

Wabash's release from arboreal imprisonment occurred at nine o'clock in the evening on Saturday, January 24, 1856, when a train of passenger cars pulled in on brand-new tracks that paralleled Hill and Sinclair streets halfway between the two. The editor's anticipation had been building for some time. Locally the railroad had been a topic of speculation, planning, and expectation since at least 1852. On January 21, 1856, the *Gazette* had reported that a train's whistle could be heard in town even though the near end of the track still lay well to the east. Previous to that there had been news of blasting a cut through a ridge of rock about a mile east, between Wabash and Lagro. On Monday, January 19, a construction train from the East had arrived at that cut. On Thursday, January 22, a train was within half a mile of town. Two days later the great event occurred. There was no formal ceremony as there had been with the canal's arrival, but the next morning, Sunday, hundreds of the "curious" streamed to the site to marvel at the huge locomotive for hours as daily progress was made in extending the tracks westward and congratulated themselves as if they had personally engineered the line. They admired the "poor Irish laborers" for their brawny arms and patient endurance and extended to them the feeling of goodwill that pervaded the resident populace.[2]

Six days after the train's arrival the *Gazette* was still crowing: "[we are] no longer shut out from the rest of mankind . . . now we can travel in winter."[3] The Lake Erie, Wabash and Saint Louis railroad was a miracle created of steam and iron. Suddenly it was possible to travel to Toledo in eight hours and to Cleveland in fourteen hours. The East Coast, once a trip that might require two weeks of clinging to a saddle in open weather, or longer in a horse-drawn wagon, could now be reached in a few days while seated, sheltered, and in relative comfort. For the first time since 1837, the fastest way to get to Lagro from Wabash was no longer by sleigh over the frozen waters of the canal.[4]

The advent of the railroad was the crowning event in a fourteen-year span, 1847 to 1861, that saw Wabash come "out of the woods" in more ways than the improvement of long-distance travel. Almost every aspect of community life seemed to blossom in those years. The telegraph arrived, spreading "electric news" of distant events the same day they occurred. The Gold Rush made its impact locally, drawing some citizens west. Banking and the economy grew more complex and sophisticated. The credit system in local merchandising began to give way to cash-and-carry. Downtown business streets bustled with activity day and night. A tax-supported school opened its doors, and its imposing building symbolized a new importance for education by commanding the highest ground in town, its stubby twin towers soaring above the courthouse. Congregations began to build permanent churches, also on high ground. Houses multiplied, though not fast enough for the demand, some springing up outside the Original Plat. Oil lighting became a possibility. Politicians seemed more feisty as they addressed the rising national issues of slavery and the viability of the Union. Enormous effort, controversy, and expense were invested in attempts to create a plank-road system that would further ease the horrors of travel. Formally organized social and cultural events began to claim the attention and discretionary incomes of citizens by offering attractions that were possibly more enriching than the ordinary tavern diversion.

If locals did not fully appreciate the positive developments taking place in the 1850s, the local *Gazette* in 1855 attempted to inspire their civic pride by reprinting a piece from the *Indianapolis Journal* about "Wabashtown." The

Journal estimated the population of Wabash to be 3,500 (it was closer to one thousand) and described it only in glowing terms:

> Wabashtown is pleasantly situated—water good—and in close proximity to the best of stone and other building material. Its business houses are mostly commodious, and of brick. Its warehouses are filled to overflowing with the products of the farmer . . . awaiting . . . transit to the lakes . . . and the East. Its streets are well filled with sturdy farmers. . . . Its Lawyers and Doctors are young men and mostly, I judge, from the Eastern states . . . and rank equal to those of any city. All in all, Wabashtown, in commercial . . . business, and professional capacity and talent, may be placed in the FIRST class . . . decidedly the handsomest town on the river . . . thriving and beautiful.[5]

The railroad, which was still a year away when the *Journal* piece appeared, was fiercely desired. However, no one seemed about to forget the canal. It remained a source of pride and promise for Wabash throughout the 1850s. Merchants and farmers continued to make use of it and continued to think of it as competitive with the railroads. For a while it seemed to be so. The canal, however, faced insurmountable challenges. A canal boat could not travel more than six miles an hour, and trains were much faster. The canal was subject to frequent service interruptions because of flooding from the river or because its berm had sprung leaks. And it was seasonal, closed to traffic during the winter months. The Wabash and Erie had been in operation at Wabash for nineteen years before railroads made it to the interior. The canal continued to compete with varying success for roughly another decade, but after that it slowly became an artifact, good for skating in the winter, for supplying water to nearby factories and to fight fires, and for breeding mosquitoes.

Despite the upbeat spirit about Wabash in the years 1847 to 1861, there were lingering, seemingly intransigent, obstacles in play. The greatest of these was mud. A visitor to town in 1855 wrote of it, "The Best Houses and the Worst Streets of any Town in Indiana."[6] Mud continued to be the bane of existence in Wabash because it was the difficulty that was least amenable to leaders' ordinances and citizens' good intentions. Nature put it there and for a long time it seemed that only nature could get rid of it. In wet seasons residents could not venture from their homes without taking into account the omnipresence of mud. A contributing difficulty was the bluff. Mud on level ground is an inconvenience, but mud on a steep street is potentially lethal. Even in dry seasons, the steep streets posed difficulty, especially if a wagon team of horses became a "runaway" and tore downhill helter-skelter with helpless passengers aboard. Wabash struggled with its streets, and mud, throughout the 1850s and beyond. A great many additional difficulties that needed to be addressed were not Mother Nature's fault but human nature's, including an almost toxic disregard of communal sanitation, sporadic bickering about public works, and a rather fickle sense of civic pride among property owners.

The knight in shining armor who rode into town to champion good and challenge evil was a twenty-nine-year-old graduate of Pennsylvania's Jefferson College, Naaman Fletcher. Although admitted to the practice of law in Ohio, Fletcher had turned to journalism in 1852, the year before he and his bride, Elizabeth, moved to Wabash. More than any other journalist in this period of Wabash's development, he represented that genre of editors and publishers who make it their business to advocate progressive causes, to denounce perceived wrongs in a community, and to do so in plain language without fear of libel. The influence of such journalists in emerging communities probably cannot be overestimated; all they needed was a circulation healthy enough to create a broad audience. A newspaper and its editor could be for a community what a teacher is in a classroom, what a preacher is to a congregation, and what a coach is to a ball team. Fletcher was such a journalist, untiringly "prophetic" in the Old Testament sense of holding a whole community to account.[7]

Like the best of his breed, Fletcher was able to do this with intelligence, passion, and humor. His vocabulary was close to salty at times; words such as "jackass," "worm," and "skunk" sometimes erupted in print as enemies were named and ridiculed. He once devoted four columns to skewering his archrival, Daniel M. Cox, editor of the *Wabash Intelligencer*, as a "dishonorable man . . . our bitterest and most unscrupulous enemy."[8] Although it was only on his deathbed that Fletcher may have professed a religious faith, as an editor he had promoted all kinds of religious endeavors, such as Sunday schools and the temperance cause, and was himself in attendance at worship at least occasionally. It is not known if Elizabeth's Presbyterian background was influential with him. Fletcher was undoubtedly temperate in a literal sense, meaning that he imbibed alcohol carefully and was not given either to overindulgence or to abstention. That he was not a teetotaler, that is, a "total abstainer" married to strict sobriety, is strongly indicated by a story passed down through at least four generations in the Stearns Fisher family. Fisher was the well-known, highly respected superintendent of the canal who lived four miles west of Wabash but who was yet very much a "man about town," visiting frequently and hobnobbing with many of its residents. Fisher descendants remember that their ancestor and Fletcher were "drinking buddies." Presumably on the basis of that relationship, Fisher provided space for Fletcher's remains in the Fisher family plot when the journalist died unexpectedly at forty years of age in 1864. At his death he left a wife and a five-year-old son. They soon moved from Wabash, perhaps to Ohio, perhaps to Iowa, and their subsequent fates are unknown.[9]

In any case, the circumstances preceding Fletcher's death serves to illustrate his courageous public advocacy of causes he considered important. Fletcher and his newspaper supported the Union, the North, and Republican Party politics, positions that undoubtedly helped circulation in Wabash during the Civil War. However, the populace was not seamless in its approbation of such positions. Off to the east, in Huntington County but also along the eastern edge of Wabash County, there was measurable interest in a quixotic, quasi-insurgency fraternity called the Knights of the Golden Circle. The knights sympathized with the South, supported the institution of slavery, and opposed the war. Locally it allegedly threatened the lives of any who opposed them, including Judge Calvin Cowgill, a strong Wabash Unionist. The situation was dangerous. Cowgill's house was being guarded with troops when the opportunity arose for the judge to address citizens in Huntington on current affairs.[10]

Cowgill deferred to Fletcher as a man who was best qualified to field the issues that were so divisive. Fletcher agreed to speak. The night of the speech Cowgill faced the audience with a brace of pistols that he placed on the podium, declared he would shoot the first "damned secesh" who made a disturbance, and introduced Fletcher. Fletcher delivered what was described as a "strong talk." Many of those present congratulated him. Cowgill opined that he had never heard such a cogent defense of the Union. The two left Huntington for Wabash. Fletcher was perspiring from the pressure of speaking. The weather turned unexpectedly cold, and Fletcher became chilled. Back at his home near the fairgrounds on the west end of town he came down with pneumonia and died within a few days. It was a typical premodern death: easily contracted symptoms, gradual complications over a day or two, no antibiotics or effective medicines, a lingering uncertainty between hope and despair, and then death.[11]

If the advent of the railroad meant that Wabash was "out of the woods" in a physical, geographic sense, the advent of newspapers, under men such as Fletcher, meant that Wabash had already come "out of the woods" in quite another way, beginning in 1847. The newspaper brought a deepened sense of both consciousness and conscience to the community, of both awareness about the larger world and awareness of local civic duty.

Fletcher was not the first Wabash publisher and editor nor was his *Gazette* the first paper, but until Fletcher's arrival there had been little stability in the local news industry. Newspapers began with John U. Pettit's and Moses Scott's *Upper Wabash Argus* in 1846, though surviving copies for that year consist of few editions. Fletcher later said the *Argus* had been "Democratic to the hilt."[12] Alanson P. Ferry soon replaced Pettit and then sold out to George E. Gordon. Gordon and Scott discontinued the *Argus* and created the *Wabash Weekly Gazette* in its place as a Whig publication. John L. Knight, who replaced Gordon in the late 1840s, maintained some continuity in the editorial position until September 1853 when he turned the *Gazette* over to Fletcher. Scott, who had stayed with the paper as a kind of manager, eventually joined with Horace P. Peters and Daniel M. Cox to found the *Wabash Intelligencer.* Editors and publishers of the *Intelligencer* came and went until 1858 when a fire destroyed Fletcher's *Gazette* office. In the process of recovering from that blow, Fletcher took a big risk and bought the *Intelligencer*, merging the papers into the *Gazette and Intelligencer.* The new paper was clearly a Republican publication that flew the complicated motto "A Family Newspaper—Devoted to Politics, Literature, Agriculture, Education, and General Intelligence" under its masthead. Fletcher soon substituted "the Good of Mankind" for "General Intelligence."[13] Complicated or not, it was a motto the new editor and publisher took seriously. The *Wabash Plain Dealer* (which survived into the twenty-first century) was created in 1859 by W. C. McGonigal as a Democratic party rival to Fletcher's *Gazette and Intelligencer*; but as the threat of Civil War began to loom, McGonigal switched allegiance to the Republicans and the Unionist cause. After Fletcher's death in 1864, the *Plain Dealer* absorbed the *Gazette and Intelligencer.*[14]

Fletcher also was not the first journalist to raise concerns about the town's liabilities. As early as the late 1840s, sanitation and streets were typically in the forefront of some editors' minds. In February 1849 the *Gazette* started reporting on the frightful assortment of rotting organisms in town. Cart-loads of decaying offal from the slaughterhouses, the paper warned, would send up a "noisome stench." In the bottomland south of the canal, the paper noted, were "not a few" dead hogs and dogs, and throughout the town, in alleys and open lots, there were hundreds of hogs heads lying about.[15] The editor, John L. Knight, blamed thoughtless businessmen. By July the situation was worse: "[There were] masses of filth about [citizens'] doors and streets, to say nothing of the back grounds [backyards], the cellars, the piles of chips, and stable manure, saturated with animal excrement, and privies without vaults . . . not a matter of small amount."[16] Besides that there were forty to sixty rods of holes and ditches that had become hog wallows where dead rats, cats, and hogs had been cast. Knight noted a small victory in that while hogs still had a free run of the place a new town ordinance provided for a late-fall roundup of the animals. He supported a law that would limit the number of loose hogs to two per owner and allow the sale of those that were unclaimed. A letter to the editor from an anonymous "Pry" complained of shingles, hewn timber, and other rubbish piled up on Hill Street that, he said, should be used to fill a "stinking hole" at the corner of Cass and Hill streets that was a "prophylactic" of cholera. Given the location of the hole and the concern about cholera, one surmises the letter was from James Ford, who loved to write for the public about health issues.[17]

Knight also took on the issues of streets, sidewalks, and the town's general appearance that later were favorite topics for Fletcher. Citizens were using the streets to store boxes, wood piles, and old stoves. Knight backed an ordinance that required "each and every citizen" to work one day—eight hours—improving streets and alleys or pay $.75.[18] Because folks were driving wagons and riding horses through town too fast, he recommended the *trot* as Wabash's earliest speed limit. Feeding horses on Canal Street was to be limited, perhaps as a way of cutting down on the manure along that busy thoroughfare. The *Gazette* backed restrictions on the "squads of dogs" that ran in packs through town.[19] Because Knight also served as town clerk he may have had the political clout to see that sanitation and safety ordinances were enforced by the town marshal. Knight also believed that a better legal incorporation of the town would help improve standards. He encouraged property owners to take more pride in their homes' appearances and hoped for laws that would require the planting of shade trees and other landscaping improvements. Sidewalks were generally nonexistent or poorly maintained. At best they were planks thrown together to offer a place where pedestrians could avoid the muddy streets. Ordinances addressed the issue by levying a fine of $2.00 for driving a cart or riding a horse on sidewalk space, which was to be an area ten feet wide between lot boundaries and streets; provision was made for merchants to use three feet of the sidewalk next to their buildings as display areas. The *Gazette* advocated all these improvements.[20]

By the time Fletcher bought out Knight's paper in 1853, the problems the latter had addressed still existed and may even have intensified with a rise in population. Fletcher launched into an unrelenting campaign to change things for the better, displaying even more passion than Knight, chiding citizens for their miserable standards of behavior and, alternately, writing in visionary language about what Wabash could be. He himself could be goaded by a visitor's negative impression of Wabash, but he was also quick to bring such impressions to the attention of his readers. In November 1857, for example, Fletcher reprinted a piece from the *Peru Sentinel* that rather smugly summarized Wabash's faults and liabilities. The *Sentinel*'s editor blamed Mother Nature for giving Wabash citizens nothing except the "opportunity to overcome obstacles," the main obstacle being that "ugly limestone rock bench" (the bluff) that rose forty feet high and ran parallel with the canal the whole length of the town.[21] It was picturesque, the editor supposed, but not desirable, especially for trade. Furthermore, the place needed a thorough system of grading streets, which would cost $2,000 a year and require new taxes. The town council ought to improve one street at a time and force property owners to put in sidewalks and curbing. In addition, someone needed to be coaxed into investing $10,000 or $15,000 dollars for a good hotel near the courthouse. According to the *Sentinel*, if Wabash accomplished all of that it might have something to crow about.[22]

It probably irked Fletcher considerably that someone from Peru would berate Wabash about the very issues that consumed Fletcher. If there was scolding to be done locally, he believed he was the one to do it. At times he averted his eyes from the obstacles at hand and measured the progress that, in some seasons, seemed evident. "The whole town is undergoing a complete metamorphosis," he wrote in 1855; "the Corporation is wide awake to its duty in improving the streets, building side-walks, etc."[23] In the same article he rejoiced that a seminary was to be built, that the merchants were cheerful, that the grain and pork markets were up, and that "mechanics" (manual laborers) were prospering. At other times he was so mindful of all that needed attention that his rhetoric could become visionary. "Look ahead," he advised in 1858, describing a future Wabash that existed only in his mind. It was reminiscent of Saint John's vision of the New Jerusalem, minus the gold. Every street was graded and graveled. Every sidewalk was paved with flagstones and shaded with rows of beautiful trees. Elegant and tasteful shrubbery adorned neat, commodious, and substantial homes. Each congregation had a stylish church, and students had adequate classrooms. Four thousand "industrious and sober mechanics" were gainfully employed, and the downtown streets buzzed with business. On the public square a new courthouse worth $40,000 rose up surrounded by a beautiful iron fence. Mr. Pawling and Mr. Stitt abandoned their Center House and Indiana House respectively and moved into three-story hotels.[24]

Despite bursts of optimism, Fletcher was more inclined to scold. As a newcomer, he remembered, he had hardly dared to comment on local conditions, fearful of being regarded as the town's "perfect Ishmaelite," an outsider.[25] Soon enough, however, he was treating his newspaper like a pulpit, preaching the gospel of civic pride and its corollary, the sin of civic irresponsibility. Favorite topics were temperance, religion, education, economic development, roads, bridges, the schoolhouse, churches, machine shops, sidewalks, shade trees, graded streets, and well-painted houses and fences. By 1858 Fletcher had run out of patience on the sidewalk issue and plunged in with diatribe and advice. "There is not a town in the United States," he wrote, "where good stone pavements can be made cheaper than here in Wabash."[26] Citizens had only to look between their feet, for paving was available precisely where paving was needed, except that it was two feet below the surface of the mud. All a homeowner had to do was dig downward in his own front yard to find "the broadest, thickest and smoothest flag-stone that can be found anywhere." Cellars were built on it, yet the town lacked sidewalks. Streets were "as destitute of pavements as . . . [the] Democracy is of righteousness, as the Somerset road is of dry spots."[27] A year later he was asking, "Is it possible" that another winter will pass without a good pavement [sidewalk] from downtown to the top of the hill?[28] He had already cited the good example of residents on East Main Street who had installed sidewalks which, he demanded, should soon be extended by others to create a continuous pavement from the junction of Huntington and Main streets to Wabash Street and thence to Canal Street. This was significant, he claimed, because three-fourths of the population traversed the hill three and four times daily, yet there were few sidewalks. The men responsible were not poor, and, besides, the cost was only a penny a square foot if the town had to pay for it. What was the point of having Wabash incorporated if the situation continued?[29]

The sidewalk issue was critical because the streets remained so horrific. Before the town council began to lay pavements at corner crossings, a little rain could make streets impassable throughout town. On Cass Street a two-horse team sank so deeply that Hugh Hanna had to bring his oxen to drag it out. Similar problems abounded. Residents on East Market "complained bitterly" about their street, in part because on muddy Sabbaths women could not make it to the Methodist, Baptist, or Old School Presbyterian services. Children who made the mistake of crossing a street risked having their boots sucked off their feet by the goo. At least one store in town touted its gum overshoes as being helpful in mud.[30]

The bluff exacerbated the problem, of course. Wabash Street was so steep north of Market Street that those climbing it could see into the second stories of surrounding buildings. This was the street that was supposed to be the main avenue, leading north through town from the canal bridge and main dock. Its slope was especially steep between Market and Hill streets but continued to rise rather dramatically well past Sinclair Street. As a result, traffic tended to use Miami and Cass streets, which, at that time, rose more gradually than Wabash Street. In 1859 Fletcher urged town officials to make Cass Street their first priority and get it graded from Market Street to Hill Street. He was also concerned that while some stumps left in the middle of streets were rotting, others remained, even in blocks where there were houses on every lot. Local opinion said that Hill Street had become "*the* fashionable street of the town." Fletcher, however, was reserving judgment until it was properly graded.[31] By the end of the 1850s Fletcher was able to report that his badgering was having a desired effect. It was possible by then to walk almost anywhere in Wabash on good flagstone pavements. Canal Street had been graded, graveled, and lined with gutters that were paved with boulders. There was scarcely a "square" in town that was not being improved to some degree. New board fencing surrounded the courthouse, and the public square was filled with young forest trees—maples, walnuts, and elms—for shade and ornament.[32]

The town needed more improvements than just decent sidewalks and streets. Fletcher addressed them all. The cemetery was a disgrace. Its gate was ineffective and the fence was damaged, allowing cows to graze there. The ground was rough, and parts of it were covered with rubbish. Gravestones were broken, many graves had sunk, and others were overgrown with "vile weeds and briars." The graves were bunched together without any order. Fletcher wanted a public meeting called about the cemetery's neglect and its "absence of good taste." He admired its location, so near to town, and its beautiful trees that had never been disturbed and that, he advised, should never be cut down.[33]

Fletcher was concerned about housing and the appearance of older buildings. He had never seen such a demand for new homes. There were more than a hundred unimproved lots in town where houses could be built. It was unfair that property owners were selling rentals "over the heads" of their renters, thus ejecting the latter into homelessness. Such people had to move in with others or leave town. With house construction "there must be no more delaying the matter."[34] At the same time Fletcher believed it was vital for citizens to mind the condition of aging buildings. Wabash does have "beauty of location," he preached, but that was worthless if houses were "unpainted," "motley," and "dilapidated," their fences were falling apart, or their yards were void of shrubbery and hosting stagnant, festering pools, stumps, and frog ponds.[35] He chided two businessmen by name in the *Gazette and Intelligencer* for wanting to erect new buildings downtown before they had removed "an everlasting eyesore," the burnt ruins of their former buildings.[36] Remarkably, citizens on the receiving end of Fletcher's verbal pitchfork possessed no ready defense against it, save for a letter of remonstrance to the editor; and the general public seemed to allow journalists the privilege of acting as the town's prosecutor, judge, and executioner in matters of civic rectitude.

Being aware, as all good homileticians are, that honey catches more flies than vinegar, Fletcher often shifted into praise for the populace. He was delighted when a tree was planted, a house painted, or a vacant lot cleared of trash and reported it to his fellow citizens. He noted that, in the mid-1850s, a public well was operating at the corner of Market and Wabash streets; it was sunk forty-seven feet deep, forty of them through rock; the water was clear, cold, and pure. At about Christmas time in 1858, Gordon and Thurston's, a downtown store, presented Fletcher with a new lamp for his office. It was fueled with coal oil that, despite some concerns about odor and heat, burned slowly, gave a clear, steady light, "cost not a whit more than a stinking tallow candle," and was an ornament to any room.[37] Fletcher was aware that Fort Wayne was already lighted with gas, so by reporting on his new lamp he was indirectly encouraging locals to be open to new technologies. At one point he had been close to sounding giddy in a column titled "Town Improvements," in which he celebrated the fact that four brick storerooms were under construction, two of which were seventy-five feet long and three-stories high. At the same time, he noted, Hanna's new steam sawmill was about to commence operation; uptown, the Old School Presbyterians were planning to rebuild after the unfinished brick walls of their new church had collapsed in a windstorm; and, downtown, Canal Street had been graded, covered with gravel, and bordered with gutters. As the decade progressed, Fletcher had his eye on 1860 when the new bridge over the Wabash would be completed; it would cost eight to ten thousand dollars. A dozen laborers were quarrying stones measuring up to sixteen inches thick that were hauled by teams to the river and then floated to the site. It may also have been at this time that town officials began to move unwanted dirt, logs, and rocks south, across the canal, to the floodplain. The material would be used to build up a levy that would extend Wabash Street across the bottoms to the bridge, making it higher than most floodwaters; the project extended beyond the 1850s. Sometimes Fletcher could not help injecting a little reservation into his praise, as when Doctor Peters refurbished a frame building on Wabash Street. "The color," the editor drolly observed, "is rather fanciful. It is Cerulean blue, not more handsome than it is conspicuous."[38]

With a great many of the causes that Fletcher embraced, it often seemed as if he were a lone prophet, the proverbial voice crying in the wilderness. This was not necessarily true, although it is possible that no one was quite so interested in painted houses and shade trees as he. For many of his other campaigns, however, he was frequently acting in informal tandem with the town council, members of the business community, and the clergy. To a large degree he was their voice, articulating for them a shared vision of community progress and whipping up support. Furthermore, Fletcher knew his audience. He was the kind of editor who left his office during the day to visit with fellow citizens and to gather local news. The idea that he may have tipped drinks with Fisher, as earlier noted, should not leave the impression that he hung around saloons at night to gather his material, for he was a family man and truly temperate in his habits. Rather, the nature of his publication supports the idea that he was on the prowl looking for stories much of the daytime, popping in and out of shops, stopping folks on the streets, and running down leads wherever they might take him. Probably no one in Wabash more accurately had a finger on the pulse of the place.

His "personals" columns were a major part of his writing—who was sick, who was getting married, what products were merchants pushing, who was traveling where and why, who was visiting town, who sold the best sodas—often delivered in good-humored brevity. He kept up with marriages, sometimes listing them under a column titled, "HYMENIAL." Following the marriage of a young local jeweler, E. G. Sackett, who was known for keeping strict business hours, Fletcher reported that the morning after the nuptials a sign on the door of the jewelry shop read: "He is not dead, but sleepeth."[39] He also repeatedly reminded bridal couples of a journalistic tradition, that there would be a much more laudatory account of their marriage in the paper if some of the wedding cake had been delivered to his typesetter. Thus, there appeared a June 1855 report, "On Tuesday . . . [married] by Rev. Mr. Skinner, Mr. Wm. H. Wells to Miss Henrietta Stepp . . . Mrs. Henrietta did not forget the printer—a large and delicious cake was the result. Thanks, beautiful, charming, *fascinating* Henrietta."[40] This was a somewhat more winning practice of the tradition than Knight's earlier dictum: "No cake no compliments."[41]

Although the canal and railroad had improved transportation dramatically by 1856, distant travel by roads was still a daunting experience. Fletcher weighed in. One wet November the *Gazette* moaned, "Now is the winter of our discontent." All roads leading into town were "so abominably bad," so impassable, that the town's commerce was down by a third.[42] Both town and county, both merchant and farmer, suffered. Conditions were not much improved in summer, when tracks became dry and dusty. In getting to Somerset "on the hardest road this side of Jordan," one went "up, up; down, down, down; jolt, jolt; plunge, rear, jostle, shake, creak, strain, break down, smash up, collapse"; the situation was "execrable," Fletcher wrote.[43] The panacea for both wet and dry surfaces was to be plank roads. There had been talk of gravel or crushed rock (macadamized) roads for several years, but either the mud was thought to be too liquid or the technology too new. Folks were used to jolting over short spans of corduroy, logs thrown down crosswise over boggy ground and small streams. Planks, which could be laid over corduroy, may have seemed like the next logical stage, and, clearly, there was plenty of lumber. Plank-road technology was broadly understood, and the reports of the economic advantages were believable. In any case, inspired by New York State's road laws, the Indiana legislature had adopted its own provisions in early 1849. The laws allowed citizens to incorporate plank-road associations, elect directors, oversee construction, maintain gates and tollhouses, and, of course, raise money for their projects. The first Wabash County company was formed a year later with capital stock of $6,000, with each share worth ten dollars.[44]

Understandably, these developments captured the attention of Wabash folks throughout that first year as the newspaper disseminated information about the new roads. In a February edition of the *Gazette*, Knight ran six full columns packed tight with facts and figures about the construction techniques involved. For plank roads to be profitable it was thought that they should "wear out before they rot out."[45] After a year of use the surface developed an elastic coating of tough, woody fiber that resisted speedy wear. The roadbed needed to be only roughly graded and cleared, with ditches on either side to divert rainwater. The dirt taken from the ditches was used to keep the road at a decent elevation. Planks—normally eight feet long, eight to sixteen inches wide, and three inches thick—were laid across the road side by side on a track of stringers. It was not necessary to attach planks to stringers (though they could float away under certain conditions). Oak, walnut, and yellow poplar were used for both planks and stringers. If hemlock were used, a road surface might last seven years. The stringers—normally four inches thick and four inches high—could outlast two or three plank coverings, so it was possible for well-laid stringers to last for twenty-one years.[46]

Cost estimates varied, but in 1849 some locals hoped that a good pike could be built for $1.00 per rod length (16.5 feet). Another kind of estimate, for a road from Wabash to North Manchester, put that cost at $15,000. It was expected that in time tolls would cover construction costs and then produce a percentage yield promising enough to entice subscribers. The financial estimates could be exceedingly complicated because volume of usage was guesswork. For example, one of the earliest estimates published locally put the cost of a road from Wabash to Eel River at $1,250 per mile. This would require a total in tolls (for an unspecified length of time) of $7.10 a day (excepting the Sabbath), which sum would pay for the construction and yield a profit of 10 percent. This estimate further conjectured that the $7.10 daily toll income needed would be met if, in a single day, the following minimum traffic used the road: 1 four-horse team, 1 three-horse team, 8 two-horse teams, 2 buggies, and 8 horsemen, all traveling the full length of the road. Furthermore, if regular traffic did not always meet this standard, the income gap might be made up by tolls on cattle and hogs that were driven over the road. The toll for twenty cattle, for example, was five cents per mile. It was the same for horses; other animals were cheaper. Two tollhouses have survived in Wabash, one at the west end of Hill Street and another on the northeast corner of the intersection of Cass and Stitt streets.

While construction required some cash up front, it was possible for landowners along the route of a road to buy into the scheme by contributing timber and labor. The great economic advantage to farmers, especially those close to the road, would be the ability to move heavier loads more quickly to town. If the limit on a load of grain over mud or corduroy had been twenty bushels, over plank it would be forty bushels. Other promising statistics made print: the power to move one ton on a dirt road would move 3.5 tons on a plank road; if one load of wheat on dirt roads was thirty-five bushels, on plank it would be 140 bushels; in addition, wagons and harness would last longer. Such technological and economic information moved the anticipation of plank roads quickly forward in Wabash minds.[47]

Speculation about what roads would be built where and when fueled considerable angst as Wabash sensed that Lagro and other towns were moving quickly toward construction. By early 1849 "Lagrosians" already had two roads in mind, though not yet laid out: one south to Marion, one north to Warsaw. If they went into operation before Wabash roads were up and running, then farm produce would flow to the canal at Lagro, new merchandising would follow there apace, and Wabash would become "a moldering, lifeless village." The situation was a "life & death matter." It was even possible that the county seat would relocate to Lagro. Knight's *Gazette* turned up the pathos: "Let us bestir ourselves."[48] Several different routes from Wabash came under discussion. Ideally there would have been four: one leading south to Mount Vernon or Somerset and toward Marion; another going northwest toward Roann or Gilead; a third aimed at Laketon and, possibly, North Manchester; and a fourth running east-west.

A great many local men of means and/or influence stepped forward to be prime sponsors of various road projects. These included Hanna, James D. Conner, William Steele, D. M. Cox, Robert Cissna, Madison Whiteside, and Knight. Given the leadership in place and its apparent eagerness for a new system it is remarkable that relatively little happened and happened so slowly. The Eel River Toll Road was first to be organized. The Wabash and Mount Vernon road company soon followed. When R. V. Skinner completed his map of the county and of Wabash in 1861, he showed only these two. The first left town headed northwest as an extension of Cass Street. The second began at the south end of the river bridge at the foot of the bluff, which throughout the nineteenth century presented a solid and precipitous face without any southward cut for a road. The new plank road turned west from the bridge, followed the site of the future Columbus Street up the bluff, and turned south on what would become Vernon Street.[49]

Even at the end of the 1850s, ten years after conception, neither of the two plank highways was complete, though it was believed that they were marginally profitable for a time and certainly temporarily advantageous to travelers, merchants, and farmers. In 1859, when the Mount Vernon road was still only "progressing," contractors began making more use of crushed rock and gravel. Over the next decade, as planks wore out, these macadamized surfaces increasingly replaced them.

Perhaps one reason plank-road construction did not go forward with the rapidity that attended canal and railroad construction was the local fuss it kicked up among Wabash leaders. Suddenly faced with the prospects of funding two or more roads, men of normal goodwill fell to feuding over what roads to support and how these roads ought to transect the town. Hanna may have presented a dark side of his personality when he touted the idea that any northern plank road should commence at the northeast corner of the public square. It was an idea with relatively few admirers. Though it was not stated explicitly, one speculates that he badly wanted one of the new roads to travel north on Wabash Street toward the other town he had founded, Laketon, to shore up its somewhat feeble prospects. Hanna's group was called "the friends of Wabash Street," representing the "upper town" route vs. a "lower town" group in pursuit of the plank road to Mount Vernon. Those supporting the road toward Roann, while technically of the "northern" persuasion, opposed Hanna's Wabash Street starting point, wanting their road to enter town down Cass Street. The *Gazette*, under Knight, while complaining about divisions in the leadership and the paucity of generous investors for projects so essential to Wabash's future, observed that Hanna "didn't give a cent" to plank road subscription.[50] It was a slam Hanna may have deserved if, in fact, he was using his influence to pursue selfish ends, and if, in doing so, he fueled a feud that slowed progress on the plank roads. His reputation, however, seemed never to get permanently tarnished.[51]

The spring of 1859 brought the possibility of another kind of change for Wabash. The state government developed the idea of locating its northern penitentiary nearby. Part of the attraction was the easy accessibility of good building stone. Rail and canal connections were also selling points because prison officials expected to market products manufactured by inmates. The first potential site to be considered was just west of town in the vicinity of the future City Park. Then Fisher expressed willingness to sell his farm and quarry in order to locate the facility four miles to the west. Fisher's good friend, Fletcher, was not sure on which side of the scale, good vs. evil, to place the prospects of a major prison even that close to town. At one point he was modestly positive: "If the prison had to be near us it might as well be with us." Later in the same column he was less certain: "It may be a blessing or it may be a curse."[52]

The Board of Control for state prisons visited Wabash a few weeks later and left the impression among locals that Wabash would be its choice. That impression may have been wishful thinking. In the absence of her husband, who was away on business, Mrs. Fisher apparently had spoken convincingly of the advantages of a Wabash location. It happened, nonetheless, that as board members left town by rail after their visit, their train wrecked while crossing a ravine east of Fisher's property. At least three cars were derailed. There were injuries but no deaths. It is not certain whether the crash influenced the board's decision, but the search for a prison location subsequently continued elsewhere. Lafayette, Logansport, and Peru had also been under consideration. After the prison was finally in place at Michigan City, Hanna was made a prison director, an appointment that some saw as a sop to the town that had lost the prison because of a train wreck.[53]

A Wabash citizen of 1859 or 1860 who climbed the bluff on the south side of the river across from the end of Wabash Street would have been able to take stock of the changes occurring in his town. Looking downward forty feet or more, between his feet, this citizen would see the Wabash Street bridge, possibly still in construction and still side by side with its predecessor. Stretching north would be a slightly elevated Wabash Street, crossing the floodplain and the canal, then disappearing uphill somewhere beyond Sinclair Street at the top of the north bluff. In the valley before him, between him and the canal, and on either side of the South Wabash Street levy, lay the stretch and stench of bottomland, redolent perhaps with rotting hogsheads, offal, and other nasty castoffs from town. Acrid smoke may have risen from garbage fires in the area, for it was probably still the town's dump.

Between the bluff and the bottoms, life abounded, morning, afternoon, and evening. Canal Street swarmed with people, with farmers and their produce, and with citizens trying to get somewhere without sinking in mud and having to lift ladies out of buggies onto newly laid sidewalks. Approximately fifty shops, saloons, warehouses, mills, blacksmiths, slaughterhouses, stables, barns, hotels, banks, law offices, groceries, dry goods stores, barbershops, drugstores, bakeries, and multipurpose outlets lined Canal, Wabash, and Market streets; many of their buildings were made of brick. Canal boats waited at the dock. Farm wagons waited to unload produce.

Looking at the town in a broad, horizontal scope, there would still be unbroken, lush forest framing the place, west, east, north, and south. But within the town plat—if Fletcher's concern for planting shade trees means anything—a certain baldness would have infested the Original Plat, along business streets certainly and on the bluff where householders had hacked away at the forest to make room for their homes. New houses would dot the bluff, here and there, perhaps especially along the bluff-top line of Hill Street. Many homes were surrounded by fences to protect yards and gardens from wandering pigs and cows. The new Old School Presbyterian church steeple at Miami and Hill streets struggled to pierce the skyline. East of it the original jail and the old courthouse still marked the public square. Trains puffed through the bluff top. Telegraph lines followed the train tracks. And way on top, rising above it all, was a new symbol of progress, of something more spiritual than brick and mortar and planks, something beyond entrepreneurial get-rich schemes, something of a loftier form of civilization and of real hope for the future: the towers of a first-class public education establishment—Union School.

6

Taming Tawdry Town

In the December 12, 1855, edition of the *Wabash Gazette*, Naaman Fletcher made a hopeless, King Canute-like attempt to turn back a flood: "Let no person come to town tomorrow." He could have saved the printer's ink. Between two and six thousand people jammed Wabash the next day, concentrating on the public square. It was the largest crowd in town yet recorded. The hotels had filled up with nonresident guests the evening of the twelfth. Neither the rain that fell in torrents on the thirteenth nor the sloppy, muddy streets seemed to deter anyone. People were wet, cold, and irritable, but they began gathering west of the courthouse before noon, pressing close to a fence on the south side of the jail. Their numbers and their unwillingness to heed the advice of Fletcher and his kind indicated that not even the arrival of the canal or of the railroad had stirred up the level of public excitement as this event did. For the profligately ghoulish, in particular, it was surely the most important local event of the century.

Wabash County was scheduled to hang John Hubbard by the neck until he was dead that next afternoon, December 13, 1855. At the appointed time, just after three o'clock, the prisoner, the sheriff, the deputy sheriff, the prosecutor, clergymen, physicians, and a clutch of official witnesses took their places in a fenced space south of the jail on the public square. Hubbard ascended the gallows. On his behalf the Reverend Mr. Skinner addressed the gathering, relaying Hubbard's repeated claim of innocence in the murder of Aaron French. The sheriff positioned the noose, covered the condemned man's face and, at Hubbard's request, granted him two more minutes to live. The prisoner complained that his legs were shaky. Skinner came forward, shook Hubbard's hand and bade him farewell. So did the deputy sheriff. Then Sheriff Pawling sprang the trap door beneath Hubbard's feet. He fell, but the fall did not break his neck. The body twitched for a time, and his heart continued to beat for sixteen minutes. He was pronounced dead after twenty-five minutes. About five hundred adults in the crowd pushed through the compound to view the body as it remained hanging—minors were not permitted. Forty-five minutes after the hanging, the body was cut down and carried into the jail. The crowd dispersed. Hubbard's trial and execution cost the county $461.72 and, save for a postscript or two, completed a fourteen-month long, gradual revelation of murder most foul.[1]

Aside from attorney, court, and jail costs, the most expensive item ($13.50) in the final list of official payments for the event was for the construction of the fence around the gallows. Given the thousands who witnessed the execution this was ironic, for the fence was erected specifically in obedience to a statute mandating that the execution be a private affair, witnessed by a handful of county officials and appointees. The local newspapers—both D. M. Cox's *Wabash Intelligencer* and Fletcher's *Gazette*—raised the issue of community propriety in the matter. After the fact, Cox rallied against the execution as a "disgusting relic of barbarous ages" and castigated the thousands who flocked to it "with eager hearts and gloating eyes" to "enjoy" the spectacle. He suggested that instead of sending missionaries to Christianize "benighted heathen" abroad it might be better to convert the heathens at home, for the locals had hooted, jeered, and raved like wild savages "thirsting for the life-blood" of a victim.

Fletcher, for his part, used the execution as an opportunity to promote debate in the community about the morality of capital punishment. In an article, "How the Gallows Educate," he argued that executions teach only brutality, a point of view considerably ahead of his time. In addition to his plea for folks to stay home on the thirteenth, Fletcher also published verbatim the section of the statute that provided for private executions that set the number and positions of persons who could witness such an event, roughly a dozen. Such effort was a whisper in a windstorm, unheeded. The following week, December 19, Fletcher covered Hubbard's execution in an extensive report that scarcely missed a detail, including news about the condemned man's last brandy and last cigar, which the sheriff had kindly provided. However, the editor also published his analysis of what had gone wrong with the privacy issue. Although Fletcher related only the facts as he knew them, he seemed eager to imply that the crowd's ability to satisfy a loathsome curiosity was due entirely to the unnamed officials who, consciously or unconsciously, failed to provide the right height of fence around the gallows. The purpose of the fence was to create a space shielded from exterior scrutiny. It was ten feet high, which might have sufficed in the average county seat where a jail would be surrounded by level ground. Given the terrain in Wabash, ten feet was inadequate, and Fletcher believed it should have been twenty. Apparently the ground south of the jail fell away precipitously enough that, on that side of the compound, the gallows was clearly visible to all who gathered there.

Residents in homes along the south side of Main Street also had excellent sight lines to the spectacle. The nearby courthouse provided convenient shelter for scores more viewers. In addition, near the jail workmen had left a large pile of discarded wood that was high enough for good viewing. It is indicative of the crowd's intense interest that two or three hundred people stood on the wood pile for nearly four hours in cold and rain. Growing impatient, spectators shouted "Bring him out," "Hang him up," "Put the rope around his neck," "Hang the damned old scoundrel," and many other "wicked and disgusting cries." Other spectators closed in on the compound and began to pry its boards apart. Younger, more agile types simply scaled the fence and perched along its top, though, reportedly, the fence gave way with them at the same moment Hubbard dropped to his death. The privacy standard was never an option. The execution was wholly public, contrary to law.

The ghoulish fascination with the Hubbard hanging is perhaps understandable in the context of the fact that his crime was unusually heinous and had held the town's attention since spring. His career as a murderer, moreover, had begun even earlier, on October 7, 1854, when John and his wife, Sarah Hubbard, murdered all seven members of the French family: the father, Aaron; his wife; and five children (John, Sarah, Louisa, Tilghman, and an unnamed infant, whose ages ranged up to thirteen years). The murder weapon may have been an axe, a hatchet, or the two-headed mallet that became part of the Hubbard collection at the Wabash County Historical Museum. In any case, the victims' heads were bashed in. Aaron was known to be quite ill before his death. The Hubbards—John, Sarah, and their "idiot" son, Richard, age sixteen—were boarding with the Frenches at the time, in a humble cabin just east of Richvalley (Keller's Station). The Frenches themselves were squatters, not landowners, but they were unassertive, likable, and needy folks toward whom their neighbors showed charitable concern. One neighbor, Stearns Fisher, was among those surprised to be told by the Hubbards, on or about October 8, that the Frenches had left in the middle of the night with Aaron's brother, who allegedly had arrived unexpectedly with news of an inheritance of land in Iowa. The fact that Aaron had been so ill so recently cast some doubts on this story at the time, but as there was no evidence to the contrary, the Hubbards' story went unchallenged.

Truth began to dawn in late March 1855, as winter's freeze broke up. While throwing a seine for fish in the canal near Richvalley, young fishermen snagged the body of a man who had been dead for an extended period of time. Wounds on the back of the head indicated murder with a blunt instrument. It proved to be the corpse of Edward Boyle, a railroad laborer who had disappeared the previous December. Boyle was known to have been carrying a large quantity of cash, which was not on the body, and to have been boarding at the Hubbard (previously French) cabin. It was also remembered that Hubbard had told folks that Boyle had moved on to Peru where he was teaching. Officials happened to question the Hubbards while the two were under the influence of strong drink; there were contradictions in their stories. John and Richard were arrested on suspicion of Boyle's murder and jailed. Richard was subsequently able to substantiate his innocence and was released. In order to strengthen the case against John in the Boyle incident, his jailers eavesdropped on conversations between him and Sarah during her visits. Learning that convicting evidence might lie in the Hubbards' cabin, a search ensued, with the result that the Boyle murder became a mere footnote to a much larger crime. Approaching the Hubbard/French home the search party met neighbors who reported a noxious odor emanating from the place. Officials broke in, easily verified the presence of the odor, and began to open up the plank floor that was laid across logs beneath. By probing the loose dirt between the logs, which was about a foot and a half deep, the men soon discovered the body of an infant and by working until late at night uncovered the bodies of its siblings and parents. Both John and Sarah were arrested for this newly discovered crime. In the following August a grand jury indicted them for the murder of Aaron French. John, an émigré from England, was in his midfifties; Sarah, from Canada, was in her late forties. John's trial lasted from September 3 to September 7, resulting in conviction and the death penalty, with execution scheduled for December 13. Sarah won a change of venue to Marion where she would also be convicted by the same evidence but sentenced to life in prison.[2]

At least two postscripts attend the Hubbard story. According to an article by Steve Jones published by the *Marion Chronicle-Tribune* in 1994, "the hangman's rope wasn't the only rope that went around Hubbard's neck."[3] A small cabal of county physicians from Wabash and Somerset, and apparently including LaFontaine's Doctor Dicken, sought to obtain Hubbard's body in order to dissect it for study. Doctors from Huntington and Fort Wayne had the same idea. The local group, apparently with the cooperation of both the sheriff and the superintendent of the county's Poor Farm (where indigents were housed), arranged for an expeditious body snatching. Following the execution, the sheriff loaded Hubbard's corpse into a wagon and took it to the "paupers' field" at the farm. He buried it there in a shallow grave, marking it for easy location.

At four o'clock the next morning the local physicians arrived at the farm to launch what, in retrospect, might qualify as a gothic comedy. Their fears that the other gang of doctors was en route to the same place intensified their frustration as they became disoriented in the rain and the dark, stomping around in fields and woods for an hour trying to locate the marked grave. No sooner did they find it than it dawned on them that none had brought any equipment. One man stayed to guard the grave while the rest scurried to the farm's buildings to scout for shovels, picks, and rope. Long minutes passed, and the rival medical collegium arrived, taking up a position within earshot of the grave, shouting threats of gunfire and demanding possession of the corpse. Undaunted, the locals dug down to the coffin, opened it, put a rope around Hubbard's neck, dragged him to the surface, trussed him to a fence post they had requisitioned, and began trudging through a woods toward their wagon. The Fort Wayne/Huntington party kept up their threats, yelling after them, "Drop it or we will shoot!"[4] As if on cue, the two toting the body lost their footing in the dark and tumbled into a steep gully, with Hubbard's body landing on top of them.

It took some time to extricate the body from the ravine and load it onto the wagon. One participant remembered that "faster driving was never done" as the wagoner, unnerved by the night's activities, urged his team toward downtown Wabash. There, yet another rope was put around Hubbard's neck and the body was dragged across the canal and hoisted through a window in one of the nearby buildings. Dissection began in earnest. When young men occupying rooms in the building complained about this activity, the doctors again moved Hubbard, who was in a plural condition by this time, to space across Canal Street. Following the dissection, the doctors divvied up Hubbard's bones among themselves. Later, Dicken reputedly acquired all the bones, reconstructed the skeleton as a display for his office, and eventually gave it to LaFontaine High School. However, other speculations about the final disposition of Hubbard's skeleton have circulated from time to time. One of those speculations, that Doctor James Ford acquired the remains, has been adequately disproved.

The Hubbard body-snatching story has not gone unchallenged. It apparently first appeared in print a quarter century after the execution, on January 24, 1880, in the *Courier*, which labeled its story "A True Report" and did not question its authenticity. Granted that twenty-five years is long enough for a rumor to take on a life of its own, the many complicated details of the report have the ring of truth to them. Then, too, none of the principals, including physicians of good standing, are known to have stepped forward to deny it. It was on the basis of this "true report" that museum curator Leola Hockett and journalist Jones quite understandably constructed twentieth-century versions of the tale.

There is a caveat, however, which comes from another source Hockett used, this one for the third installment of her coverage of the Hubbard trial and its aftermath. She quoted at length from the diary of a Baptist minister, Elder Townsend, who was one of the clergymen acting as Hubbard's chaplains during the time leading up to his death. According to the diary Townsend had found himself somewhat overwhelmed emotionally while standing next to Hubbard at the moment of execution, but he had promised the man he would stay by him. Aware of this commitment, the sheriff invited Townsend to witness the laying of Hubbard's body in its coffin and the screwing down of the lid, which Townsend did. The next day, Townsend wrote, he saw the coffin put on a canal packet bound for Fort Wayne. It was only "afterwards" that he was informed that the coffin contained a log and that doctors had stolen Hubbard's corpse. "As to the facts," Townsend wrote, "I know not."[5]

Townsend's uncertainty "as to the facts" invites further questioning. For example, was Townsend duped by the sheriff who was trying to set up a witness who would believe the corpse was properly cared for? If not, how does one account for the presence of two coffins, one taken to the Poor Farm (and presumably left there) and one shipped to Fort Wayne? If the body were shipped to Fort Wayne what evidence is there of its final disposition? Where is the body? What would be the point of telling Townsend "afterwards" that the coffin contained a log if, in fact, some kind of skullduggery had not been in the works behind the scenes? Would not Townsend have recorded the day's events soon "afterwards," in which case why would there have been in that very early, primary account—Townsend's personal diary—a reference to the dividing of Hubbard's body among physicians if it were not a matter of serious speculation at the time? The last question strongly suggests that the *Courier*'s 1880 account of the body snatching was not new in 1880 but dated from 1855 and very close to the day of execution. If the body-snatching story were myth, it was myth concocted of highly entertaining yet believable details within twenty-four hours or so of the alleged event, a fact that lends weight to the story's truthfulness despite the unexplained inconsistency of two coffins.

A second postscript concerns the fates of Hubbard's widow, Sarah, and their son, Richard. In an undated letter, probably written in the early 1960s, Wabash County Historical Museum curator, Mary C. O'Hair, responded to an inquiry about Sarah. The correspondent believed that the Hubbards were her great-grandparents and that her "grandma" had been a female infant born to Sarah while she was serving out her life sentence of hard labor in the Indiana prison system. In her response O'Hair acknowledged that she, also, had heard of Sarah's pregnancy and believed that Sarah—sometimes referred to as Aunt Sally—was essentially a pleasant but amoral person who may have used her pregnancy to win clemency from some of the more rigorous prison routines. However, O'Hair knew of no positive proof of a child being born to Sarah in prison.

In her letter the curator also commented on the subsequent life of the Hubbards' so-called idiot son, Richard. After he was exonerated of his parents' crimes, he worked on the canal in the Fort Wayne district, developing a love of horses. Apparently on the basis of that interest he won the friendship of a gentleman who became his guardian. The guardianship continued with the man's son-in-law, so that Richard seems to have lived a long and peaceful life, dying in his late eighties in 1907. His reputation, according to O'Hair, is that of a harmless and industrious man. She believed he is buried in a cemetery at Poe, Allen County, Indiana.[6]

The Hubbard story, an extraordinary example of local crime, depraved behavior, death, and a public's insensitivity, serves to introduce consideration of the general quality of life in antebellum Wabash.

Certainly death, in a variety of forms, was each citizen's ever-present and fascinating neighbor. It could cast a patina of melancholy over life almost daily. Infant mortality was high. Seventy was a good long life, beyond normal expectations. Given a high female death rate, widowers were likely to have been as numerous as widows. Lethal disease might strike anyone—or dozens—at any moment, causing anxiety about cholera, smallpox, and the "flux." Fatal accidents inspired reports abloom with lurid detail. Suicides seemed to stir the greatest curiosity. It was thus common for folks in the nineteenth century to be morbidly concerned about such matters, in part, perhaps, because of Judeo-Christian considerations about the "fallen state" of humanity—illness and death were what one *ought* to expect—and in part because of everyday experiences that informed them that illness and death simply abounded the way weeds did in one's well-tended summer garden.

In September 1859 "a very quiet, sedate, good-looking young man," a twenty-one or twenty-two-year-old employee at Hugh Hanna's steam mill, was found dead along Charley Creek a few hundred yards downstream from the railroad crossing.[7] He was later described as being about five feet, nine inches tall, having black hair, and weighing 150 to 160 pounds. At the time of his death he was dressed in a black frock coat, check pants, dark speckled vest, white cotton shirt with "Marseilles" bosom and collar, a pair of "kip boots," and a black hat. A portmanteau found with the body contained some money, a banknote, a linen cambric handkerchief, a pocketknife, a pair of pocket combs, a box of percussion caps, and a black lead pencil. The news of the discovery must have raced through town, for soon about two hundred citizens gathered by the creek, eager to witness the next stages of the tragedy. The young man was lying on his back, with arms at his side, his hat near his feet, one foot crossed over the other, a Colt revolver peering from under his lower legs, and "a ghastly wound" between his eyebrows. His hair was stiff with blood and stuck to the ground. One eye was closed, one open. The mouth was open, and flies were "busy" in nose and mouth.

The deceased was Samuel Hadley. A reason for his suicide unfolded gradually. He had arrived in town in May, probably drawn by a family acquaintance already living in Wabash. He was a native of eastern Pennsylvania, southwest of Philadelphia, where his wealthy parents were faithful Quakers of good reputation. Young Hadley, who had worked for Hanna all summer, made good wages and was in excellent health. He was no spendthrift; a total of thirty-four dollars was found on the body and among effects at his boardinghouse. Although he may have been a loner, with few close friends, and not given to running with the town's youngbloods, the suicide seemed at first to be inexplicable. However, it soon became known that his father had died in June and that, the week preceding the suicide, Hadley had received an affectionate letter from his sister describing their father's death. Thereafter he had become depressed and was known to have eaten little. Presumably his was an emotional derangement, a grief that drove him to unmanageable despair. Hanna arranged for a decent burial. The newspaper article apprising citizens of all these details was appropriately entitled "Melancholy Suicide."

Much of the published news in this morbid vein was less detailed than the Hadley story, but there were weekly, shorthand accounts of the awful disasters that befell citizens. Examples abound. William Morgan, a "little boy," attended a picnic at Charley's Falls, Wabash's first popular site for such outings, and fell off the cliff to his death. In August 1852 two died of flux, one a nine-year-old, one John U. Pettit's brother, Ossian. Cyrus Dingman, a bridge inspector, was run over by a train after he tried to jump a cattle guard. Two doctors amputated much of what was left of one of his legs. A railroad engineer reported having seen Dingman lying on the track, as if asleep, a couple of days earlier, perhaps with suicide on his mind. The man allegedly said he did not care if he were run over, and it was noted that he had lately married. In 1856 a woman lost her sister, Sarah Scott, to death; in the course of one year the woman had now buried her husband, two children, her mother, her brother, and a sister. Simon Newberger, prominent clothier and general merchant, was in Cincinnati purchasing goods for his store when his eight-year-old son drowned in Hanna's millrace at Wabash. In high summer 1859 Charles Herff, another prominent merchant, and a son almost drowned in the race when the father misjudged the water level and attempted to cross in a horse and buggy. They were saved from drowning by a lad named Oliver Burson. A second Herff son, Lewis, along with the horse, drowned in the same incident. Just north of town boys hunting with dogs one winter day discovered the body of a naked, partly eaten, and mutilated female infant. But there were no clues to help solve the crime.[8]

Effusive obituaries submitted for publication by the bereaved became more common in the mid-1850s, replacing the editors' short, matter-of-fact notices that "So-and-so died in her home on Main Street last Thursday." Composers of the longer obituaries appeared to assume an obligation to usher the deceased through heaven's gates if at all possible, making particular points of any deathbed confessions, conversions, or uplifting conversations and, more valued, elaborating on the peace with which the person of proven religious faith and moral uprightness faced the end. George Cissna, for example, was only twenty-two years old and a friendly, social young man when he faced the truth that he was to be inevitably "cut down like the morning flower." His illness was never named, but it was of the wasting variety, like cancer, causing pain and precipitous deterioration. His obituary's author made it plain that Cissna's first and great business in illness was to be prepared, stating that "He sought, and we trust, obtained the pardon of his sins through the merits of his Redeemer." The young man's sins were not enumerated, but grace abounded sufficiently for him to anticipate "his approaching dissolution with calmness and composure." As the end drew near he asked all present to lock hands together in his dying grip as "a token of undying love." When a companion asked if he were in pain, Cissna replied, "Oh, yes . . . but it will soon be over." Whereupon "he sank into the sleep of death."[9]

Citizens were not only naturally prone to suffer illnesses, disasters, and deaths, they seemed also prone to engage in mischief, immorality, and bad habits. Fletcher once used the power of the press for personal reasons, as well as for the community's welfare, when he ranted in print against "the infamous scoundrel who put poison in our yard, or barn, that killed our little house dog, watch dog, and cat.[10] Many prized pets, cows, and hogs had recently been killed, and two children had suffered severe poisonings. The editor was offering a hundred-dollar reward for help in bringing the culprit to justice. Because the public school system was not firmly established until late in the decade, Wabash children often had little to occupy their time and energy. At times boys of all ages seemed to rule the streets, going at each other with clubs and stones, blackening eyes, and breaking skulls and filling the air with "disgraceful," "profane," "fiendish," and "obscene" language. Many believed that parents' neglect was at the root of this problem and that parents should be hauled before the courts for raising young blackguards.[11] Older youths and young bachelors tended to take over the downtown after nightfall. The *Wabash Plain Dealer*'s staff complained of the "drunken rowdies" who prowled Canal Street almost every night, destroying property. "Where are the Town Dads?" the writer wanted to know, asking "Wouldn't a few days boarding with Mr. Sheriff suit such fellows?"Some folks seemed intent simply on playing the cruel and heartless trick. When Miss Anne Sayre was attending Miss Willard's Female Seminary at Troy, New York, she received a letter informing her that her father, Daniel Sayre, was dead. She immediately left school for home by rail. At the Huntington railroad station she was met by both parents and fainted from shock. The perpetrator was not revealed.

Women seemed especially susceptible to cruel masculine manipulation. "I am the victim of deception," wrote a woman to the *Wabash Intelligencer* in 1855. "I adopt this method to warn [other females] against [one] . . . who won my affections."[12] She describes her husband: six feet tall, light blue eyes, sorrel hair parted on either side, scar on the upper lip, nose turned to the right side, scar on the left hand, three toes cut off his left foot. She had him pegged, but he was gone.[13]

All in all, there was an unsavory side to life in Wabash. When a man named O'Harran stood trial before a jury for stealing a coat, his defense team of John U. Pettit and Calvin Cowgill argued that their client had been too drunk at the time to have had felonious intent. This ploy of using one vice to contravene the reality of another vice was considered so ingenious it nearly won an acquittal. In the end, however, O'Harran spent two years in the state prison. Horse theft was a common problem. So were pick-pocketing, burglary, and prostitution. The last-named vice did not establish a high profile until later in the century, but it was inevitably present, though direct evidence is scarce. On the earlier rural frontier, where couples had generally married at a young age for reasons of economic necessity, prostitution tended to be relatively rare. The rise of towns changed that in some measure, depending, perhaps, on the demographics of particular communities. At Wabash the early inundation of unmarried laborers for both the canal and the railroad increased the probability that Wabash had an established history of prostitution. Even after canal and railroad construction was complete, the evening gatherings of young men in and around downtown saloons doubtlessly encouraged the trade, and the crumbling canal shanties provided handy coves of assignation. Upright citizens worried about any assaults on the sacred vows of marriage that unseemly sexual mores represented. In 1859 there were remonstrances against loose divorce laws that allegedly had made Indiana the target of mockery as far afield as New York and Europe. It was believed that couples paid brief visitations to the state to obtain easy divorces. In 1858, 150 marriages had been licensed in Wabash County and eleven divorces had been granted, but it is uncertain what influence divorce laws had on such statistics.[14]

Other moral and behavioral issues floated on the surface of community awareness from time to time. There was ambivalence about some of them because any restrictive legislation might be both unpopular and hard to enforce. Based on a general desire to keep the Sabbath sacred, one local ordinance levied a fine of ten dollars on anyone over fourteen caught hunting, fishing, quarreling, "rioting," or performing common labor on a Sunday. Exceptions were made for Jewish citizens, the ferryman, and others whose activities might be crucial to health and safety. There was also legislation against swearing, for which no exceptions were made, though rougher individuals no doubt continued to voice their own exceptions willy-nilly anyway. Dancing was an enjoyable social recreation for many. For others it was "a ruin leading from God to Satan," a vice through which "many sons became profligate" and "many daughters [were] ruined."[15] Smoking and other uses of tobacco came under heavy fire, with scant success. Ironically this was at a time when the county was paying to provide tobacco for residents at the Poor Farm and when that busy civic reformer, Fletcher, frequently lit his cigars in public, a fact that was broadly acknowledged. Nevertheless, at the beginning of the decade the *Gazette* had published the possibly alarming news that fully eighteen shops in town "sell the weed" and that one store had sold $216 worth of tobacco in the past year. Sales would continue to rise. Opposition to the weed grew frail as the age of the ubiquitous spittoon drew nearer.[16]

The negative aspects of life in Wabash—its diseases, its tragedies, its crimes, its violence, its vices, and the shoddy behavior of citizens—did not flourish without opposing and powerful attempts to tame the place. Emphatically countering the town's flaws, there existed people and organizations to foster health, gentility, intelligence, decency, and peaceable relationships, all of which probably succeeded in making Wabash a reasonably healthy and promising community.

One such person was Ford, a man with universal interests: general medicine and surgery, pharmacy, ophthalmology, horticulture, mechanics, sanitation, astronomy, architecture, construction, quarrying, journalism, geography, geology, paleontology, surveying, military service, public and higher education, and religion. He became the town's Renaissance Man, an archetype of what it means for a human being to be civilized. In sharing his broad and varied interests in speeches and in print he seemed to be demanding, politely but forcefully, that Wabash also should be highly civilized.

Though a diplomatic, supportive, and highly principled man, Ford could also be pragmatic to the point of bluntness. He once attended his critically ill daughter whom he loved dearly and told her, apparently with no preamble, "Mary, you are going to die." Mary's answer did her father justice: "Pa, I am not afraid to die."[17] Mary was a cheerful woman of strong faith, and she was probably used to accepting inevitable facts for what they were. Nonetheless, her parents were deeply grieved. Ford's communications from the Civil War front to his wife, America Holton Ford, often seemed to reflect the formality of the time and might read more like reports of military maneuvers than personal letters, a style accounted for by the fact that they were often published in the local newspaper. He was thought to be absentminded, one of his prescriptions reading, "Take one dollar every two hours."[18] He was sometimes captive to goofy theories; for example, he believed that the new telegraph lines of the late 1840s would eliminate storms, tempests, and tornadoes by using up the electricity that clouds need to produce such weather. But he could also be humorous and self-effacing. When he was applying to enter Kenyon College as a teenager, a matron on the bishop's (president's) staff asked him, "Have you a mother?" "Yes," Ford replied. "Is she a good mother to you?" the matron asked. "The best I ever had," Ford stammered. The bishop's laughter seemed to seal his acceptance at Kenyon. "Bishop," said the matron, "we'll take the boy."[19]

It was the start of a stellar career of great benefit to Wabash. In 1841 James and America Ford arrived in town from Connersville, lived for a time at Treaty Ground, may have next moved in with a relative in the county, and eventually settled in a one-room house James had built just east of where the dirt trails of Hill and Cass streets crossed. (The much-expanded house is currently the Doctor James Ford Historic Museum.) Their son, Edwin Ford, founded the Ford Meter Box Company, which grew into an international concern. The family name persisted with grandchildren, great-grandchildren, and great-great-grandchildren who served Wabash as business leaders and benefactors into the twenty-first century.

The most palpable, extant monument to Ford's personal genius is the Christian Church sanctuary, less than a block east of his home. He designed it and then redesigned it when the first version proved too expensive. Its exterior wall-top frieze of bricks mimics the exterior wooden frieze on his home. He oversaw the church's construction and was personally involved in the labor of designing and producing the eighty different shapes of bricks that were required. The structure is a charming, one-of-a-kind mixture of Gothic and classic motifs with an interior sanctuary that was successfully designed to be acoustically superior. Significantly a church was more than architecture for Ford; he knew theology, argued theology, and expounded theology. Presumably he conscientiously tried to live his theology.

In his early years in Wabash Ford maintained a medical office on the Hill Street property and owned three downtown drugstores at different times. His drugstores advertised liberally, offering medicine and a variety of commodities: tea, tobacco, sugar, molasses, mackerels, nails, almonds, ginger, mace, bed chords, and wine and brandy "for the sick and for sacramental purposes."[20] He eventually gave up the pharmacy business. For a time he invested also in a nursery south of the river and then moved his horticultural pursuits to land west of Charley's Falls, where he also had a quarry. He was particularly interested in air currents, teaching that the wrong current might surround homes with unhealthy, miasmic airs. After the deaths of young relatives he insisted that the family abandon its homestead and build anew in an area of the county that he judged to be salubrious. He wrote and edited prolifically on a range of topics that he believed were important for the general public, not least of which was practical advice on raising various garden crops. Among some Miami, Ford was known as "Big Papoose Man" because in 1843, while in the countryside, he had come upon a very pregnant, but unattended, Miami woman in the throes of what promised to be a fatal delivery for the mother. Although the child was unusually large, the doctor made what he called "a few adjustments" and quickly delivered a "fine male infant." Aware of psychological factors in treating patients, Ford was not above stooping to a little professional deception, occasionally creating fake pills made of dough and bottled flavored cistern water to treat clients with imaginary symptoms. He helped organize the town's first school board, its medical association, and the county agricultural fair. He was a founding trustee of what became Butler University in Indianapolis. After the Civil War he was an examining surgeon for the government for sixteen years.[21]

Ford may stand alone in the breadth of his interests, but he is important to Wabash because he represents so emphatically that coterie of public-minded professionals and businessmen who seemed to sense that Wabash could answer to the highest possible embodiment of human nature. A great many family surnames of that early era persisted long enough for them to emit at least faint echoes of honorable recognition a century later—Hanna, Conner, Alber, Beitman, Bruner, Cowgill, Daugherty, Haas, Hackleman, Lumaree, McNamee, Pawling, Pettit, Ross, Sayre, Sivey, and Thurston, for example. As the nineteenth century matured, more names were added—such as Atkinson, Baylor, Bigler, Carpenter, Goodlander, Hunter, Little, Mackey, New, Plummer, Sharpe, Walter, Wilson, and Yarnelle. Whether they arrived on the scene early or late, these folks were quite naturally driven by personal ambitions—financial, professional, or both—and seemed also to sense, without having to reason about it, that their destinies would be enriched by a progressive community. Thus they were deeply involved in fraternal, social, political, cultural, and religious associations that promoted creativity, responsible citizenship, and reasonable moral standards. Possibly they were drawn as adults to such obligations by friends and associates, but it is more probable that most had been both raised and educated toward such obligations as part and parcel of a moral code. None was an angel, none a saint. No doubt each was, from time to time, treasonous to his or her own best instincts. But each was civic-minded enough to embrace ambitions for Wabash and to engage relentlessly in activities that might improve both the place and their lot in life.

Decent medical practitioners in a town were a first-line defense against the ubiquitous threat of sickness, death, and the melancholia that crippled spirits. Ford joined several other competent physicians in creating the Wabash County Medical Association that attempted to pool individual technical expertise for the good of all. Doctors Beckner, Dicken, Peters, and Winton were early Wabash leaders in the association. Members elected officers, established standards for joining the group, issued credentials to local practitioners, held regular meetings, took attendance, kept minutes, and authorized official correspondence. Association members alerted the public about epidemics and tried to educate the public in basic health and safety procedures. It pressured the local government to pass laws that limited specific social intercourse during epidemics: levying fines that eventually rose to fifty dollars per offense. The association attacked what it called "quackery," the application of quasi-scientific methods by unscrupulous or undereducated practitioners, who were forever advertising their services locally. At least some of the association members offered free medical supplies to the poor. Because members could be relatively humble about their own levels of expertise and were aware of the changing nature of medical practice, association officers regularly appointed members to present scholarly papers on timely subjects.[22]

What the town's medical professionals did mostly, of course, was to treat people. Besides aches, pains, and colds, the most common complaint surely remained ague, a flu-like (perhaps even malaria-like) problem that caused weakness, tremors, and fever throughout the pioneer period. Ralph Arnold, a Connecticut native who settled near Wabash in 1844, said that it was "a few shakes of the ague" that made a man a Hoosier.[23] There were no good cures, though staying out of drafts, avoiding bathing in the river, and swallowing various ill-tasting concoctions were thought to help prevent it, and sweating helped cure it. Quinine grew in favor as a remedy, so much so that in the 1860s quinine was briefly nicknamed "the King of Wabash," and it was suggested that town officials should regularly ring a bell to remind citizens to take their medicine. Ague was incapacitating but rarely deadly. Scarlet fever was more serious. Physicians sometimes used tinctures of iodine to arrest "anginous affectation," or recommended that the entire body be rubbed with fat from the inside rind of uncooked bacon. The disease could be especially lethal among children, who passed it to their siblings. It was not uncommon for parents to have to bury more than one child during an epidemic. Smallpox was especially fearful, requiring community-wide watchfulness and strict quarantines. When a laborer came down with symptoms while in church he was rushed to a back room on the third floor of a brick building on Canal Street where he could be isolated. A person who had already survived smallpox attended him, but those who brought supplies were stopped at the door. Affected strangers who came to town might be driven away. There were vaccines, though supplies sometimes ran short. At one juncture controversy arose about the doctors themselves as "carriers" because they were moving from house to house while wearing clothes that had been in contact with smallpox patients.[24]

The great challenge of the era seemed to be cholera. As early as 1849 the town council, being more proactive than might have been expected, called on physicians to adopt a cholera strategy. Ford had one up and running in less than two months. The disease got a "fast hold on lungs" and produced cramps, diarrhea, and burning pains in the midriff; later symptoms were flatulence, vomiting, and odious discharges. Ford thought the solution was sanitation and diet: no alcohol consumption, no river bathing (though bodily cleanliness was critical), streets and alleys cleaned of filth, water holes drained, and animal remains buried. After the morning dew was off the land, Ford encouraged townspeople to throw open their windows and doors and air out their closets and beds. They should avoid radishes and raw vegetables but blackberries and tomatoes might be eaten "with impunity."[25]

Occasionally medical cases were just plain interesting to doctors and the public alike. Later in the century, for example, a Dr. Gillen operated on the ear of James Whiteside one morning and removed twenty-five "animalculae resembling maggots."[26] It made the papers, whose editors had always peppered their publications with such curious medical tidbits. Thus, it was reported: a wise woman would be wary of stylish boots that fit tight, for they might cause gangrene and death; a surgeon removed a tumor as large as an egg from a local gentleman's mouth; a German shoemaker's squirrel hunt in the northeast part of town went awry when his gun accidentally discharged into his upper arm, requiring Drs. Ford and Dicken to amputate; the rusty nail in the shoe of Robert Rencenberger, a tailor and printer, caused a running sore, gangrene and, finally, necrosis of the bone, a "loathsome disease"; a particle of gun cap penetrated the cornea and lodged in the iris of John Bear's eye, who was chloroformed for the removal of the foreign object; and "manhood problems" could be addressed with various potions, though none is known to have been endorsed by a local physician. All in all, between the physicians and the newspapers, after 1850 citizens became much more aware of various health dangers and the possible antidotes for them.[27]

There was another prescribed antidote to treat a condition that tarnished the town: the temperance movement. In 1855 that movement peaked in Indiana, causing political and religious ruckus in the process. When the American Society for the Promotion of Temperance was founded in 1826, temperance was mostly a religious cause promoted by the clergy and church members of those denominations that stood for broad social reforms. For these denominations temperance did not rest solely on concerns for personal moral behavior and individual sanctification; it was also a social issue. Early leaders used temperance promotion to target marital, family, and community dysfunctions. Not without cause they blamed divorce, child abandonment, squalid home life, poverty, broken health, illiteracy, prostitution, violence, and crime on the fact that too many Americans drank too much too often. This, they perceived, was especially true in the emerging communities of western states where addiction seemed pandemic. The fact that by the 1850s many politicians had joined the cause indicates that the more secular elements of society had awakened to the real dangers of intemperance.[28]

What happened in 1855 was a showdown in Indiana over the so-called Maine Law, or versions of it, which sought to eradicate the consumption of "spirituous liquors." The problem with all such laws was that a state where prohibition had been legally established might lie just across a border from places where drinking was still legal. With a little expenditure and a little travel, individuals living in "dry" areas could easily figure out how to import the liquid booty from "wet" areas and keep it privately sequestered at home. Enforcement was often haphazard and unfair, the wealthy being more able both to travel long distances and to procure larger amounts than the average laborer. Then, too, there were plenty of respectable citizens who gave temperance lip service without much conviction. In Wabash the temperance cause was probably introduced by the Presbyterian missionaries in the 1830s and 1840s, but the Methodist and Christian churches were not far behind. Physicians tended also to recommend temperance for health reasons. In time Whigs and Republicans took up the cause, leaving Democrats, backwoods Baptists, and a great many Roman Catholics to represent leniency on the issue. What had begun as admonitions toward temperance (abstaining from hard liquor or drinking very moderately) became campaigns for total abstinence (the teetotalers) and then, finally, efforts at prohibition (outlawing manufacture, purchase, and consumption). In Indiana escalation toward prohibition had begun in 1839 and culminated in 1855 when the Indiana General Assembly outlawed the manufacture and sale of intoxicants. Almost immediately, however, the Indiana Supreme Court ruled the measure unconstitutional.[29]

For a brief span in the summer of 1855 Wabash was dry, or, rather, legally dry. Prohibition went into effect on June 12. Liquor vendors and saloons were closed down. It was the culmination of several years of local wrangling over the temperance issue. Various schemes to limit drinking in Wabash (as elsewhere) before this time had been proposed—and some tried—as attempts were made either to control licensing or to suppress sales by the drink. In 1847, for example, the Wabash Lyceum, a debating society, scheduled a public debate of a proposed "license" law. That proposal, depending on its version, would either outlaw sales by township votes or provide for restrictive license fees. Ford, a Whig, spoke in favor, and William Steele, a Democrat, opposed. Three years later William Johnson (the county's original sheriff) had been indicted for selling whiskey by the gill—one-fourth a pint—rather than by the quart or more. The court records name thirteen of his customers, from which it may be shown, for example, that a Jerome Morgan enjoyed three gills of whiskey on January 18, 1850, and paid a total of eighteen cents. More significant, however, is the fact that the official summonses to court were professionally printed, fill-in-the-blank forms, with the specific offense of selling by the gill preprinted. This indicates that "gill-drinking" was rampant at that time and that the law was in hot pursuit of offenders.

Perhaps more effective than legal attempts at control had been the voluntary ones. There was, now as earlier, keen interest on the part of churches to encourage folks to become teetotalers or at least to sign temperance pledges. In addition, this was the age of temperance fraternities, such as the Sons of Temperance and the Washingtonians. These were groups of men who met regularly for social interaction, encouraged each other in the pursuit of sobriety, did good works in the community, and sought to increase their numbers. The Washingtonians were locally the most active, claiming the loyalty of some of Wabash's leading citizens, including Benjamin Sayre, Alanson P. Ferry, and Stearns Fisher.[30]

Matters came to a head in the spring of 1855 when the general assembly finally promulgated its prohibition law. As June 12 that year approached, temperance supporters planned a jubilee, but they were also aware that a law on the books did not necessarily mean compliance and feared that moderate drinkers in particular would attempt to skirt it. "Enforce the law!" became their war cry.[31] For those who had supported the cause the approach of general sobriety was a welcome relief. No doubt Fletcher expressed the hopes of many community leaders when he wrote that the liberty "of getting drunk and making fools and paupers and murderers of our fellows will have an end." For a while the euphoria held. The effect of prohibition was "peace," "quiet," and "tranquility." There were men observed going home sober in the evening for the first time in recent memory.[32]

There were also signs, however, that, as many expected, folks were finding ways to drink. Liquor traffic at the state's border was brisk. The *Gazette* reported that "Hoosiers are found to be importing mysterious looking packages."[33] The rival *Intelligencer*, which had tended to be less enamored of prohibition, said that Indiana was no longer the Hoosier State but the "Jug State," and that the law had failed to reduce drinking because people were forced to import large quantities and drank more than they had before. It ran figures from the local liquor agency to illustrate the point that even in Wabash the retail of whiskey remained substantial. In one month in the summer of 1855, more than eighty gallons of liquor were purchased in 329 separate sales, most of which were theoretically for medicinal purposes, the remainder were for "chemical" and "mechanical" use. None of it, according to this accounting, was imbibed for pleasure. These sales figures did, however, compare dramatically with those collected before prohibition during two weeks in June 1854, when just one merchant sold 660 gallons of whiskey.[34]

The general assembly, not anticipating that its law would be overturned in November, had no backup legislation to control liquor consumption on a statewide basis. After November regulation was the exclusive domain of local governing bodies. Meanwhile, as repeal became a looming possibility, the *Intelligencer* rejoiced that "Good times may be anticipated."[35] Even that newspaper, however, was unprepared for the negative fallout. In the new year, 1856, it declared that "the reign of Bacchus" had broken loose in the streets of Wabash, with "debauchery . . . enough to stagger sober men."[36] Fletcher was especially appalled, reporting on January 26, 1856, that the town was disgraced by "more drunken men on the streets than we have ever seen. Whooping, swearing, blackguarding, reeling, staggering and disgusting affections were displayed in such abundance as to make the heart sick."[37] This explosion of insobriety had been caused by railroad hands striking for higher wages. Fletcher observed sadly that many of the drunks that day had been sober since June 12 and wondered if anyone could now dare say that the prohibition law had not done great good.[38]

The aftermath of the prohibition debacle so far as the temperance cause was concerned developed in two directions. The first was local enforcement, endorsed locally by Judge George Gordon, who declared that prohibition was still in force in Wabash. That did not stick. Instead, there were repeated efforts to curtail drunkenness through license fees, fines, and forbidding the sale of "spirituous and malt liquors" in quantities less than a quart. The idea of licensing caught on, but by-the-drink sales continued. The second direction temperance reform now took was a rekindling of "moral suasion." Churches, temperance societies, and temperance fraternities carried on the effort through preaching, publication, and various limited demonstrations against taverns, saloons, and other vendors. In some sense this was a return to the original strategy begun earlier in the century. Certainly in Wabash the temperance cause was far from dead, though legalizing prohibition was moribund for the foreseeable future.[39]

Perhaps no civilizing agency is more powerful than a good public education system. For the first two decades of its existence Wabash had none. There were small private schools, as earlier noted, but it was a system of short terms, limited curricula, no enforced attendance, no tax support, little administration, and no standard qualifications for faculty. The later, township-based common schools had public funding but their standards of operation were not high. Common schools were criticized locally for being "ill-ventilated establishments to which boys and girls are sent to acquire algebra and lose their lungs"; the term "lose their lungs" probably referred either to the poor ventilation or to instruction heavily dependent on classes reading and reciting out loud together.[40] Without a better control of the situation "the amount of ignorance, error, vice, and corruption [was] truly lamentable."[41] For a great many citizens the traditional condition of boys loitering in the streets all day, being neither in school nor at work, was becoming unacceptable. Nevertheless, during 1854–55, Noble Township spent only $571.50 on 1,191 students. Of those students an average of 403 attended daily, and the number of days schools were in session amounted to a total of two months a year. It was time for an overhaul.[42]

The answer was a statewide, tax-supported, comprehensive, graded school system. Such a system was created by the general assembly in 1852, but not without opposition over issues of taxing powers. The tax levy was ten cents on a hundred dollars worth of appraised real estate. The hope of the law's advocates was that there would be a well-equipped brick schoolhouse in every neighborhood. However, as would happen to the prohibition law in 1855, the education bill was declared unconstitutional. This effectively postponed Wabash's plans to erect a comprehensive school building. Following three more years of debate, a new law created a state-based educational system, putting taxing powers in the hands of local school corporations.[43]

The tangible result locally was the rise of Union School to crown Wabash's skyline. The school's prominent location—facing south toward town from the highest elevation on Miami Street—was possibly a conscious decision. Certainly it was a symbolic one for the building became, for a time, visually the most important structure in the town, as if its presence announced great aspirations for the place. Its message seemed to be that if Wabash's tawdry quality of life were to be overcome, it would take more than improved health conditions, religion's guidance, progressive enterprise, or reliable transportation connections with the larger world. It would also take a population so well educated that it could and would support an enriched and enriching local civilization. Union School embodied that sentiment in brick and mortar. Indiana's ability to tackle the education issue in the early 1850s, albeit in starts and stops, had pushed Wabash in a noble direction.

The decision to build Union School, however, had not been automatic. Town leaders had fussed about it in public debates since 1852. That year at least one Union School meeting was held at the New School Presbyterian church, a fact that hints at an undertow of sectarian division on the school question. John Pettit, a prominent New Schooler, complained in print about the "oppugnation" of George Gordon of the Old School church, saying "We want good schools first, and shabby, lying men, calling themselves Presbyterian afterwards."[44] Given leaders such as Ford and Elijah Hackleman, it is quite likely the Christian Church was allied with the New Schoolers. It is less certain where the Methodists stood at the early stages of debate. Although, as expected, the *Gazette* was the more vociferous advocate for a new school, in fact the two newspapers represented a growing consensus that dramatic educational reform was both needed and expected and that a new schoolhouse was inevitable. Both the *Gazette* and the *Intelligencer* frequently published articles from Caleb Mills, the first state superintendent of education and a former Wabash College professor, who almost single-handedly shamed the general assembly into action by publicizing the dearth of literacy in the state. Mills's name was a byword for progress in education, the kind of progress Union School was meant to embody.[45]

After seven years of mildly contentious prelude the cornerstone of Union School was laid with appropriate ceremony on May 18, 1850. For Wabash it would be a massive structure, matched in size only by ungainly warehouses or mills along the canal. Built of brick and with generous windows, it rose three stories and contained space for twelve classrooms, plus a chapel/assembly hall on the top floor. Above it all rose two towers, one of which must have held the school bell that alerted students and the town to the day's schedule. The bell's charm wore off for some neighbors who complained that it rang too often and quite inappropriately late at night. "Won't somebody stop it?" one wrote, and "What is the sense of it?"[46] The building cost approximately five thousand dollars, a princely sum. It was backed, financially, by the fact that there were two thousand Wabash inhabitants holding taxable property worth approximately $600,000, reportedly enough to support the educational needs of an estimated five hundred students. By June 1855 the school tax had risen to fifty cents on one hundred dollars worth of appraised property.[47]

Someplace in the structure there may have been space—perhaps no more than a desk—designated for administrative work because both a superintendent of schools, William E. Spillman, and a high school principal,

S. L. Eastman, worked there, though these administrators would also have taught in the high school department. There were six additional teachers, all unmarried women. Students, ranging in age from six to the lower teens, made up the primary and intermediate departments. The high school was a three-year program for older teenagers. Soon after the school opened, a Miss King, in charge of the primary department, accosted the president of the school board, Albert Pawling, demanding a large supply of baby cribs for her room. She needed them, she said, because parents were bringing children to school who were too young to learn. Pawling took her point and made certain children under six stayed home.[48]

For its three to four hundred students Union School was a place of precise schedules, clearly stated rules, and a full academic agenda. Classes met from 9:00 a.m. to noon and from 1:00 p.m. to 4:00 p.m. Tardiness was almost a worse offense than absence. For a late entry into class the only acceptable ticket was a written excuse from parent or guardian. Tobacco was not allowed in a classroom. Nor was it permissible to deface furniture, to use profanity, to fight, to be rude, or to be slovenly. Students were to go directly home after classes. It is doubtlessly true that such rules would not have been so clearly defined if the offenses proscribed were not regularly committed. Continued acts of disobedience resulted in exclusion from school for an indefinite period of time. Thrashings were a common form of corporal punishment. Conforming to rigid schedules and rules was admittedly difficult, especially for boys who were used to roaming the town at will for much of a day. It seemed to be almost expected that a boy might keep a "Barlow" knife secreted in a pants pocket; as class work droned on, out came the Barlow for a little surreptitious whittling or, perhaps, some artistic carving on a desk. The curriculum was not designed to entertain the pupil but to refine him or her. It was heavy on reading, writing, and arithmetic, of course, but as the grades ascended it accumulated sophistication: orthography (spelling), articulation, vocabulary, gymnastics, literature, history, geography, higher mathematics, music, rhetoric, and introductions to various sciences.[49]

Nevertheless, many community leaders understood education to be something more profound than attending classes and taking courses. For example, as Union School began its second decade of operation in 1860, the *Plain Dealer* reminded readers that "the greatest education takes place in the home where newspapers and books are placed before youngsters so that a child may begin to enjoy the life of thought.[50] A year earlier, before the first term of Union School, while officials were still waiting for the installation of desks and other furnishings, the editor of the *Gazette* published a brief statement of purpose for the new school. The school existed, he wrote, "to improve the morals, elevate the tone of society, and promote, generally, the interests of the people."[51] In other words, education in Wabash was intended to be not so much about equipping individuals for their personal futures as it was about reforming a whole community, beginning with the quality of home life. As with the practice of medicine, the pursuit of temperance, and other causes, Union School was about bringing Wabash out of the shadows of its tawdry past.

7

"Arma Virumque Cano"

In late August 1865, when the drama of the Civil War had become mostly a matter of soldiers returning home and reviving normal life, Wabash citizens witnessed their own stunning finale to the great national saga. It began with news that one of its most colorful citizens, war correspondent and soldier Stockton Campbell, was dead. The *Wabash Plain Dealer* noted his three years of military service and praised his usefulness as a reporter, his "jovial disposition," and his kindheartedness. He had been one of those classic journalists who made it his business to know his town from the bottom up and scouted for stories day and night in all parts of Wabash, especially downtown. He had moved in and out of shops, saloons, offices, mills, and sports events, swapping stories with anyone who would stop to chat, collecting items of human interest, amusing anecdotes, and gossip. He probably knew most folks in Wabash on an informal basis. And now, having survived the guns, cannon, and cavalry charges of war, he had met with a fatal accident en route home. While aboard a Mississippi paddle wheeler plying the river northward, Campbell had either jumped or fallen from a deck. A witness reported that he had seen Campbell bob to the surface of the river after his plunge but that, almost immediately, the boat's paddle wheel had struck him. He sank beneath the surface and was not seen again. Stock's grief-stricken father immediately left for the South to try to locate his son's body to bring it home for burial.[1]

Some days later, on Sunday, August 20, a *Wabash Plain Dealer* reporter, who was also quite possibly its proprietor, S. M. Kibben, attended worship at a local church, likely the Old School Presbyterian on Hill Street. Another worshipper, a Mr. Kennedy, let it be known among those gathered that a gentleman staying at the Indiana House hotel downtown had claimed to have spoken recently with Campbell. Sensing a story, the *Plain Dealer*'s reporter left the service before the sermon began, hoping to interview the stranger before the latter had a chance to leave town. The newshound's instincts had been right. The stranger had a story worth pursuing. There had been a resurrection.

Thus, on page 3 of the August 24 edition of the *Plain Dealer*, immediately following an updated account of Campbell's alleged demise, there was a column written by the deceased himself on the topic "Why I didn't drown." The editor promised, "We know it will be rich." Campbell told readers they could believe he was dead if they wanted to, but "I don't," and challenged those who needed further proof to invite him for supper because he had a "darned good appetite for a ghost." The article must have been the best reading of the week for Wabash citizens, not only because it was a piece of self-effacing, humorous journalism that helped put the horrors of the last four years behind them, but also because Campbell's recent adventure was entertaining in its own right.

His epic return from the war began in Shreveport, Louisiana, where he had been detained through much of June and July with a raging fever for which he was heavily medicated. "I became a wholesale Drug Store," he wrote, "a physic shop, an animated medicine chest." As soon as he was strong enough he left Shreveport for Baton Rouge and New Orleans, where he pursued the bureaucratic processes that would muster him out of the army on July 28. That having been accomplished he boarded, appropriately, the *Indiana*, a steamboat headed for Louisville. He was still unwell, but feared to remain where he was because yellow fever and smallpox were rampant in the area.

The *Indiana* was a crowded boat. As it stopped at ports on the trek north, it took on scores more soldiers who were leaving the front for home. When the boat was about fifty miles from Memphis, Campbell's fever returned, and he became delirious. At midnight he imagined that the other soldiers on board were murderers intent on killing him. Insane with fright he jumped into the Mississippi River. Sudden baptism into the "Father of Waters" apparently squelched his fever. Later he clearly remembered submerging once, then twice, then thrice. When he survived the third submersion, which popular lore told him should be fatal, Campbell concluded that the river had rejected him. Reason further argued that since he was not dead he might as well relax and enjoy the ride. He let the current float him gently south into the darkness. By this time he was naked except for a shirt.

After floating a few miles he became aware of an island with willow trees overhanging the river. Paddling toward them, he pulled himself into the trees and settled down as best he could for the night. Referring to Psalm 137, Campbell observed that he had not "hung his harp on a willow," but he had certainly hung himself on one. The night was excruciating. "Delegations" of mosquitoes visited his exposed body to obtain "little pieces of flesh," mementoes (he claimed) of the man who had "whipped the mighty Mississippi." Then the fever returned, and it was two and a half days before his mind again cleared. Able at last to explore his environs, he soon discovered a house, but its owner, mistaking Campbell's mosquito bites for smallpox, forbade him to approach any closer than to pick up a small contribution of clothing. The gift was a used silk hat with no crown. He wore it, reminding himself of a defeated Confederate colonel whose entire uniform had been reduced to a collar and spurs. Campbell was now attired in a crownless top hat and a checked shirt. At a second house, however, the gift was an almost complete outfit, a Rebel jacket with matching trousers. The latter had been patched and repatched but proved adequate for the most egregious exposures.

Campbell's next human contact was with woodsmen who provided a skiff by which he could reach the mainland. He was still in the former Confederacy but his fortunes now rose quickly. A plantation owner, a Dr. McGavitt, took him in, hosted him for a week of recovery, and then booked passage for him on the *Commonwealth*, which was headed for Yankee country. He reported arriving in the North thirteen days "after my immersion" and said he was returning home a veteran of the "other world" beyond death. Poignantly, Campbell arrived back in Wabash the same day his father also returned, having failed to locate his son's corpse. There is no known report of their reunion.

For most of the nation, including Wabash, the Civil War did not have the clean, happy outcome Campbell's personal journey illustrated. Yet war would be the main story, the Rubicon experience, in the individual biographies of those soldiers who grew into old men with long memories of the "Southern Rebellion." The Grand Army of the Republic was founded after the war on the premise that a brotherhood of Union veterans must forever honor its call to duty and not allow the horrendous sacrifice to be forgotten. The fact is that for Wabash, as for the entire nation, North and South, the Civil War turned into a nightmare neither side had envisioned. Both sides had assumed it would conclude after a few months, if not weeks, of dignified military engagement. It took four years of undignified maiming and dying. Armies were riddled with common illnesses, many of them deadly, that were not attributable to wounds but to miserable living conditions. It is estimated that one in twelve soldiers contracted venereal disease from prostitutes in the towns and camp followers in the field. Indiana alone lost more than 24,000 soldiers during the war. Of those, more than 19,000 died of disease, proving that the battle camp was more lethal than the battlefield. Wabash County lost at least 350 men in the war. If the state's statistics apply to these local numbers, then approximately 276 Wabash County soldiers died from disease rather than battle wounds.[2]

Such statistics, however, did not dent the idealism about war that was firmly planted in the minds of American Victorians. War was still noble, or should be. Enthusiasm for it served as the ultimate measure of a person's and a people's patriotism. It was an idealism that was not widely challenged until it met the charred realities of the First World War, after which the demonstrated efficiency of the twentieth-century military slaughter further negated idealistic instincts as reasons for war. Bloody battles might still be practical necessities at times, and warriors could still be true heroes, but there would no longer be much good to say about war in principle. As late as 1883, however, when Thomas B. Helm wrote his *Military History of Wabash County*, nineteenth-century idealism was still in high gear. He introduced his work with a paean to the essentiality of war in service to human progress. Quoting Virgil, *"Arma virumque cano"* ("I sing of arms and the man") he championed the notion that "cannon and the sword have opened the way for the car of progress." War would forever be the forerunner of civilization. It is the "military feature" in the histories of nations that form their "distinguishing characteristics," whether those nations are ancient or modern.[3]

Helm was right to this extent, that in 1861 a "military feature" became the "distinguishing characteristic" of Wabash and the nation. Though the fuse leading to war had been burning for decades, growing dangerously short with Abraham Lincoln's election, the explosion that rocked Wabash was touched off by the Confederate bombardment of Fort Sumter on April 12, 1861. News from Sumter reached Wabash the next day, forwarded to William Thurston by George Gordon, who was in Indianapolis when the word arrived there. Thurston was manning the railroad depot's telegraph, eager for the activity of that machine to tell Wabash how the Sumter crisis was unfolding. Throngs of men, women, and children had stood around the depot waiting anxiously for hours. After Gordon's message arrived, there were immediate calls for local action, beginning with a meeting that evening at the courthouse. "The town was wild with excitement and every man and boy was eager for action. Speeches were made and applauded," and "Old men and women . . . wept." Some faces were pale, others flushed, and there was cursing "in a profane dialect that would have done honor to the army in Flanders."[4]

On April 14 local attorney and politician Charles Parrish led efforts to open a recruiting office in Wabash. He correctly anticipated events: on Monday President Lincoln authorized state militia numbering 75,000 soldiers, and Governor Oliver P. Morton called for 10,000 Hoosiers to take up arms. Parrish also joined the county clerk, Elijah Hackleman, in a countywide campaign to scout for volunteer recruits. Their efforts culminated in a second community rally at the courthouse Monday evening. James D. Conner presided, and the town clergy participated. Plans for a company of volunteers were bandied about, and it was announced that a number of citizens had already agreed to bear arms. By the end of the first week, 150 men had agreed to go to the front. Wabash was at war.[5]

Naaman Fletcher's *Wabash Gazette and Intelligencer* was soon reporting that Wabash had taken on aspects of a garrison town. This was the first case of war fever to strike since the spring of 1846 when a small company had been recruited for the Mexican War. This was different. This was a general outburst of intense patriotism. The place was crowded with folks wanting news from the front and about local enlistment efforts. From morning to night small companies of men paraded to the music of fife and drum. There were public meetings almost every night, with speeches and songs and opportunities to sign up on the muster roll. During the day, business slowed toward a halt as folks stood around in groups talking. Canal Street became so crowded that women complained about the difficulty of pushing their way through groups of garrulous males. On Saturday, April 20, Parrish planned to lead his volunteers to Indianapolis for induction into Company H of the Eighth Indiana Regiment, a three-month enlistment. Parrish, however, had reckoned without the women of Wabash, who complained that a weekend departure date was unacceptable. The women wanted the departure postponed to Tuesday so that they could plan a suitable farewell with a dinner and presentation of a regimental banner.

Saturday was nonetheless a big day. County residents flooded in, making it a "lively," "animated" place. There was regimental marching and drilling, with the troops followed closely by cheering crowds. The volunteers met briefly at the courthouse behind closed doors to elect officers: Parrish, captain; Joseph M. Thompson, first lieutenant; Frank Dailey, second lieutenant; and John R. Polk, third lieutenant. On Sunday morning the clergy took charge. There was preaching in every church plus the courthouse. It happened that New School Presbyterians from out of town were meeting in Wabash; they were dispersed to speak at various churches. At 3 p.m. the president of a Marion college preached at the courthouse from Revelation about the ultimate, cosmic battle between good and evil. Fletcher pronounced it "thrilling and eloquent." An aged veteran of the War of 1812 also spoke.[6]

On Monday, April 22, the troops continued to parade through town in front of enthusiastic crowds. Banners now flew from public and private buildings. At 7 p.m. a canal boat from Lagro arrived, bearing a crowd and a brass band that led a procession of citizens to the courthouse and then to Union School, where Mrs. R. C. Helm made a speech and presented the soldiers with a flag. Parrish accepted the flag, tried to speak, but was overcome with emotion. The volunteers then marched upstairs to a "capacious room" on the top floor of the school where a magnificent supper awaited. After dining, the troops broke rank to mingle informally with those present. A solo by a Miss Lessig closed the evening. At 4 a.m. the next morning, Tuesday, April 23, Parrish led his soldiers through a tearful crowd and many "God bless you" farewells onto the train to Indianapolis. The town, Fletcher wrote, now seemed deserted.[7]

The initial call for volunteers may have been for a three-month tour, but the next one was for three years. After three months it was evident the Confederate forces were not going to run away before Yankee armies. Wabash's soldiers met the enemy on several fronts, and individuals among them were present at famous clashes throughout the war, but no large concentration of area men was present at any of the monumentally noteworthy battles such as Bull Run or Gettysburg. Rich Mountain was the first battleground for Wabash soldiers. In mid-June 1861, after two months of training in Indianapolis, H Company of the Eighth Indiana Regiment was dispatched by rail to Clarksburg, West Virginia, then still a part of Virginia. The troops arrived "tired, dirty, hungry, sleepy, [and] mad."[8] They may have had good reason for anger. Doctor James Ford, the accompanying surgeon, believed that leadership was slipshod, with the results that morale was low and insubordination was high. Ford was especially incensed that some of the officers "think more of their gin cocktails than anything else." He did state, however, that the Wabash men were better behaved than most.[9]

On arrival the troops were issued only dry biscuits and water for nourishment, allowed a couple of hours sleep, and then put to work unloading heavy artillery and preparing for battle. As a mountainous, rocky, forested challenge to military maneuvers, the terrain was inhospitable, especially in the task of hauling huge artillery by rope up rocky cliffs. Joining the Tenth Indiana Regiment and a brigade led by Brigadier General William Rosecrans, Company H searched for a Confederate army of four thousand men (some reports say fewer). The Confederates were found hunkered down at the base of Rich Mountain behind a secure barricade built of felled trees. The Union forces attempted to sneak around the enemy along a trackless mountain passage through the forest, only to discover that the Confederates, aware of the ploy, had sent 2,500 soldiers and three cannon to the mountain peak, above the Yankees. Rain poured down as the Confederates unleashed a bombardment of cannon fire, cutting off the tops of trees above the Yankees' heads. At some places the terrain was so rough and so thick with trees and bushes that musket fire was not dangerous, but neither could men maneuver easily. When Union forces tried to feign a retreat by running downhill they fell pell-mell among boulders and bushes. The effect of this confusion, however, was to convince the Confederates that they had the advantage. They left their entrenchments in hot pursuit only to be mowed down by the Enfield and Mini rifles of their enemy. Fixing their bayonets, the Indiana men chased the remaining Southerners for about three hundred yards, deactivating their cannon in the process. When their cannon ceased to roar, the Confederates who had stayed below believed their day was lost and scattered.[10]

For the Hoosiers and for Rosecrans's brigade it was a clear victory. At least 135 Southern soldiers died and another six hundred surrendered. Most of the dead had been shot in the head, their features mangled. They were immediately buried. The North collected the enemy's discarded horses, mules, wagons, tents, guns, cannon, and provisions. Wabash's Company H came away from Rich Mountain almost unscathed, but not quite. Lemuel Busick and Jacob Sailors, both scions of well-known Wabash families, were wounded. They would undoubtedly have been treated by Ford, who was in charge of the Rich Mountain battle hospital (where the most common complaint was not wounds but diarrhea). There was one death, James H. Emmett, killed in action. In 1883 Post Number 6 of the GAR was named for Emmett, Wabash County's first Civil War martyr. There was also one deserter, John Ballinger. On July 27 Company H reached home by rail from Indianapolis. The town's bells rang out a welcome. A crowd of enthusiastic and proud citizens gathered at the station to welcome its heroes. So far the Civil War was living up to Wabash's expectations.[11]

The Eighth Indiana was soon reorganized on a three-year basis, although some of its volunteers were still being recruited for only three months. The field of operations this time was with Major General John C. Frémont's Army of the Southwest, an area that included the Missouri and Arkansas front. Wabash men participated with a number of Yankee companies in some indecisive skirmishes with a Confederate army near Springfield, Missouri, and then pursued it toward Bentonville, Arkansas, in the northwest corner of that state. There, at an elevation called Pea Ridge, the fighting became deadly. Union troops were outnumbered three to one. Fighting lasted more than three days, March 6 to March 8, 1862, and in fairly short order it appeared as if Yankee casualties would continue to mount with about a thousand men put out of action early in the encounter. The soldiers became tired and cold, collapsing to the ground at night and sleeping on their rifles and without the warmth of fires. At daylight they reformed their lines and waited for the onslaught. As engagements unfolded, however, the North played its tactical ace in the form of Major General Franz Sigel, a tough militarist of Teutonic origins who was a master of artillery fire. Whether his troops were on the offensive or the defensive, Sigel was able to lay down a murderous barrage of artillery grape and shell that not only kept his men relatively safe from enemy fire, but also inflicted lethal damage on the enemy. Across dozens of miles the front seemed to move back and forth, but whether advancing or retreating the Confederates got the worst of it, so that in the end their lines broke. According to historian Clarkson Weesner, Sigel went on to become one of the tactical geniuses of the Civil War, known especially for brilliant, honor-saving retreats. Men who fought under him bragged about it: "I fights mit Sigel."[12]

Following the battle of Pea Ridge, those companies comprising Wabash men marched south to join Brigadier General Ulysses S. Grant in Louisiana. Over the course of the Civil War, Wabash County soldiers served in more than thirty different regiments and artillery battlements. In this diverse service, they were deployed for action in such places as Port Gibson, Missouri; Jackson, Mississippi; Vicksburg, Mississippi; and as far away as Fort Esperanza, Texas. In relatively small numbers they bore arms also at Shiloh, Corinth, and Chickamauga. They were present near the so-called massacre of Fort Pillow, where the feral Confederate, General Nathan Bedford Forrest, a former slave trader, allegedly slaughtered African American prisoners (an allegation taken as gospel in the North and by Weesner but disputed in other histories). Wabash citizens were also involved in skirmishes in Georgia and Virginia, at Chattanooga, at Gettysburg, at the battle of the Wilderness, and at Petersburg where African Americans from Indiana participated in a desperate charge. Finally, a few county soldiers were present at Appomattox when General Robert E. Lee surrendered.[13]

The Civil War gave Wabash its share of heroes and future leaders. First among them was Parrish, "a true friend and impartial officer," who was elected captain of Company H during the earliest days of conflict and by war's end was a brigadier general.[14] A native of Ohio and a graduate of Kenyon College, Parrish moved to Wabash in 1854 to open a law practicethat quickly prospered. He became the county's prosecutor two years later and James D. Conner's law partner four years after that. He seemed to have a natural interest in military science, organizing a local company called the Wabash Guards as early as 1857. Probably Parrish would have risen to prominence in Wabash anyway, but his war experience clearly polished his reputation. After 1865 he became a leading lawyer, a state senator, and finally mayor. To some extent his rise represents that advantage Civil War veterans enjoyed in politics, locally and nationally, late into the century. On the national stage, the likes of presidents Grant, James Garfield, and Benjamin Harrison would enjoy the same advantage.[15]

Another well-known name of the age was Alexander Hess, a man who dropped his law studies to join Company H of the Eighth Indiana. He fought at Rich Mountain, returned to Wabash, and almost immediately signed on for three years with the cavalry. He was assigned to General Don Carlos Buell's army and rose to the rank of captain. Toward the end of the war, while he was in the vicinity of Atlanta, Hess's horse was shot out from under him and he became a prisoner in Charleston, South Carolina. When released in a prisoner exchange, Hess was mustered out and returned to Wabash. He studied law again, now under Conner, and began his own practice in 1866.

As the years passed, he became prosecutor, member of the state legislature, and clerk of the supreme and appellate courts of Indiana. His public career did not end until 1900.[16]

Local citizens who were much in the news and frequently on the minds of the Wabash public during the Civil War years included Colonel John U. Pettit and Quartermaster Calvin Cowgill. In 1862 they organized Camp Pettit (Camp Wabash), located south of the river to the east of the new Wabash Street bridge, sprawling on both sides of the Somerset Pike (Columbus Street) that climbed the bluff there. The camp was well drained by the terrain's slope and well supplied with water from a spring. A comely grove of trees provided shade. The camp was used as a training base for recruits, as a mustering ground for those en route to the front, and as a rallying point where both soldiers and citizenry could meet for patriotic and martial demonstrations. A relatively level field on top of the bluff—formerly the site of a Miami village—served as a parade ground. Typical of the town's involvement with Camp Pettit was a Thanksgiving service held there in August 1863. The call for such events across the nation had been promulgated by Lincoln; church members and clergy organized it locally. There was a parade to the camp, songs, prayers, choir anthem, an address by Pettit, and a culminating feast prepared by the women of Wabash.

Both Pettit and Cowgill were political bigwigs and successful lawyers. Each founded a Wabash family that enjoyed unusual prominence into the twentieth century. Cowgill's career will be considered in a later context. Pettit was a native of New York who settled in Wabash in 1841 and was soon practicing law. In the early 1850s the U.S. government sent him to Brazil, where he supervised ten American consulates. On his return he entered politics, so that by the opening salvos of the Civil War he had already completed three terms in the U.S. Congress, representing Indiana's Eleventh District. Near the end of the conflict he was elected to the Indiana General Assembly and subsequently became Speaker of the Indiana House of Representatives. About the same time he helped establish a home at Knightstown, Indiana, for the care of soldiers' orphans. In the 1870s Pettit crowned his career by becoming circuit judge for Wabash and Miami counties. Meanwhile, his son Henry Pettit grew into a worthy successor of his father. The younger Pettit studied law under Cowgill, married into the prominent Stitt family, and became a partner in the Stitt and Pettit law firm. Henry was elected to the city council and served one term as mayor. In 1900 President William McKinley appointed Henry a U.S. Marshal for Indiana.

Parrish, Hess, Pettit, and Cowgill represent a much broader coterie of high-profile citizens—men such as B. F. Williams, Meredith H. Kidd, Will Stitt, and the very popular John R. Polk—who were locally celebrated for their military leadership. Many such veterans—matured, hardened, and inspired by the war years—proved to be catalysts of change in Wabash during the latter decades of the nineteenth century.[17]

As noted earlier, local support for the Union's cause in the Civil War had not been seamless. As the conflict wore on, those relatively few known to be emotionally or intellectually disdainful of the cause must have felt increasingly marginalized by the burgeoning patriotic fervor. The Knights of the Golden Circle, that fraternity of Confederate sympathizers present in the eastern part of the county, were still vocal and still threatening violence well into the war's third year. Theoretically the Knights and other similar groups should have been concentrated in Indiana's southern counties where Dixie pedigrees were strong. However, Logan Esarey, in his history of the state, showed that the Knights were scattered evenly around Indiana. According to Fletcher it was "established fact" that there were three or four "castles" or "temples" of the Knights in Wabash County, one of which was in the county seat. "Be prepared for them," he warned. "Scour up your old rifles, pistols and shotguns . . . put down treason right here," Fletcher warned.[18]

This was strong language from a man as levelheaded as Fletcher seemed to be, but fear of diverse opinions, if largely unfounded, was real in many locations in the state. Given the intensity of the current brand of patriotism, treason was a charge bandied about with little discretion. In that sense even Democrats were not entirely safe from suspicion unless they were clearly Unionists, allied with that wartime amalgamation of Republicans and Democrats who supported Lincoln. There were also those young conscientious objectors (or just frightened teenagers), caught in a hyper-patriotic atmosphere, who were torn between volunteering for the trenches and risking the ridicule of their neighbors. Twenty-four known objectors lived in Noble Township in 1862, and there were a dozen more in the county. Criticism of such men could be withering. That same year Fletcher advised youths that their attractiveness to females was in the balance. There was a growing opinion among women, he reported, that men who do not enlist "are chicken-hearted cowards."[19] As late as 1867 the *Plain Dealer* pilloried a "calf of unsteady nerves" who had skipped out to Idaho during the war but was now back home with "Ma." The "calf's" story, the article stated, was too disgusting to print.[20]

A more common example of those who did not share a narrow Yankee patriotism were the so-called Butternuts. Because Butternuts desired the reunification of North and South but were opposed to Lincoln's policies of emancipation, they were commonly labeled as Southern sympathizers, Copperheads, secessionists, or traitors. Their nickname derived from the butternut dye used in the manufacture of homespun cloth for Confederate uniforms. Citizens who advertised their Southern sympathies by daring to wear small butternut emblems could face potentially violent opposition. The emblems were pins made from slices of white walnut seeds, and the interior configuration of the slices was said to symbolize North and South united by common bonds. As such they were popular with Copperheads; some folks also spread the rumor that the butternut pin was an official symbol of the Democratic Party.[21]

In May 1863 the *Gazette and Intelligencer* reported on a Butternut brouhaha that, though it occurred in the country and not in Wabash proper, illustrates the volatility of feelings. Several women had appeared at a Sabbath School class at a Dora church wearing "their little diadems" (butternut pins) on their hats. Eyes rolled and fierce glances flashed between relatives of soldiers. When class was dismissed some of the Union supporters took up a position at the far end of a small bridge near the schoolhouse, awaiting the approach of the "Misses Butternuts." When the Butternut women arrived at the bridge, the Union women demanded that they remove their "butternuts," but they refused. "'Then we will take them off,' quoth the Union ladies." What ensued, according to the reporter, was such a scene that his pen could not do it justice: "grabbing and scratching, pulling of hair and tearing of hats . . . a perfect smash up among bonnets and hats, and a considerable fall of butternuts." Then a male Butternut took up the cause, vowing to "whip three of the best d___d abolition women there was in the crowd." The Unionists, sensing that matters were out of hand, welcomed a chance to retire. It was provided by a Union "boy" who caught "his gal" by the arm and said, "Come, Lizzie, they will tear all your clothes off if you stay here." Contenders "skedaddled," but it was not the end of the day's excitement. Soon after the morning's church service got under way, a Butternut woman and a Yankee woman launched a shouting match in the vicinity of the pulpit. Screamed the Butternut, "What did you do with my hat?" "I threw it in the gutter," came the loud reply. On it went: "What did you pull off my butternut for? . . . What did you wear it for? . . . Because I had a right to . . . You are nothing but a durned secessionist. . . . You are a liar."[22]

Gradually decorum returned and worship continued. But that afternoon, at the two o'clock singing school, the Butternut women were "saucier than ever" and claimed they would wade knee deep in blood before they removed their butternuts. "The fire now blazed." Singing ceased as the confrontation escalated. Outside nearly fifty men representing both sides fell into a general melee, presumably of fisticuffs. A Butternut man who began to lose ground pulled a revolver and swore to shoot any challenger. When a Union man stepped up to take the challenge, cooler heads began to prevail. A contingent of Butternuts dragged their armed compatriot away, and the Unionists took the opportunity to give three cheers for their side, three groans for the Butternuts, and quietly went home. It is possible, indeed likely, that this report was colored in favor of the Unionists because of the reporter's personal convictions. It is also probable, though not necessarily verifiable, that such open dissent of the war—such as Butternuts had expressed in Dora and the Knights had exhibited elsewhere—was more easily vocalized in the relative isolation of the countryside than it would have been in Wabash. In any case, there is little evidence of overt dissent of the war in town, even though citizens with Southern sympathies must surely have been among its residents.[23]

By the first spring of the war, 1862, when it began to appear that the conflict might be neither brief nor easily won, the home front swung into action. For example, Hezekiah Caldwell, the kiln master and president of the Agricultural Society, distributed cotton seeds to farmers so that the area could become independent of the cotton lords of the South. There were soldiers, soldiers' widows, soldiers' orphans, and collateral dependents to be cared for by the hometown. For the first time in Wabash's history women stepped up as high-profile community leaders in relatively large numbers. They had remained unsung as the hearts and hands of churches, of various social endeavors, and of the schools. But now they sought to galvanize the home front in providing palpable support to the battlefront. Archibald Stitt had long been a popular, jovial character about town, a canal contractor, an erstwhile hotel manager, and, more recently, a supervisor for the construction of the new river bridge. He seemed to be a man who went with the flow, engaging opportunity as it came to him. His wife, Catherine, however, knew how to organize the distaff side, how to get her causes publicized, and how to wring money out of the town. As much as any woman, and more than most, she represented a new breed of leadership in Wabash that war inspired. Women could not fight but they could be taken seriously in new ways, and as wives, mothers, and sisters they were appalled by the cruel lethality of war and by the abominable conditions their men on the front endured. Catherine became especially sensitive to such matters when her son, Will, joined the cause and was wounded at Chickamauga.[24]

Catherine probably did not think of herself as part of an innovative wave of civic leadership. She sensed a great need about the same time her female friends also sensed it and fell to the task of doing something about it. The "something" was the Soldiers' Relief Society, a volunteer civilian organization that operated in many communities. In Wabash it had started small but grew stronger as the war's miseries deepened. It is instructive, for example, that in a week late in the war, when J. A. McHenry was attempting to lure women into his downtown store by advertising his supply of five hundred hoop skirts, Catherine, Mrs. McKibben, Mrs. J. B. Lumaree, Mrs. E. P. Peters, and Mrs. Josiah Daugherty—all wives of prominent Wabash men—were down the street at McKibben's Hall divvying up the society's latest collection. Twenty-six dollars of it would go to soldiers' families locally, twenty-six dollars to Memphis Hospital, forty dollars worth of fruit from Busick and Brothers to the front, and seventy-five dollars worth of various goods in barrels and boxes to Indianapolis for shipment to Memphis. It is uncertain how often such sums were collected but they likely represent the efforts of several weeks. In times when a high quality hoop skirt cost $2.50, these were not small amounts to have squeezed from the general public or, for that matter, from Wabash men, who, after all, controlled most of the cash.[25]

Collecting hard cash was not the totality of the women's enterprise. The society unofficially existed to keep the soldiers' needs at the forefront of community awareness and to offer a variety of opportunities for citizens to "do their part" for the boys in blue. To that end there were offshoots of the society for handling special projects and a readiness on the part of the founding women to share the limelight with anyone who supported the cause. Sometimes the women encouraged prominent men—such as James D. Conner, J. C. Sivey, J. D. Miles, J. W. Essick, and Elijah Hackleman—to take official positions in such organizations as a way of popularizing their work. As news of pending battles reached Wabash, the society and its friends might send out a plea for medical supplies or for the volunteer services of nurses and doctors. Women and men together were involved in "Sanitary fairs," created to solicit goods that would relieve soldiers' hunger, physical discomfort, and want of proper hygiene. Thus, in late 1863, the society advertised for donations of socks, yarn, mittens, quilts, comforters, and a variety of foods: butter, eggs, dressed chickens, turkeys, and ducks. (When canning fowl for shipment in ways that would preserve them from spoilage proved to be too daunting a task, the cry had to go out: "Send no more.")[26] Sometimes pressure was applied to the county's farmers. Noting how generous the town had been, a Mrs. J. M. Vanatta laid it on fairly thick when she pointed out to county residents how scarce firewood could be in an army camp and that it was a commodity that every farmer could spare. And, always, there was a need for bandages, which could be ripped from all kinds of cloth and used clothing.[27]

It is evidence of the serious—even professional—standards of the women of the Soldiers' Relief Society that they met at McKibben's Hall every Friday, perhaps to plan strategy and tactics, perhaps to do related chores. Yet, as the war progressed, home-front efforts multiplied. Probably every church in town had its own committee working similar ground, including its "Mite Society," which sent funds to help the sick and the wounded at the front. Unpredictable fallout from war created unpredicted areas of need. Eventually there was a Freedmans' Aid Commission formed that sought to ameliorate the hardships of former slaves. The commission divided Wabash into wards—northeast, southeast, northwest, southwest—in order to facilitate the collection of used clothing. When news reached town that the war had cast up fifty thousand homeless "unfortunates," of whom three-fourths were women, children, and "superannuated men," the commission searched for donations of bedding, clothing, cooking utensils, medicines, and any household article that might be useful to a homeless person. Local politicians also got into the act of caring for the war's unintended victims. They had often been supportive of volunteer soldiers by endorsing funds for bounties, sometimes authorizing as much as one hundred to four hundred dollar payments for enlisting. However, it became increasingly clear that dead or critically wounded soldiers were leaving behind widows, orphans, or dependents who had no ready means of support. Officials enlarged the county's welfare system by subsidizing the war's victims on the home front. They paid a needy wife or widow $5.00 a month plus $2.50 for each child under age fourteen; a widowed mother of a bachelor soldier also received $5.00; and motherless children under age fourteen received $2.00 to $5.00, depending on their sibling order, the first-born receiving the highest sum.[28]

As the war wore tediously and tragically toward its victorious conclusion, Wabash's communal spirit seemed to have remained high, stoked as it was from time to time by patriotic public gatherings; by official days of humiliation, fasting, and prayer; and by occasional thanksgiving feasts. For some of these events, industries and businesses closed down so that none had a reason for not participating. The only measurable hitch in the prevailing patriotism came late in the war when it proved increasingly difficult to fill draft quotas with volunteers, as had been successfully accomplished hitherto in most parts of the county. Throughout the conflict it had been necessary to offer bounties to encourage recruitment. The system had worked with remarkable smoothness, despite an occasional spate of "bounty jumpers," men who took the money but shoved off for other climes without serving. In September 1864, however, the bounty ploy failed to produce the quota. Calvin Cowgill did what had not often been required. He ordered up "a neat walnut box" about two feet long, a foot high, and a foot wide, which he installed in a room above a downtown bank. The box had a hole in the top large enough for a man's hand. Names of qualified candidates were written on slips of paper and placed in the box that was shaken and turned over and over. A curious and anxious crowd jammed the room in orderly fashion to watch a blindfolded man pull out names one at a time. The "picker" handed each slip to the local magistrate, Judge Knight, who examined it and recorded the name. The process took a long time. The quota was met.[29]

Life on the home front was not all about the war, the soldiers, the unintended victims, quotas, or the draft. It was also about building houses, turning a buck, improving the public infrastructure of the town, and acquiring a little more community sophistication now that the pioneer period was emphatically history. The population of Wabash in the early 1860s was in excess of two thousand people and rising; and most of them were probably engrossed in a normal civilian existence that was only intermittently affected by distant battles.[30]

Of the total population approximately eight hundred were young, under age twenty-one. Families were large and housing was scarce. The war may have temporarily retarded early marriages and childbearing, though probably not dramatically. In any case, by early 1861 new families were moving into town at a fast clip. In February that year, eight or ten houses were under construction, but the next month Fletcher proclaimed a crisis: "One hundred dwelling houses wanted."[31] It seemed to him that scores of folks decided to move to Wabash all at once. Anything that vaguely resembled a house was bulging with one or more families. One man was trying to locate a military tent he could live in, and it was anybody's guess what the poor were going to do about basic shelter. In June the *Plain Dealer* noted that houses were "going up in all directions" and praised specific home owners for their good taste: Ira Stanley's two-story painted dwelling, John Wilson's modest and comfortable little cottage, and the Gamble family's "neat cottage" next to the Widow Dutton's nice place.[32]

Probably most of these new dwellings, being quickly built, were of wooden construction. The Wabash County Historical Museum owns a photograph of the relatively new Union School taken from a high point somewhere along Maple Street, possibly from the cupola of Elias Hubbard's house. The photo shows frame homes on the north side of Maple. They are modest, two- or three-room affairs, plus small outbuildings that must have housed middle-income folks and were probably built in the late 1850s or early 1860s. Brick was preferable to wood if time, labor, and money were in good supply. David Kunse's brick classic on Wabash Street (the Walter house) had established a standard for elegance in the 1840s, its brick possibly originating in Kunse's own kiln. The Sailors house (Hipskind house) on Hill Street, just north of Court Street, and the Federalist-style Alber house (the Crace house) on East Sinclair, are extant examples (2010) of brick homes that date from the same era. James Ford's original one-room brick, in the block west of Sailor's, had grown substantially and sported a flat roof-top space that would eventually be developed as a decorative widow's walk. John C. Sivey's home, built on the eve of the Civil War, was not brick but was possibly the most stylish dwelling of the time. It sat "west of town" in the center of four lots adjacent to Hill Street and Carroll Street, where the Reverend James Thomson had earlier built a log cabin in the woods. Sivey's home was a deeply gabled, batten and board, and highly decorated Gothic-revival affair that mimicked a Swiss chalet. A nearby grove of trees—possibly locusts—served as an early community gathering spot for picnics. Even farther west on Hill Street Josiah Daugherty built his spacious two-story brick that lay within easy walking distance from one source of Daugherty's wealth, his hog-butchering emporium on Charley Creek.[33]

News editors made special note, also, of businessmen who, having prospered, were improving the prospects of the downtown. One reporter was especially pleased when two or three burned out, derelict shops were replaced with "fine buildings," probably of brick because of its fire resistance. Although the general economy was not predictably steady and remained subject to occasional panics, new residents and new construction sparked a boom that extended the entrepreneurial vitality of the late 1850s. The local pork dealers, Josiah Daugherty and his partner J. M. Lumaree, maintained both a downtown outlet and the abattoir on Charley Creek, processing thousands of swine each season. They were not alone. In one year, during the 1850s, Wabash butchers had packed more than 700,000 pounds of pork. Goods tended to fly out of stores, often sold on credit because cash was scarce. Some merchants stopped extending credit because of the risks and the paperwork, but doing so could discourage business in a town long used to casual, buyer-friendly sales approaches. In 1863 merchants arranged with the local branch of the Bank of Rockville to issue "shin plasters," locally printed paper money in denominations of five, ten, twenty-five, and fifty cents. There was general acceptance of this currency because it relieved the pressure for small change.[34]

Meanwhile, shops, mills, foundries, and other businesses provided every possible material essential and a few luxuries besides. Not surprisingly, given new home construction, items such as wallpaper, furniture, pots and pans, tools, and building materials were heavily advertised in the newspapers. Commercial Row, a block-long line of shops and businesses on the north side of Canal Street east of Wabash Street, continued to be typical of much of downtown, offering a variety of goods and services during the 1850s and 1860s. A person needing basic merchandise such as clothing, fabrics, plows, tinware, drugs, furniture, books, magazines, dishes, carpets, boots, shoes, seeds, gardening equipment, stationery, musical instruments, watches, ice cream, jewelry, law offices, insurance brokers, bakery goods, blacksmithing, groceries, and hotel accommodation would find it there or nearby. The person in search of something more indulgent might stop by the daguerreotype studio to have a portrait taken, or climb Wabash Street hill to purchase oysters fresh off the train from Phillip Alber near the depot, or mount the bluff across the river to enjoy an "Electro Therapeutic Bath" under the auspices of Doctor D. D. Miles at his spa. The daily hubbub of enterprise in town was augmented by the arrival of trains and canal boats and by the presence of farmers with wagon teams eager to do business at mill or foundry. Though nothing could match the drama, or importance, of the battlefront, the home front obviously had its own kinetic energy. On the eve of the war, Fletcher wrote that Wabash was "a perfect jam from 10 o'clock in the morning until about 4 o'clock in the evening," and, indeed, that was the tenor of the place throughout the rending national conflict.[35]

The establishment of a permanent fairground at the county seat also captured the attention of the home front. Agricultural fairs, taking place in late summer near the old Treaty Ground (between Hanna's millrace and the canal) had enlivened that season since the early 1850s. By the time war broke out, however, the Treaty Ground had long since proved inadequate. There was not enough space for the burgeoning number of attractions created or for the hundreds of town and county citizens who crowded in to enjoy shows, booth sales, food, races, speeches, sermons, and other distractions from their normal routines. Early in 1860 the county fair board became aware that a new town addition was being carved out of the remainder of Chief Charley's section, and after a narrow vote, bought land in that section. The minority had wanted to rent land because of current prices, but the desire to build permanent fair structures, especially a "floral hall," won the day. The board was soon looking at ten to fifteen acres between West Hill Street and the railroad bridge spanning Charley Creek, land which, much later, became the Wabash City Park and the location of the Women's Club House. The facts that the site was near town and was bordered by a "stream of pure, living water" sold it, in preference to a second possibility along the road to North Manchester.[36]

Once purchased, the eastern half of the new fairgrounds was fenced. There was a permanent pair of gates at the fence's western end and, at the eastern end, a walnut stile that accommodated passage over the fence. Within the fenced compound were the floral hall and spaces designated for booths and various agricultural displays; this section was eventually reserved for pedestrian traffic only. The western half of the property provided for horse-and-buggy tethering and a one-third-mile long, oval race track located just south of the top of the Charley Creek bluff. The track survived into the twenty-first century as an asphalt road surrounding the park's large, steel-strutted Chautauqua and picnic pavilion. When horse racing grew into one of the most popular activities of the fairs the governing board constructed a large set of permanent bleachers, which was placed at the track's east end, approximately where the main drive into the park runs (2010). So quickly was the town expanding westward that in 1862 county officials began considering building a road that would connect Hill Street and the new fairgrounds with the Peru Road (Mill Street). Hill Street had at last stretched westward far enough to descend to the floodplain on that side of town.[37]

Folks living in the east of Wabash and those traveling out of town toward Lagro had long complained of that egregious public disgrace—Hanna Cemetery, later the Old Cemetery. As previously noted, its fence was forever in disrepair, it was overcrowded, and it was so poorly maintained that skeletal parts all too often worked to the surface or were accidentally cast up during new burials. The place was also hemmed in between the Lagro road and the railroad, limiting expansion. Something needed to happen. The subdivision of Charley's section may have inspired town leaders as it had inspired the county's agricultural fair board, for they began to look at land northwest of town as a possible site for the New Cemetery, later Falls Cemetery. The fact that Falls Avenue was then becoming important as a connection from Sinclair Street in town to the northwestern parts of the county made a new cemetery along that route attractive and, presumably, there would be acreage available for expanding such a cemetery for the foreseeable future. The great attraction, however, was the land itself. It swept upward from Charley Creek in a series of knolls and was heavily forested with shade trees that provided "a splendid resort for the living as well as a resting place for the dead."[38] A cemetery association elected officers, issued shares at a dollar apiece, and collected about five hundred dollars to get the project launched. The New Cemetery became reality in 1862. One of the early burials there was Fletcher's (1864), who had championed the kinds of civic improvements that the cemetery represented.[39]

The home front's most ambitious projects were street improvements and an assault on the steepness of the bluff. There were still "oceans of mud" both in town and in the county. "Oh, for a . . . little cold weather," folks would say in rainy times, being hopeful that the mud would gel or freeze and become passable.[40] Teams got mired, and street surfaces could run like thick, watery ooze. To walk along the Canal Street sidewalk was to run a gauntlet of sloppy conditions, including the viscous splash from horses' hooves. Visitors to town were not favorably impressed. Those responsible were sometimes as mired in disputes about the problem as teams were mired in mud. Fletcher had forthrightly and persistently blamed "unwilling factions" and "selfish owners of real estate" who held up progress.[41]

Little by little, however, it had become clear that steps would have to be taken. In 1861 the town trustees appropriated funds to grade Wabash Street from the canal to the new river bridge (which was almost complete but not quite). That section of road was not yet built up high enough to clear serious flooding. At the same time there was growing interest in doing something about the steepness of north-south roads between Market and Hill streets. Wabash Street was especially difficult to navigate, rising more precipitously to Hill than other streets, dipping where the railroad tracks had plowed through, and then continuing to rise sharply to Maple Street. It dawned on some officials that two problems might be solved with a single project, by building a levy or causeway from the canal to the river with material dug out of the streets on the bluff. Though that specific solution may not have worked out as easily as envisioned, eventually five hundred dollars in private and public funds were spent to create the desired causeway across the floodplain.[42]

The issues involved seemed to have sparked a renewed effort. The town council promulgated a spate of ordinances dealing with "pavements" (sidewalks), grading, "bouldering" (street guttering), and graveling, with specifications for each. Privies closer than eight feet from the street were forbidden. Property owners were generally the ones responsible for sidewalks in front of their homes or businesses. There were also tax assessments for other improvements, though a citizen short on cash could work out his share with labor or goods. The flagstone pavements used for walks, which were locally available in large quantity and sometimes could be had for the taking from creek beds and banks, were to be at least 1.5 inches thick and were to be laid seven to ten feet wide, depending on location. Some streets seemed to blossom under relatively little care. Once it received a gravel coating, for example, Elm Street became one of the most desirable residential stretches in town, at least for a while. The council specified that Canal Street, which was especially heavily traveled and the first graveled street in town, should also have "gutters" along each side by the curbing. At the edge of the gutter the street gravel should be seven inches thick and rise to eleven inches in the middle of the street. The expectation was that rainwater would run off packed gravel into the gutters formed by the larger stones or boulders. Similar treatment was scheduled for other downtown streets. In addition, town and county officials joined in appropriating several hundred dollars to replace the canal bridge at the foot of Wabash Street. It was to be a double-track bridge with pedestrian walks on each side.[43]

The south-north ascents of Wabash, Miami, and Cass streets had been graded many times, although not seriously reconfigured. Grading seemed mostly to have been a matter of smoothing out the bumps in the dirt surface, getting rid of rocks and stumps, and creating enough central rise in the surface that water might flow to the edges. For several years Miami may have been a preferred south-to-north thoroughfare because its rise was more gentle than that of Wabash Street. In the spring of 1863, however, the town took on the monumental engineering challenge of subduing the Wabash Street hill, a feat that may have resulted in the most dramatic topographical change in the town's early history. The truth of such a statement depends on exactly how much dirt and stone were moved from the area where Wabash and Main streets crossed. One report in the *Intelligencer* suggests that the bluff at that point was lowered by nearly twenty feet. It is unfortunate that the earliest photograph of Wabash (1866), in which the old courthouse seems to stand quite high on the southeast quadrant of the Public Square, does not show anything of Wabash Street itself or the recent work that had been done on it. The street's rise from Hill to Maple, also more formidable than it appeared in later years, was cut down by several feet. Whatever the exact proportions of the change, the result was a much more gradual ascent from downtown to uptown. The work likely facilitated construction of public buildings and businesses along the ascent of the Wabash Street corridor. It was surely the largest earth-moving, bluff-carving project in Wabash before the "cut" was made through "Limestone Hill" near Paradise Spring.[44]

The Civil War came to a welcome end on April 9, 1865, with the surrender of Robert E. Lee at Appomattox Courthouse. Wabash exploded with jubilation, the town's bells rang out, and citizens poured out of their homes to celebrate. Among the celebrants in the streets were several members of Ford's family, but not the doctor himself. He was confined to bed, being well into his second year of recovery from a desperate bout of typhoid fever contracted at the battlefront. But the momentous event at hand and the pandemonium he could hear from the streets inspired Ford to attempt something fit for the occasion. Still dressed in night shirt and armed with his musket, he managed the steep stairs to the flat part of the house roof, where he fired the musket in celebration. When Mrs. Ford returned home to check on her husband, he had disappeared from his sickbed. It was some time before family members located him—out cold on the roof, knocked unconscious by the recoil of the gun.[45]

Ford recovered fully to live until 1898, but less than a week after that musket shot a pistol shot killed Abraham Lincoln. Wabash and the rest of the North sank into shock and grief. The date was April 14, 1865. Bells tolled. At the courthouse's offices the next day, county clerk Elijah Hackleman, public servant and historian, stopped changing the date of the wood-framed calendar that hung on the wall, keeping it set at April 14 as a memorial to Lincoln and as a reminder of a tragic postscript to a terrible war. The calendar survived an 1870 fire and became one of the prized artifacts of the county's museum. Hackleman also traveled to Indianapolis later that month to watch Lincoln's funeral procession pass through the city. "I saw him twice," Hackleman reported; "Looks very natural—one vast concourse of mourning."[46]

Throughout 1865 and 1866, every time a company of soldiers returned home Wabash greeted it with public acclaim. All were grateful for the men's safety, proud of their accomplishments, and mindful once again of those who did not survive. One such reception is especially poignant. On a Monday evening late in January 1866, a particular company of soldiers arrived in town to be honored and feted as so many others had been at Wabash and around the country. The town hosted a dance at Union Hall downtown. The honored guests were Hoosier soldiers (their local origins unspecified) who had fought deep into the Confederacy, some of whom had survived a bloody confrontation at the siege of Petersburg, Virginia. These "boys in blue" happened to be so-called colored soldiers, African Americans who had served their nation well and were now welcomed back into the bosoms of their state, counties, and towns. Here were citizens for whose race the Civil War had largely been fought. January 1866 was not yet the era of Jim Crow laws, nor of seemingly intractable racial segregation, nor of the necessity of civil rights demonstrations in America's streets. No doubt there was unchallenged, assumed racial segregation at that dance; for example, blacks and whites would not have danced together. Yet, it seems also to have been a fete graciously hosted by a mostly white community for its black brothers, with both races participating and interacting.

In that sense the Union Hall dance was a dance about the future. It was a brief, incomplete, but shimmering glimpse of how things might some day be in a nation that had just committed massive slaughter in order to effect massive changes in human relationships. It was a dance about that still-far-away day when minorities of any stripe might be welcomed joyfully and enthusiastically into the hearts, homes, and families of the majority.[47]

WABASH COUNTY HISTORICAL MUSEUM

South Side Female Academy, 1870s, sited at the present-day corner of Vernon and Pike streets.

From the main canal dock looking northeast, late 1860s: (left) Hanna's Corner, occupied by the Palace of Fashion; (center) a major office complex; and visible on the bluff three houses that are extant in the twenty-first century, including at the east end the homes of W. G. Sayre and J. D. Conner.

Canal Street, looking east from Miami Street, circa late 1850s–1870s. The photographer, Samuel Moore, was active in the 1860s and possibly earlier.

THOMAS B. HELM, *HISTORY OF WABASH COUNTY, INDIANA* (CHICAGO: JOHN MORRIS, 1884), 127

Wabash County Courthouse, artist's rendering, circa 1879–83.

WABASH COUNTY HISTORICAL MUSEUM

View of the 1883 flood, south from the courthouse roof.

WABASH COUNTY HISTORICAL MUSEUM

One of many Wabash barbershops, circa 1890s.

WABASH COUNTY HISTORICAL MUSEUM

The orphanage, circa 1890s. It was later the hospital and then the Women's Club House.

WABASH COUNTY HISTORICAL MUSEUM

The Goodlander (aka Commercial) Hotel on Canal Street east of Huntington Street, one of three or four hotels operating at the end of the nineteenth century.

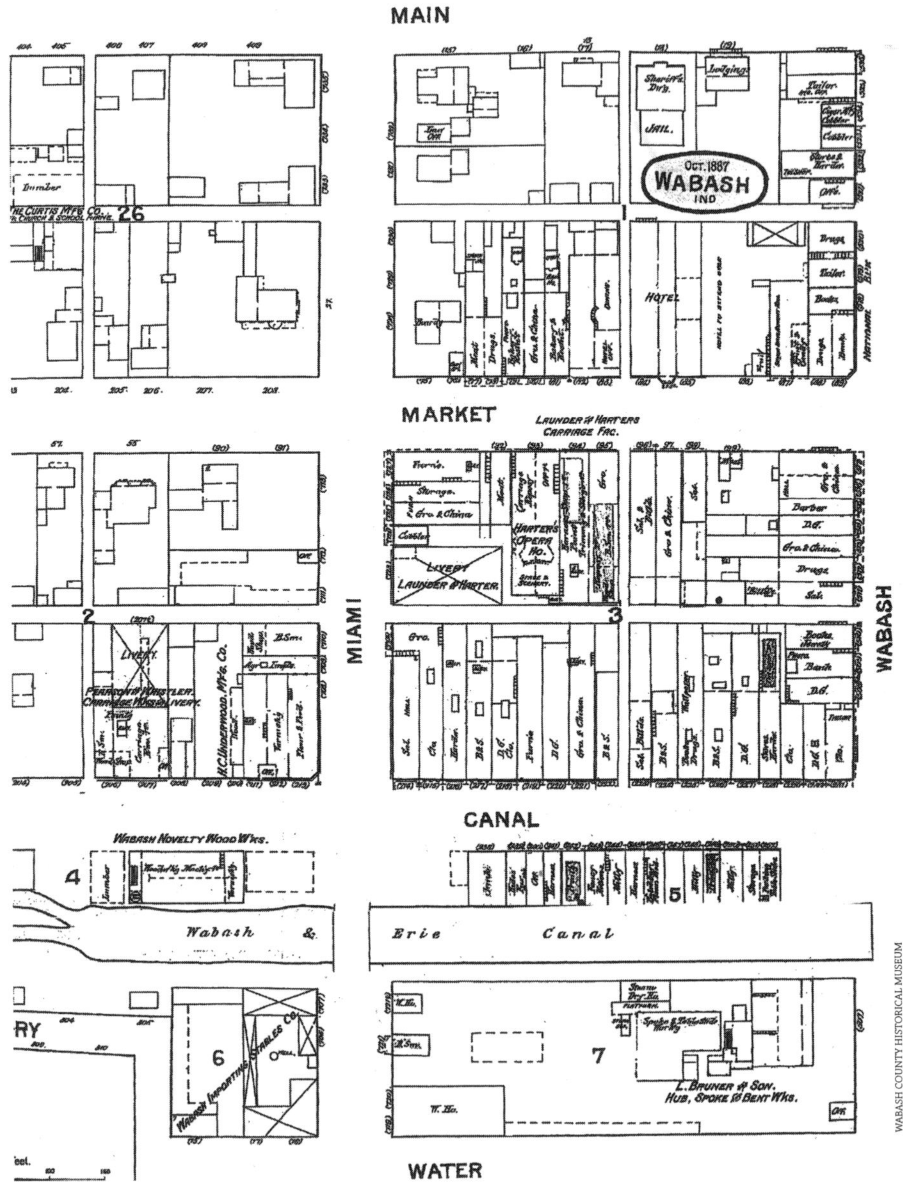

A section of an 1896 Sanborn insurance map showing a portion of the business area south of Main Street and west of Wabash Street.

CLARKSON WEESNER, *A HISTORY OF WABASH COUNTY*, 2 VOLS. (CHICAGO: LEWIS PUBLISHING COMPANY, 1914), 1:307

City Hall, Masonic Temple, 1880s.

WABASH COUNTY HISTORICAL MUSEUM

A political rally, 1884. The Haas novelty and dry goods shop and the Presbyterian church are in the background. Republican presidential hopeful James G. Blaine was reported to be present.

WABASH COUNTY HISTORICAL MUSEUM

Charles Little as a young man (1872) and as an older man (1897).

WABASH COUNTY HISTORICAL MUSEUM

CLARKSON WEESNER, *A HISTORY OF WABASH COUNTY*, 2 VOLS. (CHICAGO: LEWIS PUBLISHING COMPANY, 1914), 2:816

Leewell Carpenter.

WABASH COUNTY HISTORICAL MUSEUM

One of the oldest photos of Wabash (1866), showing a northern part of the town prior to the fire of 1870, explained in chapter 8.

8

A Photo, a Fire, and a Future

On a snowy December day in 1866, Samuel W. Moore carried his photography equipment along Canal Street to the Hyman Building, probably located on the north side just west of the central alley. Michael Hyman and his family were among the earliest Jewish residents of Wabash, arriving in 1852, and were active in the synagogue (Rodef Shalom) formed in 1868. The Hymans were merchants, specializing in clothing, who later expanded into oil and wool milling. Their Canal Street building was possibly three stories high, with the upper stories likely used for storage and rental. Moore climbed to the top level, stood before a window overlooking the alley, aimed his camera toward the north, and snapped a photo of central Wabash. The result is the oldest known image of a major portion of the town. Of the twenty or so structures visible in the photo, only one survived to the twenty-first century. The rest represent a face of Wabash that has disappeared, save for alleys, streets, and the bluff. Among many interesting aspects revealed in this view of the town is the fact of so few trees. Granted, it is a winter scene, bereft of foliage generally—there is one lone tree of respectable size growing in the middle of an alley—but the overall aspect of the place indicates how booms in home building must have stripped the forest from the center of Wabash. It also suggests that Naaman Fletcher's campaign to encourage citizens to plant shade trees had not yet taken root. Indeed, two years earlier Fletcher's *Wabash Intelligencer* had printed a remark that much of Wabash looked like a "vast clearing."[1]

Posterity is grateful not only for the survival of Moore's unique photograph but also for the fact that thirty-one years after it was snapped an enterprising reporter from the *Wabash Morning Times* interviewed Moore at his home on Ferry Street. The reporter wanted identification of buildings in the picture. Having milked Moore's memory on that score, the reporter then spoke with Elijah Hackleman about the photo. Moore and Hackleman provided the *Times* with clear identification of homes, businesses, and public buildings, as well as a few vignettes related to some of the structures.

Near the center of the photograph is a large house that stands at almost the highest elevation in town, sporting an ornate cupola or widow's walk. It is Doctor Elias Hubbard's home, built just prior to the Civil War. Hubbard was the county treasurer in 1866, and two years later he was ensnared in a scandal over his use of public funds. His political enemies claimed he had embezzled thirty thousand dollars. His friend and attorney, John L. Knight, agreed that Hubbard had foolishly gambled away sixteen hundred dollars on the Chicago commodities market but that the total sum missing from the county's coffers was only about eighty-five hundred dollars. Either way, these were huge sums. Hubbard's defense was absent-mindedness; he had, he said, kept putting old soldiers' bounty vouchers in an unsecured desk drawer, from which they had been filched. Knight organized enough character witnesses to get Hubbard off on the basis of his promise to repay the eighty-five hundred dollars, with interest, within two years. After the scandal died down Hubbard may have left town for a time to practice medicine in Lagro, but in 1897 Moore believed he had been living in his Wabash house in the intervening years. The house in the 1866 photo stood on the west side of North Wabash Street not far from the Maple Street corner. It may have been sited on a somewhat elevated patch of ground that has since been graded down.[2]

To the far left of the photo on ground slightly higher than the Hubbard lot rise the twin towers of Union School, later called Central School, which had been built in 1859 and was, at the time of the photo, the town's only school, housing all grades. In front of the school and toward the east is the only building in the 1866 photo to have survived to the twenty-first century. The perspective of the photograph makes it appear to be quite close to the school when, in fact, it is located almost three blocks south, at 54 West Hill Street directly across from Court Street. It was the Jacob Sailors home in 1866. For many years in the twentieth century it was owned by Homer Hipskind, a local hardware dealer. Subsequently it was turned into an office building. Sailors arrived in the Wabash area in 1841 and became a successful dry goods merchant, served as a county commissioner, and, in 1876 and 1877, was a representative to the state legislature.

Across Hill Street from Sailor's house stood the jail, a two-story brick structure that subsumed within itself the older, single-story log jail. A high stone wall shored it up on its southern side. It contained two cells on the first floor and an upper, one-room bullpen where the more serious offenders were incarcerated. Supervision of inmates was not always professional. According to Hackleman, a horse thief once slipped out when Sheriff James Furrow opened the door to feed the inmates and ran north toward the woods. Brandishing a weapon and shouting threats, the sheriff gave chase but failed to secure the jail door behind him, so a second horse thief walked out and sat on a fence to watch the chase. When the jailer returned, the second prisoner was still there. "Why in thunder didn't you run?" Furrow asked. "The race was so interesting," the man replied, "that I didn't think of it." The sheriff pushed the man inside the jail. "Humph," he said, "I don't believe you know enough to steal a horse."

To the far right in Moore's photograph is the New School Presbyterian Church. Its steeple contained one of the first bells in town, which was rung not only as a call to worship but also to alert the town to fires and other important events. After the congregation sold the church structure the bell became the community's official fire alarm when the courthouse was temporarily housed there. Eventually Saint Matthew's Congregational Church acquired the bell, housed it in its steeple at Huntington and Walnut streets, and moved it in the twentieth century to the new sanctuary of Saint Matthew's United Church of Christ at 1717 North Wabash Street. There it hangs in the twenty-first century, still an ecclesiastical ornament. Except for the Sailor house it is the only extant artifact represented in the 1866 photo. According to Hackleman, the church in the photograph had stood quite high above the street level—possibly left at an ungainly height when the hill was severely graded downward during the Civil War—but in subsequent years the church was lowered and moved a few feet to the south.[3]

The most prominent structure pictured is Hugh Hanna's 1839–40 courthouse. The angle of its dome-top flagpole speaks of the increasing dilapidation of the building, though it was only twenty-five or twenty-six years old. However, Hackleman remembered its grounds as a beautiful park where children frolicked all year long, building snow forts in winter and playing games in summer, with the girls wearing bright dresses and the boys in knickerbockers. During the Civil War volunteers drilled in the park. At one drill session the officer in charge, forgetting the terrain, fell to his death over the retaining wall. Hackleman also commented on the popularity of the Wabash Street hill for winter sledding and noted that the town's decision to restrict that activity to Miami Street was not popular, presumably because that street was a bit tamer in its descent.

In the middle foreground of the 1866 photo and situated east of the alley and north of Market Street is the commodious house built by Madison Whiteside, a prominent businessman. Moore was a fan of Mrs. Whiteside's garden around this house, stating that citizens made a point of taking visitors from out of town to see its flowers, which bloomed abundantly from early spring until frost. Whiteside also owned the building across Market Street to the south. He was to sell that property for $750 worth of horses; folks thought Whiteside had made a good trade. It was later acquired by a member of the Herff family, a successful group of Jewish entrepreneurs. The Whiteside home was eventually sold also, for $6,000 cash, to become the Tremont Hotel, which would later be replaced by a larger building under the same title.[4] The Tremont name survived into the twenty-first century as the Tremont Parking Lot, located where the hotel had stood.

South of the Whiteside property, along both sides of the north-south alley between Market and Canal streets, are several frame buildings. The three on the west side of the alley, north to south, are thought to be, respectively, William Launder's blacksmith shop and carriage factory, a stable, and, in the foreground, apparently behind the Hyman Building, a small shop where Charlie Herff later ran a liquor store. Two of the buildings on the east side of the alley were not identified by Moore or Hackleman, but Moore remembered that the largest and southernmost structure was a clothing store that later became a saloon. The name of the saloon was The Blue Front, possibly because of its paint job, but temperance advocates called it "The Blue Ruin." Just to the east of it, but not in the photo, was its competitor, "The Red Ruin."[5]

Moore's photograph, plus his and Hackleman's explanations of it, are especially valuable because they reveal the town just prior to a transformation. Concurrent with Moore's photographic view of Wabash is a written one that appeared in the *Cincinnati Gazette* and was reported in the *Wabash Plain Dealer* in May 1867. It was titled "Letter from Wabash." The reporter wrote of the "elongated" appearance of the town, running east to west along the canal. He was struck by the adjacent limestone hills, the surrounding woods, and the "fountains of clear, living water." It was one of the "prettiest, liveliest towns in the state." The whole place seemed to be "paved" (had sidewalks) in limestone. Citizens were sprightly, fashionable, and intelligent, although not so social as some in remote villages. The canal was still in good working order, with many boats loading pork and timber. There was a great company of businessmen and "neat and commodious" churches and schools.[6] This essentially was the town, described in words, that Moore had captured on film six months earlier. Three years after "Letter from Wabash" appeared and three and a half years after Moore's photograph was taken, significant portions of Wabash disappeared forever in the fire of 1870. In three or four decades, everything in the photo except the Sailors house was gone.

As with all towns in the nineteenth century, fire was a source of enormous anxiety. Wabash's advantage against it was the canal, a ready source of water. However, delivering that water quickly and in sufficient quantity to the site of a fire was a perennial frustration. Brick had become the building material of choice because of its fire resistance; yet roof beams, shingles, and floors were still highly combustible. Then, too, the bluff presented its own special challenge. Even after the town could afford professional firefighting equipment to siphon water from the canal with reasonable efficiency, the upper reaches of Wabash remained outside the range of effective water delivery. In addition to canal water the only sources in the early decades were the natural springs, such as Paradise Spring, and the wells homeowners and businessmen sank on private property. A "Fire Company" existed from the 1850s, but whether it used canal, spring, or well water, its delivery of a steady stream of it to a fire site frequently required a bucket brigade manned by a host of volunteers.[7]

The 1870 fire epitomized the specter of fear that all earlier Wabash fires had raised—the idea that a fire might not be contained at its source but would leap from building to building. In that sense the Mammoth Building blaze in 1849, while it destroyed Commercial Row's major retail anchor at the northeast corner of Canal and Wabash streets, and was undoubtedly the talk of the town for many days, had disrupted commerce and folks' lives in a relatively contained way. Not so was the spectacular Bruner and King fire of 1861 that began in J. L. Bruner's hardware emporium, located on Canal Street. On a Sunday night George King, Bob Polk, and a Mr. Taylor were all sleeping in a room above the ground-floor store. About midnight King woke up in thick black smoke and roused the other two. They could not get the backstairs door to open. Not having time to dress, the men grabbed their clothes and made for a front window. With Polk almost overcome by smoke, the three dropped to the street. Help quickly arrived. When the front door was broken in, however, the fire was already too hot to approach. In a half hour the front of the building was consumed. Flames spread to the back where they were fierce enough in spots to melt supplies of nails but, conversely, left many hardware items in good condition.[8]

Adjoining businesses were in jeopardy almost immediately. The roof of the Hyman brothers' building caught fire. There were no ladders available just then to reach that high, so the whole structure was lost, including, presumably, a new iron front that was being attached at the time. The Lumaree Building, a three-story brick that shared common walls with the west side of Bruner and King, was soon aflame on its second and third stories. A substantial metal roof saved it from destruction by containing flames until water arrived. However, one hundred to two hundred feet of roof and much of the second floor interior would have to be replaced. A building owned by a Mr. McGuire also sustained severe-to-total damage. Farther east on Canal Street, owners such as James D. Conner began emptying their stores and offices of books, papers, and other portable valuables. Even Hanna's Corner, at the extreme east end of that block, was threatened, and firefighters unnecessarily broke its upper windows as a preliminary step in saving the place. On the other hand, "a perfectly calm atmosphere" among other firefighters was credited with saving Hanna's wooden sheds and stable at the back of the property. In the end damage along Canal Street was estimated to be in excess of $10,000, with about one-third of it covered by insurance.[9]

The tumult, excitement, and anxiety were at times as intense as the flames, especially among those who understood that the whole business district, if not much of the town, was threatened and so pitched in accordingly. It is also true, however, that the Bruner and King fire revealed another side of local character. The editor of the *Intelligencer* wrote a blistering attack on those who saw the fire as only so much entertainment, who watched but did nothing to help. At one point he estimated there were about two dozen of these "noble specimens of the genus homo" who, with the "gallantry of bears," stood around with their hands in their pockets.[10] At another point he pushed the number to "hundreds" who proved worthless. Meanwhile, those who did their share of time in the bucket brigade could not manage a consistent supply of water in sufficient amounts to quench the flames. The one tactic that did prove beneficial in the case of large buildings was hauling water to the rooftops, where it seems to have helped contain the conflagration.[11]

Time and again such fires threatened Wabash, though only one or two were as potentially disastrous as the Bruner and King fire. It is remarkable, though not unusual for the times, that Wabash had electricity and telephones before it had a modern water system, the former being generally available by the early 1880s. It would not be until about 1887 that a fully operable firefighting operation, with one hundred hydrants, would be in place. Until then improvements materialized only slowly and in fits and starts. A fire brigade organized (or reorganized) in 1866 used a horse-drawn pump and later added a hook-and-ladder component. As the century progressed, large cisterns capable of holding up to eight hundred gallons of water were located about town in a systematic pattern so that no area would be without protection. In this way even buildings on the bluff were theoretically within range of fire hoses. The Fire Department, as the brigade was now minted, moved into City Hall in 1885, placing it halfway between downtown and uptown. Despite advances, those who fought fires were long dependent on scores of citizens willing to move water in bucket lines. It was also true that early pumping devices frequently proved faulty in one way or another, if not in the mechanical pump itself, then with the hoses attached to the machinery. Perhaps typical of the attendant frustrations was the response of a band of firefighters who, in disgust at their pump's repeated failure, threw it upside down into the canal.[12]

Like the great Chicago fire a year later, the great Wabash fire of 1870 seems to have started in a barn and was whipped into a fury by prevailing winds. It originated in the southwest end of town where Charles Herff owned a barn located near a foundry, some wooden sheds, a wagon shop, and at least one sizable storehouse. It is believed that on Thursday afternoon, April 14, 1870, a cinder from the foundry wafted into the barn, settling on the dry hay there. The barn was soon afire. A wind from the west picked up its flaming shingles and "light combustible matter" and spewed them eastward. The sheds caught, then the wagon shop, and then the storehouse. Hundreds of citizens turned out. So did the Fire Department, "one bucket strong," according to Thad Butler of the *Wabash Republican*. Firefighters manned a hand engine, a pumping device that sucked up canal water. Butler admitted that the pump, formerly the subject of public derision, paid for itself that day, although the hose attached to it was problematic. The barn, the sheds, the wagon shop, and the storehouse all collapsed in flames. The winds began carrying burning material to the business district along the north side of Canal Street.[13]

Just then came a break. The winds subsided or shifted direction. Canal Street was saved. Confidence grew in the belief that the day was won. Such confidence reckoned without consideration of flying, flaming shingles. One such shingle had floated high over the downtown and lodged in the cupola of the courthouse. Others followed. As the courthouse burned "handsomely," the drama shifted again to the downtown. Canal Street was safe but not Market Street. The former Whiteside residence [the Tremont Hotel] caught its share of floating flames and was largely destroyed, despite intense efforts to save it. A bystander, befuddled into mindlessness by the crisis, rushed daringly inside, ran upstairs through flames and smoke and rescued a piece of stovepipe. A half block west of the Tremont, at the corner of Miami and Market streets, the home of a Mr. Sweetser caught fire. On an opposite corner of the same intersection so did the Payne Furniture House. That fire was contained, broke out again, was contained, broke out again, and finally was extinguished for good. Meanwhile, back at the Tremont, a stable combusted, taking with it the sole fatality of the day, a mule.

Now the fire of 1870 spread into a truly memorable event. The courthouse was already burning. Next to it the one-story building housing county offices caught the flame. Many years earlier, not long after Hanna finished the courthouse, the state had mandated that the records of all counties must be given fireproof accommodation. In compliance, county commissioners had built a three-room office building on the public square northeast of the courthouse; a fourth room was added later. To make the offices fireproof, or at least fire retardant, they covered the ceilings with eight inches of sand, adding a sprinkling system to keep the sand moist. It worked. County records survived the 1870 fire. So did Hackleman's memorial to Abraham Lincoln—the calendar he had stopped the day of the assassination, at April 14, 1865. (The day of the fire was, coincidentally, the fifth anniversary of Lincoln's death. If we did not have Hackleman's testimony to the contrary, it would be easy to have assumed that the calendar was from 1870 and not 1865, since it did not record the year.)[14]

Meanwhile flaming shingles and other debris were flying everywhere. The New School Presbyterian Church, across Wabash Street from the courthouse, was burning, along with the railroad freight depot, a grain house, and several buildings north of the tracks. At one point every building in the block east of the courthouse was on fire. Although Hackleman stated that "about fifty houses [were] on fire at one time," the bulk of them east of Wabash Street, this was likely an overestimate based on how desperate the situation appeared to be at the height of the drama.[15] Most of the many house fires must have been extinguished by the property owners, and fairly quickly. The newspaper credited women with being at the forefront of the effort, doing their share while putting to shame the "Its" who stood on corners with their hands in their pockets. The point was that, for a brief spell, it must have seemed as if flames ruled. Hanna had died the year before. Was Hanna's town largely doomed as well?

It did not happen. Either because the winds died and shifted or because Chief Hezekiah Caldwell's firefighters persevered against great odds, or both, the crisis abated about four o'clock in the afternoon. There had been no deaths, and there was very little looting during the crisis. But there were stories to share, which the editor of the *Wabash Republican* latched onto with poorly disguised glee. While the fire was raging, two ladies living in the western part of town, well out of the fire's range, pumped water into every container they could get their hands on and took them to the roof of their home, determined to save it. When Market Street was in flames, a citizen rushed down the hill toting a bucket with no bottom to it. A farmer who happened to be in town stopped his team at the corner of Market and Miami streets to watch spellbound what was unfolding, oblivious to some boys who were disengaging his wagon from the horses because it was on fire. Such stories perhaps lightened the load a trifle for those who, in fact, lost a great deal. Preliminary estimates by the *Republican* put the loss to businesses at more than $5,700, of which about roughly half was uninsured. The county treasurer lost a packet of money totaling $92.60. The loss of the courthouse was anyone's guess. Thad Butler of the *Plain Dealer* called it "an old shell" and put its value at between ten cents and $125,000. In the same vein, the *Republican*'s office, he thought, was worth at least one shirt collar and a suspender button.[16]

The great Wabash fire of 1870 provides a useful marker in the town's history, between what had been and was to be. Economic and cultural changes had already gained momentum by the 1860s, but now the town would never look the same. It might never feel quite the same again either. Much of what was lost to fire were shabby remnants of a more primitive past. This was especially true of the courthouse. Long before 1870, citizens had complained that the "old barrack" was an eyesore. It was forlorn, rudely patched in places, brown with age on the outside, grimy plaster falling, and furniture broken on the inside. Its passing symbolized that Wabash had truly entered its postwar era—decades of generally accelerated prosperity and beautification. Across the nation as a whole, forces were coming together for change. Railroads, the steel industry, oil and mining investments, new inventions, growing markets, and ready money transformed communities after the Civil War. Although America's economy would hit periods of hard times in the next thirty years, and Wabash's with it, the Gilded Age was under way. Much of the rest of Wabash's story in the nineteenth century reflects the aggrandizements of that period. The 1870 fire surely accelerated the desire of many Wabash citizens to put the rugged, log-cabin past of the frontier forever behind them. Like others in America they now strove for much more than ways to make ends meet. They were primed for acquisition, comfort, style, and wealth. Such goals were frequently achieved, though poverty, racism, gender inequities, crime, and various forms of unsavory human behavior managed to keep apace beneath the gilded veneer.[17]

Was Wabash ready for its Gilded Age? Was it equipped to become something far more sophisticated and modern than a maturing but still somewhat rustic village? No surprise, much remained that was reminiscent of an ungainly past: streets turned to mud in a downpour; public sanitation remained minimal in some parts of town; and homeowners had to surround new shade trees with osage orange fencing to protect them from the ubiquity of roaming cattle and hogs that chewed on the bark. Fortunately changes punctuated by the 1870 drama were already under way, powered by an economy and by local governmental structures that had been maturing for several years. On those scores rustication was fading fast.

Wabash's pork industry had stoked the town's economy even before the Civil War. By 1860 Wabash was a colossal abattoir, a veritable killing ground during the peak winter seasons. The leaders were the prince of pork, Josiah Daugherty, and his partner, J. B. Lumaree. They had been in the business since the mid-1850s, but during the war their enterprise expanded at two locations, one downtown and one on Charley Creek west of the fairgrounds. Downtown they built a two-story brick packinghouse, forty by sixty-six feet, at the corner of Market and Wabash. It stood over a cellar that, if it resembled its neighbors, was dug deep between thick foundation walls of local limestone.[18]

The Charley Creek complex was nestled at the base of the bluff about a hundred yards north of where Hill and Mill streets later intersected. There the stream made its last sharp turn to the south before burbling straight toward the river. A physical remnant of the enterprise is visible, though not obvious, in the twenty-first century in the form of a limestone foundation corner jutting from the bottom of the hillside. Although some packing may have been done here, it was primarily "a splendid slaughter house," forty by one hundred feet and two stories high. Inside were a massive boiler and "improved modern apparatus for slaughtering and [for] rendering up the offals [*sic*]," entrails that could also be processed for market.[19] Grounds adjacent to the building covered seven acres, representing the western end of what became City Park. During the 1860s the prices paid to farmers for their animals ranged broadly, from between two and seven dollars per live hundredweight. At peak season the firm employed sixty to seventy men, who earned $1.75 per diem. They regularly slaughtered four hundred fifty hogs a day and could produce twenty-seven barrels of lard in the same time. Waste material was dumped into the creek, to be flushed out to the river when the water flow was high and, doubtless, to fester odoriferously in dry weather. Nevertheless, the editor of the *Plain Dealer* pronounced the place "clean" and "sweet" when he toured it in the winter of 1867.[20]

The firm's products had plenty of competition, not only from other towns but also from packinghouses in Wabash. In the 1866 season, for example, J. D. Miles and Company processed five thousand hogs, each of which averaged three hundred pounds gross and two hundred thirty-five pounds net. Local competition was not especially critical, however, because the long-distance markets were hungry for pork. Wabash pork probably graced tables as far away as New York City, and it certainly did in Cincinnati with some regularity. Indeed, according to one report, an annual comment at Cincinnati markets was "the big drove from Wabash is coming."[21]

Because pork slaughtering was largely seasonal, men such as Daugherty pursued other interests. Daugherty, for example, was involved in banking, in woodworking and lumber businesses, and in canal boat transportation. He became the chief director of the huge and hugely successful Wabash School Furniture Company after 1873. Clearly Daugherty was an early representative of those nineteenth-century entrepreneurs who were not satisfied with a single career. He and many others pushed themselves to create multiple sources of wealth that, in turn, multiplied local jobs and raised the wealth of the whole town. In the twentieth century the Daugherty name would be remembered locally for an entirely different sort of enterprise. Josiah's daughter, Marie Daugherty Webster, became nationally famous as a designer of quilts and quilt patterns.[22]

Wood production and manufacture, more than pork, was the backbone of Wabash's nineteenth-century prosperity. In 1867 Kokomo boasted shipping 60,000 feet of lumber in a single week, but in the same timeframe one Wabash firm shipped 100,000 feet and three firms shipped 75,000 feet each, "and it wasn't a good week for lumber either!"[23] George Duck, who with his partner, W. V. Pressler, established a lumberyard on West Canal Street during the Civil War, represented another component of woodworking. Duck and Pressler manufactured screen doors, shingles, lath, sashes, blinds, wainscoting, scroll work, and various versions of "dress lumber." They brokered unfinished timber in large lots, shipped lumber out of the county, and were contract builders at home. Duck and Pressler claimed that it could "contract to build a house entire, and deliver the keys to the owner, with the house ready for occupancy."[24] Later in the century, Wabash's Duck and Yarnelle families intermarried so that the Duck and Pressler wood retail business continued uninterrupted into the twentieth and twenty-first centuries as the Yarnelle Lumber Company, still on West Canal Street.

The behemoth of Wabash woodworking was Thomas F. Payne's factory on Wabash Street just south of the canal. His storehouse and display rooms were on the southeast corner of Miami and Market streets. Payne began in Wabash in 1849 as an independent, twenty-three-year-old carpenter, branched into coffin manufacturing, then into a full line of funeral goods, and finally into a complete wooden furniture industry. As much as any Wabash biography, Payne's has overtones of that American dream in which a person of humble origins becomes a wealthy, respected citizen. As if to confirm for himself the reality of his success, Payne temporarily laid aside tools and account books for the first time in his adult life and, in 1883, set off on an extended tour of Europe. He was clearly an early Wabash version of the self-made American whose wealth supports a broadening interest in a world beyond work, one symptom of life in the Gilded Age. These early lumbering concerns such as Daugherty's, Duck's, and Payne's—were the vanguard of an industry that bolstered the local economy for decades, though some long-lived lumber businesses of note—W. P. Jones Company and B. Walter and Company—were not founded until later in the century.[25]

According to a report compiled in the 1870s, sawyers, cabinetmakers, and carpenters were in the medium-to-high range of pay for laboring men, below brick masons and paperhangers but better than stonecutters and railroad hands. They earned around $1.85 per diem. That range of pay suggests that Wabash could attract and keep a workforce able to maintain a home and family and, just possibly, get ahead in the world financially, albeit modestly. An unknown twentieth-century scholar of Wabash's nineteenth-century woodworking industry compiled an unpublished study that compares the wealth of fifty-two individual woodworkers in 1850 with their wealth in 1870. For example, as a twenty-three-year-old cabinetmaker in 1850, Payne had a total wealth, both real and personal, of $150. At age forty-three, now listed as a furniture dealer, Payne's real wealth was $24,000, and his personal wealth was $17,000. Sanford Honeywell, a twenty-year-old carpenter in 1850, was worth $1,200 in real wealth. By 1870 he was listed as a retired farmer with a personal fortune of $14,000. (Sanford was the father of Mark Honeywell, Wabash's future industrialist and benefactor. Aside from carpentry skills, Sanford was well known locally for the strawberries he grew and often shared.) William Whiteside, carpenter turned furniture dealer, increased his total wealth from $600 to $9,000 in twenty years. John Wilson's $85 grew to $13,000. Not all the laborers fared so well as these examples, but the increases in wealth generally are impressive enough to allow the conjecture that Wabash's economy was not only growing substantially, but that it was not leaving behind laborers in the woodworking industry. It might not be too large a jump in reason to speculate that laborers in other lines of work were also able to prosper, though at this juncture the scholarship on that has not been compiled. In any case, it is an indication of respectable social progress that many in the laboring section of the population worked in favorable economic conditions.[26]

Besides pork and lumber, a variety of other industries helped build the postwar economy. An inventory published by the *Plain Dealer* in 1867 listed the following manufacturing concerns: a chair factory; a wooden pump maker; two saddle and harness shops; two foundry/machine shops; two tin and sheet iron processors; two firms in the blacksmithing side of the carriage trade; a host of boot and shoemakers; two tanneries; a marble preparation shop; two brick kilns; King and McCrea's flour mill; at least three saw/planing mills; three coopers; Rettig and Alber's brewery, reputedly the biggest "this side of Toledo"; Whiteside, Steele and Company's canal-side woolen mill; and

Michael and Leonard Hyman's oil mill. At about this same time William H. Launder was turning out buggies, wagons, drays, and various blacksmithing articles in his building on Market Street.[27]

As these manufacturing enterprises prospered so did the numerous and quite competitive retail businesses. They were filling up storefront gaps along Canal, South Wabash, South Miami, and Market streets. Some stores were quite large, forerunners of later department stores. Gordon and Thurston's kept a huge inventory both in basement storage and on display on two floors above ground. This included lamps, cutlery, jewelry, wallpaper, clothes, paints, cigars, drugs, two thousand cases of quinine (for reasons medicinal), and (allegedly for the same reason) "imported wines and brandy."[28] Such merchants strove, seemingly with considerable success, to cater to any material whimsy on the minds of Wabash customers, offering merchandise and styles that were au courant in eastern urban centers. Perhaps all one needs by way of illustrating the economic and stylistic changes at hand is to know that, at about this time, the clothier, Henry Herff, rehabilitated the storeroom of the then-ancient Hanna's Corner and called it "The Wabash Palace of Fashion." Herff was importing goods from the East and from Cincinnati.[29]

This reach toward elegance extended to more than household goods and clothing. When W. D. Jones yearned for a new carriage in 1864, he contacted a Wabash man acting as agent for an Ohio buggy firm. Jones chose to order the Crane Neck Family Model, but he might just as easily have acquired the Phaeton, the Slide Seat, the Rockaway, the Spring and Market, the Jenny Lind, or the Prince Albert Trotting Buggy. Had he desired it, Jones could have taken his new buggy from his South Wabash residence to a shop downtown to have its exterior expertly and exquisitely detailed in gilt stenciling. Downtown was home also to three flourishing hotels—the Indiana, the Tremont, and the Center—that attracted a mostly respectable out-of-town clientele and offered restaurant and barbering services to the locals. The Tremont boasted of a "buss" that carried guests to and from the railroad depot. Unfortunately, the "buss," like other horse-drawn vehicles, was subject to the jeopardies of the Wabash Street hill where "runaways" could threaten life and limb by tumbling passengers into mud, gutters, or sidewalks. Such events were "frightfully frequent and common." It may be one reason a new hotel—the Passenger House—was in the works near the depot in 1868. Significantly, however, the local papers began more frequently to print flattering comments about the downtown area that had for so long been the target of journalistic barbs, though it is also possible that such comments appeared only in dry or freezing seasons when mud abated from the streets. Nevertheless, it was noted that local retailers were hanging merchandise outside along the streets, giving it good exposure and increasing sales. Furthermore, the shops' new exterior awnings shaded sidewalks and provided shelter from rain, making downtown strolls quite pleasant. Indeed, in the summer of 1867, the *Plain Dealer*'s editor, being fed up with braggadocio claims of progress from other towns, totaled the past year's sales of just five downtown businesses. It came to $293,968 (worth more than four million dollars in 2010 figures). Five short years later the *Republican* announced that the total worth of Wabash business activity for the previous year (1871) exceeded two million dollars (more than thirty-four million dollars in 2010). This was not antebellum Wabash.[30]

As if to signal that an accelerated economy was truly on the march, a second railroad—variously called the Cincinnati, Wabash and White Pigeon, the Cincinnati, Wabash and Michigan, and, more permanently, the Cincinnati, Cleveland, Chicago and Saint Louis (the Big Four)—stirred the place with its presence just two years after the conflagration of 1870. The Big Four had already been in the works for several years, so that just one month and five days following the fire a surveying team for the new railroad reached town, a significant milestone. The slow, deliberate approach of the line was faithfully reported to the public. First, trains had come as far south as North Manchester. Then, grading had reached two miles south of Urbana. Next, construction gangs were tackling the "greatest task," bringing the line down an eight hundred-foot-long cut to the bottomland, "through resistant clay," from a fifty-foot-high elevation.[31] In late July 1872 Thad Butler rode by train from north of Wabash to Goshen through North Manchester, Silver Lake, and Leesburg. The ties were well laid, he wrote, so that the ride was very smooth. Soon after Butler's ride a train from Grand Rapids, Michigan, was the first to arrive at a new Wabash depot on the extension of East Market Street.[32]

Being a north-south route that complemented the older east-west railroad, the Big Four put Wabash at a transportation crossroads, making it a considerable railroad burg. The town also happened to be located at a midway point in northern Indiana, was equal in population to other towns on the line, and had the canal as a water source. These factors contributed to the location of a roundhouse and maintenance shops on what, in 1872, was still referred to as the Hanna estate, previously called the Treaty Ground. Over the coming decades the shops supported scores of Wabash families. Their presence also caused a complete reconfiguration of topography at that end of town. What had once been a sylvan Miami watering place, then the locus for the 1826 treaty, then the headquarters for newcomers, then the site of derelict log cabins, and then the fairgrounds was now filled in and leveled over to accommodate immensely heavy train engines and cars. There is some evidence that by the late 1870s the old Paradise/Hanna Spring was largely forgotten, its covering collapsing, as wagons crossed over it. Creation of the 1896 cut through the limestone bluff completed the transformation. One estimate is that the elevation of Paradise Spring Park (2010) is at least three feet higher than the original Treaty Ground because of cinder, rock, and rubble fill.[33]

That indomitable civic leader, Calvin Cowgill, was the primary mastermind behind both the creation of a new rail line and the location of the shops. A personal reason Cowgill may have championed the north-south route was the inconvenience of having to go to Peru first in order to travel south, as he often needed to do. It is also true that his Wabash compatriots, John L. Knight and Warren G. Sayre, had tried to get to Indianapolis in 1871, only to end up with Sayre having to ride in a boxcar for part of the trip and Knight resorting to a sleigh. In any case, Cowgill was Wabash's point man in a struggle with the courts to obtain state approval of countywide taxing for the north-south railroad; these taxes raised the needed $6,000 per mile to pay for construction through the county. Cowgill was also among those local politicians who convinced the Wabash Common Council to appropriate approximately $45,000 (for a variety of projects) so that the Big Four would develop extensive rail yards on East Market Street that would create jobs for Wabash men. At about the time the Big Four was reaching Wabash, Cowgill was also in consultation with folks who wanted to press for a railroad to Kokomo in order to gain access to coal and wood. Both commodities were important to Wabash industries, coal for firing furnaces, wood for the lumber and woodworking concerns. Kokomo already had a rail line going west to coalfields and, presumably, there were untimbered forests in that direction. If Wabash could connect with that source in an economically advantageous way it would enhance the town's prospects even more. Cost was estimated at $4,000 per mile. Apparently the task of financing one railroad was enough. Enthusiasm for a line to Kokomo waned and disappeared.[34]

In order to understand how this new prospering and expansive city of Wabash was to be organized and governed through the rest of the nineteenth century, it is necessary to look back at its political and organizational roots. The basic characteristics of the town's political climate and of its governmental components grew out of antebellum conditions, but the Civil War itself did much to confirm certain realities of the past, especially the political ones.

Necessarily, as the town had grown from a village, governance and the politics of governance became more obvious and more complicated. Although parts of the county, such as Lagro Township, had been heavily Democratic from the start, the county seat began life as a Whig (later Republican) stronghold. However, so long as pioneer and village conditions prevailed, politics had remained fairly personal rather than partisan, in the sense that the community had tended to depend, first, on its founding fathers and, second, on succeeding prominent citizens to be its political and government leaders. Hugh Hanna had fairly and openly been selected first treasurer of the county, but he did not actively campaign for that position. It fell to him in what was probably a small, friendly tavern caucus of the county commissioners and was a natural choice more than a political one. The same was true of so many other important officers. If one were heavily invested in the start-up of Wabash, or in its early growth, that person might logically be tapped for an official town function. Officeholders had tended to be folks nearly everyone in town knew either by name recognition, by sight, or by both.

In early 1849 the state legislature approved the town's first incorporation papers, providing for an elected board of trustees with power to levy taxes, issue licenses, authorize public improvements, impose fines, punish offenders, and appoint a number of the town's officers. This just put an official stamp on what was already being done in Wabash. In this system the highest official in town was the president of a board of trustees named by the elected board. Daniel M. Cox was the first president. John L. Knight was clerk, William O. Ross, treasurer, Albert Pawling, marshal, and Henry B. Olin, assessor. (Ross and Pawling—and possibly Olin—all have direct descendants who, while not sharing their surnames, persist under equally prominent surnames in Wabash in the twenty-first century.)[35]

The first incorporation was followed, in 1854, by a more complicated one that sliced the town into five narrow north-south wards or districts whose trustees oversaw the well-being of their respective areas. This version of government proved to be only a stopgap because it did not provide for enough comprehensive planning to satisfy a growing town. As the population neared 2,900 souls, the *Plain Dealer* raised the cry, "Shall Wabash Be a City?"[36] The

Fifth Ward, which lay west of Cass Street, was by far the largest with more than a thousand residents, an indication that the town was bulging westward toward the fairgrounds. Annexations in that direction had already taken place.[37]

By act of state government, Wabash technically became a city in 1866. The ward boundaries were redrawn and reduced in number. The new status gave the city authority not only within the corporation boundaries but also over parts of the county lying within two miles of Wabash. City laws applied only to the city, but Wabash could maintain rudimentary law and order in the surrounding area and, presumably, could effect annexations from it more easily. City status also meant that Wabash would have a mayor and a common council. Joseph H. Matlock was the first mayor. Although not a resident of long standing, he was a well-known lawyer, having served as both a prosecuting attorney and a judge. Even better known, because of activities in business and/or education circles, were several of the earliest councilmen: Joseph Mackey, William Steele Jr., J. D. Miles, and Josiah Daugherty. It seems clear that Wabash's governance was still very much in the hands of folks who were movers and shakers in nonpolitical venues and whose hold on high office prevailed deep into the century. As mayor, Matlock was followed by Warren G. Sayre, Clarkson W. Weesner, and Charles S. Parrish, each a substantial citizen in his own right. No doubt these were men savvy in political matters, but they did not have the aura of rough-and-tumble, professional politicos.[38]

Not surprisingly, however, the political activity behind the outward, rather stately succession of natural leaders became intermittently contentious as years passed. During the 1850s the prelude to the Civil War had torn folks apart as they argued over the issues of popular sovereignty, abolitionism, and the specter of secession. Before war actually broke out, Wabash Democrats generally voiced tolerance of the South's institution of slavery as a way of preserving the Union and eschewed the thought of secession. Although Stephen A. Douglas of Illinois spoke for many local Democrats in the 1860 election, he did irrevocable harm to his candidacy in Wabash when he passed through on a train in September that year. Interested citizens had gathered at the depot to hear him. His train ran two hours late, not arriving until almost one o'clock in the morning. The great man came to a car platform in his stocking feet and bareheaded, said something like "My fellow citizens!" and headed back to bed. Wabash Republicans called him "little fellow" and "little sucker." He did not carry Wabash.[39]

Republicans of the period were, by comparison with Democrats at least, the liberal party of progress and, as such, were united in opposing the extension of slavery. Robert Cissna and Alonson P. Ferry, both prominent citizens, were two of the very few Republicans whose names were connected with the term abolitionist, a label for the far-left wing of the party, though whether Cissna and Ferry fully qualified is uncertain. There were other citizens whom Democrats accused of being "Black Republicans," meaning that they were as close to being abolitionists as was possible without actually declaring it. Relatively few abolitionists, however, were so radical (for the times) as to be antiracist. Many of them would have been happy to free all the slaves so that they could be promptly shipped to Africa. Most Wabash Republicans, by contrast to abolitionists, were in the Abraham Lincoln camp from the start of the campaign because he clearly stumped for the preservation of the Union and the curtailment of slavery. Emancipation was not yet on Lincoln's public plate. In the minds of leaders such as Hanna and Conner there had never been any other candidate once they returned from the Chicago convention that nominated "Old Abe." Cowgill and John Pettit turned part of their law office over to be used as a Republican headquarters in Wabash and Hanna hoisted his Lincoln banner at Hanna's Corner. As the election of 1860 neared, the *Plain Dealer* did its part to get out the Republican vote, calling for mass participation in public rallies and crying in print, "Remember the Ides of November are upon us!"[40]

Local Republicans were helped immensely when W. C. McGonigal, the *Plain Dealer*'s publisher, flipped his paper from the Democratic side to the Republican in the summer of 1860. The national issues were tough on Democrats locally, for no matter how "soft" they may have been about slavery and its extensions, they could not bring themselves to continence secession and were fearful of sounding wishy-washy in support of the Union. George Ruddle, a local Democrat, was very proud of an American flag he had purchased in Cincinnati. His brother, a Unionist, asked him what he would do if someone desecrated it. "By the eternal I would shoot him," Ruddle replied. Retorted the brother, "No, you wouldn't. You would compromise with him and settle the matter."[41] The fact is that during the war many Wabash Democrats put up with being labeled as Unionists, that alliance of Democrats and Republicans who supported Lincoln as a way of saving the Union. By the time of an 1863 election, the Unionists captured a 964 majority in the county and a 416 majority in Noble Township (including Wabash). Although individual races for local offices could stir up animosity, in general the Unionist cause thinly papered over normal political divisions while the war raged.[42]

In the end Lincoln carried the county in 1860 by 1,100 votes and Noble Township (including Wabash) with 800 votes out of 1,076 cast. Rain canceled a victory celebration the weekend after the polling, but the following Monday citizens poured into the public square. Some came bearing a twenty-foot-long-hollow sycamore trunk, which they filled with tar, resin, pitch, turpentine, rails, shavings, and wood. About 5:00 p.m. the Lagro brass band arrived by train. The crowd swelled further. Many from out of town were connected with residents who would provide them lodging for the night. When it was dark someone fired the "torch," the sycamore, which reportedly lighted the whole town. Here and there rockets and Roman candles went off, and boys threw turpentine balls. There was tremendous cheering. Conner, that stalwart Lincoln Republican, was the speaker of the evening.[43]

Lincoln's elections in 1860 and 1864, plus the wavering of Democrats such as McGonigal because of war issues, confirmed a Republican hold on Wabash that lasted for the rest of the nineteenth century, long enough for the Grand Old Party to grow more conservative nationally, while the Democrats moved left on many issues. Locally Republican domination was never unchallenged because many Democrats—William Steele, M. H. Kidd, Phillip Alber, John Wilson, John Whisler, and J. H. DePuy are examples—were high-profile citizens who were able to put their kind into local positions on a regular basis. The very first common council, for example, may have been dominated by three Republicans, but it also had one Democrat. That was something of a template for town election results. Wabash's nineteenth-century mayors were almost predictably Republican. It played out for national elections, too. Just as the nation knew an almost unbroken line of Republican presidents during the remainder of the century, a majority of voters in Wabash and Noble Township invariably supported the Republican ticket in every presidential race between 1860 and 1900. Twice Wabash was out of sync with the national choice, voting against Grover Cleveland twice, in 1884 and in 1892, and supporting the Republican losers, James G. Blaine and Benjamin Harrison.[44]

William G. Sayre was mayor of Wabash at the time of the 1870 fire. Elected mayor three years earlier at age twenty-three, Sayre was prominent in Wabash and Indiana affairs for the rest of his life, serving several terms in the statehouse, including a term as Speaker of the House. President Harrison appointed him to the Cherokee Commission in Oklahoma, where he worked for Oklahoma's statehood. In 1904 he ran unsuccessfully for governor. His handsome, commodious brick home on the bluff survives at 143 East Main Street, albeit in somewhat shabby condition, just west of the James D. Conner (Halderman/Hetzner/Duffey) house. Sayre walked daily from his home to the courthouse, a block west, until poor health forced him to give up his law practice in 1926. He died in 1931.[45]

Sayre's mayoral administration was presumably responsible for responding to the 1870 catastrophe. Remarkably then, when the common council met a few days after the fire, it took no official action and its minutes for that meeting, as for subsequent meetings, are silent about the event. This is possibly because responsibility for the damage was almost exclusively in private and county hands rather than in city hands. Losses in the business district along Canal and Market streets and in residential areas on the bluff would have been borne principally by property owners and their insurance carriers, if they had them. Likewise, the county's commissioners had to decide what to do about the loss of a courthouse. Nonetheless, the fire had driven home the need for improvements in fire protection for town and county properties. In the expanding western part of town, for example, there were virtually no public cisterns in place. In May 1870, a month after the disaster, a new volunteer fire company was formed, called the Hoosier Fire Company Number 1. There were enough volunteer members to operate the city's hand pump but not many more. Before Sayre turned over his office to Clarkson Weesner in 1876, the Rock City Hook and Ladder Company materialized with forty volunteers, possibly including a good representation of the town's young adult males.[46]

As it turned out, a full decade passed before Hanna's humble courthouse had a permanent successor. Meanwhile, Providence, playing no favorites between secular and religious entities, came to the rescue with an interim solution for both the county commissioners and for the Presbyterians. The New School (First Presbyterian) Church building was just across Wabash Street from the public square and had sustained only minor fire damage. It happened that in 1870, the New School and the Old School wings of the Presbyterians were reunited on a national basis. They had been separate denominations since 1837, when Presbyterians tore themselves asunder over theological and polity issues. Since then the fevers of Calvinistic asperity had cooled. With reunion, Wabash Presbyterians determined to worship together in the Second (Old School) Church's sanctuary, a quite handsome brick building erected at the corner of Hill and Miami streets in 1855, and to use First (New School) Church's hymnals. This was likely an easy compromise because the First Church sanctuary was showing age (and, just possibly, because First's hymns were livelier or because their hymn books were in better shape). The reunion happened locally a month prior to the great fire, in the wake of which the county desperately needed space for a temporary courthouse. The deal was struck. For $3,500, money that First Church could put into its new home, the county acquired a well-situated, quite handy facility, equipped with a bell to warn of future fires. It would be the county's home base for the next ten years. After that decade the new seat of county government, replacing both the modest Hanna structure and the equally modest First Presbyterian structure, soared above the cityscape in quite exquisite good taste, if not, by comparison, with downright opulence.[47]

9

Of Gilt and God

It was Wednesday, September 22, 1880. Downtown at the Haas Opera House (soon to become the Harter Opera House) on the south side of Market Street scores of citizens, dressed in their formal, elegant best, gathered for the final act of an event that "for weeks and months [had] been the chief topic of conversation in Wabash."[1] Nearly two dozen of the participants were guests from out of town, some from as far away as Virginia and Philadelphia. It was already late into the evening. Earlier folks had gathered at 7:00 o'clock in one location, moved to a second, and at a third were seated about tables at Haas's for the finale. The stylish throng had not yet had dinner. For that reason they may have sought their assigned seats eagerly, and if some among them desperately were wondering what sustenance might eventually arrive, they had only to consult the contents of one of the envelopes placed at each plate. Inside was "a specimen of the engraver's art," a menu inscribed, "Wedding banquet. Compliments of Mr. Isaac New to his daughter Hannah and Simon L. Barth." New was a leading merchant in town.

The caterer, George Edwards, had written the menu in French, which the *Wabash Plain Dealer*'s editor rendered, as best he could, into English:

Hitherto such epicurean opulence had been rare in Wabash. It represent-

Huites en Coquille
(Oysters on the half shell)
SOUP.
Potage aux Clams (Clam soup)
Potage aux Huitres (Oyster soup)
FISH
Truite au Court Boullion
(Trout with Court Sauce)
ROAST
Filet de Boeuf aux Champignons
(Fillet of Beef with Mushrooms)
Dinde Farcie
(Stuffed Turkey)
Coteilettes de Perdreux
(Sliced Partridge)
Canard Sauvage, Sauce aux Groseilles
(Wild Duck with Currant Sauce)
VEGETABLES
Pommes de terre farcies
(Baked Potatoes)
Puree de pommes de terre
(Stewed Potatoes)
SALADS
Salade de Volaille
(Chicken Salad)
Salade de Crevettes
(Celery Salad)
DESSERT
Crème Glacee, a la Vanille
(Vanilla Ice Cream)
GLACES
(Ices)
Jelly Rolls. Lady Fingers. Lady Cake
Gold Cake. Fruit Cake. Coconut Drops
Bride's Cake Ornamented. Grapes. Pears.
Assorted Nuts. California Plums.
French Candies.
BEVERAGES
Tea. Maderia Wine. Coffee.
Havana Cigars

ed a new standard of elegance and sophistication. Nor was dinner the end of the evening. "Wine flowed freely." Toasts were tendered. Henry Herff, a close friend of the New family, read more than forty telegrams that had arrived from distant friends and family members. One had come by cable from the groom's relatives in Germany. About fifteen guests responded to the toasts with brief speeches, beginning with Rabbi Ferdinand Becker, who had officiated at the wedding. Doctor James Ford and local journalists Lee Linn and Thad Butler also spoke. These latter three were among the Christians in a largely Jewish gathering.

Following these formalities, the floor was cleared of tables and opened for dancing. Local dignitaries functioned as floor managers, presumably to make certain that musicians and guests were comfortably accommodated around the dance floor and that no crude behavior marred the evening. The Culp "full orchestra" of Logansport, having played opera tunes during dinner, struck up a series of dances. The bride and groom, now Mr. and Mrs. Simon L. Barth of Staunton, Virginia, led the grand march and danced to the opening waltz. The music, comprising at least twenty tunes, "was deemed by all to be the finest music for dancing ever heard in Wabash." It was approaching daylight when the festivities ended.

The *Plain Dealer*'s account of the previous evening was three columns long. It was so detailed as to suggest that its author had gathered many facts well ahead of time. He must also have invoked the aid of a female amanuensis, a bridesmaid perhaps, to help craft descriptions of "the ladies' noticeable toilets." That "cynosure of all eyes," the bride, was swathed in "dove colored gros-grain silk," a court train, a veil that fell to the floor, orange blossoms, lilies of the valley, and diamonds. Nor could a mere male have dreamed up the variety of fabrics, colors, and styles to account for the haute couture of the female guests. Silks, satins, brocades, and lace dominated. As for colors, black was a favorite. Both the bride's mother and the groom's mother wore satin yards of it. Some of the black gowns were rescued by contrasting colors, as with Mrs. Jake Hyman's heliotrope top. Other redemptive colors were "ashes of roses," "dregs of wine," "gas light blue," and "white momie cloth." Noticeable toilets, indeed. Miss Stella McGuire had the good sense to wear cardinal satin and white bunting.

The estimated cost of gifts on display was two thousand dollars. The newspaper provided an incomplete list of items for the curious public. It included, but was scarcely limited to, silver and gold cream spoons from the groom's grandmother in Germany, matching butter knives and cheese forks from a German aunt, a huge variety of solid silver dining utensils and table ornaments, more than two dozen pieces of majolica including a pair of majolica spittoons, pitchers, vases, goblets, cake plates, tea sets, woolen blankets, oil paintings, carpets, linens, a chamber set, a fish shovel, a sideboard, a piano, a bedroom set, a silver pickle castor, a silver nut cracker with a dozen pickers, and a small container for odds and ends called a "tidy."

Although the *Plain Dealer* account of the wedding gave generous coverage to the final festivities at the opera house, it also covered nuptial activities at the two preceding locations. All important was the wedding ceremony itself at Synagogue (Temple) Rodef Shalom (which the reporter insisted on calling a "church") located on the corner of West Sinclair Street and Falls Avenue. Three hundred friends and relatives had been invited, and "Hundreds" had accepted. Most guests arrived in horse-drawn carriages for the 7:00 o'clock service. Organist Mrs. Jerome Herff played Mendlesohn's wedding march as the bride and groom presented themselves. Rabbi Becker addressed the gathering with a wedding homily and blessed the bride and groom with the words "*Adonai Imochem*," "May God be with you." He descended from the pulpit, briefly explained elements and symbols of the service, led the bride and groom through their vows, invited them to share wine from a common cup as a sign of their shared life, whether of joy or of sorrow, and pronounced them husband and wife. Following the service at the synagogue there was a reception at the Lutz Hotel on the north side of Market Street. There the parents of the couple greeted their guests while that hotel's staff made last-minute preparations at Haas's and guests had a chance to meet and mingle informally before moving across the street for dinner.

Given the studied profusion of the evening, plus the prospect that "nought but happiness appeared possible" for the couple's future, it is an ironic and sobering fact that Hannah and Simon Barth's marriage lasted only four months.[2] Simon died in January 1881 in Staunton, Virginia, from an unexplained illness. The "cultivated and handsome" widow moved back to Wabash to live at her father's home, located at what is now 112 East Main Street. In time she pursued her interest in music and became socially active in town once again. She died in 1887 of an ailment that attacked both body and mind. Hannah's tombstone stands near her father's in Rodef Shalom Cemetery. He died in 1907. One of the young men at the wedding, the bride's brother, Alexander New, memorialized his parents, Isaac and Henrietta, by commissioning the Abraham Lincoln statue on the courthouse lawn. It was erected in 1932.[3]

This reprise of a Wabash wedding is of historical interest for at least three reasons. First, it is simply a verbal artifact of the times, a primer on style and social custom among a fortunate elite—some of the gilt of the Gilded Age. Second, it signifies how sophisticated and advanced—some would say complicated and expensive—the standards of social intercourse could be now that Wabash had some real prosperity to flash at the world (such a wedding would not have been contemplated twenty years earlier or even ten or five). Third, it clearly illustrates the position of Jews in Wabash's communal life. In that sense the most telling fact in the *Plain Dealer*'s coverage is the reported presence of Christians such as Linn, Butler, and Ford, who apparently were intimate enough with members of the Jewish community to have been included as guests. Nor were these three men alone in that representation. McCreas, Rettigs, Caldwells, Sayres, and Zeiglers—mostly Protestants from leading families—were also present. Clearly Jews were well-established citizens, openly accepted business and social leaders, and numerous enough to make religious diversity a reality in Wabash.

If there is then a fourth reason to review the New-Barth nuptials, it would be for the purpose of introducing consideration of Jewish life in Wabash and, by extension, consideration of the religious, ecclesiastical, and spiritual climate of the town in general.

The Simon and Rebecca Newberger family were the first Jews to settle in Wabash, arriving in 1846.[4] Simon opened a dry goods and grocery store on the north side of West Canal Street. It was a shop that, typical of the time, branched beyond the basics to include such inventories as hardware, dinnerware, boots, and shoes. Almost as soon as there was a local newspaper, Simon was advertising in it, promising greatly reduced prices, offering an extensive assortment of goods, and soliciting produce to sell. He represented a host of energetic Jewish immigrant merchants who had escaped to America from Europe in large numbers after a succession of social, political, and economic upheavals, culminating in the revolution of 1848. By the time of the Civil War, there were roughly three thousand Jews in Indiana. A very large percentage were Germans of the Reformed Jewish tradition. This meant that, in comparison with orthodox or conservative Jews, they were free to acclimatize themselves to American Christian manners and customs. Many went so far as to surrender Jewish practice altogether, marry Christians, or assimilate so completely in other ways that they were no longer identified as Jews.[5]

On the American frontier, however, there had been influences such as the widely acclaimed Cincinnati paper, the *Israelite*, which published news and articles that encouraged Reformed Jews to become Americanized without forfeiting practice of the faith. Most Jews who followed the Newbergers to Wabash were of this latter persuasion. One of their time-honored traditions was observance of the Jewish Sabbath, from sundown Friday through Saturday, a tradition that bowed to the fact that Christian Americans liked to shop on Saturday. Most Jews in Wabash probably accepted this reality and kept Saturday hours. Another tradition was establishment of a Jewish cemetery. A third was the foundation of a synagogue. The ability to function as a recognized congregation with a synagogue, however, depended on the presence of ten adult males, the minyan. For this reason it was several years before the congregation called Rodef Shalom existed.[6]

Typically Jewish settlers arrived in a "steady trickle."[7] That was true for Wabash Jews. Soon after the Newbergers, Michael and Julia Hyman also arrived in 1846. Again, it was dry goods and groceries for the Hyman store. Charles and Hetty Herff arrived in 1850. Six years later David Bach came to town, married Rachael Hyman, Michael's sister, and bought his brother-in-law's business. In 1866 he paid $700 for lot Number 88 on the corner of Cass and Market streets, where he probably erected a dwelling. Subsequently Michael and his brother, Leonard Hyman, established a linseed oil mill on Canal Street, the oil being useful in the treatment of wood and for medicines. From then on the Jewish "trickle" begat a stream of enterprises: the Star Woolen Mill; Wolf and Beitman clothing (later the long extant Beitman and Wolf); Simon Brothers; and the Simon Cook dealership in junk, hides, pelts, furs, tallow, feathers, glass, tin, and clothing on Water Street (eventually, after 1926, the Abraham Sposeep business, of which the stone building, though empty, endures in the twenty-first century). Later in the century the Wabash Importing Company, forerunner of the Belgium Draft Horse interests, was an important Jewish enterprise. So was Harmon Wolf's Pioneer Hat Factory, which by the 1890s employed more than forty workers. Other nineteenth-century Jewish concerns included the Staadecker millinery shop, the Wabash Screen Door Company, and the Wabash National Bank.

Establishment of a cemetery designated exclusively for Jews normally preceded the founding of a congregation. It was part of Jewish sensitivity to be especially mindful of the dead and the welfare of their survivors. The presence of a cemetery signified that a serious and viable Jewish community was in the works, even though a minyan did not yet exist. During those early years of uncertainty, when one or two Jews in a Christian town might feel a strong tug to surrender religious identity and meld into the pervasive Christian order of things, organizing a cemetery society could rescue their identity. Such a society might involve collecting dues, establishing bylaws, electing officers, and holding meetings—activities that focused members on a common concern and counteracted assimilation. In the case of Wabash Jews the need for burial ground may have first occurred when the Newbergers' eight-year-old-son died in 1848. Yet, it was not until spring 1854 that Charles Herff and Michael and Leonard Hyman bought land west of town from members of the Sayre and Whiteside families. They named the place Rodef Shalom (pursurer of Peace). It eventually received a total of about three hundred burials. Names on the tombstones are a palpable catalog of Wabash's Jewish families: Adler, Bach, Beitman, Block, Blumenthal, Bochman, Cook, Doob, Goldreich, Herff, Hyman, Isaacson, Kahn, Kaufman, Kern, Levy, Mandelbaum, Marks, Meyer, New, Newberger, Oppenheim, Rosenthal, Savesky, Simon, Spero, Sposeep, Staadecker, VanBaaler, and Wolf. In the twenty-first century the cemetery is well maintained, moderately wooded, and surrounded by a wrought-iron fence that had once enclosed the public square. However, only one or two of the families named there have survived among twenty-first-century Wabash citizens (2010).[8]

The Rodef Shalom congregation dates from 1868. It disbanded in 1946, after Wabash's Jewish population had dwindled to a few families. Initially the faithful had worshipped in private houses, but for most of the congregation's existence its physical home was the synagogue at the corner of Sinclair Street and Falls Avenue. It had been constructed as a Disciples of Christ church (New Lights) in 1869. After 1946 it reverted to sheltering successive Christian congregations, including a spiritualist group and the Missouri Synod Lutherans. The Jewish congregation purchased the building from the Disciples in 1883. It was (and is today) a simple but pleasingly proportioned brick structure with long narrow windows and a handsome central entrance. An old photo reveals that it had once supported a disproportionately bulky steeple above the front entrance and had been surrounded by slender trees and a wooden fence. A floor plan of the interior shows double aisles down the nave, thirteen long center pews, and twenty-two shorter pews plus two stoves abutting the walls. At the north end were spaces for a choir, an organ, and an elevated "desk" or pulpit. Although the services of permanent, long-term rabbis were difficult to secure, beginning in 1877 a series of clerics presided over the congregation for brief terms.[9]

Sigmund Reyf was one rabbi, also known as Simeon Frey. In the inconsistency of his name lay a potential scandal that aroused the curiosity of locals. Synagogues proved no more immune to human follies and the resultant gossip than any other religious body. Reyf had taken charge of Rodef Shalom in February 1886. It is unlikely that any other cleric in Wabash history arrived with more prestigious credentials than Reyf, for he came equipped with the strong endorsement of Rabbi Isaac Mayer Wise of Cincinnati, a scholar of national and historical standing and the publicist of the influential *Israelite*. For a year all went well. The faithful seemed uniformly pleased with their rabbi until March 1887, when letters addressed to congregational members began to arrive charging Reyf with being a fugitive from the law, a characterless adventurer, and a heretic. Congregational consternation erupted, and town tongues wagged. The situation was soon exacerbated by the letter writer's revelations that she was Reyf's estranged wife, Clara Netter Frey, and that her husband's true name was Simeon Frey.

In fairly short order Reyf (Frey) also received an epistle from his wife. She announced her intention of coming to Wabash and remaining until she had ruined him. Frey had never hidden the fact of his marriage, but he had tried to keep his distance from Clara, for she had attempted to ruin him in other locations, including Philadelphia. Frey now threw in the towel and prepared to resign his post, fleeing to Cincinnati and seeking the counsel of Rabbi Wise. Wise advised him to return to Wabash and lay his case before the congregation, admitting to marital chaos but asserting that his wife's charges were unfounded. Perhaps more important, Wise publicized his own defense of Frey, explaining that the man had been forced to change his name in order to throw his "termagant" wife off the scent, and that he, Wise, had endorsed Frey's idea of rearranging the letters of his name from Frey to Reyf.

Upon his return to Wabash, matters began to reorient themselves in the rabbi's favor. At base his congregation probably wanted to believe him. Frey took the initiative by calling at the *Plain Dealer* to tell his story. The bare bones of that story were that Frey was a native of Austerlitz, that he had received a superior and varied European education, that he was trained in medicine, and that he had immigrated to Pittsburgh where he taught languages. Enter Miss Clara Netter, and Frey married her. "She proved a regular demon," according to Frey. She quarreled, had fits of rage, and engaged in violent attacks upon the furniture of their home. Charging that her husband already "knew too much," she burned his books, valued at three hundred dollars. This last act compelled his departure. He returned to her once, for fourteen days, then escaped again, eventually coming under Wise's mentoring in Cincinnati. Clara did not give up. The "pestilential woman" subsequently hounded him, by letter or in person, to Innsbruck, Austria; to Erie, Pennsylvania; and to Akron, Ohio, where the quarry changed his name to Reyf.

The *Plain Dealer*'s sympathetic publication of Frey's story ("A Virago's Vengeance") helped reestablish his local reputation. Clara's visit to Wabash, where she openly tried to discredit her husband, failed. He was honored, rather, as one who had contributed generously to the synagogue and given liberally to the poor. There was speculation that Clara would sue for divorce in Ohio and that the rabbi would, wisely, not contest it. It began to be assumed that Frey's re-election as rabbi was a foregone conclusion. Nevertheless, Harmon Wolf and a few others went on record as saying that their continued financial support of the congregation depended on Frey's reinstatement.[10]

Nineteenth-century Wabash Jews were reticent to seek public office. One possible reason is an unspoken fear among them that the heat of elections would stir up quiescent anti-Semitism. Such a fear would reflect Jewish memories of anti-Semitism in Europe. Nor was it an entirely unfounded fear. The expected appointment of a Jew as postmaster for Wabash in the 1880s caused murmurs of anger among some citizens. Nativism of this ilk existed largely sub rosa locally, but it would surface in hateful ways during the Ku Klux Klan era in the early part of the twentieth century. A second and more practical reason Jews may have eschewed active politics was their identification with the Democratic Party, which, in Wabash proper, was a disadvantage for candidates on election day. The relatively rare public expressions of disapproval between Jew and Christian arose over the occasional reluctance of Jews to shut down their businesses every time a Christian holiday might dictate closure. It is also true that the posting of numbers on buildings in town—in order to facilitate postal, firefighting, and police work—temporarily alarmed a few Jews for whom the marking of a doorpost in a secular way had negative religious significance. As has been noted, good friendships and cordial business relations between Jews and Christians were common, and, indeed, Jews were welcomed into predominantly Christian-weighted organizations such as the Masons and the Odd Fellows. Nevertheless, there was some exclusivity based on ethnic lines. There was a chapter of B'nai B'rith, for example. Also, Jewish women had their own literary society while other women in town, after 1880, had Round Table, which seems to have had an entirely Christian membership in its early years. In addition, marriage between a practicing Jew and a Christian would have been very rare.[11]

As a whole, the Jewish community seemed to have been more mindful than the average citizen of the potential for graceful living in Wabash, and they often had the financial resources to achieve upwardly mobile lifestyles. The best gauge of this may be the homes Jewish families built. At one time all five houses along the north side of Hill Street between the Christian Church and Cass Street housed Jewish families. Judging from the three that survived late into the twentieth century they were neither small nor plain. Two were duplexes, illustrating how more than one generation of the same family often dwelled under a single roof. Of these houses only one, the massive Simon home at 142 West Hill, survived the twentieth century. Three of them fell to the construction and subsequent expansion of the Carnegie Library, and a fourth was sold to the Christian church for a parsonage and, later, was replaced by the church's education building. Of the five, the house that sheltered its original family longest was the Benjamin and Julia Wolf home at 156 West Hill, which had been built in 1879 and occupied by Wolfs through most of the twentieth century. There would be substantial Jewish residences in other parts of town, also, particularly on East Main and North Wabash streets.[12]

Of particular interest is the present-day Honeywell House, 720 North Wabash Street, dating from 1880. Strictly speaking it was not a nineteenth-century Jewish residence; it was purchased in 1920 by Isaac Beitman for $3,600. In the twenty-first century it is enjoying its fourth or fifth incarnation, having become an elegant venue for cultural and social events. It was built on the northeast corner of Hill and Spring streets. In 1921 the Beitmans decided to move the house to their property on North Wabash Street, naming it Brookwood. Reportedly they undertook this move rather than build a new house because it was important to them for spiritual reasons to live in a place that had already housed human beings. Difficulty in transporting the house over interurban and/or railroad tracks on Wabash Street necessitated cutting the house in half. Beitman moved both halves to the new location, connecting them there with a spacious central hall. Under the ownership of succeeding residents, including Eugenia Honeywell, the house was radically altered twice and was then restored after a devastating fire that took Mrs. Honeywell's life in 1974.[13]

Although Wabash Jews were formidable for their numbers they were, nonetheless, a clear minority among religious groups. Christianity, by comparison, was an unofficially established religion. Christian parsons were forever preaching or praying or moralizing at public gatherings, as omnipresent as the stars and stripes. Closet atheists, agnostics, and cynics stayed in the closet or close to it. Among Christian denominations, the Presbyterians had been prominent since 1836, but they by no means had a monopoly on the Christian enterprise in Wabash. Presbyterians had been followed by Methodists, two versions of Campbellite Christians (Disciples of Christ), Baptists, Roman Catholics, African Methodist Episcopalians (AME), and Quakers (Society of Friends), all of whom gathered communicants, helped shape the moral climate of the town, defended their doctrines and theology, and strove to raise up impressive sanctuaries. Several of these sanctuaries were worthy of the Gilded Age and, in their attractiveness, served as tools of evangelism.

As the nineteenth century matured, each church staked out a permanent location. The first Christian Church moved from a schoolhouse northeast of town to the courthouse, then to the Baptist building at Cass and Hill streets, and finally to the northwest corner of Miami and Hill streets, where its acoustically superior "audience room" (achieved by curved end walls and cornices) was ready for use in 1867. As with other structures of the day, this building may have owed some of its features to architectural plan books that were in broad circulation among contractors. As noted earlier, Ford had overseen the design. Begun as a building in a Gothic style with spacious interior vaulting, it turned into something unique as church leaders wrestled with difficult structural and financial issues. Reportedly its graceful cupola, completed in 1869, is so integrally an extension of the south façade that the former cannot be removed without collapsing the latter. The sanctuary windows, probably installed in the 1870s, may be of more primitive design than the high Victorian art glass of other local churches, but under full morning sunlight the untamed intensity of their colors dazzles profoundly.[14]

In 1862 the Methodists moved from their twenty by forty-foot structure on the north side of Main Street (west of Miami Street) to the northeast corner of Sinclair and Cass streets, where their new building was dedicated in 1863. By 1880 membership growth had dictated some dramatic alterations. A second floor was added plus a steeple, containing the largest bell in the city. For years the bell rang eight times between 8:00 a.m. and 8:00 p.m. on each Sabbath: four times to alert the faithful to upcoming events in the daily schedule and then four times to mark the beginning of each event. These events included two Sabbath Schools and two "preachings." In the twentieth century the bell was sent to a mission in Africa. In the late 1890s Saint Bernard Roman Catholic congregation acquired the building, which accommodated its multiplying numbers for the next half century.

The Methodists took their bell and moved across the street into a stylish, newly completed "wedding cake gothic" edifice of "vitrified" brick and stone. It had forty-two rooms, fifteen sets of stairs, and was equipped with both electric and gas lighting. The fact that it was, at base, a squarish structure was aptly camouflaged by the architect's exuberance for arches, apses, entrances, gables, dome, and massive, upward thrusting windows. The art glass of the windows and dome is a combination of religious scenes and decorative designs that feature boldly colored glass jewels. The sanctuary floor plan copied the then-popular Akron style, with chancel and organ pipes in the southeast corner facing a sloping floor of curvilinear pews that were arranged diagonally northeast to southwest. A combination of balconies, sliding walls, and generous doorways made it possible to accommodate eighteen hundred worshippers. The cost for building, pews, windows, and land was $32,170 in 1898, though for the next five years there were fees paid for litigation over poor workmanship. The decision to build anew on that spot also caused a church split, with about two hundred members choosing to form the Wabash Street Methodist Church.[15]

A number of other congregations also vied for a material presence in Wabash's spiritual life. The Baptists held ground briefly on the southwest corner of Hill and Cass streets. Later their building there was a very temporary home for the original Christian Church and, then, for a longer period served the "other" Christian congregation, known as the "New Lights." The latter eventually built on the corner of Sinclair Street and Falls Avenue (the future Rodef Shalom). Just around the corner from that location was the tidy, brick Saint Bernard Roman Catholic Church on West Maple Street that Bishop John Henry Luers of the Fort Wayne Diocese dedicated in late 1867. This original Catholic structure survives in the twenty-first century, though it has served many nonecclesiastical purposes and is in poor shape. Abandoned by the church late in the century, it served as an annex to the nearby West Ward school, housing the first and sixth grades, and later was a garage for city buses. Saint John AME Church was founded in 1869. The AME members worshipped at various locations until the end of the century when they began raising funds to build a church on the north side of East Sinclair, between Huntington and Allen streets, not far from the depot. Portions of the white community helped in this and other efforts, though, with few exceptions, segregation was mostly an ineradicable part of Sunday worship. One place the African American congregation had worshipped in its early years was the Friends (Quaker) church on Market Street. The Friends, however, did not stay at that location permanently. Although they were stronger in the county than in town, they claimed the then-separate community of South Wabash as the locus of their urban manifestation. They eventually built a succession of four church buildings there, from which they cast a broad influence in a conjoined Wabash (north and south) in the twentieth and twenty-first centuries.[16]

By the 1880s several of these churches counted membership in the hundreds, two or three hundred formal adherents being considered quite promising. Such numbers, however, did not take into account the possibility that actual attendance on Sundays could far exceed the number of names on church rolls. For reasons of respectability, entertainment, and socialization, church was the place to be on Sunday morning. A teenager or a young bachelor, for example, could find no more socially acceptable way to pick up a date than to spend some worship time surreptitiously scrutinizing young females in the congregation; then he might stand on the church steps after worship with a welcoming arm crooked by his side, hoping that the right girl would put her arm in his and accept his offer to walk her home. No doubt older folks also found self-serving reasons for attendance, in addition to sincere spiritual ones. Sanctuaries reflected this reality by providing for a seating capacity in excess of the needs of member communicants, sometimes anticipating crowds of more than a thousand at special services. Presbyterian, Methodist, Christian, and Roman Catholic churches would all had ample balconies to accommodate nineteenth-century overflow. A couple of churches that had begun with every chance of growth and endurance faltered along the way and eventually disappeared. This was true of the early Baptists and of the second Christian church.

Although divided in doctrine, theology, history, worship styles, and the location of their buildings, Protestant denominations shared passions for evangelism, religious education, and social reforms. Occasionally their congregations came together in joint efforts to lift up the standards of piety or moral behavior in town. An annual Week of Prayer and occasional community Thanksgiving services, led by the town's clergy, were common examples of ecumenism. So, too, were efforts at mass evangelism. In 1869 the Methodists, Presbyterians, and Christians joined together for evangelistic services that alternated among their buildings. As public interest increased, services continued night after night with no definite end in sight. In fairly short order the Methodists had taken in 153 new members and the Presbyterians zero. This lopsidedness was explained by the Presbyterians' having offered no opportunity for anyone to join either of their two congregations. Possibly an aloof Calvinist theology made them awkward in such matters. A month later, however, the New School Presbyterians enticed more than forty of God's predestined elect to their fold and baptized six infants into the Covenant of Grace. By this time converts to both Campbellite churches totaled eighty-four. The Methodists' harvest rose to two hundred. Old School Presbyterians, who again scored zero, could claim a disadvantage because their sanctuary was closed for repairs.[17]

Not content with their vigorous indoor evangelism program in 1869, the Methodists also promoted preaching in the streets and in saloons as a frontal attack on drunkenness. The idea was to reach the "hundreds" who never ventured near a church door. Methodist women took up positions on downtown street corners and invited local clergy to preach there on the evils of drink. Sometimes they invaded saloons en masse, as they did at Eby's Saloon after a Monday night church meeting. There is some indication that the Haas saloon, on Wabash Street at the time, surrendered unconditionally under the threat of such an invasion, going out of business, at least until the passions of reform had cooled. Dramatic efforts of this kind represented what was left of the more politically oriented temperance movement of the 1850s. Prohibition having failed as a way to cut off the taps, moral persuasion became the weapon du jour. The Woman's Christian Temperance Union became a powerful ecumenical movement nationally about this time and eventually had active representation in Wabash. Even the Roman Catholics, not generally credited with enthusiasm for temperance, established the Saint Bernard Total Abstinence Society in the 1870s.[18]

One man who believed that temperance was a political issue as much as a personal and moral one was William J. Essick, the last minister of First Presbyterian before its merger with Second Presbyterian in 1870. A fellow clergyman called him "the skillful reaper." Encouraged by the *Plain Dealer*, which provided space for his "Temperance Column," Essick sought to reinvigorate the cause in the aftermath of the Civil War. He enlisted influential citizens such as J. D. Conner, Cary Cowgill, and Mayor Warren Sayre in the effort. Cowgill, who was prosecuting attorney in the spring of 1867, not only used his office as a bully pulpit, speaking publicly for temperance, but also made certain that laws were enforced locally and that convictions were publicized. In March 1866, for example, the *Plain Dealer* cited the case of a young man who had recently paid $64.80, a massive fine, for illegally selling three drinks. The same report stated that twenty-one people from the so-called law-abiding class had been fined an average of $15 for illegal tippling, buying, or selling. Their names were spread before the reading public.[19]

At this early stage of his campaign Essick declared that Wabash children deserved to be able to grow up in a town where the use and sale of liquor had become "odious," and he kept trying to measure progress to that end. It was a good sign, Essick wrote, that over the course of eight months one pharmacy in town had sold only one barrel of whiskey and twenty-four gallons of brandy. Sales by two other druggists were also low, something that was especially encouraging because these retailers supplied drugstores and physicians throughout the county: "The smallness of the above quantities will astonish our good citizens."[20] He encouraged the public by reporting the beneficent changes in town: several "drunkard making establishments" had closed their doors; places where liquor was sold were now orderly and respectable; public drunkenness had declined noticeably; public officials were no longer afraid to enforce temperance laws; and candidates for office had all declared themselves to be temperance men. In 1871, after Essick had moved on, his ally, Sayre, refused to let the city council lower liquor licensing from $300 to $150 a year. It had been a tie vote in council, which Sayre broke, but the final pro-temperance decision seems in retrospect a tribute to Essick's tireless work. As Essick's pastorate had neared its end he organized huge public temperance meetings, ecumenical affairs that met in churches. Every congregation in town was officially on his bandwagon, as were some of the fraternal lodges, and each sent a representative to the Temperance Central Committee that planned strategy and tactics. Among the representatives were Stearns Fisher, Leewell Lee Carpenter, W. A. Elward, Robert Cissna, and Peter King, all of whom carried enough local stature and clout to broaden the influence of men such as Conner, Cowgill, and Sayre.[21]

Whereas in earlier temperance efforts the Presbyterians had been especially fervid—witness clergymen such as Essick—there emerged signs in the 1870s and 1880s that Methodists, Campbellites, and Baptists comprised a new vanguard in Wabash. It is perhaps instructive, then, that on Tuesday noon, June 4, 1878, Presbyterian elder Erwin G. Sackett was observed carrying a pint of whiskey toward his East Hill Street home, presumably for his wife's medicinal needs. Unfortunately the good elder subsequently sustained bruises and a sprained wrist by tumbling down his cellar stairs. The *Plain Dealer* moralized, tongue-in-cheek: "Presbyterian Elders should not be found carrying whiskey about[,] even for their wives."[22] Although Sackett, who was a leading elder of his church for years to come, was probably innocent of the implied intemperance, this vignette illustrates that as the town prospered, segments of its upwardly mobile population probably found reasons to be somewhat offhand about the temperance issue and, just possibly, to be less abstemious than once they were. For instance, the fact that "wine flowed freely" at Hannah New's wedding dinner in 1880, plus the fact that members of prominent Protestant families were among the guests, leads to the speculation that not all those Protestants present abstained that night. In addition, it was not reported that any guests were so disapproving of the libation offered that they walked out of the festivities in righteous protest. No doubt hundreds of Wabash citizens were faithfully teetotal during these decades, but the idea that at some point there existed a seamless loyalty to the temperance cause, even among the church-going crowd, cannot be sustained.[23]

Issues other than temperance surfaced with regularity in, between, and among the churches. The Christian church represented by the Reverend L. L. Carpenter and the Christian church led by the Reverend P. Zeigler used letters to the *Plain Dealer* to battle it out over which of their churches should be known as "The Christian Church" of Wabash, both claiming that moniker. The paper's editor finally had to put the brakes on this theological verbosity, first, by limiting debate to a single column of print and, finally, by announcing that nothing more on the subject would be published. Sunday Schools were another important item on congregational agendas, as they had been with some churches since pioneer times. Before public schools existed the Sunday Schools had championed basic literacy as one of their objectives. Now they continued to tout basic scriptural knowledge and decent moral behavior. It was largely an ecumenical cause spurred on by multidenominational institutes, rallies, and picnics that drummed up community and parental support.

One July day the entire Wabash Sunday School crammed into a boxcar "like cattle" for a "not pleasant but brief" trip to a "pic-nic" at Lagro where the sojourners were met by a Sunday School band from Huntington.[24]

Such activities partially addressed a need for youth ministry before the age of great national youth movements—Christian Endeavor and Epworth League—had fully dawned. Aside from Sunday Schools there were tentative local attempts to meet the spiritual needs of older youth. The Presbyterians, for example, created a ninety-seat "chapel" for young people on its property. Others hoped that a "Reading Room" for young men might provide an alternative to evenings of drinking. Any exposure to religious or cultural involvement was viewed as an inoculation against that crude and virulent behavior of the young that had wagged tongues since pioneer days, the smutty, vulgar talk of "young sprouts" on public streets. Around the Tremont Hotel, for example, young men and women frequently loitered, engaging in "disgusting" talk and "silly chattering." It was all very irritating, according to a local editor, who advised the offenders to find some other place to "do their cooing." Another hot spot in town, at least during the Civil War years, had been the railroad depot between Wabash and Huntington streets. "Why do parents let boys go to the depot at night?" asked a concerned citizen.[25] It was allegedly a hangout where children and teenagers, ages nine to seventeen, fraternized with a dozen "bad boys." If a youngster went there "good," he would come home "bad." He would have learned to swear and fight. Parents should keep their boys at home in the evening. Sayre reflected the value system of the ecclesiastical establishment in 1872 when he sponsored and signed a city ordinance that made it illegal for saloons and billiard halls to allow minors to loiter on their premises. Religious folks in Wabash were often passionate in targeting external signs of moral tawdriness, especially among the young.[26]

Religion was meant to mold the whole of life, its leisure hours as well as its more serious endeavors. To that end the Reverend A. S. Reid preached a sermon in February 1871, titled "Amusements." Despite a nasty snowstorm, there was a full house. One of the attendants that morning, the *Wabash Republican*'s Thad Butler, was inspired to take notes from his seat in the balcony. Butler had come expecting the minister to attack dancing, and he was not disappointed. Amusements, like flowers (Reid began), can exist for our good, especially the good of the young. When not abused, amusements are a blessing. The test lies with whether an amusement pleases God or whether it harms humankind. The preacher suggested baseball as an example: it is good unless it is "elevated to a profession," meaning, presumably, unless it is taken too seriously. Such amusements then become "hurtful excrecenses [*sic*]." The arts, by contrast, are not mere amusements because pursuit of them demands skill and study. Prizefighting, on the other hand, violates biblical principles. So does gambling. Card playing stultifies the intellect. Then he got to Butler's concern. Dancing, Reid said, should be avoided because it is too often connected with evil by offering personal liberties not otherwise allowed. Many public balls are indecent; some participants want to dance with Christians to shield themselves from shame; such events are a "growing evil among us." One suspects that Butler was no stranger at balls and had just heard the condemnation he expected. In an earlier news article he had mischievously suggested that Reid might condemn croquet or euchre or other games of chance or skill; if he did so, Butler wondered, would the preacher be able to suggest substitute amusements. Butler seemed bemused by Reid's narrowness, or perhaps even angered by it. In any case, Butler's recording of Reid's sermon is a small window on a larger truth, that a serious divide of values and desires—with the attendant tensions—inevitably existed at times between churches, church leaders, and their communities. It was supposed to be that way. Much of the local churches' raison d'etre was to urge Wabash toward more respectable forms of communal life. If, in this case, the reporter was doing his job, so was the preacher, however dated his standards of decent behavior may seem in retrospect.[27]

As the decades passed, religious groups became stronger and more permanent players in community developments. Their success rose partially from the fact that they were hives of regulated interaction among like-minded and, indeed, high-minded folk; probably no newcomer got further faster with regard to general acceptance in town than one who quickly found a niche in a church. In the beginning Christians theoretically sorted themselves out ecclesiastically along theological and doctrinal lines, the Reformed glomming onto the Reformed, the evangelicals to the evangelicals, the immersionists to the immersionists, and so on. As years passed, however, it is likely that a sorting out by social connections—even by what might be labeled snobbishness—also came into play. Inevitably some people joined churches simply on the basis of friendships. Others studied the business, cultural, or social landscape to determine which church offered their personal ambitions a leg up. To that end a church's appeal depended partially on an accounting of who already belonged. Strong lay leaders who happened also to be prominent in the community added luster to a church's attractiveness. The Christian church's Ford, Elijah Hackleman, and A. M. Atkinson are good examples of such leaders. So are the Presbyterians' Conner, McNamee, Sayre, and Stitt families. There were also Saint Bernard's W. A. Elward; the Jones and Miles families of the Friends; Stearns Fisher of the Baptists; Rodef Shalom's Hyman, Beitman, or Wolf families; and the Duck, Bruner, Payne, and Wilson families of the Methodist church; to name a very few among many.[28]

Compared with many prospering white neighbors, Wabash's African Americans had missed out on the affluence of the Gilded Age and, yet, overall they seemed to be economically stable, spiritually healthy, and growing slowly in numbers. In 1877 there had been only eight thousand adult black males in Indiana and only forty-two in Wabash County. Six years later Wabash had at least enough youthful black males (the "Black Diamonds") to beat an all-black Kokomo team in baseball. The AME church, Saint John, undoubtedly boosted black solidarity and confidence locally. Its presence also inspired white Christians to contribute to the financial health of that parish, which they valued as a source of community tranquility. Notable exceptions to such tranquility may have been, first, the Republican tendency to accuse Democrats of "buying" black votes, and, second, the newspaper-bantered reputation of a few black miscreants, such as "burly Negro" John Boswell who was frequently arrested for brawling and theft. Over the years, however, the Jefferson, Thurman, English, Furguson (Ferguson), and Lewis families planted roots that supported a viable and respected black presence deep into the twentieth century. The Furguson family in general was especially well known as a pillar of Saint John's and as a vital part of the town's workforce. The male population of town eagerly patronized the Furguson Barber Shop, which boasted one of the earliest public baths in town. They probably also patronized Saint John's "Cake Walks," a fund-raiser introduced to Wabash by that congregation. One prominent black citizen, noted for his oratory, Daniel Furguson, broke with the Saint John's congregation and attended the Presbyterian church where he seems to have been well received.

In spite of theoretical and legal equality, however, Wabash was no more free of entrenched racism than any other Northern town. The terms "nigger," "darky," "descendant of Ham," and "colored" were in common—and largely unquestioned—usage. Entrenched custom limited social intercourse or marriage between the races and dampened the kind of career ambitions that many whites took for granted. But in the post-Civil War era radical antiblack, racist terrorism did not seem to have a local footing, as it would in later decades when the Ku Klux Klan became active in Wabash County and throughout the state. Most citizens seemed to accept the legal standing of blacks and to value their contributions to the community. Emblematic of that attitude was the rowdy welcome Wabash gave the news that equal citizenship for African Americans had been affirmed by passage of the Fifteenth Amendment. Its passage was joyously announced by the firing of cannon at 2:00 o'clock on a Sunday morning.[29]

In addition to encouraging lay leadership and strong families, churches were able, from time to time, to bring to Wabash towering personalities in the form of installed clergymen whose theological acumen encompassed a genuine interest in the welfare of the whole town. On this score the Methodists were at a disadvantage. Their rules of polity moved ministers so often that few had a chance to establish memorable influence in town. Between 1837, when the itinerant Methodist J. B. Meshon preached in Wabash, until the end of the nineteenth century, thirty-six clergymen served the First Methodist Church, their tenure averaging less than two years apiece, scarcely time for a man to become acquainted with his flock, let alone the entire town. Of the thirty-six, probably none was more memorable than the Reverend William J. Vigus, who remained for five years, 1870 to 1875. A native of Virginia, a former store clerk, teacher, and medical student, Vigus turned to the ministry at age twenty-four. He served briefly as a chaplain in the Civil War, then joined the Methodists' Northern Indiana Conference, coming to Wabash in 1870. In Wabash, as elsewhere, he was a sensation as a revivalist, bringing 312 converts into the Wabash fold during his tenure. His obituary credited him with a year (after his Wabash tenure) in which he averaged one convert for each day of the year. Vigus's success seemed undiminished by the fact that for Methodists at this time a profession of faith was not necessarily sufficient for membership. For years the church maintained a fairly strict "probationary" policy that subjected prospective members to a long period of testing and observation before they could enter "full connection" with the church. After leaving Wabash in 1875, Vigus worked the Northern Indiana Conference as a pastor and revivalist, becoming in time the superintendent of the Wabash district. In his forty-fourth year of ministry he returned as a resident of the town in order to serve as pastor of the Middle Street Methodist Church on the south side. He died in 1910.[30]

The week following Vigus's death in February 1910, his contemporary, friend, and fellow Wabash pastor, Leewell Lee Carpenter of the Christian church, also died.[31] Carpenter had been far more prominent than Vigus, approaching whatever status amounted to Protestant sainthood in Wabash minds. In statewide reputation he even towered above that other Wabash Christian church pastor, Ira J. Chase, who had gone on to become governor, 1891–93. The Carpenter family's speculation had been that, as a seventh son, Leewell Lee was destined for medicine as a profession; but after stints sawing wood, pursuing odd jobs, and teaching school, he matriculated at Bethany College in West Virginia with his future still undetermined. He had grown tall and rangy, naturally intelligent, and articulate. At some point he earned the nickname High Pockets because of his stature. A fictionalized biography labels him "the tall sycamore of the Wabash." At Bethany he studied under Alexander Campbell, the nationally famous founder of the Disciples of Christ or Campbellite denomination. Although the Disciples had roots in Calvinism they were strong revivalists, practicing baptism by immersion. Carpenter converted in 1854, dabbled in Republican Party politics, missionary and Sunday School work for several years, and then, in 1867, launched a brief career as an itinerant preacher. In 1861 he married an Ohio girl, Mary Eve Funk. According to Carpenter's grandson, it was Mary who had taken the initiative and made a marriage proposal. The union was fruitful, producing seven children, of whom the four boys (Erret, Willard, Frank, and Arthur) all became productive citizens of Wabash. Carpenter's grandson, biographer, and namesake, Leewell H. Carpenter, had a distinguished career in the twentieth century as superintendent of Wabash schools and as a Republican state legislator.

Carpenter became pastor of the Wabash Christian Church in 1868, when the congregation was in difficult straits. Elijah Hackleman had met Carpenter at a regional church meeting and brought him by train to Wabash, where Ford helped convince him to seek the local pastorate. The church's building was incomplete and its debt was two thousand dollars. In his first year as pastor Carpenter brought 150 new members into the fold and inspired the faithful to pay off the debt. In the following two years the building was completed and paid for. Although he maintained a permanent residence on West

Maple Street in Wabash and was perennially active in local church matters, the bulk of Carpenter's subsequent work with the denomination was serving as an evangelist, Sunday School organizer, and missionary society official throughout the Hoosier State. Toward the end of his career he and Mary traveled extensively in the Near East, the Holy Land, Egypt, and parts of Europe. By the time of his death he had organized and/or dedicated 752 churches and raised two million dollars for church extension purposes. He had also delivered 17,136 sermons, conducted 492 funerals, baptized 3,425 converts, and welcomed 1,598 others into his flocks. It was a monumental career. His tombstone in Falls Cemetery reads:

> A Preacher of the Primitive Gospel
> And a Defender of the Faith
> Once and Forever delivered to the Saints

Carpenter was an affable man with a lively sense of humor. A friend who lived opposite the Christian church on Hill Street was the equally affable Charles Little, pastor of the Presbyterian congregation, beginning in 1872. The two clerics probably enjoyed digging at each other over theological and ecclesiastical differences. Sharply contrasting methods of baptism—sprinkling vs. immersion—was always a hot topic. One day Little and Vigus visited Carpenter as the latter was watering his garden. "Why now, Brother Carpenter," said Little, "I always thought you did not believe in sprinkling." "I don't really," shot back Carpenter, "but I believe it is good for cabbage heads."[32]

Topping even Carpenter's stellar reputation and lofty standing among Wabash citizens, Little was more immersed in the Wabash community, more popular, and more revered than any other cleric of the period. Indeed, at the beginning of the twenty-first century, eighty years after his death, there have been elderly Wabash citizens who clearly remembered him from childhood or recalled the day city schools closed for his funeral in 1921. Among Presbyterians in particular he remained for decades the very icon of their churchly success. Clearly much of his reputation is attributable to the longevity of his pastorate. He occupied the Wabash pulpit for more than forty-nine years, dying suddenly and unexpectedly in office just a few months short of a half-century tenure. It would be unfair to Little, however, to suggest that his success was only a matter of his staying put for a long time, similar to monks of old. In addition to being an intriguing preacher and an able scholar, he was a social animal, an active participant in community affairs, a personable and loving pastor, a gifted leader, and, apparently, a capable administrator. Unofficially he was considered to be the dean of Hoosier clergy. Quite officially he was elected national head of his denomination in 1910.[33]

Little was a scion of a clerical family that included his uncle, Henry Little, an early missionary in southern Indiana and, for a long time, state agent for the American Home Missionary Society. In that latter capacity Henry visited Wabash in its early years and probably preached from its New School pulpit. Henry's brother, Jacob (Charles's father), had also preached in Wabash. No doubt the Little family's grapevine worked efficiently in 1872 to inform young Charles, newly hatched from Lane Seminary in Cincinnati, that the recent merger of Wabash's Old and New School churches (in 1870) had resulted in a single church with good prospects. Even better, its pulpit would soon be vacant. In September 1872 the *Plain Dealer* announced that "the Rev. Charles Lyttle [*sic*]" would preach at both morning and evening services the following Sabbath. Apparently these were "candidating sermons," successful ones. He was installed before the end of the year, succeeding Reid.[34]

Connected as he was through his family with the American Home Missionary Society and being a graduate of Lane, Little represented the more liberal Calvinists of the day, meaning that although he was inevitably a stout moralist, he was likely to be less dogmatic in theological matters, more open to social issues, and less austere in manner than earlier clerics. Typical of successful clerics, Little was undoubtedly able to massage his interpretation of scripture in ways that made his views acceptable to his public. Then, too, he cemented his relationship with Wabash by marrying a local lass, Annie Thurston, daughter of a prominent businessman. They had three children. One of the two boys, Robert Little, became pastor of Fort Wayne's First Presbyterian Church in the 1920s. Over the years Charles collected two honorary doctorates, a Doctor of Divinity from his alma mater, Marietta College, and a Doctor of Law and Letters from Wabash College, as well as a host of denominational and local accolades.

An 1876 photograph reveals Presbyterians' newest pastor as a slender, somewhat unkempt bachelor with a dark scraggy beard and mustache. Another photograph of Little, ca. 1910, shows a portly Edwardianesque gentleman with a full, gray, and carefully squared beard. The latter portrait is somewhat too serious, too adulatory, tending to hide what must have been a fairly merry disposition in a man who was extremely gregarious and, very likely, quite happy with his lot in life. He liked to participate in picnics for young people, parishioners, and friends. He played baseball well into his middle age and sang with choruses at public events. His activities became a perennial topic of local news reporting, so that it seemed as if he were seated on the speakers' stand of every important community celebration. When Governor James P. Goodrich came to town in 1917 to address laborers and officials at the truck factory, he shared a makeshift platform with only one man, Little. Little seemed, at times, to be pastor to the whole community rather than only to those who paid his salary, for he was repeatedly invited to assist at the funerals and weddings of folks who were not of his flock. Remarkably, there is no known record of other ministers in town resenting his presence or his standing, although it would be straining credulity about clerical dispositions to imagine none existed.[35]

Typical of newspaper reports of Little's activities is a *Plain Dealer* entry for October 10, 1899. On that day Little performed the marriage of Olive Lutz to Sanford Honeywell's son, Mark Honeywell, at the bride's home on the southeast corner of Market and Cass streets (immediately east of the present-day Honeywell Community Center). Little, the paper observed, did his work "in his most happy manner." Then, apparently skipping out early on the reception, he traveled uphill to Bossler Walter's house on North Wabash Street where he wed Daisy Williams to Clarence LaSalle. He "performed" this way for fifty years, apparently creating goodwill in his wake. It is no wonder that the community's attention to his funeral rites in 1921 was effusive.[36]

His congregation, of course, flourished during his tenure, growing to more than five hundred members in the 1900s, which for nonevangelical Presbyterians—who scarcely knew how to invite someone to worship—is a significantly high number. Since the merger of Old and New School denominations in 1870, the Presbyterians had occupied the Old School's building across from the Christian church. In September 1880, eight years after Little's arrival, a local paper reported on his congregation's new building project: "The Presbyterian Church is rapidly looming up, and our people now begin to realize what a massive and splendid building it is to be."[37] The new building not only seemed massive, but it also was of a classic design and, save for the location of the new courthouse, it commanded the most prominent heights in town. It was designed by Fred Grant who likely used a current architectural plan book for his inspiration. A stereo-optic photography collection at the Wabash County Historical Museum includes the image of an unidentified church that was surely the inspiration and template for the exterior of the Wabash church: high peaked roof, soft-red brick, large rose window, and slender steeple. The Wabash version is an American Gothic Revival that is uncluttered, yet strong and decorative in its public presentation. Interiorly, it succumbed to the fashionable "auditorium" design, meaning that its nave floor is slightly bowed (east to west) as it slants downward (north to south) toward the chancel. (In this design the Presbyterians were perhaps trying to rival the neighboring Christians whose sanctuary was so acoustically advanced by appropriate curves.) Sloping, bowed floor aside, the lingering impression of the church's interior was of vaulted space, timbered ceiling supports, plenteous organ pipes, and, eventually, tiers of choir lofts rising from either side of a central pulpit. The lofts could accommodate a seventy-five voice chorus or a hundred fifty additional worshippers.[38]

Most churches acquired parsonages during this period, normally next door to the sanctuary. It is perhaps emblematic of Little's status in town and of his roots in the Hoosier missionary cause that by the 1890s the church's manse (Scottish term for a parsonage) was considered inadequate, though it was neither small nor antiquated. The fact is that while Little's family was not large, his ecclesiastical connections were often considerable. If a missionary, fellow pastor, presbytery official, seminary friend, or relative came to town, Little needed to put him up and feed him. Little also liked to entertain local or regional clergy in his home. The new Queen Anne-style Wabash manse, completed about 1894 at the cost of six thousand dollars, had three generous reception rooms—one with a grand, two-tiered oak staircase. The manse also had a formal dining room, a study/office with private entrance hall, a butler's pantry and supply pantry, a full kitchen, five large bedrooms, maid's quarters, four-room cellar, full attic, bath facilities, five exterior entrances, appropriate porches, and a large stone stable with loft. It was certainly competitive with the most avant-garde, stylish, and exuberant houses in town. As such it was a testimonial to Little's measurable success and to the material triumph of religion in Wabash in the nineteenth century. The Gilded Age had arrived, for better or worse, even in religion.[39]

10

The Guilty and the Gilt-less

However much Wabash society may have advanced in sophistication and sanctification in the Gilded Age, the place had a flip side, as all human communities surely did and surely do. For every dozen-or-so God-fearing, law-abiding, morally responsible citizens there were honest cynics, a criminal or two, and probably a few whose moral compasses regularly spun askew, at least by local standards. There is reliable evidence to suggest that such aberrations were not confined exclusively to any one class but were democratically scattered across the social landscape.

Early in the twenty-first century the house at 388 West Hill Street—on the northwest corner of Hill and Fisher—went on the market, not for the first time in recent years. It is an example of small-town domestic splendor for its period. Warren Bigler built the house in the 1890s. Designed in the Queen Anne style, it has retained its ample art-glass windows, a unique turret reminiscent of Carcassonne, and hints of Moorish influence. With Bigler's yen for rare rugs and tapestries the place became "a veritable storehouse for his treasures" during his lifetime. Though Bigler died in 1930, his widow and/or their descendants lived there through much of the remainder of the century. After passing out of the Bigler family's hands, the house changed owners with some frequency, survived brief periods of decrepitude, and was finally restored to quite respectable condition.

In 2005, as its owners were cleaning the house prior to moving out, they discovered a cache of letters hidden beneath the attic eaves. Most of the letters seem to have been addressed to Bigler, though envelopes are often missing and many of the letters lack addressee or correspondent names. A few appear to be rough drafts of Bigler's replies. Those that are dated were written in the 1880s and between 1899 and 1902. Although neither the context nor content of the letters is so transparent as one would hope, the collection is valuable because it provides intimate, if sporadic, glimpses into the life of a nineteenth-century Wabash citizen who was, if anything, very prominent, influential, popular, and highly respected.[1]

Bigler died at age seventy-nine near Hays, Kansas, on Sunday, September 28, 1930, in an automobile accident. His sudden death may be the reason his sequestered letters were not destroyed, as one or two of his correspondents had occasionally requested. Being chairman of Indiana's school for the deaf at the time of the accident, Bigler had been en route to Colorado Springs, Colorado, to attend a national convention about educating deaf people, just one of his many interests.

It would be difficult to find a more authoritative example of a pillar of society than Wabash's Bigler. One expects the local obituary for such a man to be abundant in praise, eschewing all foibles, and the *Wabash Plain Dealer*—that he had helped guide as a corporation officer—quite justifiably pulled out special stops. His original career had been the practice of law in Shelbyville. Coming to Wabash in 1875, he founded the Wabash Abstract and Loan Company, a major player in that business throughout the twentieth century. Later he helped organize a consortium of local entrepreneurs called the Board of Trade, using its influence to entice important industries to Wabash, including United Paperboard, Wabash Cabinet, and the Pioneer Hat Factory. With his partner, A. M. Atkinson, Bigler founded a long-standing farm loan business. He probably also owned part of a southern timber plantation. As years passed, his community service became as intense as his business interests. He was a longtime member of the Wabash school board, serving as its president for a number of years and proactive in the decision to build the new high school in 1894. He was present at the creation of a viable public library and was credited with having helped convince Andrew Carnegie to invest in a town so small as Wabash.[2] Although he never ran for office, Bigler influenced Republican politics. His service included terms as Republican county chairman, as secretary of the Republican state committee, and as state auditor. He counted presidents William McKinley and Theodore Roosevelt as good friends.

In evaluating Bigler's personal traits, the *Plain Dealer* emphasized his intellectual pursuits and kindness toward others. Both traits are verified in letters he left behind. With regard to his intellectual life it would be easy to speculate that he was the best-read person in town. He had built up a huge private library and read broadly in philosophy, theology, science, the arts, and both classical and modern literature. Many of his friendships were cemented around discussions of books and authors. He seemed intimately familiar with works of such literati as Emile Zola, Edmund Spenser, Charles Darwin, George Bernard Shaw, Henrik Ibsen, Gerhart Hauptmann, Maurice Maeterlinck, and Gabriele D'Annunzio, writers whose appeal would have been to a fairly narrow stratum of well-educated citizens. Of these authors Bigler identified often with Zola, Spenser, and Darwin. Zola was a modern novelist, a purveyor of sensual and fatalistic themes. Spenser was a sixteenth-century poet who emphasized the secular values guiding a person's moral and emotional life. Darwin was the nineteenth-century scientist whose theory of evolution was considered to be iconoclastic in many religious circles. Given that these three were among Bigler's favorite authors, it is fair to suggest that he was not only deeply intellectual but also demonstrably esoteric in thought and values, an anomaly for his time and place.

The letters also illustrate his kindness. A large number of letters in the collection are from Hazel Harter. She was vice principal of Wabash High School when Bigler was president of the school board. Between 1900 and 1902 Harter took an indefinite leave of absence from her position in order to live with family members in Colorado Springs, Colorado. Health concerns may have prompted her departure; in any case, in the high altitudes her physical condition deteriorated, forcing her to move temporarily to California. To support herself and help her family, she returned to Colorado Springs to teach. During her absence from Wabash she and Bigler carried on a lively correspondence. It was mostly about literature. He would recommend books for her to read. She would report on her reactions to them, or complain that they were not available at her local library, and keep him informed about her health and her family's welfare. Here was a very busy, prominent, and successful community leader devoting considerable time and thought to Harter's well-being by promoting her self-education, encouraging her self-esteem, and supporting her professionally. At one point he lent her three hundred dollars to see her family through an economic difficulty, and throughout her extended absence he seemed determined to hold open her vice principal position in Wabash indefinitely. Harter was probably in her thirties. Bigler was beginning his fifties. Their letters account for at least thirty-three of the eighty-three letters (and partial letters) in the collection. Although it is mystifying why he saved her letters (and rough copies of a few of his responses), there is no hint of anything romantic in their relationship. They were on a friendly but formal footing; her letters normally open with "Dear Mr. Bigler" and close, "Most sincerely, Hazel Harter." Every indication is that this was correspondence between two friends who had literature and Wabash High School in common, nothing more.

The same evaluation does not apply to other papers in the collection, some of which open tiny windows into Bigler's privacy, revealing the man as more devious and perhaps less honorable, certainly more susceptible to the human condition than he appears to be either in the Harter correspondence or in his laudatory obituary. For example, at least one letter casts a shadow upon the state of Bigler's marriage to Carrie Major Bigler. Carrie was also from Shelbyville and was a close relative of Shelbyville's Charles Major, author of the classic *Bears of Blue River* and a national literary figure at the turn of the twentieth century. It is possible, then, that Carrie came from a highly literate background that prepared her to be attractive to, and attracted by, a man such as Bigler. They married and moved to Wabash in 1875. Their only child, Herbert, was born four years later. Although Herbert married and produced a daughter, he spent time in the state mental facility in Logansport and died in 1916, while still in his thirties.

The year after Herbert's birth, in September 1880, Bigler received an unsigned letter from a Wabash resident warning him of his wife's deviant behavior. The letter has the flavor of the sort that deserves to be destroyed immediately and forgotten, a Nosey Parker's attempt to make trouble where no trouble really exists. Perhaps significantly, perhaps not, Bigler did not destroy it. "Dear Friend," the letter begins and then suggests that Bigler's work, industriousness, and goodness have kept him from knowing the truth. The "truth" is that his wife, often accompanied by a Miss Clare, is "in the streets every evening flirting and talking with the boys." Bigler may be aware that "she is down town more than any married woman," but he does not know how she acts when out of his sight. Not only does she "run around to catch beaux" in public, she also entertains men at home, men who would claim to be visiting her unmarried women friends there but who actually had come to visit Carrie. The writer claims not to be impugning Carrie's virtue but notes that her behavior has made her persona non grata among the married women of her social class.

Charges then become specific. One of the men Carrie was seen consorting with was "a travelling man . . . a pimp and associate of prostitutes" who was recently arrested in Logansport in "a house of ill fame." This man, Miss Clare, and Carrie had recently ambled west along Market Street to the Tremont lot where Carrie and the man were overheard to speak playfully about whether Carrie were really married. The traveling man then proposed that she ought to be married "at least for a little while" and winked at Carrie as he said it. There was much verbal interchange also between Carrie and a second man. Notwithstanding the fact that the latter was someone prosperous and of good reputation, the two were seen deep in conversation while Carrie leaned against him, putting her head on his shoulder. On the prior evening, the writer continued, Carrie was overheard to be having a conversation with a man in which the word "arrangement" recurred several times, "as if they were arranging a meeting." Soon thereafter he and another man, in saying goodnight to Carrie and Miss Clare, stated pointedly, "'Wabash depot in one half hour' as if they were to all four meet at the depot" at that time. The men and women then parted, but the letter writer, in following the women up Wabash Street hill in the direction of the depot, lost track of them. "Read carefully and reflect" are the writer's closing words.

If Carrie was, in fact, a woman who played fast and loose by local standards of behavior, this letter is all that is known about it. At worst it can only testify to coquetry on her part and might suggest that the private lives of the Biglers were less smooth than Warren's public and professional life seemed to be. The letter does exactly what the writer probably intended: it raises suspicions without proving a thing and may have been no more than a form of entertainment for its author.

There are other letters in the Bigler collection that bear witness not to Carrie's possible infidelity but to his. These are maddeningly vague while, at the same time, being undisputedly suggestive of serious liaisons between Bigler and one or more women. Two accompanying envelopes give the appearance of Bigler's having assumed the pseudonym of James H. Martin, at Wabash Post Office box number 435, for the purpose of receiving confidential correspondence. To that address an unnamed writer communicated from Winfield, Kansas, where her temporary housing (she reports) is both crowded and dismal but where apricots are in bloom and the general surroundings are romantic, like Italy in America. She quotes sentimental love poetry ("seize the passion") and uses mostly guarded language or literary references until near the end when she alludes to the "conquest," which has left her thinking, day and night, of the recipient and resenting their separation. Another brief note from an undisclosed location, but in the same handwriting and using the same purple ink as the former letter, recalls the pleasure of "keeping the 'Tryst.'" She has inferred that he may be tiring "of our little arrangement" but assures him that as they are not man and wife it can be easily broken off. In a third epistle that seems to be by the same hand and posted in Wabash, the writer speaks of the importance of fidelity between a husband and wife, makes a point of Bigler's marriage being five years old, and expresses the fear that his wife is now jealous of this correspondent so that her visits to the Bigler house must cease.

This correspondent was apparently not Bigler's only conquest, if conquest it was. Several communications are suggestive. In one note from another unidentified hand, the writer fairly screams her fury at his breaking their relationship: "And this is the end! This is friendship! . . . Have I not fulfilled all my promises to you? Have you heard even the slightest allusion to anything wrong in regard to my conduct? . . . All hope is gone . . . life is a blank and a wreck—what is there to live for?—Nothing!" She makes one last request, for "a few moments conversation with you this evening—at our house." It is signed "Your Friend." A yet more intriguing epistle, dated October 1880 from Hot Springs, Arkansas, is from another "Friend" who has traveled from Wabash to the spa city to put herself under the care of a Doctor Gebhart. The physician believes he can work a cure of her ailment in two to three months. "His examination," she reports, "revealed a terrible fact—one which I cannot tell you—it is so terrible that if I had my baby here you would never see me again. . . . He said that I had been terribly imposed on and that had I not come here when I did my life would have been short." She promises to tell Bigler everything when she returns home, but he must burn this letter and keep its content to himself. "All I ask is for you to think kindly of me—& pity me—oh pity me in this dire trouble." A photograph in the collection may have accompanied this letter. If it is of the writer, she was at the time a slender, dark haired woman, perhaps in her thirties and photographed in a stylish black dress of the period.

One probes the Bigler collection apologetically, aware of intruding into intimate spaces. The historical significance of these letters—these glimpses into quite private matters—is their illustration of life as it could exist beneath laudatory obituaries, sanitized church histories, and elegant soirees. For example, in one of his rough-draft responses to Harter, Bigler styles himself as a disciple of Spenser and Darwin who believes that there is no sin except sin against one's self, a concept not easily meshed with orthodox Christian doctrine. Bigler was a trustee of the Presbyterian Church. Clearly there may have been a disconnect between Bigler's public persona as a believing Calvinist and his private scruples. This is not surprising. It indicates that in a time when religion is in ascendancy men and women join churches not only out of conviction but also for reasons of communal solidarity, with doctrine and theology playing a minor role in some folks' loyalty to a church. Conversely, the modernizing tendencies in theology during this period, of which he might well have been aware, could have encouraged a man such as Bigler to think in more liberated theological terms. He could have been both an honest cynic and a faithful Presbyterian. His pastor, Charles Little, would surely not have approved of any extramarital liaisons Bigler may have pursued, though Little presumably was not privy to them. And what Little might possibly have applauded in Bigler's intellectual journey we cannot guess because, unlike Bigler, he left no known cache of private letters revealing the minister's own interior spirit.

Bigler was neither the first nor the last nineteenth-century Wabash citizen of prominence to have slipped into suspicious relationships, though few are documented. A documented case from earlier years concerns William R. Winton. Winton was a physician who had set up practice in Wabash about 1851. He was a graduate of Oxford Academy in Ohio and a trustee of Wabash College at Crawfordsville. For his 1873 obituary a *Plain Dealer* journalist interpreted a crusty professional exterior as cover for less obvious virtues: Winton was "open" and "plain spoken," could not abide evasions and was "blunt"; but he also had a "sympathizing heart" and kept current with advanced medical procedures. However crusty he may have been, he was popular in spite of it. Although he had been out of circulation for two years prior to his death, being confined with paralysis and "softening of the brain," his funeral at the Christian church drew a full house, with clergy from three denominations presiding.[3]

In 1858 Winton ran afoul of his church's local governing board, which had authority to serve as a "court" or judicatory with oversight of communicants' spiritual health and moral behavior. This judicatorial power had been especially useful to churches on the earlier, rough frontier where secular court and police systems were not yet powerful enough to bring a sense of order and responsibility to community life. Churches were often equipped by their denominational polity to order life rigidly among the faithful. It was the surviving net of that ecclesiastical practice that snared Winton. Ironically, the board's clerk at the time was Judge John L. Knight, who had acquitted Winton in 1853 of an assault and battery charge before Wabash's Court of Common Pleas. Despite that brush with notoriety Winton had been a church member in good standing prior to 1858. It is Knight's notes that provide documentation of the Winton case. The charges against the doctor were multiple, all relating to inappropriate pursuit of females. When "public rumor" could no longer be ignored, elders of the board gave Winton the opportunity to request an investigation. He declined, stating that he was powerless to refute the charges because of the nature of them but that he would not resent the board's exercise of its duty.[4]

In consequence the church officers drew up three specific accusations that needed testing, all alleging that Winton had committed "gross immorality and Unchristian conduct" by "proposing and attempting scandalous familiarities, and illicit connections, with different women at different times and places, within the last two or three years." The first accusation stipulated that in 1856 Winton had forced himself upon Mrs. Henry C. Miles by entering her rented room uninvited and "proposing an embrace to her." The second charged that the accused had accosted Frances Bishop in one of the upstairs rooms of the county Poor Farm in September 1858. The third specified "proposals and declamations" made to Mrs. Frederica Moses by the accused at Winton's office in February 1859.

The following month the church board summoned witnesses, including Miles, Bishop, and Moses, to testify as to the authenticity of the charges. Copies of witnesses' testimonies were subsequently handed to the accused, who concurred that a trial should go forward. On March 8 Knight wrote out the board's opinion: "Resolved—That we find from the evidence before us Brother William R. Winton guilty as charged thus far, and <u>no farther</u>, viz., that he has been guilty of attempting such unbecoming familiarities with ladies, as lead us to believe his designs therein, to have been grossly immoral and wicked." There was also a sentence. Winton was excluded from church privileges until such time that he had given satisfactory evidence of repentance. Essentially Winton was excommunicated. In "the interests of Religion," there would be no publication of the trial or its results except for a copy of the board's resolutions that was to be handed to Winton.

Given the board's attempt to keep its proceedings under wraps, the case might have ended there had Winton not taken matters into his own hands.

He appealed his conviction and sentence to his denomination's regional judicatory. In April 1859 that body criticized the local court's handling of the case, but sustained the results. Winton was still an excommunicant. He nevertheless stood his ground, appealing to yet a higher church judicatory, one governing ecclesiastical matters across the state of Indiana. This time he was exonerated by a reversal of the decisions of the two lower courts. By late October 1859 Winton was officially back in good standing with his church.

And, yet, it was not over. Apparently, in the wake of Winton's appeal, the local board's attempts to keep the case quiet failed utterly, to Winton's disadvantage. The "minds of the greater part of the Church," according to Knight's notes, had been turning the matter over, with the result that new rumors and fresh evidence emerged. The board had reason to suspect that Winton was "guilty of . . . unchristian conduct" in the months since his recent trial. Pending an examination of these new charges, or Winton's repentance of them, the board admonished him "not to go to the Lord's Table." On October 25, 1859, Knight recorded Winton's capitulation. The man requested in writing that his name be stricken from the list of church members, "a request that will be best for all concerned."

As with activities illustrated in the Bigler cache, Winton's moral aberrations point the finger at Wabash's so-called upper class, those who had made money, succeeded socially, or were in enviable positions of influence. This stratum was clearly not immune to the call of sexual adventures outside the bonds of marriage, yet little of it is recorded. Most such activity lies beyond verification, versions of it passing down through family stories and inherited gossip, much of which would have sprung from grains of truth if not from whole stalks of it. In such stories lie promiscuity, bigamy, infidelity, prostitution, and even murder. For example, a scion of a prominent family, on a ride with a young friend in the family buggy that he was driving north on Wabash Street, showed his companion a neat trick by dropping the reins and saying, "Watch this." The horse continued north and, without direction from the driver, turned west on Stitt Street and, a little farther on, turned north into an establishment run by Madam Lum Hong (as she was popularly called), stopping at a hitching post at the rear of the two-story, duplex-like residence. This place may have been the memorable (but, again, quite undocumented) "House of the Blue Lights," a venue for prostitution.[5]

The significance of the son's experiment with the reins was, of course, to demonstrate to his friend that his prominent father frequented Madam

Hong's so often his horse knew the way instinctively once its course had been set northward on Wabash Street. To the degree this story is based on fact, it corroborates the assumption that extramarital liaisons such as Bigler and Winton pursued were not unusual among the town's gentry, may have been commonly acknowledged by close friends or family members, and were more widely practiced in Wabash than local news editors and other sources willingly revealed. Given its modus operandi, its location, and some of its clientele, Madam Hong's alleged business might have received a modicum of local respect for tastefulness and discretion. Indeed, a footnote to this part of the Hong story says that Madam liked to fill her buggy with a few of her stylishly dressed "girls" and drive them to the Pioneer Hat Factory on Manchester Avenue at closing time on pay day so that they could solicit business as the men left work. According to this line of thought, Madam was Wabash's premier, top-of-the-line demimondaine.[6]

There is nothing in these undocumented tales, however, to prove that Madam Hong ran a bordello or even that she was a prostitute. Nevertheless, the woman had a dark side that was documented. Her husband was a respected, popular laundryman, Lum Hong, whose downtown business had been at various locations, including East Canal Street and the Masonic Lodge basement on Wabash Street. A native of Pekin (Peking, Beijing), China, he had immigrated to the United States in 1878 and worked mostly as a cook and restaurateur before settling in Wabash ten years later. In 1904 he applied for naturalization, but for unclear reasons was unsuccessful. His wife was the former Irene Glass of Plymouth, Indiana, and Chicago. They were married in the Windy City in 1891, where he had relatives, and returned to Wabash. Lum Hong died at age fifty in 1909. His home address was on the northwest corner of Stitt and Miami streets, within a block of the possible site of the "House of the Blue Lights."

Meanwhile, however, tragedy struck the Hong marriage, making front-page news in Wabash in a way that must have wagged tongues for days if not longer. On July 20, 1896, Elijah Hackleman made a typically succinct, understated entry in his diary, noting that William P. Moore had shot the "Chinaman's wife" and then killed himself. A thirty-five-year-old bachelor, Moore had fallen passionately in love with Madam Hong, who was then in her early twenties. Mr. Hong was far from sanguine about this relationship, which cast him into the role of an angry, jealous cuckold. Moore was from a respectable family living in the west end of Wabash. Will and two brothers shared a house on Alena Street. Though a popular, likable chap, he was afflicted with an addiction to alcohol and, as it turned out, to the Madam, who did little to discourage his attentions. Evidence obtained later from private correspondence indicated that at one point in their relationship they were both infatuated, giving each other the nicknames "Papa" and "Mamma." The newspaper described her as a handsome woman in the face and form, so attractive that several young Wabash men had "worshiped at her shrine." Moore's brothers and other members of the family, out of love for the man, had paid to have him undergo various cures for alcohol addiction.

In the summer of 1896 Moore was a resident of Warsaw, taking one more cure for alcoholism, though public speculation was that the family's real motive had been to remove him from Madam's immediate presence. That ploy failed. Moore was able to sneak back into Wabash by train to meet her. His credit was good enough for him to order transportation ahead of time: a horse and buggy ready at the Big Four station in case the couple wanted to travel to Peru or to other distant places. Moore engaged liveryman Lynn Dawes as a contact when he wanted to make secret visits to Wabash. On one such visit he and Madam Hong had to speed away in their buggy to avoid being caught by her enraged husband. More than once Moore arranged to meet with Madam at the home of Henry Graves whose house was conveniently located a block from the station on the northwest corner of Allen and Market streets. According to the press it was a recognized "house of assignation."

At 8:45 p.m. Monday evening, July 20, 1896, while the Graves family was absent from home, five shots rang out in that vicinity. Even though a domestic employee in the house thought the shots had come from outdoors, those who were loitering at the Big Four station quickly determined that the shots came from indoors. A *Plain Dealer* reporter was one of the first to enter the house. He immediately saw Madam robed in night clothes and seated in the front room, though later reports indicated that she may have collapsed to the floor. She was pallid and covered with blood, with her right arm already in a sling. Moore had shot her, she said, and then turned the pistol on himself. She had received four slugs, one through the left arm, two through the right arm, and one in the back that exited near the naval. Powder burns from the last shot were on her clothes; that shot was potentially fatal, depending on internal damage. Later examinations concluded that while the liver had been damaged the bowels probably had not; the woman was critical but not moribund.

Madam was lucid enough at the scene of the crime to say that she and Moore had earlier gone upstairs to bed. There Moore insisted that she divorce her husband and marry him. She refused, perhaps not for the first time. Moore reached for his revolver that was hanging with his clothes. He fired in the dark while lying in bed, which explains why his shots seemed poorly aimed for murder. She was beginning to flee when he shot her in the back. The victim was taken away in a hack, which she ordered to be halted at Hong's laundry so that he might be apprised of the situation. He "cracked his fists" in consternation but hurriedly left to meet his wife at their Stitt Street address.

Two policemen and two marshals were the first to reach Moore. He was in the front upstairs room sprawled on a bed in his own blood. Nearby lay a six-shot Smith and Wesson revolver. He begged the officers to hand it to him so he could finish killing himself. Instead they carried him to his father's home where he received medical care. The bullet had lodged near his heart. Nothing could be done to save him. He died at 5:00 a.m. the next morning.

Although this episode was not Madam's only brush with the law over prostitution, the Hong marriage lasted until his death thirteen years later. It is uncertain how long her recovery from the Moore shooting was or how complete. Nor is it known what effect the scandal had on her business interests. What is known is that the Hongs joined Saint Bernard Roman Catholic Church in 1901. Whether that signaled a shift either in their marriage or in her reputation remains a matter of speculation. It is known that she later married Edward Moss and that they had a daughter. Irene Glass Hong Moss was buried at Plymouth, Indiana, in 1960, at age eighty-six.

Until the shooting of Madam Lum Hong, the local newspaper had reported relatively little about her or her alleged career. The same was not true with regard to the downtown houses of ill repute. They seemed to incorporate the worst of the human condition: poverty, overcrowding, health hazards, abused children, violence, and, of course, promiscuity. They were easy targets for the press. The *Plain Dealer* complained bitterly about the likes of a "Degraded old wretch," Henry E. White, a "monster," a "professional debauchee" who cohabited with the "vilest wrecks of femininity."[7] He had been spotted near the river bridge with a "degraded harlot" whom he met by appointment. He reeked with disease. It would be good, opined the journalist, to assign him to the "yawning abyss" of hell in the near future. Meanwhile he had been arrested and fined forty dollars, notwithstanding his defense that his wife was an invalid. His fine was fairly stiff. Henry and Malinda Snyder, alias Vandyne, had had to pay a fine of twenty-five dollars each, plus costs, for keeping a house of ill repute.[8]

By the 1880s prostitution was well established in the downtown area. It differed from that of earlier decades mainly by being slightly better housed—gone were Irish shanties along the canal—and by a potentially steadier supply of customers—permanent employees of downtown enterprise rather than transient canal and railroad laborers. Local residents were certainly aware what was going on and where. When "Uncle David Thompson" was conned out of fifty cents at the Methodist church by a fellow who claimed to be a printer, a prospective church member and down on his luck, a suspicious citizen followed the man far enough to watch him disappear with Thompson's money in "close proximity . . . to a bawdy house."[9] Some of the "bawds" were well enough known locally to merit their own publicity, as when the *Plain Dealer* alerted readers that "The Big Girl that slung hash" at Roann had moved to Wabash.[10] At a hotel called the Sherman House two women, Amanda Bennett and Mattie Howard, were under constabulary surveillance for much of 1883 before an officer caught them "in flagrante delicto" with Jason Tucker and William Stone who had stopped by to indulge in "unhallowed intimacy." The former was a bartender and the latter a laborer at the Cincinnati, Wabash, and Michigan railroad shops. The women, not the men, were arrested, although the proprietor, Henry Unger, was charged with operating a house of prostitution. Unger had kept part of the women's fees. His policy was that "the girls could make as much as they wanted to upstairs" so long as his wife did not find out.[11]

Wabash had already developed an unenviable reputation for prostitution beyond its own borders. In the spring of 1878 the *Indianapolis Sentinel* ran a "Personal" item that read, "Wanted by four frolicsome feminines, four or more fun-loving fellows." Those interested were instructed to contact "Sophrona, Sabina, Serina and Salina" at Post Office Box 460, Wabash. The local editor dismissed the item as only a "tease," but it was rather too elaborate a tease not to raise suspicions that business in Wabash was brisk.[12] Although the local law enforcement kept an eye on the trade, occasionally closing houses and/or fining their proprietors (as in the case of Unger), it also unwittingly abetted it at times by running competition out of town. When two prostitutes from Marion came to "take in the sights" of Wabash and were followed through town by five young men, the marshal jailed the women. They won their release by promising to leave town at once.[13] With prostitution a high-profile scandal in town, it is interesting that, unlike law enforcement, the churches did not address it, at least not with the directness with which they had attacked alcohol consumption. A very popular, earnest, and fiery evangelist, James Bitler, who came to town under the auspices of the Methodist Church, led a public session on moral issues for men only. Apparently Bitler said little about the obvious temptations of local fleshpots, zeroing in instead on what he considered to be the despicable impurity of "self-pollution," the current euphemism for masturbation and an alleged cause of insanity.[14]

In later decades Wabash's prostitution industry centered around second-rate hotels in the eastern end of downtown, but before that time a particular hot spot was West Canal and West Market streets. No place was more notorious there than the "Barracks," a long, low tenement built for two families that often held more than that. The Barracks was just one of five houses of prostitution in the district in 1883, but it had become a synonym for vice and debauchery. A variety of crimes were perpetrated by couples who lived temporarily at the Barracks and who were infamous not only for prostitution but also for sending their children into the streets to steal and to beg. Apparently some of the neighboring houses of ill repute were owned by respectable citizens who had trouble getting rid of disreputable tenants. H. B. Lasselle tried vigorously to oust one Jane McNeil from his house in order to quiet neighbors' complaints about her, but he failed. T. C. Hutchins rented his house to a Mr. and Mrs. Bones. Mrs. Bones was the former Tish Higgins, a hooker of established reputation. Hutchins tried to dislodge the Boneses because Tish kept soliciting in broad daylight in full view of employees of a pork house. On one occasion Mr. Bones did not approve of his wife's client, so he knocked the man into Charley Creek and walked off arm in arm with Tish, true love seemingly triumphant. Again, the law tried sporadically to suppress this West End prostitution, but the effort was uphill and frustrating. At a time when the Barracks was in full operation the town's deputy marshal sought to arrest a "boarder" who was a well-known citizen and family man, thinking perhaps that such an arrest would put a dent in future traffic there, but his quarry skipped out the back door. Long-suffering neighbors tried to support the law by organizing a citizens' stakeout that would discourage visitors to the Barracks. It worked for one night only, when no one showed up, but after that it was business as usual.[15]

Prostitution was not the only form of misbehavior rampant during Wabash's Gilded Age. Drunkenness continued to plague the place, as it had in prewar days. Neither legal nor moralistic campaigns were permanently potent against it. At times the problem seemed pandemic. In April 1883 the "unsullied pages" of Mayor George Stephenson's court record were "now Teeming with [cases related to] Drunks," raising the query, "what are we going to do with them?"[16] The calaboose was repeatedly filled up. The scoundrels' wives, who worked hard over washtubs, had to spend their money paying fines. The mayor was giving thought to forming a chain gang, or even using the lash, as means of making a lasting impression on the perpetrators. Meanwhile, in one thirteen-day period Stephenson jailed ten men for drunkenness and fined each of them $9.05 plus costs. The following month the mayor hired an experienced law man from Ohio, W. C. Worthington, to be deputy marshal. He became a terror to the criminal element, deriding namby-pamby treatment of drunks and promising to arrest all offenders, no matter their status. He jailed the inebriated left and right, including those who had successfully defied the law in the past.[17]

With drunkenness came public rowdiness. A well-known case in point was that of Milton Sims who was "not a bad man"; indeed, he was muscular, courageous, agreeable, and obliging when sober. However, once he made "too free [a] use of liquor" he could set records for getting into skirmishes. After one thirteen-month-long communion with sobriety, Sims launched "a grand row." In the middle of the night he attacked two friends sharing a room above the Jones and Ditton Saloon. They subdued him and turned him over to the mayor's court, where he was fined five dollars the next morning. By afternoon he was back at the saloon in a noisy mood. Ditton asked him to keep quiet, but, instead, Sims attacked him. By the time the marshal arrived, six men were brawling. Sims was dragged off to the mayor's court again but not until one of the other brawlers had assaulted Sims with a "slung-shot [*sic*]." The mayor imposed a bond and ordered Sims back to court the following week. As he left the mayor's office he met Ditton on the street and struck at his neck with a knife. Ditton warded off the blow to his neck but sustained a deep stab wound above an eye and lost a little finger. This time the mayor imposed a two thousand dollar bond, fined the drunk another five dollars, and bound him over to circuit court for trial. Sims tried to counter by asserting that the "slung-shot" attack had been done with intent to kill.[18]

The problem in Wabash was that while Sims may have been more erratic than most, rowdies of his kind were legion. True enough, not all transgressions in this category were of the sort that merited attention in a later age.

For example, in October 1871, twenty-six people were convicted on a variety of charges, all but one—maybe two—of which seem ludicrous in retrospect: gambling, horse racing, Sabbath breaking, illicit fishing, and retailing liquor to minors. But beneath those transgressions lay a genuine concern for communal tranquility and decency. When Marshal Bruner was unable to quell a row between "roughs" from Wabash and those from out of town in early 1883, the crowd jeered him and laughed, the whole street echoing "with a loud guffaw." Bruner tried to force his way through the melee, to no avail, and then attempted to deputize a few men who were there, again failing. Worthington, the next to try, proved somewhat more effective. The "gilded youth" who indulged in "bug juice" thought they might have the best of him also. One drunken ruffian even fired a couple of shots at Worthington. When the latter threatened to club the youth the crowd cried, "Shame!" but he was also gathering broad respect from those who realized that "He ain't paid to run a gospel temperance society."[19] But even Worthington was up against a growing force of street roughs who thought they owned the night. Regularly the silence of the evenings was shattered by boisterous and obscene shouting, and there were nights when street intersections in the residential parts of town were gathering points for rowdy and drunken youth.[20]

While drunken youths and slightly older miscreants were major irritants, a few chronic offenders were neither young nor from among the unprivileged "roughs." A favorite target of the *Plain Dealer* was John H. (Doc) DePuy who had settled in Wabash late in the 1840s. It was said of him at his death that he had arrived with $6.00 and then accumulated $150,000. Doc and his son Romeo DePuy erected two of the premier houses in Wabash, side by side on Sinclair Street. Both are extant in the twenty-first century. DePuy was a physician, an investor in real estate, a close friend socially of other prominent men in town, accompanying two of them on East Coast and European junkets, and—according to the newspaper—a reeling drunk. It is possible the *Plain Dealer* made much of DePuy's drinking because the man was also a leading Democrat in town. The paper implied, for example, that DePuy had inspired a Democratic plot to get voters drunk so they would vote as told. Whatever their motivation, editors would not leave the man alone, skewering him in print repeatedly and recording his casual visitations to local saloons. When the county fair was under way in 1880, a reporter wrote, "All the drunken men in Wabash were arrested during the fair except Doc DePuy. Doc was cavorting about the streets and on the fair grounds calling people sons of bitches, denouncing Republicans as damned liars and scoundrels, and inviting any and everybody to kiss the most prominent part of his anatomy—but the officers apparently didn't hear a word of it."[21]

More deserving, perhaps, were jabs about DePuy's reputation as a cruel landlord. According to the newspaper, he owned a "miserable hovel," a shanty at the corner of Cass and Canal streets. It had sustained fire damage, was missing half its windows, suffered a roof so leaky it looked "like a ventilator," had a defective flue, and needed a lot of plaster and weatherboarding. A previous renter had removed his Jersey cow from the place because it was unfit even for animals. Into this hovel DePuy moved a man named Daniel Browel (also known as Samuel Brower), his wife, and a daughter who had been tenants of a farm north of town before DePuy sold it out from under them. Browel had worked the farm but he was old and had a crippled arm. When he tried to obtain a financial settlement from DePuy for his downward shift in living conditions, DePuy offered him ten dollars. The family's alternative was the county's Poor Farm but Mrs. Browel refused, asserting pluckily that she was able-bodied and knew how to work; if the county could just give them sugar and coffee they would survive. Within a week, however, Browel was dead. The county buried him in the Old Cemetery. According to the *Plain Dealer* death was quite likely attributable to exposure in DePuy's "miserable shanty." It was "A sad commentary on human justice," the paper moralized, "By their fruits ye shall know them."[22]

In addition to drunken and rowdy behavior, burglaries and break-ins were common. So was pickpocketing, especially during any large public event or when a traveling circus was in town. Gangs of so-called footpads occasionally made residential areas dangerous, in particular for women outside after dark. The "awful Anderson gang" from out of town did not always bother to hide under cover of darkness; when they were not busy thieving, gang members relaxed openly in local saloons, where their boisterous behavior and obscene threats presented a special challenge to the town marshal. The gang claimed the law would never incarcerate its members, but in one showdown Bruner and Worthington, working together, got the "nippers" on the right wrist of the gang leader, only to discover that the man was a left-handed slugger and still dangerous. While friends cheered him on the culprit pulled out a Smith and Wesson with his left hand and fired off two shots. He missed everyone and faced both a fine and the grand jury.[23]

Folks were especially excited by an assault on Mrs. Alf Harter who, on a spring evening, had left her husband downtown and walked alone toward home along Hill Street. She passed a short, burly man in a slouched hat standing by a gate. When she reached Comstock Street he caught up with her, grabbed her by the wrist, pinned down an arm, and ripped from her grasp a purse containing $2.50 in silver, a key, and a few other items. She screamed for help. Because of dark shadows cast by a new streetlight, identification of the assailant was unclear, but the next day Constable Frank Lines took on the case. At the corner of Hill and Thorne streets Lines came upon two suspicious-looking men, one tall, one short. "You --- --- ---, we want you!" yelled the constable. He drew his revolver and fired. The ball went into the ground. The two suspects fled. "Halt, you --- --- ---," yelled Lines again. The men drew their revolvers and fired back, with one bullet buzzing close by Lines's cranium. One of the two then emptied his revolver completely, to no effect. The quarry escaped. The constable was left with a shoe size taken from a footprint, but back downtown next day he could find no matching shoe sizes among the potential suspects. When shortly thereafter another woman was stopped near Maple Street by a "rough" who stuck his "ugly phiz" in her face, the general opinion about town was that Wabash had become a favored stopping off place for thugs. It was further speculated that crooks liked to come to town on one evening train, do their dirty work, and then take the next train out.[24]

The modus operandi of burglars and sneak thieves seemed especially brazen. They walked into houses, barns, and shops both day and night, picking up whatever attracted them. There seemed to be no end of them. Barns were easy to break into, and almost all home owners kept a ladder on the premises, which facilitated second-story invasions. Not surprisingly the first inmate of the new county jail in 1881 was a thief, Anthony Baker, who had snatched George Schultz's crosscut saw. One June night a man entered Mrs. Wade's boardinghouse, on Main Street just west of Wabash Street, where nineteen youthful boarders were sleeping soundly and, going room to room, made off with three hundred dollars. Another nighttime intruder liked to toss chloroform generously around the bedrooms of his victims so that they would not interrupt his work, but when he splashed some on Mrs. Jerry McCarty as she slept, her sudden coughing spoiled the effect. A female burglar, Mag Hayes, deserved a prize for nonchalance. She specialized in towns along the Wabash River, wore stylish clothes she had stolen, avoided hiding from the public, and operated during daylight hours. One day she carried a carpetbag into the home of Mrs. J. M. Tilford, went upstairs for watches and gloves, climbed to the attic for clothes, descended the back stairs to the kitchen (where she asked a servant girl for a glass of water), and, then, finding the back gate locked, left by the front gate. Mrs. Tilford was home at the time. Alerted, an officer caught up with Hayes at a downtown hotel. It would not be her first time in court locally. She was known always to win her case. As far back as the 1860s "citizens [had been] thoroughly alarmed" by such crimes and were admonished to have guns and pistols ready and to "shoot the scamps as you would shoot a dog."[25] By contrast, however, there were those thieves who were so comparatively harmless, or so coy, that they almost became pets of the news reporters. One was nicknamed "The Festive Burglar." He once entered Henry Herff's home on Hill Street, turned on the kitchen light, visited an icebox on the back porch, fixed a meal, had a smoke, then stole some overshoes and the coffee, but not the silver. He left the overshoes in the alley.[26]

Infidelity, promiscuity, prostitution, and criminality touched all Wabash directly or indirectly to some degree, but as in any community Wabash citizens also experienced unwholesome human conditions that were unrelated to immorality and crime. Simply put, grisly things occurred, some curious, some tragic. And there were individuals whose lives, through no special fault of their own, had not been enriched by the Gilded Age in ways the wealthy and prominent had been. Now and then existence showed a grim side and, for some, that condition seemed unfair, personal, and permanent.

A man named Smith, one of Ed Bechtol's tenants on East Hill Street, caused a sensation when he dug up a human skull while digging a hole in his yard. It was the second week of June 1883. Smith took the skull to a physician, Doctor Smith. The doctor cleaned the skull, revealing signs of blood stain. A bone at the base of the nose was broken, and there were contusions on one side. It was the skull of an adult white male, age forty to fifty years old. Doctor Smith suspected murder, and he, or someone else, remembered that there had been a "bawdy house" near the Bechtol property "years ago." Further digging ensued, and the newspaper published mounting speculations about the case. Was the skull that of Jacob Pearson who had last been seen in 1871 or 1872? Did it belong to a boarder in the boardinghouse that a Mrs.

Bittner had kept at the address? The unnamed boarder had also disappeared, leaving his boots and his pantaloons. Were Pearson and the boarder one and the same? The case for murder solidified. The following week additional witnesses emerged with confusing testimony. Ed Skully said that Pearson had never lived at the place, though he ate supper there on occasion, and when he disappeared he had left a coat, a hat, and boots. Bittner denied any knowledge of Pearson.[27]

Then—the fourth week in June—Thomas Fowler, who had formerly occupied the premises, revealed all. He had buried the skull. He had found it with other bones eighteen months earlier in the Old Cemetery at the east end of Hill Street. Because of his interest in physiology Fowler had taken the skull home for study. Eventually he threw it into his back yard where it was occasionally "kicked around." His wife found that irritating, so he buried it. He speculated that the bones were from a burial about forty years earlier and that, in the course of a more recent interment in the overcrowded plot, the earlier remains had been deposited near the surface. He had found them sticking out of the soil. Fowler's revelation had the salutary effect of alerting the town once again to the chronically decrepit condition of the original cemetery. Gravestones were broken, weeds were rank, and cans, rubbish, and brush abounded. But it would be a new century before a permanent solution was adopted.[28]

Inevitably public interest in individual misfortunes was always intense, something reporters exploited in almost every newspaper edition. Nor was it the current journalistic style to censor grisly details. Lizzie Hildebrand and other women employees of Whiteside and Lee's Woollen Mill had been advised against wearing their hair loose at work. On a late November work day Lizzie had failed to heed the caution. Suddenly, as she worked, a belt on a large piece of machinery caught her tresses, yanking her upward, high above whirring machinery almost to the upper floor. Another worker, Kate Hildebrand, caught Lizzie's dress in time to save her from critical injury, perhaps from death. Half her hair was pulled out, leaving her bald on the left side of her head, her fingers were crushed, and one had to be amputated. The company agreed to pay her wages until she could return to work or until the mill reached its seasonal shutdown.[29]

The railroads were also chronically dangerous, mangling the careless. Charles Sheridan's death in May 1896, made especially gruesome reading. He was forty years old. On the evening in question he was reportedly drunk, but not suicidal as circumstances might have suggested. He apparently wandered along the alley just north of Hill Street to a spot behind the Sailors family barn, about halfway between Wabash and Miami streets. He lay down with his head on the south rail of the track, a hand cupping his head. A train came. His brains scattered. When Coroner Gibson arrived he found a teaspoon of brains still lying in the cupped hand.[30]

Before central heat and electric lights were common in homes, house fires flared frequently. A Miss Bruner was dressing at home, upstairs, when she knocked over a coal-oil lamp, setting her clothes alight. Fortunately, friends who had been waiting for her downstairs ran upstairs to find her under the bed in flames. An acquaintance named Mary dragged her out and threw a bucket of water on her. All her clothes were burned off, but her flesh wounds, thought serious, were not fatal. She was expected to recover under the care of Doctor Winton.[31]

The streets that Hugh Hanna and David Burr had created going straight up the bluff on the Original Plat continued to be inhospitable to traffic throughout the century, even though Wabash Street had been radically graded to a more manageable slope in the 1860s. On a July day in 1883, at about 11:30 in the morning, Mr. and Mrs. A. S. Kilby left their home at Maple and Huntington streets for a buggy trip downtown. The buggy had been newly purchased, and the horse belonged to the Reverend L. L. Carpenter. As the couple began to descend Wabash Street, Mrs. Kilby opened her umbrella, startling the horse, which began to run. As the horse and buggy careened downhill, Mrs. Kilby was thrown to the street without serious injury. Mr. Kilby tugged the reins, trying to bring the animal to a halt, but to no avail. The horse swerved to avoid a pile of building stones in front of the new city hall that was still under construction at the corner of Main Street. The maneuver threw the buggy and its driver onto the stones. The horse was stopped at the bottom of the hill, but Mr. Kilby had to be carried to a nearby grocery and then to his home. So severe were his injuries that several physicians attended him. There were compound fractures to a leg, a knee, and an arm, his head was cut, and there were internal injuries. By press time reports on his condition were encouraging. Nevertheless, he died.[32]

Not in the least associated with grisly matters, but of perennial bemusement, was the local curiosity known as Nancy Everly, a woman untouched by the material blessings of the Gilded Age who was, nonetheless, virtually legendary by the dawn of the twentieth century. She had come to Wabash in the early 1840s and died in her home on North Cass Street in 1893. For most of that half century she was the widow of Peter Everly, a kinsman of Hugh Hanna. In the last twenty years of her life Everly lived off county welfare, although the Presbyterians may also have subsidized her existence in small ways. Like so many impoverished citizens she would have been soon forgotten were it not for an eccentricity she exhibited in public for twenty-five years.

Whenever she was out about town she took with her a walking stick to which she had affixed a white flag, presumably as a symbol of purity. Such a flag may have been a common symbol of the day but, apparently, not a universally admired one locally. Tish Higgins, the notorious bawd of West Market Street, caused a public ruckus by attempting—unsuccessfully—to tear down a white flag of purity flying in her neighborhood. But Everly had been undeterred in her cause. When she met another pedestrian she would lift the flag, telling the person that only by passing under the white flag would he or she be able to enter the Kingdom of Heaven. This eccentricity might have passed quickly from public remembrance had not famed Wabash County author Gene Stratton-Porter immortalized it by naming one of her novels *The White Flag* in which the character Crazy Becky is based on Nancy Everly.[33]

Everly's existence is a reminder that a great many citizens passed their days in poverty or near poverty, dependent on public welfare, private charity, family care, or menial employment. As has been indicated, the poor also included the prostitutes, much of the common criminal element and their families, and the families of habitual drunks. Most of the poor, however, must have been quite respectable citizens who lived long decades in economic restriction. Exact percentages of the truly poor are difficult to determine. In the early 1870s and again in the 1890s hazardous national economic conditions exacerbated the hardships of local populations generally. Although in most years most Wabash adult males were employed and generally safe within a broad middle class, serious financial pitfalls were always plentiful in an economy that was basically laissez faire, there being no broad, tax-funded safety nets beyond local welfare. The fortunate laboring citizen worked until he or she was too feeble to do so and then lived with relatives. Reasonably secure also were those unmarried females who had found employment as domestic help or, such as Lizzie Hildebrand, as part of a workforce in light industry. A woman's best chance for security was, of course, marriage to a hardworking man.

None was so poor, so cast-off from the Gilded Age, as an orphan. Helpless orphans were thrown upon the public's compassion by bastardy, by abandonment, or by those vicissitudes that sent parents to graves prematurely. In early years such children were either indentured or housed by the county at its Poor Farm, where adult indigents also lived. Out in the county Quakers founded White's Institute south of Wabash for educating Native American children and, later, orphans and delinquents from the general population, but the city developed its own solutions more slowly. At mid-century an outside organization called the Children's Aid Society sent agents to Wabash with orphans for hire or adoption. One such agent arrived on a Friday in 1859 with forty-eight boys aged eight to seventeen. These were housed and fed at the Center House hotel where, in a sense, they were on public display for that weekend. Their high spirits and apparent self-confidence were selling points. By Saturday night only three of the forty-eight remained at the Center House. Most had been taken to homes in the county where, presumably, they would work as farmhands and develop the advantages of life in a family.[34]

Such efforts, while admirable, ignored the fact that Wabash had its own crop of children who were regularly born without benefit of home or decent adult care. In the mid-1880s citizens began to address the issue with fresh creativity, which included cooperation with the Woman's Christian Temperance Union and with county officials. Accepting responsibility for nine children who had been living at the county Poor Farm they housed them in a south side building that had formerly been used as a business and a school. At one point in its brief history this orphanage housed more than fifty children. Maria Burke was matron. Three years after it opened the orphanage burned down. A temporary shelter in the old fairgrounds buildings on West Hill Street also burned. Arson by one or more of the orphans was suspected.[35]

It would be three more years before a permanent replacement was ready. It was a two-story, red-brick building, newly constructed for $7,548, and located "at the extreme end of West Hill" on four lots purchased from the agricultural society. According to an 1896 report, the structure itself was "not beautiful," but it was spacious and was set in the midst of a magnificent lawn that provided areas for vegetable gardens and an orchard. There was a "very pretty, broad reception hall" on the first floor, where kitchen and dining room were also located. Other architectural features on that level had not been well planned. Parlors and library were small. There was one large shabbily furnished playroom, which had an extension that could be used exclusively as play area for more than a dozen "tots" or babies. In the basement were a furnace room, bathrooms, laundry room, and vegetable cellar. Sleeping rooms were on the second story—one for boys, one for girls, one for babies, and one for a matron. Porches on the back of the building were added as a memorial to local businessman Leonard Hyman.

Oversight for operations fell to an eighteen-person board of directors. Esther Walter (Mrs. Bossler), an early president of the board, addressed the need for improvements to the new building. Those needs included fire escapes and beautification of the interior. Each school-age child was to be provided with three sets of clothing, one for play, one for school, and one for Sunday. Two or more physicians were on call for the home. Walter also pursued township trustees for help in finding permanent homes for children. Top capacity for the home was probably between fifty and sixty children, though it tended to house fewer than that. In 1895, when there were thirty-four residents, twenty were boys, eighteen were "half orphans," and nine had both parents living.

The board carefully regimented life at the orphanage. The children ate together at four dining room tables. Breakfast was at 6:30, consisting of bread, butter, milk, and hash. Dinner was at noon, offering a fare of meat, a vegetable, gravy, and bread. Supper, at 5:30 p.m., consisted of bread and milk, augmented three times a week by a "picnic supper" of cold meat, bread, butter, cheese, and fruit. Policy was to feed the children until they were full. Babies were carried off to bed at 7:00 p.m. In the evenings the older children enjoyed piano playing and singing, or they were read to by the matron. They went to bed at 9:30. The regimen included various chores on the premises, including work in the garden and orchard. In October 1896 the matron, Mrs. Hall, reported that with the help of many of the thirty-two residents that year the home's seasonal production was eight bushels of beans, twelve bushels of tomatoes, seventy bushels of potatoes, three bushels of beets, eight bushels of sweet potatoes, fifty heads of cabbage, twelve bushels of pears, three bushels of onions, ten gallons of black and red raspberries, and forty-six gallons of strawberries.

For economic reasons the county closed the orphans' home in 1903 in favor of using White's Institute. During its eighteen-year existence the home succeeded in placing 169 children in homes. More than a hundred were returned to their natural parents. A few had to be sent to a reformatory or to a home for the mentally impaired, and twenty-three finished growing up at White's. The brick building on Hill Street passed to other important uses, as a hospital first and then as the Wabash Women's Club House. The balance of the orphans' home bank account in 1903, about $2,300, went to the hospital to help pay for orphans' medical costs.

11

Fun and Games

In the springtime of 1871 a man from another town visited a Wabash resident whom he considered to be an "elegant friend." He readily accepted his friend's invitation to stay for dinner. At the dinner table the guest confronted something unfamiliar to him, a linen napkin at his place. Not being used to napkins he kept putting his into his pocket like a handkerchief instead of on his lap. This error would not have led to anything socially calamitous had the man not earlier removed a sock that was pinching his foot and stuffed it into a pocket. During dinner, perhaps when a bit of sauce ran down his chin, he "went for a napkin and flourished a sock." Reflecting later on his deep embarrassment the guest said, "I felt so mean that I wanted to spit in my own face and kick myself to hell."[1]

Although this vignette illustrates how styles and manners evolved, sometimes faster than the average citizen could master, it also illustrates that folks of the period loved to entertain at table. It headed the list of the town's pleasant pastimes. By the 1870s the place settings and the menus might be racing ahead of the rudimentary standards of early Wabash, but both friendships and community spirit continued to be courted over shared food. Sometimes a crude repast of the past was deliberately wedded to meals of a more refined present, as in the fare presented at a meeting of the Possum Eaters in 1896. Three friends met for dinner on a Saturday evening at Charles Davis's house on East Hill Street. Before them lay the centerpiece, an opossum killed the previous day, and a three-course banquet, served on white Haviland china with silver tableware. The first course featured soup, wafers, broiled steak, escalloped potatoes and oysters, stewed apples, bread, pickles, and coffee. Course two was the opossum, with sweet potatoes, parsnips, mixed pickles, bread, jelly, salad, and wafers. The third course offered mince pie, cheese, ice cream, fruit salad, and cake. It took the guests two hours to work their way through these courses. The men ended the feast with cigars.[2]

Feasting could bring the races together socially. The public seems to have been invited to the nuptials of "Miss Annie Alice" and the popular lawn mower Lewis Williams. In any case, the public showed up, and Saint John's church was crowded. Reverend Hill presided. Annie Alice appeared in a pale blue gown of the latest fashion. Williams was attired in full dress suit. According to a news reporter who was present, at the conclusion of the service Hill moved to "salute" the bride with a kiss but was interrupted by the new husband who declared that the first kiss was his, a claim met with loud applause. Hill's parsonage was the scene of a public banquet and reception. Afterwards the "swellest cab in town" took the bride and groom to their new home on Market Street.[3]

The *Wabash Plain Dealer* specialized in making a fuss over entertainment stories, as if there were some kind of competition among hosts and hostesses to create the most lavish or the most clever cuisine. In the same year as the Williams nuptials at Saint John's, Mayme Atkinson received her King's Daughters sorority sisters at her father's mansion on North Wabash Street (later renovated to become a Ford family home). Twenty-one young women met to eat and to be entertained. There was piano playing, singing, a cakewalk, and a parlor play called *A Case of Eviction*, all preceded, according to the news account, by a five-course "sumptuous" dinner. Likewise in the following month when Clio, a literary and social club, met at the Aaron Simon house the newspaper published the carefully conceived courses: cereal compound, churned cream, cold canard, curious cucumber combination, cider cured carefully, complete chocolate cake, China cordial, and coffee clarified. Possibly it was only because oysters did not start with the correct letter that they were omitted from this dinner, for they were consumed enthusiastically from canal days throughout the nineteenth century. In the single winter of 1881–82 Arch Stitt sold forty-three hundred cans of oysters, and he was only one purveyor.[4]

With or without banquets, a number of fraternal and sororal groups offered social distractions. Exemplary among them were the Masons and the Odd Fellows, both well known nationally, perennially strong locally, and begetters of offspring organizations for females, such as the King's Daughters. Before the Civil War there was a national organization called the Sons of Malta, a quasi-military fraternity that attracted as many as seventy local men to its ranks. Although the Sons of Malta had sometimes met at the courthouse they eventually established a lodge on West Canal Street. They liked to dress in white-and-black robes, black scarves, and dark masks. At five dollars per member the dues were exceedingly high for the times, but much of the organization's resources went to purchase supplies for widows and poor families, a fact that was not lost on the general population. The Sons of Malta were remembered especially for their annual midnight marches, during which they distributed supplies to the needy. Large numbers of Wabash citizens lined the streets to watch the march.

There was also a more rambunctious, rascally side to the Sons of Malta. Initiation into the fraternity's so-called vale of mystery was highly theatrical, entertaining for the cognoscenti, and possibly terrifying for the initiates. In November 1859 the Sons of Malta inducted eight to ten men, one of whom (calling himself "Jeems") later revealed the highlights of his rite of passage. He was thrown into a tub of cold water. "Big men" stuck pins in him, and others attacked with hot molasses that they poured into his hair and his boots as they kept a stream of cold water splashing over him. A black-robed Son of Malta shoved a snuffbox in his face until he sneezed "vociferously," while the fraternity laughed and cheered. Shoved deeper into the gathering, the initiate was grabbed by his hair, nose, and coattails and then stripped naked. In that condition he was forced to shinny up a soaped pole to avoid further jabs with pins and sharp sticks. His ordeal lasted two hours. At one point Jeems banged his head so hard he saw stars. In the end he was given a large helping of liverwurst and let go. The Sons of Malta disappeared after the Civil War.[5]

No one needed to belong to a fraternity or be able to afford an elegant spread in order to enjoy a summertime picnic. In the early days, if townspeople did not want to travel far into the country for a picnic there was a pleasant grove of trees (possibly locusts) just west of John Sivey's property, on the south side of what became West Hill Street, between Carroll and Fisher. In fairly short order, however, this spot was superseded in popularity by a grove adjacent to Charley Creek's picturesque falls. Before Falls Avenue developed as a residential street, before the creation of the New Cemetery in 1862 and before a bridge was built over the creek at the Stitt Street and Falls Avenue intersection, the falls site was a preferred locus for all kinds of community and private outings. Boys loved to scramble over the rocks and up the cliffs of the gorge, sometimes to their peril; churches used it for outdoor services and dinners; and in the 1850s it was where the town sometimes celebrated the

Fourth of July. In June 1855 the *Wabash Gazette* reported that twenty-five hundred people had congregated at the falls for a recent religious gathering. The table that day was three hundred feet long and "covered beautifully with good substantial food." A Peru minister spoke, the crowd sang temperance songs, and no one became intoxicated.[6]

Oddly, Fourth of July festivities were not inevitable. "Wabash, as usual, will not celebrate the glorious Fourth," announced the *Plain Dealer* in late June 1883.[7] Rail travel and roads had become so dependable in dry weather, and local plans for the holiday so skimpy at times, that citizens sometimes preferred to celebrate in neighboring towns or to observe the day quietly with friends and family at home. When there was a public celebration, however, the choice location after the 1850s was the county Agricultural Society's Fairgrounds. In some years there were huge patriotic parades, featuring bands and military formations that led the citizenry to the fairgrounds from a downtown gathering point. In other years people simply streamed west down Hill Street on their own. Either way thousands were expected and thousands usually attended, including many from out of town. For horses and buggies there was parking at the west end of the grounds or, later, north of the Orphans' Home.

The grandstand at the east end of the fairgrounds's racetrack provided a center for formal programs. Bands played, the crowd pledged allegiance to the flag, the Declaration of Independence was read, and then Charles Little, John U. Pettit, a Civil War hero, or a politician delivered a patriotic address. On at least two occasions, in 1870 and again in 1879, the Fourth was marked by hot-air balloon ascensions, both of which failed. In 1896 when Mayor James E. McHenry promoted a celebration that would re-create "an old fashioned Fourth," he specified activities such as sack racing, wheelbarrow racing, greased pole climbing, pig chasing, platform dancing, and, as a nod to modernity, bicycle racing. A favorite feature on the Fourth and at other times in summer was horse racing on the one-third mile oval track. In the early 1870s Hugh McKahan's racing stallion Old Pete vied repeatedly with Asher Gray's Hoosier Bob, each winning two out of four races and tying for one.

In late summer or early fall, the Agricultural Society's annual county fairs attracted thousands, providing the premier opportunity for townspeople and country folks to interact. Apart from the social opportunities the main draw was the enormous variety of displays featuring farm, garden, and domestic products. Sheep, pigs, cattle, horses, fowl, corn, wheat, shrubs, vegetables, fruits, flowers, honey, quilts, embroidery, and crafts and hobby projects vied for attention and prizes. A Mr. Twining and his Bee Circus might put in an appearance. Businesses and industries also participated, with venues for saddles, wagons, carriages, jewelry, cabinets, photography, boots, farm machinery, inventions, or any product manufactured in Wabash's Canal Street industrial center.

In 1870 a new organization, called the Old Settlers, began meeting about the time of the county fairs each year. James D. Conner, J. C. Sivey, Stearns Fisher, and Elijah Hackleman were among the founders of the Old Settlers. The objective was to gather the county's pioneers annually for social interaction and to promote the preservation of their reminiscences. The original members were divided into three classes: those who had settled prior to 1836, those who had settled between 1836 and 1841, and those who had settled between 1841 and 1846. The Old Settlers club lasted well into the twentieth century. It kept splendid records of its proceedings and of participants' reminiscences. The *Old Settlers' Book*, containing these records, is in the Wabash County Historical Museum archives.[8]

Wabash's downtown also had its popular attractions. Balls held at Center House hotel, McKibben's Hall, or Union Hall attracted both the young and the elite of Wabash. That "Prince of Landlords," Archibald Stitt, might prepare supper for such occasions, after which participants danced into the wee hours, even until dawn. In 1858 the Wabash Guards, the town's pre-Civil War military unit, participated in a target practice outing during the day and met in full dress uniform for a "grand ball" in the evening. The following spring the guards launched a fife and drum parade, after which it distributed snacks consisting of candy, raisins, peanuts, and "gimcracks" to the public. This was followed by a "May Party" in one of the halls. An 1872 masquerade ball cast John H. DePuy as Shakespeare, Harvey. B. Shively as a burgomaster, Cary Cowgill as a schoolboy, and Colonel J. R. Polk as a Chinaman.[9]

Of considerable importance to many citizens were the concerts, musical performances, and dramas that graced Wabash's social halls and the long-extant opera house usually known as Harter's, though its name, with its ownership, occasionally changed. Harter's Opera House stood on the south side of Market Street halfway between Miami Street and the next alley east. It was not especially fancy, but it was often busy and provided performance space for local volunteers such as the Wabash Union Choir Association, the Wabash City Band, a local brass band, young people's concerts, and various instrumentalists. Although such an event is not specifically recorded, it is likely that Sanford Honeywell may have been among those who performed on the violin at the opera house or one of the local halls. Harter's also attracted traveling companies, the quality of which was chancy at best. Tickets to such attractions were going for thirty-five, fifty, and seventy-five cents in 1890.[10]

Whether posted at the opera house or one of the other halls, playbills heralded dramatic presentations by local amateur groups, lectures by itinerant scholars, school performances, exhibitions, Christmas festivities, church programs, and road shows with at least a modicum of national reputation. For example, in 1860 a local literary society sponsored *The Drunkard*, a drama that had survived 124 previous performances nationally, about the downward path of an inebriant who then discovers the upward path to sobriety—sobriety being forever a worthy social value. The musical tastes of some citizens may have remained rustic throughout the century. In 1896 a crowd gathered near the river bridge because a "crazy lady" was ranting at the top of her voice there. Police were called. They identified the woman as Gertrude Lodge, a visiting soloist for a local performance of *Faust*. She was vocalizing outdoors because she could not do so at her hotel.[11]

For open-air entertainment that spiced a dull summer, nothing promised more than a circus. But based on the town's past experiences with circuses, previews were mixed. In announcing the expectation of another circus in 1855, the *Wabash Intelligencer* fielded a question on many minds: Is it a blessing or a curse? Once the tents had folded and left town, journalistic reviews were often cutting. The long-anticipated Sells' Circus arrived in late July 1883. When it was gone the *Plain Dealer* complained bitterly. The clowns had been a "nuisance," their jokes stale and coarse. Only half the animals advertised appeared. The coal-oil lamps cast a "sickly glare" over the performances. The Punch and Judy show was "hideous." As feared, the circus had attracted drunks and pickpockets, so that special police had to be sworn in for the duration. The G. F. Bailey and Company Circus seemed to have enjoyed a good reputation locally but most were as bad as Sells. Circus employees and itinerant hangers-on were "filthy," "scabby," and "lousy." There was not a clean rag among them by way of clothing. They were "whiskey bloats," "bawdy-house pimps," and a "moving pestilence." Worst of all, a circus could come to town and leave without noticeably improving business for the downtown merchants.[12]

Nevertheless, thousands attended, flocking to the river-bottom flats where circuses often set up. Neither the heat and dust of summer nor a drenching rain nor sloppy mud could discourage the crowds. A parade through town ahead of the main show in the big tent was one of the ways circus managers drummed up business. Thirty-four hundred tickets were sold for an 1855 circus, which surely guaranteed a packed tent that day even though the skies had opened up with a downpour. If performances in the big tent were disappointing, or the parade less than inspiring, an accompanying menagerie of uncommon beasts and birds might be worth the twenty-five or fifty cent entrance fee. One local reporter was especially taken with the Van Amburgh "mammoth menagerie," featuring not only a live crocodile but also a "tremendous jawbone of an a—hem, we don't know what."[13]

From earliest pioneer days Wabash males were sportsmen. In the beginning this mostly meant hunting and fishing for pelts and food. Gradually the impetus became entertainment rather than sustenance. Great numbers of men continued to gather for foxhunts well into the 1880s. These were not like the legendary British hunts with horse, hound, horn, and strict dress code. Dogs were used but the men were mostly on foot and dressed commonly. Typically a hunt might start at the South Side Female Academy (the corner of present-day Vernon and Pike streets). There hunters and dogs formed a long, north-south line that noisily worked east toward Treaty Creek across an area covering much of the bluff top. At the creek it would reverse and work west. There were no guns involved and the dogs were initially kept leashed. Premature unleashing could carry a five-dollar fine. When the hunt marshal gave a signal, the dogs were released to chase any foxes that had been flushed out. Once a fox was taken down by a dog, it would be sacked and sold on site. By the mid-1870s there were not large numbers of foxes in the wild, but hunters were still legion. In February 1872 five hundred men joined a hunt north of town that yielded a single fox and one turkey.[14]

Undoubtedly the most popular sport continued to be fishing, though by the end of the century supply no longer outstripped demand as had long been the case. In 1896 a local paper asserted that there were more fishermen along the bank of the Wabash River than there were fish in the river and that consideration should be given to restocking upstream. Contrarily, enormous catfish, one weighing in at thirty pounds, could still reel in men to the river. Alex Hess was bitten so severely by a catfish that he had to have some fingers amputated. More amazing was the discovery of twenty-seven black bass trapped in a hollow log that had floated downstream on high water. The bass were valued as "fine and gamey fish" that had become scarce. True enough, a fisherman could still catch respectably large pike in the river well into the 1870s, but increasingly fishing parties tried their luck in Indiana lakes farther north rather than close to home. An 1896 oil spill in the Salamonie River tributary killed all the fish in that area. It was a bad omen, foreshadowing the deadening of the Wabash through much of the twentieth century, a tragedy caused mostly by unregulated sewer and industrial discharge into the river. Gone was the "clear bright water over pure white rocks" that had given the town its name.[15]

The open river bottom south of the canal, when it was not hosting circuses, floods, burning trash, animal carcasses, or cornfields, was home to baseball, Wabash's favorite team sport. It was property that may have been legally secured by a consortium that met regularly at Sam Moon's Cigar Store. The prominent Alf Harter was one of those intent on acquiring space for a ball diamond. In spite of such efforts, for most of the nineteenth century the game was probably underorganized, surviving summer to summer only because a handful of the faithful bullied other chaps into participation. In 1871 the *Wabash Republican* announced that baseball was dead in Wabash because most young men were "too lazy to indulge in the game."[16] This was a comedown from four years earlier when men such as Cary Cowgill and Civil War hero John R. Polk had been directors of a local club that fielded two teams and held regular practices on the bottomland. For the general public games were a source of "considerable merriment," a fact that may have sparked a revival of interest among potential players. Team names were always in flux, changing with some frequency. One early name was the Alerts, which played under the motto "Win, tie, or wrangle." Other names were Red Stockings and The Zig-Zag Club.

Early in the 1880s a short-lived Young Men's Christian Association in Wabash succumbed to lack of support ("a stiffened corpse with its toes turned up"). It was replaced by a regular schedule of baseball games with teams from other towns, though regionally applicable regulations and rules were in a state of flux. In 1883, the year Wabash beat Peru 25–23, the practice of teams' fielding their own umpires came under criticism, accompanied by a suggestion that umpires should be recruited from neutral towns. In 1890 a more sophisticated organization emerged with the formation of the Indiana Baseball League, which held a meeting at Wabash's Tremont House that February. The league assigned Wabash to a multitown circuit in the north-central part of the state and charged each team fifty dollars to belong. The circuit included Warsaw, Huntington, Fort Wayne, Peru, Kokomo, Marion, Anderson, Muncie, and Bluffton. Team managers could be paid, but not more than five hundred dollars a season. Except for exhibition games, Sunday competition was forbidden.[17]

Near the end of the century organized team sports achieved new importance and permanence with the creation of the Wabash Athletic Association. Over the next several years H. B. Hutchens, owner of a laundry and cleaning firm, became a major player in that organization. He and his associates were especially interested in promoting football. The strictly amateur squads that they organized not only played teams from other cities and towns but also those of small colleges, such as Earlham and DePauw. In addressing a gathering of the Wabash Athletic Association in 1912 Hutchens credited Henry Wolf with kicking off a football craze twenty years earlier when he proposed the idea of a town gymnasium for young men. In fairly short order the gymnasium became a reality, situated on top of the bluff near the corner of Main and Huntington streets. The gym was such a draw that a much larger facility was added to the property in the early twentieth century, after which the older building was used for club rooms and billiards. From the start the Wabash gym was valued as a way to siphon the energy of "young blades" by engaging them in physical activities.

As citizens in the 1890s anticipated their first gym, the "germ footabus ballibus" emerged from dormancy, infecting the population strongly enough to support a team. In the beginning players had to pool their own money to buy a ball and were expected to furnish their own moleskin jerseys or go without. The opening game of Wabash's football history was against a North Manchester team, played on an old hog lot on West Canal Street. Wabash won, 44–0. Pumped up by that victory Wabash challenged Huntington and chartered a railroad car to travel to the game. Decked in "pickle dish" hats of an earlier style, the Wabash men paraded triumphantly through Huntington's streets, then lost the game by twenty-eight points. Hutchens expressed the opinion that the game could have been won if the team had put as much effort into it as they did the parade. By the end of the century schools were into the gridiron craze. For a time a Wabash High School squad and the WAA squad competed for practice space, which had to be used before darkness fell.

Hutchens and his WAA associates resolved the conflict by installing electric lighting for the practice field in 1900. Organized sports was entering its age of repletion.[18]

A lot of the fun people had was unorganized, serendipitous, and spontaneous. Bossler and Esther Walter were a few among many who enjoyed an informal evening of whist with friends. Downtown ice-cream parlors did a brisk business with customers stopping in on the spur of the moment. Boys were enthusiastic for games of marbles. For a short while some men entertained the general public by sporting a new hairstyle in which the top of the head was shaved from the forehead to the crown. Five young men were spied together in a single barbershop submitting to the fashion. When Ed Tolan followed suit the *Plain Dealer* was unkind enough to point out that his cut did not count because he was going bald anyway. Folks were amused by the ubiquity of bloomers worn by the "gentle sex," noting that horses also wore a version of them to keep flies off their legs. The increased popularity of bicycling in the 1890s promoted that of bloomers. Young teenagers and boys often took their fun in ways that did not please their elders. At the Lutz Hotel on Market Street a few boys hooked the establishment's telegraph batteries to the front-door handle and then watched in glee as people entered. The victims decried it as a "scandalous arrangement." When fourteen-year-old George Houston threw a bucket of water on a Canal Street shopkeeper, the man picked up Houston by the collar and the seat of the pants and threw him in the air. Houston, it was reported, turned four somersaults before landing in the canal. Smoking, a "disgusting and dangerous" temptation, gained popularity among boys. The town's council fought back against the "shroud pins" (cigarettes) with taxes and licensing laws, but it was also fighting the profit motives of merchants.[19]

Some of the fun followed the seasons: May Day outings, Halloween shenanigans, New Year's Day festivities, and Leap Year parties. On a June evening a crowd might gather at S. J. Payne's greenhouse on Comstock Street to observe the night-blooming cereus, a type of cactus. Summer Sunday buggy rides were popular, despite the reservations some held about its appropriateness on the Christian Sabbath. "Buggy Riding on the holy Sabbath," pontificated a news editor, "may be made hurtful, but *per se* I cannot so regard it."[20] In winter the canal offered an excellent skating surface, smooth and handy. Between January 1 and January 9 (Saturday to Wednesday) in 1895, Hackleman's diary reported "fine skating," "Everybody skating," and

"Best skating for twenty years," although by that year a lot of the old canal had been abandoned.[21] The most popular of winter pastimes was sleigh riding. For young males it provided courting opportunities. Ideally one started with a warming meal of pancakes and a punch called "Thomas and Jeremiah." Thus fortified inwardly, and outwardly warmed with robes and fur blankets, a young male hoped to have "something pretty, plump and palpitating by [his] side." If, by chance, politeness dictated that others should pile into the sleigh—there always being "room for just one more"—that was no loss; it meant she would have to sit on his lap and he could "hold her slender form firmly in [his] arms."[22] In 1887 Wabash held a Sleigh Riding Carnival in forty degree weather. Beginning at 1:30 p.m. on January 19, and led by a band, 107 horse-drawn sleighs pulled their passengers west along Canal Street, then back east on Market Street, then west again on Main Street and "so on until [the] whole city had been traversed."[23]

Weather also changed with the seasons, of course. For Wabash citizens it provided a perverse source of entertainment, perverse because the worst weather was also the most fascinating. Autumns—being not too hot, too cold, or too wet, and therefore far too pleasant—merited relatively little comment from citizens or press. Not so the other seasons. No one had Mother Nature more meticulously pegged than the indefatigable Hackleman. For forty years, 1861 to 1901, Hackleman kept a diary. The entries are maddeningly terse, unadorned with detail or emotion. When a beloved family member, his daughter, lay critically ill in his home, Hackleman's daily reports ran, "Alice has lung fever," "Alice, still bleeding of the lungs," "Alice very feeble, just able to ride in buggy," and "Alice—Died at 7:40 A.M." He was only slightly more forthcoming about the weather, but there is no doubting his interest in witnessing to nature's more dramatic moods. Between Hackleman and the newspapers the weather record is reasonably complete.[24]

The entertaining enemies of summer were heat and drought. On July 13, 1871, church services were canceled because thermometers inside buildings were reaching 98 degrees. In 1872 fires broke out because of drought. In July 1878 Hackleman recorded 98 degrees in the shade and 124 degrees in full sun. In 1887 his garden dried out, the grass died, and his celery was threatened even though he watered it every evening. Sunstroke was not unusual. Some summers it was not the heat that annoyed or destroyed, it was flies and caterpillars, against which there was little defense. Greater oddities, and not necessarily seasonal, were cyclones and earthquakes. Hackleman recorded them all, plus a lightning strike that knocked out his new telephone in 1883.[25]

By contrast came winter's freezes. On February 6, 1856, temperatures dropped to 26 degrees below zero. Some winters the sound of sleigh bells in the snow was so constant as to become annoying. Canal water froze several inches thick, providing quick, smooth sleigh transportation to Lagro. On New Year's Eve, 1863, it started snowing when the thermometers read 30 degrees above zero. Then dawned a new year, "the most disagreeable day ever experienced in this country."[26] First came sleet, then snow, then more sleet. It got colder, with more snow, and the temperature dropped to 24 below zero. "All the horrors and discomforts of a Siberian winter" set in, with wind that howled "like ten thousand weird demons." Houses rattled and creaked. People risked freezing their noses, ears, and fingers just by leaving home. House windows clouded up with "an impenetrable frost," and downtown on a Friday it was "quiet as the Sabbath," with only a single team of horses in sight.[27] The following year showed little improvement: the ground froze in mid-November and stayed solid until April, with no break of a midwinter thaw.[28]

Little about weather occupied the public's attention as much as rain, water, and floods. In a river and canal town stakes were high, especially so since a flooded river in late winter might damage canal beds and delay the canal's spring opening in March. Nothing, then, was quite so remarked upon as the amount of rain. "Tremendous Rains," the *Gazette* warned in print slightly larger than the regular text. On Sunday, November 12, 1855, a warm, summerlike rain swept in, the river rose two feet every hour, and the bottomland between canal and river was soon flooded. Two years later in the same month with the same "huge rain" the river did not rise so quickly, but bridges over streams washed out, roads were covered, and the roads' corduroy logs were "afloat by the mile."[29]

Eighteen fifty-eight became a crucial year, this time not in early winter but in the spring. It began in mid-April and continued into June: "Rain, rain, rain; one eternal, never ending, continuous rain" morning, noon, midafternoon, evening, night, and morning again, "Tremendous Rains."[30] On Wednesday, June 9, the river came up to meet the town. "Such an outpouring of water we never saw before," with "all the bottoms covered from hill to hill." Farmland drowned, fences broke apart, and a canal bank eroded. Cabins wallowed in two feet of water. Canal Street was covered. Then trees swept down river within two hundred feet of the canal, and sawn logs and boards from lumberyards floated away. By "a miracle" the river bridge stood ("its very worthlessness preserved it"), but the road from town to the bridge disappeared in places.[31] Conditions in 1858 quieted down after spring, until late in the year when the enemy became mud. "The rains descended, and the mud came, and it is now something less than four feet deep on the level."[32] One potential gain that arrived with flooding was huge deposits of sand left by the river "in front of the town" where it was claimed for construction purposes, as happened the following year. In fact, most years saw the Wabash River over its banks, and a great many years were stamped on folks' memories as especially bad—1859, 1860, 1862, 1863, 1875, and 1896, to name a few. An earlier flood in 1843–44 was also remembered as disastrous, but as that one occurred before there were local newspapers or many other records, few details survive. However, legend maintains that during this flood canal boats were floated down Canal Street to rescue citizens from their homes.[33]

Mother Nature saved her pièce de résistance in the matter of flooding for 1883. As February opened, the ground was frozen and covered with snow. When four and a half inches of rain fell, it had nowhere to go. Three to four inches of water covered streets and sidewalks. Walking through the downtown meant slogging through ice-cold water. Many folks came down with colds. One noon, during the first week of February, people converged at the Big Four railroad bridge to watch large ice cakes assault the structure as they rushed downstream. Some cakes were thirty feet square, others carried logs with them. Although the bridge trembled and lost some of its timbers, it seemed to survive, but during the night its south span was carried away.

Concern shifted to the bottomland where several dozen families had erected their homes, a decision that seems witless in retrospect but that was doubtlessly the result of cheap land in that area. Some of these residents fled to upper stories and were trapped there as three feet of water gushed into their living space. In one house Mat Jones kept pushing his cat off his bed until he heard it make a splash and thereupon concluded that the flood was both serious and personal. At 3:00 a.m. Wabash officials sounded a general alarm, calling out citizens to aid in the rescue effort. Ed Harter carried Mrs. Henry Tinkle out on his back, over her objections about leaving her home. Jack Stober was rescued but soon returned to his house to retrieve four loaves of his wife's bread. Boats plied the bottomlands for much of the day, ferrying families to safety. By this time the temperatures had plummeted. Standing floodwater began to freeze. At its peak the waters covered Canal Street as far west as Cass Street and had inched up Carroll Street toward Market Street. The fact that the levee between the Wabash Street canal bridge and the river bridge had frozen before the flood arrived saved it from washing out.

In the aftermath the *Plain Dealer* attempted to sort out the losses. Standing reserves of corn, oats, and orchard produce, three cows, and a private library were swept away. So were logs and timbers from sawmills, as were timbers that had been stacked up for a new river bridge. The contents of a safe were soaked. Hearses that had been covered in water were fished out and seemed to be salvageable. The school furniture factory and T. F. Payne's cabinet works were both deep in water. No deaths were reported. The city had to take precautions against looting that began almost immediately. Because the river had backed up behind a natural dam of ice and driftwood, the city council paid $195.57 for "blowing out the gorge" of the river so that floodwaters could recede rapidly. Meanwhile a few folks speculated on two silver linings: first, boys could skate on the bottomland and, second, sediment from the flood would help next summer's crops.[34]

For those who required more regulated entertainment than might be found in spontaneous gatherings or in the weather, there existed a plentitude of clubs: the Wabash Gun Club, the Itinerant Club, and the Franklin Club for young men, to name a few. A cooking club was organized for women interested in haute cuisine. When Mrs. Cary Cowgill hosted a luncheon for that group at her Wabash Street mansion, she decorated with yellow roses, served on Irish Belleek and cut glass, and offered her guests bouillon, scalloped fish au gratin, olives, fried chicken, Saratoga chips, salted almonds, pickled raisins, Roman punch, coffee, oyster salad, wafers, plum pudding glacé, whipped cream, and sponge cake.[35]

Men of the Cowgill social range seemed to have interests in tackling various issues of the day. In the late 1840s they created the Lyceum, with its programs open to the public. It offered a forum for lectures and debates presented by gentlemen of respected scholarship. "Does nature, unassisted by Holy Scriptures, prove their truth?" was one such topic. Others were equally provocative and/or currently pertinent: "Should males and females be educated together in our colleges?" "Were the Allied powers justifiable [*sic*] in banishing Napoleon to St. Helena?" "Is conscience innate?" and "The intermingling of the races." Such topics do not prove that the intellectual attainment of Wabash citizens was extraordinary, but they do indicate that representatives of those citizens had lively interests in thought-provoking subjects.[36]

The Lyceum died out after the Civil War but another group later carried a torch for intellectual inquiry. The Round Table was founded in 1880 by a group of well-read, socially prominent women. More than one hundred thirty years later it continues its mission. That mission began as an encouragement to women in the study of a broad range of fields: literature, poetry, art, history, religion, philosophy, science, and politics. The group was founded as an offshoot of the popular Chautauqua movement of textbook studies, but after a few years it became something of its own design and vision.

In the twentieth century the scope of the Round Table's programs narrowed somewhat, in that it centered on book reviews, art, and music. By contrast the original interests of members seemed universal in scope, and the pursuit of them was in dead earnest (which does not contradict the fact that hilarity sometimes punctuated club meetings). From 1897 to 1903, for example, the Round Table studied the following: astronomy, current events, recent scientific discoveries, education in foreign lands, George Eliot, the War of the Roses, socialism, the Renaissance in art and literature, Elizabeth I, Shakespeare, Peter the Great, American literature, American poverty, history of the temperance movement, nineteenth-century Russian history, Charles Dickens, and Frederick the Great. Occasionally the program was a debate, as when Kate Busick argued against the electoral franchise for women, and Annie Conner argued for it. Most meetings were designed around take-home reading assignments or the presentation of a scholarly paper by a single member. This heavy schedule was lightened by two special events each year, but it was expected that music would play a part in every program. The club met Monday evenings at 7:30 from autumn until late spring, suspending operations for the summer, in part because some of the women's families spent summers at Bay View, Michigan, and other cooler climes. Club discipline was regularly enforced with small monetary fines for unexcused absence, for failure to prepare a lesson, or for inability to recite assigned poetry.[37]

The Round Table's great gift to Wabash was a public library. Nine years into its existence the club lost to death one of its popular members, Jessie Stitt. Two weeks later the women decided to fund a library in her memory and subsequently created the Women's Library Association, with Mrs. Cowgill as president and a twelve-member board of directors. Their guiding objective was to provide "cheap reading for the masses." Charging a dollar for association membership, the women raised enough to purchase two hundred volumes, which they housed in the Probate Room of the courthouse and made available to the public one afternoon a week. The collection was named the Women's Library of Wabash. With the erection of a new high school building at Hill and Cass streets in the mid-1890s, the collection was joined with that of the high school's library on the second floor. Women of the association and of the Round Table continued to volunteer as librarians, as they had done at the courthouse. It was not long, however, before the school needed more classroom space. The library moved again, this time to Memorial Hall west of the courthouse.

By 1901 the library held five thousand volumes, had a board of directors separate from the Round Table group, and acquired a new name, the Wabash City Library. A number of men now served on the board, including Charles Haas of the *Plain Dealer* as president and the well-read Warren Bigler. Mrs. Nelson Zeigler was the librarian. It was about this time that Bigler, his fellow board member, Mrs. Cowgill, and possibly others began to bombard Andrew Carnegie with requests for financial aid in creating a permanent library building. These pleas fell on deaf ears, it was believed, because Carnegie was interested in investing in towns larger than Wabash. When it was pointed out to the philanthropist that larger towns could more easily afford a library building, Carnegie donated the necessary funds, contingent upon the city of Wabash assuming responsibility for ongoing support. The organization then became the Wabash Carnegie Public Library. A Herff family home, then standing catty-corner from the high school, was purchased and demolished. In its place rose a classic Greco-Roman temple to books and learning, domed and massively pillared inside and outside, which was approached by an impressive sweep of broad, steep concrete steps leading to the front entrance. The year was 1903.[38]

12

Bustling Agora

Before Wabash's 1870 fire had destroyed the old Hugh Hanna courthouse, residents had recognized that the building needed to be replaced. In early January of that year a writer calling himself "Citizen" recommended major alterations to the public square in a letter to the editor of the *Wabash Plain Dealer.* Citizen envisioned closing Court Street and purchasing the western lots lying between it and Miami Street, enlarging the public square. Bounded by Wabash, Hill, Miami, and Main streets, the enlarged public square would be developed as a bluff-top park with a new courthouse rising at its center. The jail and auxiliary buildings would be located on the south side of a widened Main Street, and the parkland around the courthouse would feature walking paths and shade trees. At the top of the courthouse would rise Citizen's pièce de résistance: an observatory so that the public could enjoy the great vistas from its height.[1]

Citizen's vision was not to be realized, but neither was it entirely discarded, for the new courthouse made good use of its elevated setting. In some minds, no doubt, whatever might have passed for a glorified pole barn in 1870, with a few windows and fireplaces, would have sufficed as a practical replacement of Hanna's courthouse. Mercifully the county commissioners had time to think and plan before they built. The fortuitous availability of the old First Presbyterian building provided convenient and adequate spaces for a temporary seat of justice, if nearly a decade can be considered temporary. It was also fortuitous that by this time officials were ready to plan in earnest for both county and city had matured, had acquired a few degrees of sophistication, and had folks at the helm who apparently believed that style and a dash of opulence were both timely and worth the extra expense. Nevertheless, the early 1870s had not been economically encouraging. War debts still dampened down discretionary revenues across the nation. So, too, locally did Wabash's investment in the new north-south railroad. By 1877 such impediments seemed less intimidating and serious planning for a new courthouse began. There was "general acquiescence" that the time had come.[2]

The first contracts were let in September 1877. The architects were the B. V. Enos Company of Indianapolis. The firm's design has been described as classic revival because of the heavy use of pillars, various other architectural details, and the dome and ornamentation of the clock tower. Some have speculated that the architects were playing on an eastern European theme, suggested in part by the minarets that originally accented the roof corners.[3] A construction company from Eaton, Ohio, signed on to complete the building for $72,900, exclusive of movable furnishings. This figure rose to $75,400 by completion time. An estimated $95,000 was the final rendering at the close of the project when all the interior necessities and extras had been added.

The county's auditor, clerk, treasurer, recorder, and sheriff were assigned offices on the first floor. The second floor was for a main courtroom, which some thought to be too small, and other judicial facilities.[4] The county invested $79.73 on spittoons, so necessary in an age of copious expectoration. The completed building covered between 10,440 and 10,716 square feet, rose to 52 feet at its cornices, and was topped with a pole on the central clock tower that could fly a flag nearly 180 feet above the square. Stone trim came from Ohio, but the 1.25 million bricks required were kilned at Hezekiah Caldwell's brickyard on North Wabash Street. Some of the cabinetry inside was built by the Wabash School Furniture Company; chairs were purchased from the local W. P. Jones outlet; and lumber came from George Duck's downtown concern. Other local contractors included the Treaty Creek Stone and Lime Company that agreed to remove the twenty-foot-high stone retaining wall from the south side of the public square. Usable blocks of stone were sold back to the county as needed for forty cents a perch.[5]

In her pamphlet on Wabash County courthouses, Mary C. O'Hair, the county's museum curator for many years, marshaled a wealth of details about the new building. For example, it was lighted with 134 Coleman gas jets, including two chandeliers with twelve jets apiece and twelve smaller chandeliers with four jets apiece. Emerging gas wells south of town had made gas an inexpensive fuel for municipal and domestic use. For the first fourteen years the courthouse floors were carpeted (partly in a large floral design), but in 1894 the carpets were replaced with patterned tile. A news reporter claimed that two tons of dirt had to be swept from the clerk's office floor when the carpet there was removed.[6] Although the county paid more than three thousand dollars for a coal-fired steam heating system, wood was also burned in the fireplaces. Later, gas was piped to those hearths. There were lavatories with solid walnut washstands but no inside toilets. Rather, a somewhat decorative "necessary" rose up on the southwest corner of the grounds, presumably available for the general public as well as for courthouse workers and clients. On a northern corner of the square was a well that supplied water for the courthouse and the jail. The new courthouse bell, replacing the old and modest Presbyterian bell, weighed three thousand pounds. Under favorable weather conditions it could be heard nine miles distant.

Two interesting components of the new courthouse were its fence and its clock. The fence defined the courthouse grounds and provided space for lawyers and judges to secure their horses and buggies. It was constructed of heavily ornamented black cast iron; it was four feet high with three horizontal rails and had a decorative spearhead on each picket. Posts at corners and gates were a foot square at their broadest dimension and constructed with solid iron sides. Other posts, so-called T-posts, were smaller and of open grillwork. Utilitarian brace posts placed every several feet helped maintain stability. The Champion Iron Fence Company of Ohio won the bid for fencing at $2.15 per lineal foot. Speculation about the fence's eventual disposition developed in two directions. O'Hair believed that it was taken from the public square to be used at City Park for a time and afterwards discarded. Others perpetuated the idea that the Jewish community purchased the fence (after its manifestation at the park) for use at Rodef Shalom cemetery. Comparisons of measurements and illustrations submitted by the fence company in 1877 or 1878 with measurements and design of the extant fence at Rodef Shalok cemetery—plus old photographs—indicate that the present cemetery fence is the 1879 courthouse fence. The major iron posts at Rodef Shalom meet the fence company's description, as do the height of the fence, picket design, and the general placement of brace posts. The only discrepancy is with the number of open grillwork posts. Although several were probably part of the original fencing, only one remains at the Rodef Shalom cemetery, on its south side.[7]

The four-faced clock on the courthouse tower was operated by a bronzed gunmetal control that was six feet high, four feet deep, and six feet long. It had been ordered by a Wabash jeweler from the Seth Thomas company, which guaranteed that it would be accurate within ten seconds a month. That accuracy was thrown into doubt, however, in an age when cities did not keep standard times, some depending on astrological time, others on railroad time, and still others, probably, on guesswork. A complaint in Wabash was that the "city time" kept by the courthouse was five minutes ahead, on "fast time." There was also "slow time," five minutes behind, so that on any given morning between, say, 6:55 and 7:05 a.m., a different bell, siren, or whistle sounded every minute, creating a cacophony that the *Plain Dealer* described as "a h___ of a time."[8] The courthouse clock weighed a ton, and its two weights were fifteen hundred pounds apiece. It was electrified in the late 1930s after one of the weights fell, smashing through a ceiling into the courthouse interior beneath.

The cornerstone laying in May 1878 attracted a huge crowd. A parade headed by several bands, officers of the Hanna Lodge and the Odd Fellows lodge, the Rock City Hook and Ladder Company (with truck), the Hoosier Fire Company (with fire engines) and the Hoosier Hose Company (with hose cart), various county officials, and other citizens assembled on Market Street and then sloshed on rain-soaked and muddy streets to the site. L. L. Carpenter prayed. The Masons and Odd Fellows placed a copper box full of historic items in its place and sealed the cornerstone. A visiting Odd Fellow spoke. Charles Little offered the benediction. One hundred sixty ticket holders then gathered at the Harter Opera House that had been decorated with evergreens and lodge symbols for a reception and dancing. Other spectators took advantage of the two or three candy stands near the public square, eyed "flirtatious girls" from out of town, or went to gawk at the six-legged "double-rumped" calf on display at the corner of Hill and Wabash streets. By day's end a fight had broken out at the downtown depot, and several "full blown drunks" were carousing about the streets.[9]

As the courthouse neared completion, skeptics who had expected it to be ugly—teasingly calling it the Sweat Box—were won over by the quality of construction, by the elegant design, and by the realization that while it had some pretensions of opulence it could not be considered an especially expensive building by 1870s standards.[10] Its dedication on July 4, 1879, was a popular event despite a torrential rain that turned streets to quagmires and drove the dedication ceremony indoors. Judge John U. Pettit delivered the day's address to a packed courtroom.

Although various aspects of the courthouse grounds remained incomplete at the time of the dedication, they were soon addressed. The old, elongated county office annex on the northeast side of the square was demolished. Walks of four-to-six-inch-thick flagstones set on gravel beds a foot deep were installed around the new building. The south lawn was terraced and sodded, features that were believed to accentuate the drama of the new courthouse's bluff-top dominance of the city. Within seven months of the July Fourth dedication, contracts were let for construction of a county jail and sheriff's residence on the south side of Main Street, a facility that served the county long into the twentieth century. This structure replaced the second (1853) jail. The cost for the new jail and residence, a combined facility, was more than twenty thousand dollars. Moving the jail and other structures from the public square helped emphasize the solitary splendor of the towering courthouse.[11]

Important as 1879 was for the advancement of civic pride in town and county, 1880 was an even more significant year. In early November of 1880, for example, President Rutherford B. Hayes and Secretary of the Treasury John Sherman (former and future Ohio senator and future secretary of state) traveled by train eastward toward Ohio so that they could vote in the presidential election that month. Because word got out that these national leaders would pass through Wabash, a crowd of hundreds gathered at the Huntington Street depot to welcome them. The train slowed down but did not stop. The reason it did not stop lies buried in presidential time schedules. The reason it slowed down is known. The president of the United States and one of the nation's leading economists wanted to see with their own eyes the wonder of the Brush arc lights atop the new Wabash County courthouse. Here, after dark, was a city the streets of which were lighted by that marvel of the age, electricity. For a brief shining moment or two Wabash held the attention and fascination of its national leaders as it displayed the very latest technical advancement in human civilization.[12]

If that perennial and popular journalist, Thad Butler, is to be believed, Wabash's launch into momentary world fame began with a silly idea hatched by Theron Keaton of the *Plain Dealer*. One night soon after the completion of the new courthouse, Keaton, surveying the structure, observed to Butler that "if you had a barrel of tar on the dome of the court house and set it on fire it would light up the whole town." Years later, in 1910, Butler claimed that this offhand comment had inspired the two men to think about electric lighting and, subsequently, to travel to Cleveland where they approached the Brush Electric Light Company about acquiring an electric dynamo and lighting for the Wabash courthouse. Presumably the inventor of the arc light, Charles Brush, was captivated by reports of the courthouse's elevated setting and decided it was a good place to test a practical application of his invention. When the Brush company guaranteed that its lights would illuminate an area one mile in diameter sufficiently bright enough for people "to get around" on the outer perimeter, negotiations sped efficiently toward agreement. Just eight months after the courthouse dedication, Wabash's Common Council paid the Brush company a hundred dollars to proceed with a test of four arc lamps on the clock tower.[13]

The test on Wednesday, March 31, 1880, proved so successful that the first reaction of the thousands who witnessed the device spit sparks and then shine brilliantly was to fall into a speechless silence of awe, followed by bursts of exultant noise. There were still skeptics on the council, but differences there were expressed civilly and even with good humor. One opposing councilman, Reuben Lutz, wanted a specification that the lights would produce two crops in each growing season. On April 8 the council agreed to contract with the light company for a permanent installation (minus the Lutz specification).[14]

James Ford may have made the most interesting comment on the new lights. According to Leewell Carpenter, Ford observed to L. L. Carpenter (Leewell's grandfather) that whereas Benjamin Franklin had successfully pulled electricity out of the sky and brought it down to earth, now, in Wabash, men had reversed Franklin's work, taking electricity from down on earth and placing it back in the sky.[15] A more common reaction was the claim, hard to prove in retrospect, that even farmers on their distant properties could read a newspaper at night by the light from the courthouse tower. It is certainly possible that a farmer in a field just south of the canal might have been able to do that. There is no doubt that the illumination in streets around the public square was considered to be intense and a highly desirable advance for the city. Downtown streets also benefited, especially in view of the fact that shops often stayed open into the evening hours, although Canal Street's taller buildings shut out some of the light there.

Almost immediately people became aware that intense light creates intense shadows and that whereas, say, the south side of Market Street was basking in new illumination, its opposite, northern counterpart was cast into a blackness seemingly darker than night, a ready cover for thieves and stalkers. Perhaps aware of both the positive and negative aspects of the new lights, citizens began to talk of needing more numerous and brighter lights. In addition, the lights on the courthouse certainly did little for townsfolk living on the outskirts who paid the same taxes as those near the public square. By early 1883 a scheme emerged to add six light towers, each one a Norway pine pole a hundred feet high. Two would stand at the crossing of Cass and Canal streets, two at the intersection of Falls Avenue with Maple and Fisher streets, and two at Walnut and Spring (or possibly Allen) streets. Each pole would produce candlepower equal to the courthouse lights. Together they would provide a canopy of light for most of the town. Sponsors of this solution believed that "soon Wabash will be thoroughly and beautifully illuminated."[16]

Unfortunately, by April that plan had been squelched in the common council over technical and financial concerns. Some complained that a surrender on the issue of creating better lighting would transform the town into a "paradise for thieves and thugs."[17] Everyone seemed to understand that electric lights were cheaper and more efficient than gas. It cost $1.15 to burn the courthouse arc lamps all night, compared with three dollars for sixty-five gas lamps burning from dusk to midnight, though it is not known if that latter figure includes wages for the town's "old lamp lighter." At this juncture, however, the town's council had much on its plate, in particular the construction of City Hall on the southeast corner of Main and Wabash streets. That project involved, coincidentally, a basement installation of powerful boiler and engine components that might possibly be used in the generation of light in the near future. Therefore, a delay in any major lighting scheme seemed wise. A larger stumbling block was probably the fact that city taxes were not yet high enough to fund all the desired improvements. It is also true that Thomas Edison's incandescent light was gaining in reputation and promised to be more efficient than arc lighting for projects such as general street-by-street illumination. In any case, comprehensive electrical street lighting had to wait for more auspicious times. Gas street lighting, which in 1878 had replaced a brief and unsatisfactory experience with coal-oil lamps, had to suffice for the immediate future.[18]

If the vision that Citizen had proposed for the public square in 1870 had come to fruition, there would have been, by the 1880s, some kind of an observation deck on top of the courthouse. Because it did not materialize, one has to imagine how residents might have enjoyed bird's-eye views of their expanding city from that elevated spot.

Such observers would have been able to track with their own eyes the many measurable ways Wabash developed from 1880 toward the new century. In those years the town's population continued to grow at a healthy clip and with it the spread of urban settlement. Wabash had increased from about 1,500 inhabitants in 1860, to almost 2,900 in 1870. It was moving toward a little more than five thousand in 1890 and exceeded eight thousand by the end of the century. Although such growth was not atypical with communities that had recently sprung from the frontier, taken as a single community's phenomenon it represented dramatic change. In the last decades of the nineteenth century houses extended, roughly, from the Old Cemetery (in the east end) west to the orphanage and City Park, and from South Wabash (south side across the river) north toward residences popping up beyond Charley Creek. Whereas Hanna's Original Plat encompassed 233 lots there were now many scores more: some were the size of those in the Hanna plat and some were larger outlots that had not yet been subdivided into single-dwelling spaces.[19]

Various extant maps record the city's growth patterns. An 1875 map of Wabash indicates that the official corporation limits—drawn arbitrarily in neat angularity—were not necessarily containing the less-neat spread of residential settlements. Although there was an Eastern Addition (essentially east of Allen Street), the preponderance of growth was not in that direction, probably because of the squeezed space created by railroad and bluff. North and west the story was different. Large outer tracts owned by members of the Rettig, Ewing, Hanna, Gillen, and Tyer families were gradually being subdivided and bought, perhaps, by those who hoped to keep a stake near the country while living conveniently within walking distance or an easy buggy ride of the center of town.[20]

J. W. Shea's 1888 map of Wabash, which hangs on the wall of the Wabash County Historical Museum archives, shows considerable "filling in" of once platless acres. It also indicates that the Ross Addition, south of Harrison Street and east of Wabash Street, was inhabited and that Stitt Street had been extended east from Cass Street to meet the Manchester Road at its Wabash Street junction, an improvement dating from 1880 that facilitated travel between the town's northwest development and its northeast area.[21]

An 1891 map drawn by city engineer Robert Woods illustrates proposed corporation line changes. The town's legal border was pushed northward beyond Harrison Avenue to accommodate the additions between Alber and Wabash streets. Likewise, a later city engineer's map, published in 1901, shows how areas that had once been sparsely developed as large out lots were becoming dense with single-dwelling lots, especially northeast and west. The fact that many new single-dwelling lots appear on maps does not necessarily mean that houses had been built on them. A subdivided area along western Stitt Street on the 1901 map, for example, probably never contained homes; it had formerly been the fairgrounds and in the twentieth century would be the locus of a truck factory, and, later, of General Tire and succeeding corporations.[22]

The greatest change in the 1891 and 1901 maps, however, lies south. On both the 1875 and 1888 maps nothing is shown of South Wabash (later South Side), which had been developing as an independent community since at least 1846, when Stephen Jones bought land there. By contrast, as Woods's map indicates, South Wabash ceased to exist as a separate entity, but its area now lay very much within the official city boundaries of the merged communities. This merger boosted Wabash's population by six or seven hundred people. It created a city sited on two major bluffs with a river running through it. That not every South Side resident believed incorporation represented progress is illustrated by the appearance the next year of a petition for deannexation, a petition that failed.[23]

Though long separated in a legal sense and by river valley topography, ties between the two bluff-bound communities had always been vital in commerce and friendships, especially so after plank (later gravel) roads toward the south and bridges over the Wabash River came into being at mid-century. Camp Wabash, which had straddled the Mount Vernon Road (later Columbus Street) during the Civil War, helped keep the north side of the river palpably aware of its southern partner in that great patriotic effort. At the start of the war the south side's David Miles and Stephen Jones, both doctors, opened a health spa, called the Water Cure, featuring a ten to fifteen foot falls of abundant, stimulating waters. It was built on land that became the northwest corner of Vernon and Pike streets. That plot—about five acres in the early years—was destined to maintain a high profile over the decades, becoming, ad seriatim, the locus for a tollhouse, the spa, private schools, an orphanage, a public school, and municipal buildings.[24]

When the Water Cure went out of existence after the Civil War, a group of Presbyterians took over the property and opened a Female Seminary (the South Wabash Academy). Housed in a handsome three-story frame structure and "quietly nestled" in shade far from the distractions of Wabash, it catered to both day and boarding students from Wabash, South Wabash, other Hoosier towns, and even Ohio. A clergyman, Doctor F. A. Wilbur, was both the academic principal and the principle stockholder. The building could accommodate between twenty-five and forty residential students who paid $5.50 each per week for room, board, and tuition. At times total enrollment was in the neighborhood of fifty. Such academies were common in the Presbyterian frontier tradition; however, coming as it did just as Wabash's public school system was up and running did not bode well for its future. While the quality of education was probably superior, enrollment was a perennial problem. Admission of the first male students in 1869 did not sufficiently improve the situation. In 1873 a consortium of Quakers bought the academy, operating it for five years as a Friends school before abandoning the effort in 1878. As noted earlier, in 1885 the old academy building was converted into the county's orphanage and then, in 1888, it was destroyed by fire. South Wabash finally got a city-sponsored school building on this property in 1897.[25]

Both religiously and commercially the south side was a lively development. Because of early settlers such as Stephen Jones, his kin, and his neighbors, it was heavily populated by Quakers, beginning organizationally in 1848 when the first Friends meeting was held there. White's Institute, located farther south in the county, represented an outlet for the Wabash Friends' deep interests in missions and education. Even though that facility was never part of the city proper, its success and influence owed much to a rising Quaker presence, especially in South Wabash. Although Methodists, Brethren, and Evangelicals also staked claims on the south side in the nineteenth century, Quakers seemed to dominate the religious climate.

In employment South Wabash men were mostly farmers, horticulturists, furniture manufacturers, funeral directors, quarrymen, merchants, and professionals such as the Doctors Miles, Jones, and E. D. Pearson. Limestone quarries made an especially ineradicable impression on the terrain, leaving deep, picturesque (and later overgrown) hollows in the ground in the northwest part of the area. The quarries' neighbors, however, are known to have complained about those quarrymen whose boisterous and profane language was "disgusting" and a "disgraceful example" in the hearing of children.[26] More felicitous residents were Luther Smallwood and Charley Thompson who ran a grocery. They were thought to be "jolly good fellows" and "capital men" whose store was a popular gathering spot.[27]

There are at least three notable South Wabash relics of the nineteenth century that continue as landmarks into the twenty-first century. One is the Big Three Building for shops and offices on the northeast corner of Vernon and Columbus streets. A second is the modest but stately brick Georgian-style home that Daniel T. Jones built on the west side of South Vernon Street. A third surviving structure of note is somewhat removed from the main part of South Wabash. It is Allen W. Smith's large brick home, named Shore Acres, which stands high on the bluff, south of the river, overlooking the town to the north. Smith was a pioneer, coming to the area in 1833 with William Steele Sr. Although he was from the Richmond area, he seemed to have been more closely associated locally with the Presbyterians than with the Quakers of South Wabash. He rose to prominence by serving in the state legislature and, later, by replacing Hugh Hanna as a director of the state prison at Michigan City. His grandson was the reclusive artist Charles Cochran who lived in the Smith home for several years and decorated its walls with murals, including one of Adam and Eve.[28]

If in the 1880s and 1890s people had actually been able to gaze from the observation deck on the courthouse envisioned by Citizen, they might have caught glimpses of South Wabash's emergence from the forest, as noted above. Glancing farther afield to the east toward "Choke Town" on Treaty Creek, viewers on that imaginary deck might have spotted in that general south-easterly direction other familiar landmarks, or they might have craned their necks to locate those that were obscured by foliage or terrain. For instance, they could have indicated to one another that up Treaty Creek's forested and rock-strewn valley lay the important water source for the town. There, artesian wells, plunged deep into the clear, abundant, gravel-filtered waters of the Teays Valley aquifer, were providing water for cisterns, for downtown horse troughs, for firefighting, and, most significant at this late stage, for the first applications of indoor plumbing and community sewage control. The city's water system was completed in 1887 and headquartered near the point where Treaty Creek flows into the Wabash, in buildings that survived to the twenty-first century. Earlier in the 1880s even high upper-class homes were still being designed with outdoor privies. For example, the Frank Blount house on West Sinclair Street (later known as the Lawrence Bird home), which was built in 1883, boasted an enviable outdoor privy that is still extant. It is located beneath an arbor and has three seats, each with a porcelain knob on its lid, with one seat having been designed for a child. A decade later, in the 1890s, premier homes of similar quality were built with indoor plumbing, including flush toilets, an enormously welcomed advance. The downside of this advance was increased pollution of the Wabash River where sewage was flushed.[29]

Casting eyes closer in, to the north bank of the Wabash River, observers atop the courthouse would notice that the arc of Hanna's millrace still scarred the floodplain, though traces of his mill were probably gone. The river's bottomland was being developed slowly, partly for housing, partly for industry; but it still grew corn and other crops and was still subject to massive flooding. Apparently citizens continued to use it also as a dump. In 1891 town officials were still contending with refuse that piled up on both sides of the Wabash Street levee. It may have been about this time that an area nicknamed "Tin Cup" sprang up at the foot of the bluff on the river side of the Lagro road just outside the east end of town. Tin Cup was a preferred dumping ground around the turn of the century.[30]

Just north of Hanna's abandoned millrace was the complicated configuration of the Big Four rail yards with a semicircular roundhouse and dozens of lesser structures that spread east of South Allen Street, beginning in 1872. Foundation stones of the yards continued to pattern the grounds of Paradise Spring Park, which was created there late in the twentieth century. At 10:45 o'clock Tuesday evening, October 23, 1894, fire erupted without warning in a machine shop adjacent to the roundhouse where engines were housed for repairs. Timbers saturated over the years by oil and oil fumes were thought to have contributed to the fast-moving and dramatic conflagration. Alerted by sirens and locomotive whistles, hundreds of citizens turned out to watch, lining Allen Street and massing on "Conner's hill" northwest of the yards as flames claimed one structure after another. The fire brigade poured multiple streams of water on burning buildings with little initial effect. Even though workers managed to move some of the enormous engines out of danger, several were lost or heavily damaged, as were boxcars, coaches, and cabooses.[31]

Harry Haygood, an African American railroad shop worker, was later praised for having had the presence of mind to save the record books in the master mechanic's office. No lives were lost; few injuries were sustained; the place was covered by insurance; and, fortunately, important buildings east of the main roundhouse were not consumed. Also surviving was the massive brick repair shop, built in 1872 near Canal Street, which later housed the Corso produce company and continues to dominate the area in the present day. The greatest loss fell on the approximately 100 to 135 workmen who were left unemployed and who, in many cases, had lost their collections of expensive tools, worth as much as two hundred dollars. City fathers immediately called a public meeting in order to organize remedial projects, including the raising of funds to replace tools, to aid displaced workers temporarily, and to initiate renewal of the railroad yards. An insurance map of the area drawn up two years after the fire shows the yards, shops, and roundhouse again intact. Those community movers and shakers who led the recovery effort included Mayor James McHenry, John B. Latchem, John A. Bruner, and Cary E. Cowgill. A township tax was expected to be levied to meet expenses not covered by insurance.

After 1896 a splendid new Victorian-designed passenger depot stood at the eastern end of the railroad yards along the base of a barren stretch of the limestone bluff. Just beyond the depot was the southern entrance/exit of a man-made chasm, up to sixty feet deep, that had been blasted through solid rock. The purpose of this so-called cut was to facilitate the approach of trains onto the downtown rails and to raise rail traffic away from the floodplain. The cut was a monumental engineering feat that obliterated substantial portions of the "Limestone Hill" that had dominated the Treaty Ground of 1826. Contracts were let in 1895, and the work began on Wednesday, February 19, 1896. Over the next nine or ten months, a huge steam engine powered at least a dozen drills used by a cadre of workers to set charges in rock that was described as "hard as flint." Eventually between 100 and 150 laborers may have been employed as their supervisors strove to meet a November deadline. Dynamite blasts shook houses in the area for months, popping pictures off walls, rattling nick-knacks, and, in one instance, shooting a rock out of the bluff into the head engineer's office. A few men suffered lacerations from flying rock chips. Much of the rock debris was used to fill in the old canal bed and to pave an eastern extension of Market Street. Apparently the bluff along the street's extension, specifically in the area of the old spring, was naturally unstable; even before blasting began part of it caved in, momentarily endangering Hanna's now-antiquated homestead above. Trains began using the cut in early December 1896. The new line of rails spelled the eventual abandonment of an old railroad bridge over the Wabash, the abutments of which survive in the twenty-first century. Construction of a new railroad bridge a few hundred feet southwest of the old one was completed in 1898.[32]

Just downstream from the new railroad bridge—where the Huntington Street bridge would one day stand—the old ford across the Wabash was still visible at low water. Farther downstream from that site, and very close to where Hanna's millrace had emptied into the river, the venerable Wabash Street bridge (1859) stretched across the stream until 1894 when it was replaced by an iron structure. In its early days it was one of the longest spans of its kind in the state. A covered, wooden bridge (decorated with advertising on its exterior walls), it angled across the river in a southeasterly direction, reaching the south bank where the G. M. Diehl Machine Works later stood. At the span's southern end Wabash Street divided into three major roads. Eastward toward Treaty Creek's valley went the Wabash and Ashland (LaFontaine) Road. Westward climbed the Mount Vernon Pike. Straight ahead a road made two or three sharp turns as it angled up the steep bluff to connect with the Walnut Tree Road that shot due south toward Marion. That road's zig-zag path up the bluff remains faintly discernible in the twenty-first century. Even farther downstream stood Carroll Street bridge, or Vernon Street bridge as South Wabashers preferred, built in 1890.[33]

However fascinating South Wabash, waterworks, millrace, railroad yards, and bridges might have been to observers atop the courthouse, probably nothing would have attracted their focus more than the bustle in the business and industrial strips visible below them at the base of the bluff: the town's agora. There was scarcely a lot along the line of the canal from Allen Street in the east to the junction of Canal and Market streets in the west that was not home to a lively industry that prospered through most of the 1880s and 1890s. Likewise, along the north side of Canal Street for three or four blocks, along both sides of Market Street between Wabash and Miami streets, and along the downtown sections of Wabash and Miami streets there was scarcely an empty storefront. On the second and third floors of the taller buildings were a variety of offices, storage spaces, and living accommodations of varying desirability.

Two or three buildings were especially noteworthy for their contribution to the agora's style. The Tremont Hotel, located halfway between Wabash and

Miami streets on the north side of Market Street, was the town's premier inn, providing dining, barbering, and bathing facilities as well as rooms. Its façade illustrated the period's growing delight in projected window bays. East of the Tremont and standing on opposite corners at the base of the Wabash Street hill (at Market Street) were two major commercial buildings: the First National Bank, of elaborate Second Empire/Italianate design, and the simpler, but still elegant Ross Block, which housed insurance offices and other businesses. These latter two were constructed of similar, medium-red brick and stood at similar three-story heights, so that together they served visually as an unintended gateway to the upper heights of town. The Tremont and the Ross Block were both destroyed in the twentieth century. The former First National Bank building (the D Shoppe) continues to be a structural anchor for the downtown area. Although these three buildings stood out as especially important to the vibrant appearance of Wabash's commercial district in the nineteenth century, they were by no means alone as examples of merchants' and entrepreneurs' willingness to invest in emerging architectural fashion. By the end of the century a great many commercial buildings brandished high Victorian panache.

Photographs from late nineteenth century show downtown streets that were still mostly dirt, a fact accentuated by neat flagstone crosswalks at the corners and by the mud ruts left by carriages, carts, and buggies. A few photos show that hefty, brown-red glazed bricks were in limited use for upscale sidewalks, some of which survive in residential areas. By the twentieth century a few Wabash streets were paved with brick or asphalt, but the emerging popular choice for general paving was gravel, sometimes called macadamizing after its Scottish developer, John L. McAdam (1756–1836). Gravel was a known quantity locally because earlier in the century it had been used to replace rotting planks in the old country turnpikes. In the late 1870s and early 1880s, when parts of Canal and South Wabash streets were also covered with it, it began to represent the solution of the immediate future. Increasingly the city's common council ordered street improvements and invested in large street machinery, such as sprinklers to keep down dust and steam rollers to smooth dirt and gravel surfaces. In any case, whether in mud or dust or on gravel, downtown was the place to be. It was a hive of productivity, commerce, and interaction from morning into the evening hours. In addition, if one were a single male in search of a strong drink or a smoke with friends after work or in pursuit of more egregious bad habits, then one's downtown visits might stretch into the wee hours.[34]

Although not all industry had settled in the vicinity of the canal, that is where the bulk of it lay. Major exceptions were the Rettig and Alber Brewery on the northwest side of town; the Pioneer Hat Factory far to the northeast on Manchester Avenue in buildings taken over by the Ford Meter Box Company in the twentieth century; the Caldwell Brick Yard on North Wabash Street at the site of the present-day Christ United Methodist Church; and the Latchem and Hildebrand Treaty Creek Stone and Lime Company (plus lumberyards) at Huntington and Sinclair streets where Wilkinson Lumber Company (later owned by the Don Lee family) has conducted business in the two subsequent centuries. The downtown area lining the old canal and Canal Street was, by contrast, a veritable industrial park, a mixed blessing that created wealth on the one hand while it polluted the skies on the other. When winds from the southwest prevailed, the lower part of the city was "not fragrant," emitting a "peculiar and somewhat disagreeable oder."[35] Along this industrialized stretch roughly seventeen major companies turned out products for the local, state, and national markets between 1880 and the early 1900s, though not all were in operation simultaneously during that period.

From the east end of downtown to the west, these facilities included the spacious Big Four railroad shops; passenger and freight depots; additional facilities of the uptown Latchem and Hildebrand company; the King grain elevator, the processing complex of the Star Woolen industry; the Payne Furniture Factory; the Wabash Screen Door Company; the Wabash Importing Stables, purveyor of Belgium draft horses; the Plumbago axle grease company; the Wabash Soap Company; the Thompson flour mill; the Underwood cabinet works; Duck and Pressler's planning mill and door factory; the Wabash Church and School Furniture Company; the Wabash Electric Light Company; the Wabash Paper Company; the Diamond Match Company; and former sheriff Bossler Walter's table slide factory. Of these only Duck and Pressler's, which metamorphosed into the Yarnelle Lumber Company, and the B. Walter Company remained operable into the twenty-first century. Each of these companies has a history, mostly lost in obscure records, but together they spell out a story of economic vigor and relative prosperity in the late nineteenth century.[36]

If one were to highlight, by way of illustration, just one of these downtown industries, the choice might logically fall on the sales department of T. F. Payne's furniture company, if only because of the detailed information available. By the 1880s the company was already venerable. Its high profile in the community symbolized how woodworking had replaced pork processing as Wabash's leading industry. As noted previously, Thomas Payne had become a relatively rich man and was ready to travel abroad, leaving behind well-organized display rooms on the southeast corner of Miami and Market streets that were both packed with the products of his labors and no doubt enticing to potential customers. On the ground floor were bureaus, bedsteads, kitchen safes, cupboards, tables, toys, and wall brackets. Upstairs were at least four more rooms. The first contained parlor furniture, chamber suites, bookcases, sideboards, hall stands, and a new style of parlor furnishings that featured black-hair cloth trimmed in red silk plush. A second room displayed stacks of chairs of various design (folding, rocking, cane seated, camp) and carpeting. The third featured lounges (nine dollars and up) and two hundred center tables topped with marble that had been imported from the South. The last room contained both baby carriages and, incongruously, undertaking goods, particularly caskets and burial robes. The Payne operation was larger than some local industries and smaller than others. The volume and variety of its products provide an anecdotal measurement of the health of Wabash's industrial marketplace in the last two decades of the nineteenth century.[37]

There were bad times, to be sure. The mid-1890s brought turndowns that temporarily shook local confidence. The hitherto seemingly robust Wabash Church and School Furniture Company, so long a leader in Wabash's woodworking industry, was threatened with bankruptcy. The Diamond Match Company was hit by the panic of 1893 but managed to rebound vigorously, its stock rising from a low of ninety dollars to more than two hundred dollars a share. On Canal Street in 1896 the sheriff closed down E. H. Murray's dry goods emporium because of a nine thousand dollar outstanding mortgage and a debt of $1,800 owed to Carson, Pirie, Scott of Chicago. By contrast, most of the century's last two decades were economically promising. Businessmen such as Warren Bigler, who helped found the Board of Trade, a generic forerunner of the Chamber of Commerce, sought to entice new enterprises to town by trumpeting the economic glories of the city. The board's magazine-style publication, *The Manual of Wabash*, which puffed the town's culture and industry at century's end was a highly professional and polished piece of community propaganda.[38]

The fact is that businesses of the era employed hundreds of men and women who, in turn, supported family members numbering many hundreds more, who, in turn, spent money almost exclusively in Wabash. Wages for unskilled laborers in 1879 had amounted to at least a dollar a day. A few specialists might have earned four dollars. By the turn of the century pay standards improved appreciably though not dramatically, with the low end of the scale being about $1.25 in 1896. What is important is that these wages, low as they appear in retrospect, were probably dependable enough to create a semblance of security among employees and to fire a local economy that seemed, on most days, to be buoyant and promising. There were undoubtedly occasions when employees and employers locked horns but these were largely skirmishes between individuals or small groups of individuals. For example, just as Hezekiah Caldwell was gearing up to provide 1.25 million bricks for the 1879 courthouse, his workers threatened to strike, asking for $1.25 a day instead of a dollar. Yet, in a generally benign social atmosphere where even the local Republican newspaper expressed sympathy for both sides, Caldwell and his employees were probably able to negotiate an amicable settlement. The age of truly proactive, massive labor movements—unions versus management—which was just dawning nationally apparently had not yet made much progress in Wabash.[39]

Up and down the streets at the bottom of the bluff—Canal, Market, Wabash, and Miami—stores often duplicated inventory, yet prospered. In a special advertising edition supported by local merchants in the early 1880s the *Wabash Plain Dealer* promoted five clothiers, two bookstores, three groceries, two jewelers, and two barbers without taking into account their several competitors in what was essentially twelve blocks of storefronts, including the two blocks on the Wabash Street hill south of Main Street. A rough count indicates that in 1896 there were more than 135 businesses operating in these storefronts, including more than a half dozen ground-floor offices, banks, and (on the south side of West Canal) the *Plain Dealer*. There were other, smaller businesses tucked away behind storefront shops and in alleys. In addition, there were the Opera House, a post office, two or three boardinghouses, and four hotels—Lutz, Tremont, National, and Goodlander. About a half dozen storefronts were vacant. Among the businesses were ten grocery or meat shops, six dry good outlets (not counting clothiers), and nine saloons. A comparative count of storefronts taken from a 1901 insurance map virtually duplicates those of 1896, except that saloons outnumbered groceries twelve to eleven.[40]

Here, then, was an area of town that was just possibly beginning to resemble, albeit in a less sanitized version, the nostalgic vision of nineteenth-century streets depicted in Hollywood films and romantic novels of later decades. There were canvass awnings over shops and barber poles and heavy iron railings around those sidewalk openings that led to dark, subterranean storage basements. Produce and retail goods filled baskets or covered stands along the sidewalks. Great stone troughs provided water for horses, and hitching posts stood ready. The streets were not bricked, but on a good day the gravel that covered the former dirt and mud surface was rolled neat and smooth and contoured just enough to shed water into boulder-lined gutters, providing a smooth surface for the Tremont Hotel's horse-drawn van as it raced to meet incoming trains at the passenger depots. Manure in the street was a fragrant lure for a thousand flies, dogs were everywhere, and a stray cow or a pig could still be found wandering about, waiting for its owner to come steer it home before the town marshal took charge.

Most of all, however, downtown was a place for people. Not only was there scarcely anywhere else to shop, but it was also an accessible and democratic venue for social contact. Merchants, shopkeepers, businessmen, journalists, bankers, attorneys, and their employees took breaks from work by walking along the streets where they met on purpose or serendipitously for conversation. Children played in the streets, splashed in the gutters, and ran along the sidewalks. Housewives and domestic employees streamed down the Wabash and Miami street hills most weekdays to buy meats, coffee, staples, and other necessities, long skirts swishing along the sidewalks, parasols snagging momentarily against awnings. As with the men, being downtown was not only about chores and errands for the women. It was also about communal bonding, friendship, news gathering, gossiping, and maybe arguing or fighting. If a person happened to be downtown mostly for the shopping, however, he or she had the choice of a great many competitors, any number of whom might be acquaintances. For example, clothing and dry goods probably led in the number of outlets, and while the founders or managers of these stores would have imported their stock from great warehouses in Cincinnati or Chicago, they were local citizens who were familiar to their customers, men such as O. W. Conner, C. E. Diehl, J. W. Busick, J. R. Bruner, Isaac New, Aaron Simon,

James McCrea, Jake or Henry Herff, Benjamin Wolf, David Beitman, and Nelson Zeigler.[41]

In determining what buildings and businesses actually existed in central Wabash during these years few sources are more interesting or more informative than a series of Sanborn insurance maps, which are rich in detail and illustrate the precise footprints of factories, shops, banks, schools, houses, and churches. The maps also indicate the location of various outbuildings on each property, excluding privies and fencing that were either not subject to fire or not worth being insured. Early street address numbers are noted, as are the locations of public cisterns. The purpose of the maps was to track the size, shape, special features, and changes in buildings that might be covered by insurers. Because the maps for Wabash were issued every few years between 1887 and 1931, they measure both significant and cosmetic alterations in the properties shown over those years. Here are two examples: First, from these maps it is possible to track the replacement of early downtown homes by commercial buildings and to date roughly the rise of other new structures. Thus, between the 1896 map and the 1901 map, the old canal dock on the southwest corner of Wabash and Canal streets vanished, and the huge Bradley Block (Jack Francis's shop, 2010) rose in its place. Likewise, between the 1893 and 1896 maps the old canal bed itself is shown to disappear. Second, from these maps one can determine the approximate years in the nineteenth century when adding such amenities as wraparound porches and decorative turrets to homes became locally fashionable. The maps are limited in their geographic scope, since many developments outside the center of nineteenth-century Wabash are omitted.[42]

As those imaginary observers atop the Wabash County Courthouse now turned their attention from a southern view of their town toward its northern aspects their line of vision might naturally have traveled upward along the Wabash Street hill, the town's main thoroughfare. If so, their eyes probably paused for a moment at the sight of City Hall, close at hand, on the southeast corner of Wabash and Main streets. It was new in 1883 and constructed on two lots of the Original Plat that had cost the common council fourteen hundred dollars.

In a sense the new city hall was oddly—even awkwardly—sited, being neither on level ground downtown nor on level ground uptown. Rather it seemed to perch precariously on an especially steep portion of the hill that had been partially tamed by bluff-grading projects in the 1860s. In fact, however, its location may have been the result of logistical genius—whose genius, specifically, is unknown, though it resulted from a council decision made late in the mayoral tenure of Clarkson Weesner (1876–78). City hall's most practical function was to house a fire department, responsible not only for firefighting along the industrial and commercial strips downtown but also in the bluff-top areas as well. As noted earlier, providing protection in the expanding residential areas on the heights of town was a long-standing challenge for men, vehicles, and horses stationed on the lowlands. Yet, the most challenging fires were likely to occur in the latter area, as the origins of the 1870 conflagration demonstrated. The location of city hall seems, in retrospect, to have addressed the needs of the whole town by providing a fire station that was centrally located. Response to a downtown fire meant a quickly efficient downward rush toward Market or Canal streets, and any response to the top of the bluff required a much shorter, easier climb than was previously required.[43]

Behind the hall's large front door there was an area on the ground floor large enough to accommodate horses, ladder truck, hose cart, and engine. Even through much of the twentieth century the space was adequate for motorized vehicles. There were lofty spaces where hoses were hung to dry. The night shift occupied upstairs quarters and when called to duty descended in record time on a shiny brass pole that held the fascination of generations of schoolboys. The ground floor held offices for the fire brigade, for telephone service, and, later, for the police department. The mayor, clerk, treasurer, and engineer had upstairs offices equipped with enormous safes for storing documents and other valuables. The city court was also upstairs. A railing that separated its public from its judicial spaces still stands in one of the offices occupied by the Youth Service Bureau.

The exterior of city hall, like the courthouse, illustrated the determination of leaders to put a best foot forward by way of a public presentation. Local contractor, Fred Grant, who won the bid at $13,850, produced a utilitarian structure that did not look like one. It reflected accepted Victorian tastes: stone foundation, red-brick walls, carved stone and wood trim, mansard roof, and timeless architectural features such as the tall arched doors and windows along Wabash Street. High, narrow windows let light pour into upper-story rooms. An iron, domed cupola topped the building. Although decorative and stylish, it housed the all-important bell that alerted the town to trouble. A flagpole extended from the dome. The cupola disappeared in later decades, but the rest of the exterior remains largely unsullied.[44]

Along the Main Street side of city hall, at the eastern end, was an exterior door. A labyrinthine route wound from the door to the council chamber, a spacious room where the mayor, four councilmen, and a clerk met officially two or three times a month and probably more often unofficially. Here these officials received petitioners, listened to committee reports, and issued ordinance after ordinance in their attempts to stay on top of the needs of a maturing city with a swelling population. They dealt with the street conditions, with trash and garbage issues, with licensing and appointments, with innovations such as telephone poles, streetlights, and water hydrants, and with myriad random issues.

Of all concerns those related to streets, alleys, and sidewalks consumed a lion's share of space in council minutes. Downtown the original flagstone sidewalks wanted replacing. Uptown residential streets needed extending, improving, or both, and alleys needed to be policed against dismal heaps of trash and garbage. Because citizens had a right to approach the council with requests about conditions in their areas, its Committee on Streets and Alleys was tapped for frequent investigative work. Sometimes residents became desperate enough for improvements to partner with the council. When Calvin Cowgill and Hezekiah Caldwell wanted an expensive upgrade on a stretch of alley lying between Sinclair and Maple streets they convinced the council to install twenty-inch-high, parallel "walls" the length of the alley. Cowgill and Caldwell then crossed the walls with planks at their expense, creating—presumably—a surface that was slightly elevated above the mud created by runoff flooding.

As the century aged the use of "asphaltum" to pave graveled (macadamized) streets became more feasible. Although in some minds brick should have vied with asphalt as the pavement of the future, the latter had the larger following. For example, news reporters sometimes commented when a local politician could be identified as proasphalt. Although brick eventually covered some stretches of downtown streets, "asphaltum" held its own, even in the new century, as the paving of choice. Such improvements, however, had materialized slowly. Hill Street, for instance, was a desirable residential thoroughfare in the late nineteenth century, yet tinted commercial photographs taken of it no earlier than 1897 and as late as the early twentieth century show it to be graveled in a very smooth and tidy way; the presence of manure in the street indicates that the photos were not touched up. It was down such streets that the first "Loco-Mobile" would be driven by a Doctor Upjohn on June 8, 1900.[45]

With one exception the mayors presiding over city hall perpetuated the town's reputation as a "Republican fortress," and the common councils were uniformly tilted in that direction as well. Michael R. Crabill, Democratic mayor from 1890 to 1892, was the exception. "Farmer" Crabill unseated Henry C. Pettit by three votes, in part because many Republicans had voted Democratic in a show of pique over the council's choice of a town marshal. Occasionally a Democratic newspaper attempted to stir up formidable opposition to the majority party. For example, in 1878 the *Wabash Courier* derided what it called "Little Jimmy McCrea's City Council," accusing it of cronyism and nepotism. James McCrea was a prominent businessman and a Republican councilman. The council, the *Courier* charged, had raised salaries of Republican city employees only and, worse, had readily hired McCrea relatives, "placing the public teat in the mouth of every worthless and impecunious male member of the McCrea family."[46] McCrea's brother, Billy, the street commissioner, it was alleged, had tried every other kind of employment and had failed. The "Republican fortress" remained largely impregnable against such Democratic surges, save for the Crabill aberration. From the 1866 incorporation to 1902 the mayors of Wabash were Joseph H. Matlock, Warren G. Sayre, Clarkson W. Weesner, Charles S. Parrish, Clarence W. Stephenson, Henry C. Pettit, Michael R. Crabill, Horace D. Bannister, and James E. McHenry. Sayre, Parrish, and Stevenson had multiple three-year terms.[47]

City hall must have been abuzz also in the hotly contested election of 1888. It roiled the whole state, not only because Hoosier Benjamin Harrison was running for president against Democrat incumbent Grover Cleveland, but also because of scandal over voter fraud. Apparently with good reason Democrats accused Republicans of paying off so-called floaters, men who would cast their votes for a price, using ballots provided by the party. The fact that some Democrats were also openly paying for votes accelerated general cries for reform. In 1889 the Indiana General Assembly adopted a uniform ballot policy and then pushed through a rash of other reform measures in the following years. Meanwhile, in Wabash, the rumor that floaters were being paid ten dollars a vote in 1888 added heat to a lively contest in which Republicans sought to give Harrison a huge plurality. Cheered on by the *Plain Dealer*, Harrison's supporters attended giant rallies in Wabash and Peru before the election and "jollified" exuberantly after the results were tallied. Although citizens of both parties might gather around "party poles" to publicize respective loyalties, it was also alleged that Democrats, hoping to avoid the Republicans' victory celebrations, went hunting on election day in such droves that "the woods were full of them."[48] Harrison's county plurality was 1,430 votes, a large percentage of them credited to that "Gibralter of Republicanism," Wabash.[49]

Emerging Republican leaders in the 1890s included Calvin Cowgill's son-in-law, Harvey. B. Shively, a future circuit judge, Alfred H. Plummer, president of the local McKinley Republican Club, and his vice president, Bossler Walter, who had once served as sheriff. It was also the decade in which Sayre, the former mayor, began to eye the state's gubernatorial contests. The 1896 election was especially exciting for local Republicans because Harrison scheduled a stop in town to stump for William McKinley. Walter organized an elaborate parade of floats and three or four bands that marched circuitously about town. After that commotion Harrison's arrival at the downtown rail station was a bit of an anticlimax. The overly short former president was introduced by that overly "tall sycamore of the Wabash," L. L. Carpenter. Harrison made a brief address and was on his way to Indianapolis in less than twenty minutes. The hoopla continued without him: the parade marched on into the evening, accompanied by torchlights, Roman candles, "cannoncrackers," and other fireworks.[50]

Wabash Democrats also had their emerging leaders, a loyal opposition that worked to articulate locally some of the issues that were important to the national "Democracy." Nelson G. Hunter, for example, was a rising figure in the 1890s. He spoke at rallies frequently, supported William Jennings Bryan for president, and stumped for free trade and against a restrictive tariff. James Whistler was building a reputation; in the new century he was elected mayor. Still around and active was Doctor J. H. DePuy, whose inebriation the *Plain Dealer* had once excoriated. In 1896 DePuy tried to inspire a free-silver publication that would be "a red hot newspaper, pure and simple in its democracy," but not much came of it. Other prominent Democrats of the period were Will Elward, a Roman Catholic and chair of the county party, and Reuben Lutz, the party's treasurer and erstwhile city councilman. DePuy was among those local politicians taunted by Republicans as "Bourbon Democrats," perhaps because, in this case, they were thought to be less than stalwart in matters of temperance, even though the term had referred to Southern sympathizers during the Civil War.[51]

Local political leaders at century's close were sensitive to the advent of another American war, the war with Spain, culminating in the United States' acquisition of the Hawaiian and Philippine Islands. This marked the beginning of American imperialism, of a global reach that probably reflected on a national scale what many citizens in towns such as Wabash were feeling about themselves in these years—confident, optimistic, expansive, prideful. The Spanish-American War was victoriously completed almost before it began and no Wabash area men lost their lives. More than two hundred of them were mustered into the companies of two Indiana regiments, the 157th and the 160th. Some recruits justly worried that the war would end before they saw action. Soldiers of the 160th did reach Cuba in January 1899 and were mustered out in April without engaging in action. Most local recruits served about a year without leaving the country. Surviving letters of the period indicate that for Wabash men the Spanish-American War seemed personally more memorable for the travel it afforded than for chances to be heroic.[52]

Perhaps Wabash's most significant human contribution to this war effort was not so much with the men who served as in the efforts of Doctor Rose Kidd Beere, who had been born in Wabash. Her father was Major Meredith H. Kidd, who had been an officer in the Civil War and subsequently a military leader in the West. Her maternal grandfather was Stearns Fisher, former canal commissioner and an early pioneer living west of town. When a war with Spain seemed certain, Major Kidd wrote his daughter about his regret that he was too old to fight and his grandsons were too young. Rose wired her father this reply: "You take care of my boys and I'll represent our family in this war. I can't raise a regiment, or carry a gun, but I can help nurse the men who do."[53] Though she held a medical degree from Northwestern University she went to the Philippines as a nurse in charge of eight other nurses, the first woman assigned to that front. Under the auspices of the Red Cross she opened a hospital in Manila for ailing soldiers. Although she reaped praise for her care of soldiers and was popular with many of them, she was also controversial. Some critics believed she had favorites among her patients, but others may have been responding to her aggressive advocacy of improved standards in the troops' accommodations and diet. She was certainly known for directness of expression. Her telegram that notified authorities of her resignation from service read "Resigned. Beere."

Late nineteenth-century observers on top of the courthouse would not have missed the Masonic Temple, a magnificent gothic pile just two doors south of city hall, housing Hanna Lodge, Number 61. It was built a decade after city hall. It was a remarkably tall building, rising four stories above ground, plus attic space, plus two short, decorative spires. Although positioned halfway downhill from city hall it nonetheless towered above the roof of that building, rivaling its cupola for attention. Its public, western face was all windows and rounded bays in a confection of articulated stonework. Until it burned in the mid-twentieth century the Masonic Temple, with its pool hall, card rooms, lounges, and abiding pungency of tobacco smoke, was a favorite haunt of Wabash males. Its size and ornateness clearly witnessed to the prominence of fraternal movements in the social life of the city in the nineteenth and early twentieth centuries. Perhaps significantly, then, the temple that replaced it would be a squat, flat-roofed utilitarian structure that was about a fourth the height of the original and considerably less inspired as an architectural presence.[54]

Wabash's princes of industry and merchandising—plus many of their employees and coworkers—and the leaders who made important decisions in the chambers of city hall did not spend their excess profits or their Sundays or their leisure time in the bustling agora beneath the bluff top. Many of them spent such fortunes and such time with their families uptown where judicial, educational, domestic, and religious structures formed an acropolis that increasingly dominated the landscape. Their pockets may have been lined by labor in the valley, but their loftier interests were served on the heights.

The Wabash "acropolis"

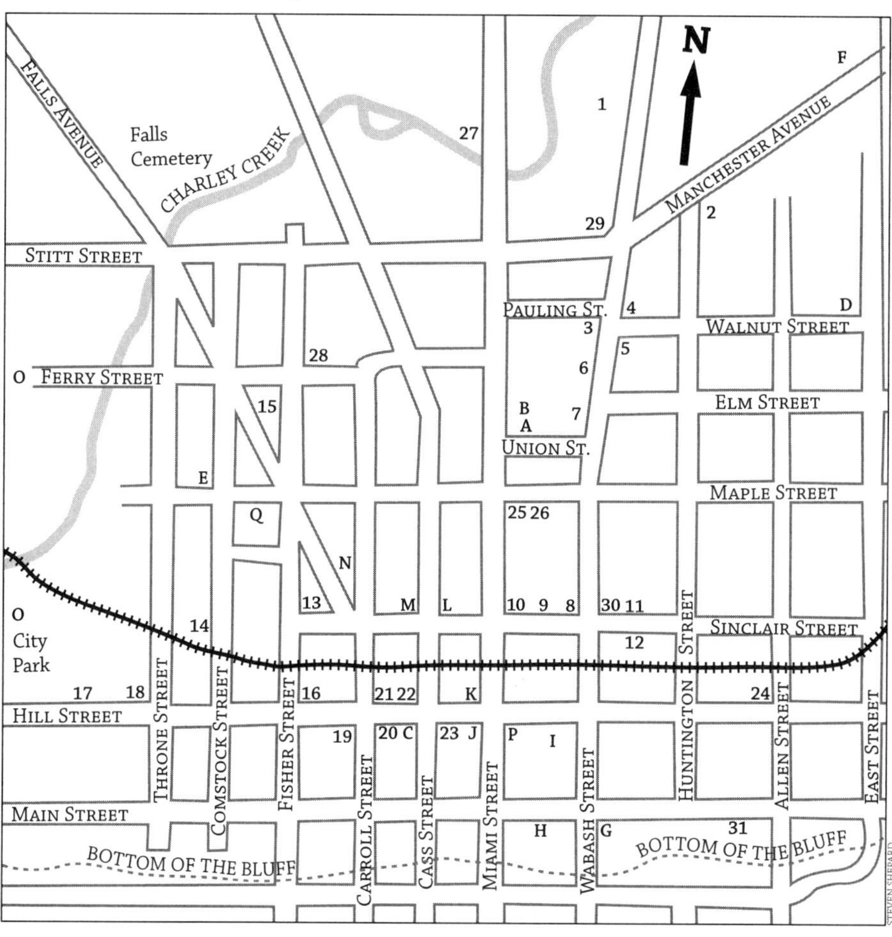

1. Atkinson-Hess-Ford house
2. John Latchem house
3. Kunse-Pawling-Walter house
4. W. P. Jones house
5. J. H. Ford house
6. William Sharp house
7. F. M. Eagle house
8. J. W. Busick house
9. Calvin Cowgill house
10. H. B. Shively house
11. Joseph Gries house
12. Phillip Alber house
13. John A. Bruner house
14. Charles Haas house
15. George King house
16. Warren Bigler house
17. Josiah Daugherty house
18. William Yarnelle house
19. Clarkson Weesner house
20. Harmon Wolf house
21. Thomas Payne house
22. Thomas McNamee house
23. James Ford house
24. W. A. Elward house
25. J. H. DePuy house
26. Romeo DePuy house
27. Alfred Plummer house
28. Site of Elijah Hackleman house
29. Site of J. D. Conner Jr. house
30. Site of Cary Cowgill house
31. J. D. Conner house

A. Union School site
B. Miami School site
C. High School site
D. East Ward School site
E. West Ward School site
F. Century School site
G. City Hall
H. County Jail
I. Courthouse
J. Presbyterian Church
K. Christian Church
L. Roman Catholic Church
M. Methodist Church
N. Jewish Synagogue
O. Fairground sites
P. Memorial Hall
Q. Former Catholic church

WABASH COUNTY HISTORICAL MUSEUM

The Richardsonian-style Wabash High School building was destroyed in the late twentieth century; ***Insets:*** *The tower and stonework details of the high school building.*

Adelaide Steele Baylor, high school principal, who became superintendent of the city schools.

WABASH COUNTY HISTORICAL MUSEUM

WABASH COUNTY HISTORICAL MUSEUM

WABASH COUNTY HISTORICAL MUSEUM

PHOTOGRAPH COURTESY OF RICHARD E. FORD

Clockwise from top: *Joseph Gries, 1890s; Calvin Cowgill, prominent lawyer and community leader; the Atkinson-Hess-Ford house, prior to 1928 when it was dramatically downsized; Bossler Walter, sheriff and businessman.*

WABASH COUNTY HISTORICAL MUSEUM

WABASH COUNTY HISTORICAL MUSEUM

Top: *Kunse-Pawling-Walter house, one of the earliest homes in town and one of the highest. At seven hundred feet above sea level, it is located one hundred feet higher than Market Street.* ***Above:*** *Gries-Hoover house on East Sinclair Street, extant in the twenty-first century.*

WABASH COUNTY HISTORICAL MUSEUM

THOMAS B. HELM, *HISTORY OF WABASH COUNTY, INDIANA* (CHICAGO: JOHN MORRIS, 1884), 238

Top: *Alber-Crace house, East Sinclair Street, an example of the Federalist style.*
Above: *George King house at Fisher Street and Falls Avenue, later a funeral home.*

PHOTOGRAPH BY W. WILLIAM WIMBERLY II

Haas-Kiefaber house, a fine example of the Queen Anne style.

WABASH COUNTY HISTORICAL MUSEUM

Warren Bigler, businessman and community leader.

WABASH COUNTY HISTORICAL MUSEUM

THOMAS B. HELM, *HISTORY OF WABASH COUNTY, INDIANA* (CHICAGO: JOHN MORRIS, 1884)

***Top:** William Yarnelle's 1902 home on West Hill Street;* ***Above:** Thomas McNamee home, Hill and Cass streets.*

CLARKSON WEESNER, *A HISTORY OF WABASH COUNTY*, 2 VOLS. (CHICAGO: LEWIS PUBLISHING COMPANY, 1914)

Thomas McNamee, banker and businessman.

WABASH COUNTY HISTORICAL MUSEUM

Elijah Hackleman, historian, diarist, county official, farmer, and community activist.

CLARKSON WEESNER, *A HISTORY OF WABASH COUNTY*, 2 VOLS. (CHICAGO: LEWIS PUBLISHING COMPANY, 1914), 2:688

William A. Elward, businessman.

WABASH COUNTY HISTORICAL MUSEUM

Doctor J. H. DePuy's seventy-eighth birthday gathering at Romeo DePuy's home (extant 2010) on West Maple Street, the "house of the seven gables." Doctor DePuy is seated in the first row, seventh from the left. **Front row, left to right:** *Henry Wenzel, John Greer, Levi Bruner, Miles Morgan, John Hoover, Dr. J. H. Ford Sr., Dr. J. H. DePuy, Albert Pawling, Thomas Underdown, J. S. Daugherty, David Bach.* **Middle row, left to right:** *Michael Hyman, R. P. Mitten, Leven Murphy, L. P. Dollison, Phillip Davis, T. F. Payne, Dr. R. F. Blout, Hon. Calvin Cowgill, Dr. M. R. Crabill, W. H. DePuy, Cornelius Lumaree.* **Back row, left to right:** *Col. J. R. Bruner, Jack Higgins, Franklin Keyes, David Coble, Judge J. D. Conner, Jesse Talbert, M. W. Ross, J. H. Talmage, Capt. J. M. Thompson, John Tyre, Phillip Alber.*

CLARKSON WEESNER, *A HISTORY OF WABASH COUNTY*, 2 VOLS. (CHICAGO: LEWIS PUBLISHING COMPANY, 1914), 2:596

A Conner family home that was built on Main Street in 1882 and destroyed in the twentieth century.

WABASH COUNTY HISTORICAL MUSEUM

Cary Cowgill's showplace, northeast corner of Sinclair and Wabash streets. It was razed in the twentieth century and replaced with a gas station.

Reuben Lutz home, a quintessential version of the Queen Anne style, on the southeast corner of Market and Cass streets, was destroyed for commercial purposes. Olive Lutz married Mark Honeywell, future Wabash benefactor, at this address in the 1890s.

James Dicken Conner, Hugh Hanna's son-in-law, as he appeared about the time that he moved the Hanna graves to Falls Cemetery.

WABASH COUNTY HISTORICAL MUSEUM

WABASH COUNTY HISTORICAL MUSEUM

Top: *Hanna's corner, late nineteenth century;* ***Above:*** *The J. D. Conner home, built in the 1850s. It was subsequently divided into apartments and later restored and occupied ad seriatim by Halderman, Hetzner, and Duffey families.*

13

Soaring Acropolis

On "Citizen's" imaginary courthouse observation deck, late-nineteenth century sightseers would now shift their positions in order to inspect the northern reaches of Wabash. Their line of vision would sweep from city hall past offices and shops along the east side of Wabash Street, taking in the stone-fronted Bigler and Dicken Building near Hill Street and then—just south of the railroad tracks—the large brick bakery and grocery complex that had earlier housed the Wabash Business College. Beyond, along the northward horizons, the undulating canopy of forest was still largely intact, and closer in, where home owners had once chopped down trees ruthlessly, maples and elms along streets and avenues had begun to mature, filling in the gaps. Especially when the foliage was gone from late fall to early spring the view from above the courthouse might clearly have revealed ways in which wealth generated in the valley was creating a certain progressive urbanity on the bluff.

There were, for starters, the school buildings.[1] By the turn of the century they dotted the landscape, their slate roofs pushing above surrounding tree branches: Third Ward elementary (built in 1872 and doubled in size in 1893) on West Maple Street; First Ward (1883) on East Walnut Street; and Century (1900) on Manchester Avenue. Wabash's First Ward and Third Ward were later known as East Ward and West Ward. Central was built just north of old Union School in 1888. It housed the high school after Union was condemned in 1887 and later became exclusively an elementary school named Miami. South Wabash—before incorporation with Wabash as South Side—had its own schools, including a high school by the 1880s. The private elementary school of Saint Bernard's parish was located on Miner Street in a small building just behind the church (which was in the 400 block of West

Maple Street) and, later, on Saint Bernard's West Sinclair Street property. In the mid-twentieth century the parish built a new, three-story school north of its sanctuary on property where the prominent John U. Pettit family had lived in the nineteenth century.

The new public elementary schools were all substantial brick structures of two stories and of Queen Anne or Italianate architectural design. Typically the buildings had eight large classrooms, one of which might be designed for convocations, and featured broad halls, hardwood floors, sweeping wooden staircases, tall windows that opened wide for ventilation, blackboards and chalk rails that stretched across interior walls, rows of wooden desks that were bolted to the floor and had built-in ink wells and hinged seats, long narrow cloakrooms where miscreants could be sent for punishment, and commodious basements to house heating equipment and toilet facilities. Outside were playgrounds of varying size, most with play equipment, some with small softball diamonds, some with great shade trees left by the ancient forest. Two recesses a day were important socialization and exercise components of education.

High school had commenced in 1871 at the instigation of Superintendent J. J. Mills who opened space in the third floor of Union for freshman, junior, and senior classes. It was several years before a fourth (sophomore) class was added. Meanwhile, with the Old Union building's condemnation in the late 1880s, desire for a new high school structure mounted, resulting in the school on West Hill Street, built in 1894. Although this new high school surpassed the elementary schools in architectural exuberance, making the latter look pedestrian by comparison, these earlier structures were, in fact, individually quite handsome as well as being conducive to educational activity in practical ways.

Given the generous use of wood for beams, floors, and stairs—plus the oily solutions used to polish wood—these schools were probably firetraps in the making, a consideration that led to the addition of exterior fire escapes and to regular fire drills. However, only one was consumed by fire, which broke out, mercifully, during the night at holiday time. On December 27, 1892, Miami went up in flames. Though it was feared at the time that the school was a total loss, the Sanborn map of January 1893 illustrates that while there was no longer a roof to the structure the exterior walls were intact. Extensive damage notwithstanding, the replacement very likely mimicked the footprint and dimensions of the original (1888) design.

The construction of six new schools in just twenty-nine years was an attempt to keep abreast of the rapid population growth in Wabash. In 1870 there had been roughly 2,900 residents, in 1900 there were more than 8,600. Demographics had changed also with regard to the national origins of citizens. Whereas those from the British Isles were still dominant, more surnames now reflected origins from the European continent. As has been noted earlier, German Jews had played a significant role in Wabash's development since mid-century. By the 1890s it was evident that other folks—of German background in particular—had helped swell the population. Many Germans affiliated with Saint Bernard Catholic parish, in contrast to the dominant Irish faithful of Lagro's Saint Patrick Catholic Church. The saints' names themselves had long spelled out the difference, Bernard having been a continental European and Patrick having founded Irish Christianity. There were also numerous German Protestants in Wabash, many of whom had settled in so-called German Town, an area east and south of the Caldwell brickyard, located between North Huntington and North Wabash streets. There was a German Protestant church at the corner of Huntington and Walnut streets. The *Wabash County Directory* for 1894 lists the names and addresses of roughly two thousand Wabash residents. Of these, approximately 150 addresses were for heads of households who bore surnames other than those associated with the British Isles. There were twenty-one addresses for the expansive Hipskind family alone and seven for the Schlemmer family. The Hipskinds and Schlemmers, along with citizens of similar European backgrounds, assimilated fairly easily and fairly quickly over the years, becoming respected and productive members of the community.

Given the upward population surge, student enrollments understandably jumped accordingly. In 1873, 620 students were enrolled in eleven regular, graded classes plus a "German School," which may have specialized in math and science. Regular classes met each weekday under increasingly crowded conditions at the Union building. It may have been a blessing in disguise that, in contrast with the enrollment figures, an average of only 569 students actually attended each day. Even so, this meant that there might be an average of more than fifty students in each of Union's eleven classes, an average that was not, of course, evenly distributed, the higher grades being smaller. Given the pressure of such figures, the year 1872 had been a watershed. The Wabash Common Council that year voted to support the construction of a new school (West Ward), taking some students away from Union School. It was a temporary fix, but it set an agenda for the near future: keep the high school at Union (or, as it turned out, at Central/Miami) and scatter the younger grades in neighborhood schools across the city, including a new elementary building for South Side, erected in 1897. By that year enrollment in public schools had jumped fourfold from 620 in 1873 to 2,587 students. The number of teachers had risen from a little over a dozen to more than forty.[2]

At about 1:00 a.m. on Tuesday, March 17, 1896, three men returning from a lodge meeting downtown to their homes in the western part of Wabash caught sight of flames in the basement of the high school, which was just two years old and stood two blocks west of the courthouse on the southwest corner of Hill and Cass streets. They rushed back to city hall to sound a general alarm and call out the fire brigade. On being alerted, M. W. Harrison, the superintendent of schools, sped to the site without bothering to clothe himself fully. Although he arrived shortly after 1:00 a.m., smoke was already pouring out of the second floor on the northeast corner where the fire was then centered, even though it had probably originated in a basement furnace room. At about this point DeWitt Payne, living at 256 West Hill Street, was awakened by an explosion on the school's second floor. There, an eastern, exterior stone wall showed signs of stress, and the classroom on the northeast, upper corner was clearly destroyed. The fire department, however, had arrived in good time. Making use of public cisterns, hydrants, or both, the men poured streams of water into the building, containing the fire and finally subduing it. Remarkably there was no interruption of the school schedule. The new building still had room to spare for the students from the classroom that had been burned out. Structural repairs cost between thirty-five hundred and five thousand dollars.

Not only did the event prove the efficacy of the town's water system and its firefighting capacity, it saved Wabash's premier nineteenth-century structure, the one that culminated the civic and cultural aspirations of the town. The courthouse and the soon-to-materialize Memorial Hall were county-based projects; the new Wabash High School was a creation of the city alone. The *Wabash Plain Dealer* called it "the pride of every citizen."[3] It seemed to rise up as a declaration in stone walls, gargoyles, grotesques, turrets, and tower that Wabash had triumphed over its rustic past, made the most of its setting, and was a city of competitive sophistication and prosperity. In that sense it was the town's signature structure. It was not practical of design or cost effective (those tyrannical goblins of a later age). It was more like a civic monument than a schoolhouse—a tangible manifestation of pride of place, of communal ambition, and of cultural yearning. Aging pioneers who thought about it—those who had camped out at Treaty Ground, watched the canal being plowed through the forests, or had slopped home through the mud of Market Street pond—must have seen the high school's tower slowly emerging in construction above the bluff-top trees and double-checked their wits to know if this were really the town where they had matured and grown old. The new structure was so very unlike the Headquarters for New comers. It screamed transformation.

This monument to a city's success was not inevitable. It had been conceived in the undeniable fact that by 1887 continued use of the old Union schoolhouse of 1859 could scarcely be defended. That building had also been symbolically important when it was built, signaling the desire of the town to improve the intellectual climate of an emerging community. In 1890, however, its weight-bearing wooden pillars were thought to be unsafe, the stairs too steep, the heat and ventilation inadequate, and the windows too small. Use of the 1888 Miami building for a high school was a stopgap solution. Perhaps a new structure should be considered. The common council was of another mind. Because of cost it "sat down hard" on the idea of another new building, ruling that there was already two much public debt.

On February 22, 1890, three school trustees weighed in on the issue with a letter to the council. They were John H. Bruner, Doctor James H. Ford (James's son), and Warren Bigler. Bruner was a successful hardware and dry goods merchant, Ford was a prominent surgeon, and Bigler was a highly literate, aggressive business leader. The three argued that Union School was past a condemnation date by at least two years and no longer usable in its present condition. Renovation would cost up to ten thousand dollars and even then lighting, heat, and ventilation would be problematic. The trio recommended, rather, that eighteen thousand to twenty thousand dollars be invested in a new structure that would house the high school, a school library, and a superintendent's office.

Bruner, Ford, and Bigler were citizens whose judgments on such matters would be hard for elected officials to dismiss out of hand. Arguably they represented the intelligentsia of Wabash and the culturally ascendant, though they were also successful business and professional men, possessing influential local connections, political savvy, practical knowledge of money, and presumed moral gravity. The upshot of their involvement was the council's decision in March to hire a Logansport architect to examine Union School. However, these decisions are not obviously laid out in council minutes but are reported secondhand by the newspaper.

The architect's analysis seemed to confirm the worst. Although Union's foundations were good and the walls were safe, the place was a disaster waiting to happen. First-floor joists were rotting and not resting squarely on foundation walls. The roof timbers were sound enough, but they were holding up a tin roof that needed repair. Ventilating shafts were unsafe. Wooden columns that supported floors were not strong enough to sustain moving loads, such as students "marching to time" during certain exercises. The outcome was inevitable. A new high school was authorized. Not surprisingly, the common council had been right on one score. It would cost almost twice the twenty thousand dollars that Bruner, Ford, and Bigler had estimated. Probably council members ultimately became enthusiastic about their decision, for when the high school seniors of 1897 expressed appreciation to city fathers for their new building they included at least one council member, Mayor Horace D. Bannister, in addition to members of the Board of School Trustees.[4]

The new school was constructed of Bedford stone with Romanesque flourishes typical of the currently popular Richardsonian style, which was a hearty nod to the perceived romance of the early Middle Ages. Much of the exterior stonework was rough faced, and much of the stone trim was deeply carved, sometimes with chubby-cheeked, half-toothless, grinning grotesques that, reputedly, were caricatures of local citizens.[5] The classroom structure proper measured 116 feet by 95 feet on the ground and 52 feet in height. On the north side were four immense, heavily ornamented stone pillars, supporting three stone arches, two of which led to the main entrances. On either side of these doors were rounded half towers with conical roofs pushing above the second floor. Inside, on the first floor, were three classrooms, a reception room, and an assembly hall with 250 seats. On the second floor were three classrooms, a library and the superintendent's office. Science laboratories and heating equipment occupied the basement. The building was lighted with both electricity and gas, used electric bells, and had ducts to help freshen the air.

A tower rose from near the center of the north façade. It was twelve feet square, narrow enough to make its upper reach appear loftier than it was: 108 feet, just over twice as high as the building proper. Gargoyles peered menacingly down from its heights. The tower's interior was virtually useless, save for a little storage space at the bottom. It housed an oak staircase that crept upward along the raw stone walls to a windowed eyrie under a pitched roof. From here there were grand views, but it was a place rarely visited. Quite obviously there was nothing utilitarian about the tower. It was pure romance or pure poetry or purely celebratory or purely art for art's sake. Perhaps it is significant that Wabash officials chose to spend public funds in so exuberant a manner and that so little protest was recorded. Perhaps leaders surmised that a community can scarcely aspire to greatness without great education, great art, and great style; perhaps they were stating that, in their opinion, Wabash had attained that status.

In the fall of 1893, ground was broken for the new school. Construction of the walls began in March 1894, and the cornerstone was laid the next month. It opened for classes on November 26, 1894, and served as the high school until 1926 when it became the city's junior high school. Over the years there were relatively few structural changes. Lockers were added, the superintendent's office moved with the high school, and the assembly hall became a gymnasium, with one set of showers for boys located inconveniently in a dungeonlike room beneath the tower. In the next century a real gymnasium/auditorium was built onto the east end. Although the interior incorporated the latest facilities, the architecture of the exterior was a vulgar distraction. The junior high, which became the middle school in the 1980s, moved out in the 1960s. After that the school corporation made various uses of the property and then abandoned it altogether. In the late 1990s the 1894 building was demolished. In its last years it was on a statewide list of architectural gems that should be preserved, and its fate was the subject of some fierce local disputes.

The person who most represented the importance of public education in Wabash during these years and into the twentieth century was a woman, Adelaide Steele Baylor. She was a granddaughter of Wabash pioneer and civic leader William Steele Sr. and daughter of a local carpenter and tanner, James Craig Baylor. Adelaide attended Wabash's elementary school and its high school, graduating in 1878, the same year she started teaching at age seventeen. She spent many summers continuing her own education, receiving degrees from the University of Chicago in 1897 and from Columbia in 1918. For eight years she taught elementary school, then served as assistant principal of the high school for five years. She became principal in 1889 and superintendent of schools in 1903.[6]

Baylor was one of those persons about whom nothing but praise has been put into print, as if she were some kind of secular saint. There is no doubt that she was deeply and broadly admired for her professionalism, intellect, strength of character, sense of fairness, and outgoing personality. She was known to have quelled a teenage student uprising with a few deft words, and she could scold individual students, and possibly teachers, in ways that made them respect her rather than resent the scolding. She supported teachers with frequent praise and professional guidance and was an organizer of a parent-teacher association. She was flexible, willing to change her opinions and policies when sound reasons so dictated. Baylor was current on studies of educational philosophy and well versed across a broad spectrum of disciplines. She was a quick thinker, an excellent public speaker, and the author of two books. Apparently she had a host of friends, many of them members of Round Table, of which she was a charter member. Possibly because her father had been an alcoholic, Baylor was active in local temperance work. She attended the Presbyterian Church and was an officer in the county historical society.

In the twentieth century Baylor's career took her far beyond the Wabash schools. Beginning in 1911 she served as assistant superintendent of the Indiana Department of Education, as a member of the home economics division of a national board of vocational education, as supervisor of vocational studies in twenty-five states, and, finally, as chief of that service for the nation. She turned down an opportunity to become superintendent of education for the state. Baylor died in Washington, D.C., in 1935. The library in the 1926 high school building was named for her, and in 1959 her portrait was hung in that library.

As the nineteenth century moved toward its culmination, the high school's new four-year academic schedule was built around a long list of required courses and a less varied sampling of electives. Typically required were rhetoric (speaking and writing), English, algebra, physical geography, economic/cultural geography, history, physics, geometry, English literature, civics, chemistry, and "higher arithmetic." The electives were: Latin (grammar, Caesar, Virgil), German, bookkeeping, American literature, biology, and astronomy. By the late 1890s approximately 190 students were enrolled in the new high school, including those from South Side. Attendance exceeded 95 percent of enrollment, and the number of annual graduates ranged in the neighborhood of thirty-five. Football was the most popular sport with students.[7]

After spotting the schools that dotted the northern range of Wabash, observers on top of the courthouse might next have taken note of two developments on the northwestern fringe of town. One was the county's new fairgrounds. The desire to expand City Park on West Hill Street had led to the city's acquisition of the fairgrounds that lay between the orphanage and the site of Josiah Daugherty's former slaughterhouse on Charley Creek. The tract included the one-third mile oval racetrack, its grandstand, and the undeveloped area sloping westward to the creek. The fair board, in turn, acquired land on the bluff northwest of the creek. It was an area of approximately eight square blocks. The 1888 city map and Robert Woods's 1891 map show the new fairgrounds developed around an oval track that is a half mile long. Within it are a baseball diamond and a judges' stand, and on the exterior south side of the track near its eastern turn is a grandstand. Responding to the rapid development of Wabash in the direction of the new fairgrounds, city officials completed the western extent of Ferry Street by bridging it across Charley Creek. It was an improvement that not only facilitated traffic in that direction but also helped end once and for all the use of that stretch of the creek by "honey-dippers" (privy cleaners), who used the site to dump the contents of the vaults they cleaned. Ferry Street now ran west to the new fairgrounds and to the industry that eventually replaced it. In the twentieth century the fairgrounds land became the locus of a series of major industrial enterprises, including the Wabash Bridge Company, the Service Motor Corporation, General Tire, and their successors.[8]

A second development in that direction was expansion of Falls Cemetery, founded in 1863, after the Hanna Cemetery (Old Cemetery) had proven to be inadequate. In 1977 Leewell Carpenter wrote a brief history of Falls Cemetery for the *Plain Dealer*, a history he based in part on the tales his father told him. The cemetery had been platted originally just east of pasture land called "Fiddler's Green," an early commons where townsfolk could picnic or tether family cows for the day. The original plat of the cemetery was twenty acres. Six of them were between the creek and Stitt Street, where a sexton's house was built. In the early decades citizens had used the cemetery almost as a public park. It was a pleasant place for a stroll and on the Fourth of July or Memorial Day residents could gather around a bandstand for special observances. Roads substantial enough to accommodate horse-drawn hearses eventually replaced walking trails, and in the 1890s, when burials were pushing the limits of available space, the cemetery association purchased twenty-seven additional acres between Falls Avenue and Colerain Street.

Along the eastern edge of this addition (which today is in the north-central section of Falls) there is a north-south line of ancient gravestones, testimony to the town's ultimate solution for conditions in Hanna Cemetery. Beneath those stones the town fathers reinterred a substantial percentage of the bodies that could be located and/or identified in the earlier burial ground. Others, such as the Hannas, were buried elsewhere in the cemetery. About 10 percent were carried to other cemeteries. Reinterment began with the Hanna family graves in 1902 (as earlier reported) and continued through 1907. It was not a tidy undertaking, due to the conditions of the remains. As many as 450 bodies may have been relocated, but the identification processes were so haphazard that random bones from multiple skeletons may have been reburied together. It is believed that thirty-five gravestones were moved; depending on how parts of some broken stones are counted, that is very close to the number present in 2010.

Hanna Cemetery was not the only burial ground to be merged with Falls. For many years there was a small Odd Fellows Cemetery adjacent to the original Falls plat on its eastern flank. In the twentieth century this cemetery, by then overgrown and untended, was added to Falls. In the same century the association purchased yet more land, which lay north of the original plat and between the line of Hanna Cemetery gravestones and Cass Street. African American citizens seemed not to have had a specific or exclusive section of Falls for their burials, although many are listed as having been interred just north of the Hanna Cemetery stones. Blacks were buried also in the Original Plat.[9]

Persons scanning the northern parts of town from Citizen's courthouse observatory in the 1880s and 1890s would easily have spotted a large number of fairly new houses, many of them quite impressive structures. Increasingly homes had been built with central heat, lighted by electricity, and equipped with indoor plumbing for sewage, bathing, and laundry. Beginning in the early 1880s streets and alleys were dotted with the poles and draped with the wires of the telephone industry, connecting residents electronically for the first time and binding the town in a new way to its larger world, just as the telegraph had once done in a more elementary fashion in the 1840s.

Residential rates for phone service were about thirty-six dollars a year, and business phone service cost twelve dollars more. Some folks complained that telephones were only a nuisance. A courthouse official reported that requests made by phone were becoming so numerous he could not get his regular work done. It is possible that by 1900 some Wabash homes of the wealthy were also equipped with phonographs, another electronic breakthrough of the age that had been introduced locally in 1890; on Saturday, May 2, Everett Carpenter gave a demonstration of the phonograph, grinding out music free of charge from morning until night at the Beitman and Wolf building downtown.

Whatever innovations the residential bluff-top of Wabash exhibited, and however stylish or expensive houses there might have been, it should not be forgotten that all citizens in that area—rich, poor, or in-between—were regularly subjected to the interruptive clamor of trains passing through town. In 1890, for example, at least five trains a day belched smoke and blared horns or rang bells on their way east at 8:00 a.m., 9:00 a.m., noon, 4:00 p.m., and 11:00 p.m.; and five more did the same going west at alternative hours. With similar clockwork regularity, both the passenger depot and the freight station on Hill and Sinclair streets, respectively, became hives of activity as people and goods arrived and departed.[10]

One way to review the work of representative civic and business leaders of the late nineteenth century is to take note of the houses they built, which, in many cases, were the most permanent and obvious relics they left behind. Something of the domestic arrangements of Warren Bigler, James D. Conner, Josiah Daugherty, James Ford, Charles Little, Warren Sayre, and a few others have already been mentioned. Their homes were typical of houses folks built if they could afford them, as many apparently could. Dozens of the nineteenth-century Wabash homes that continue to provide shelter in the twenty-first century have been architectural gems from their genesis: they are large, are of high quality construction, and once expressed the latest in architectural fashion and domestic conveniences. Not all of Wabash's movers and shakers built lavishly, and many of the homes of those who did have disappeared. Yet, an examination of a sampling of the showy homes of the nineteenth century calls to mind the accomplishments of many citizens who were important to the town's development.

The so-called Queen Anne style dominated domestic architecture in Wabash. The Queen Anne designation, however, offers such variety in subtypes and ornamentation that any number of dwellings belong to it without necessarily looking alike. Although the style lent itself to the homes of the prosperous, quite modest houses also belong to the category. Some common identifying features of Queen Anne are a steeply pitched, irregularly shaped roof, a dominant front gable, patterned shingles, asymmetrical façade, and decorative porches of moderate to large size. Variously designed bay windows were also popular. Several Queen Anne homes, such as the Warren Bigler house, are identifiable by corner turrets or by fancy towers pushing above the gutter line.

Italianate was also a popular style. It is often identified by low-pitched roofs and heavy window eyebrows. Other Victorian fashions of nineteenth-century Wabash included Second Empire, featuring mansard roofs, and Stick, which used steep roofs and intricately patterned board siding. As with Queen Anne, Stick was at times so simply executed that quite modest homes can technically fit the category. Wabash may have only one home that is of premier, classic Stick quality: the 1883 Frank Blount (Lawrence Bird) home at 44 West Sinclair Street, the address with the three-seat privy (as previously reported). Other domestic architectural types that appeared with some frequency in Wabash were Folk Victorian, a simple, uncluttered design often decorated with spindle work, and Eclectic, a catchall term for design that draws upon a number of past styles.[11]

No nineteenth-century house in Wabash was more grand or more deserving of the term "mansion" than the one Alonzo Melville Atkinson built at 540 North Wabash Street. Pronouncing it to be "palatial," the *Plain Dealer* kept close tabs on the progress of its construction from June 1883 to September 1884. Fred Grant was the architect and contractor. Grant may have been self-taught, getting his ideas from architectural pattern books of the time, but if so he nonetheless produced three masterworks in Wabash: City Hall, the Presbyterian Church, and the Atkinson place. The last named was a sprawling, three-story, bay-windowed brick edifice of eclectic and modified Queen Anne styles, decorated with carved stone lintels and other stonework. Along with Hannah New's spectacular wedding in 1880, Atkinson's "palace" marked a new high in local sophistication and elegance. It cost twenty-five thousand dollars.

Atkinson could easily afford it. Being deeply religious, he reportedly eschewed the importance of money for himself, but he nonetheless knew how to make it and how to spend it. Forced by ill health to give up the ministry, he had propelled himself into the insurance industry, becoming an executive with Aetna of Chicago in the early 1870s. He branched out into the loan business, eventually overseeing loans totaling ten million dollars. His background with the Campbellites and his role as a pillar of the Wabash Christian Church guided the use of some of his money, giving more than $100,000 to his church and to church-related causes. He was a benefactor, also, of Butler University and had served as president of its board of trustees.

Atkinson's crucial contribution to Wabash's economic base was to raise the Underwood Spool Silk Cabinet Company from near bankruptcy to viability. Apparently he was also heavily invested in house construction in Wabash, having backed the erection of a number of important residences. One was the Beitman/Wolf house on West Hill that was destroyed in the late twentieth century to accommodate expansion of the Carnegie Library. Atkinson was living in this house at the time he built his new home. His obituary mentions his building a Beitman house also on East Hill that, if accurate, could have been the future Honeywell House. Another possible house to his credit is the brick Second Empire that still exists at 189 North Wabash Street. A third possibility is John Latchem's (Heather Allen's) two-story frame at 479 North Huntington Street, near Manchester Avenue.

Atkinson and his second wife lived in the Wabash Street mansion for seventeen years, raising to maturity a son and a daughter. In October 1899, the sixty-six-year-old Atkinson and his wife traveled to Cincinnati so that he could address the faithful at a Christian Church denominational convention. He exhorted his fellow congregants to greater financial sacrifice and spiritual commitment. Just after placing his hand over a fluttering heart he dramatically uttered a command from Saint Paul, "Quit yourselves like men!," collapsed and died.[12] About two decades later the mansion on North Wabash Street passed into the hands of Wilbur Ford, James Ford's grandson. Wilbur reduced the house to two stories and removed large wings on the southwest and northwest sides. In the twenty-first century it remains a Ford family residence, being the centerpiece of Charley Creek Foundation, which Richard Edwin Ford (Wilbur and Florence Ford's fourth child) created to encourage community development.[13]

This Wabash Street corridor is rich with substantial nineteenth-century homes. One of the oldest surviving homes is at 414 North Wabash, approximately two blocks south of the former Atkinson mansion. The Kunse/Pawling/Walter house was built in 1846, and the classic Federalist abode continues to be a desirable property in the twenty-first century. Wabash's early kiln master, David Kunse, built it near the northern edge of town when wolves may still have been an occasional threat in the area. The Kunse name has since passed out of common memory, but the name of the next owner, Albert Pawling, remains enshrined in the block-long Pawling Street just north of the house. Pawling's granddaughter, Jean Graden, married Fred Walter, so that in time Sheriff Bossler Walter's descendants acquired the house and have continued to live there into the twenty-first century.[14]

Walter's father, a Pennsylvania weaver, married Lucy Bossler Hackenberg, thus the man's unusual first name. His bulky Prussian appearance may also have been from his mother's bloodlines. Yet his bulkiness did not keep him from being described in the early 1880s as "the genial and handsome sheriff" and a "whole-souled jovial gentleman."[15] The fact that twenty-first-century descendants remember that he once amused the citizenry by riding his horse mounted backward in the saddle indicates that Walter may have had an unpredictable, zany personality. Bossler was born in 1849. At age twenty-two he moved to North Manchester where he was engaged in a hub and spoke factory. He married a North Manchester woman, Esther Williams, who kept the family name polished with good works. She was of Quaker descent and had relatives who were active in the Underground Railroad movement. She was a driving force behind the local orphanage and other enlightened projects.

Walter was elected sheriff in 1882, moved to the county seat, took up residence in the new sheriff's domicile, and became a leader in Republican circles. In 1884 he bought a table slide company headquartered in Huntington, which manufactured the pieces that allow the addition of leaves to a tabletop, and moved it to Wabash. In 1891 B. Walter and Company built a 100-foot by 150-foot factory with a 30- by 40-foot wing. The building continues to be the physical core of the company's twenty-first-century presence in Wabash; there has also been an outlet in the South. The Walters had two daughters, Myrtle and Josephine, the former a musician, the latter a teacher. A son, Fred, served in the Spanish-American War and attended Purdue University. He succeeded Bossler as the head of the company.[16]

Almost directly east across Wabash Street from the Walter home, at the northern corner of Wabash and Walnut, stands a well-preserved Queen Anne house, circa 1890s, displaying many of the external bells and whistles of that style, including a handsome corner turret. In the nineteenth century it was the home of William P. Jones, scion of South Wabash pioneers. He was born in “Slabtown,” named for a lumber works on the pike to Somerset. He was three when his family moved to “Monkeytown,” at the west end of South Wabash. He later indicated that living in Slabtown and Monkeytown prepared him for life in Wabash, where he eventually settled and established himself in the family’s tradition of lumber and furniture interests and founded a long-lived family funeral business, later known as the Jones Funeral Home and now extinct.

Both in South Wabash and in Wabash Jones displayed that nimble entrepreneurial acumen that kept nineteenth-century businessmen on the top of their game.[17] Jones’s father, Mark, established the family’s lumber concerns. W. P. followed along similar lines, shifting in and out of partnerships as opportunity surfaced or changed. He began as a hired cabinetmaker, moved to investments in furniture manufacturing (cupboard, bedsteads, chairs, tables, etc.) and created a coffin trade that opened opportunities in the funeral business. Locals admired his fine collection of three hearses. Jones was a Republican who served on the Wabash Common Council in the late 1890s. He was also an active Odd Fellow and a decorated Mason. Posing as an old-style Quaker, he once sent an anonymous note to his wife, Louisa, who had just adopted bangs as part of a new hairstyle. The note read, “Thee looks like a cow.” It was some months before he was brave enough to confess that the author was not a Quaker.

Jones’s father had been prominent in the area by 1847, and Jones’s grandchildren continue to be prominent citizens in the twenty-first century, so that he represents a persisting tradition of community involvement as well as personal attainment. He was perhaps the progenitor—and certainly a purveyor—of his family’s interest in storytelling and story collecting. An example comes from his life as a preteen in South Wabash. An old man with a peg leg lived there near a lush watermelon patch. Jones boasted to his young friends that he could raid the patch and evade the law. He entered the patch hopping on one foot and balancing himself with a broomstick. Sure enough, when the melons were found to be missing, the peg-legged man was accused. Thus emboldened by success, Jones raided the patch a second time, using the same technique. Unfortunately this time he used the broomstick on the left side instead of the right and was justly nabbed for his youthful experiment in crime and duplicity.

Farther south from Jones’s Queen Anne, on the west side at 340 North Wabash Street, stands William Sharpe’s excellently preserved and bulkily impressive brick Queen Anne. Sharpe was editor of the *Wabash Times* and a leading Democrat in town. The Sharpe house, currently owned by the Kent Henderson family, has been so carefully maintained externally that the fact an open south porch was modernized in the twentieth century does not distract much from the general appearance. The property also includes an ornate and massive stable behind the house.[18]

In the nineteenth century, however, as in the twenty-first century, the Sharpe house has been overshadowed by its larger neighbor, the Eagle home in the 200 block of Wabash Street. Interestingly, the same 1899 issue of the *Plain Dealer* that reported Atkinson's sudden death also carried an obituary for Francis M. Eagle, another prominent civic leader whose name has passed from twenty-first-century consciousness. At eighty-three years, Eagle was much older than Atkinson but his demise of a heart ailment over just two days was another shock. He had come to the county as a poor young man in 1843 and taken up wool carding at a mill in North Manchester. He married the boss's daughter, Susanna Harter. Eagle was largely self-taught but he excelled in the sciences, mathematics, and as a linguist, mastering both German and French. He studied law and pursued a lively probate career in North Manchester. Later he became the principal owner of a bank in that town. In 1868 he brought his law practice to Wabash where he continued to prosper, largely by investing in farms, bank stocks, and mortgages. On the basis of Eagle's 1899 tax assessment, the *Plain Dealer* surmised that he was the richest man in the county at the time of his death. As with so many obituaries of the period, Eagle's made certain that readers had ample proof of the man's inherent saintliness, in this case his generosity toward widows, renters, and mortgage holders.

Eagle's contribution to Wabash's collection of fine Victorian homes still stands stately in the 200 block of North Wabash Street, overlooking the western entrance to Elm Street and backing onto the former Union School and Miami School lots. The property, much of it long since chopped up and sold off, was originally quite large and was surrounded by a decorative iron fence. It bordered on Union Street and encompassed several outbuildings, including a stone barn that still stands as an apartment building. The house is a massive brick Italianate affair built in 1878. Large bays face east and south. Inside were nine gas fireplaces, brass hearth covers, parquet floors, leaded glass in several windows, full basement, wine cellar, full attic, and fourteen rooms. After Eagle's death, his daughter and son-in-law, Mr. and Mrs. John

Curtner, lived there until about 1923. The Curtners added a wraparound porch and a porte cochere. A persistent rumor that John Curtner sequestered a cache of silver and jewels in the house has never been confirmed. The Curtners were childless, and after their deaths the house became, ad seriatim, a boardinghouse, a doctor's office and residence, apartments, and a one-family dwelling again.[19]

The house just over a block south of the Eagle house, on the northwest corner of Wabash and Sinclair streets, is the former home of one of the town's chief entrepreneurs, the great East Canal Street marketer, Joseph W. Busick. His Busick Block survives to the twenty-first century, although it no longer contains a bustling trade in dry goods and innumerable other products. The Busick name's prominence among Wabash merchants dates from canal days. The fin de siecle Busick fortune has been estimated at between two hundred thousand and three hundred thousand dollars. Extensive advertising in the local papers indicates that, over the years, there were few clothing, dry goods, or domestic items that some Busick did not offer for sale, the business being somewhat like a primitive version of Wal-Mart. The two-story Busick Block that bears the date 1883 was a double-wide outlet extending from sidewalk to alley and was the second version of a structure at that location. Busick was president of the Wabash National Bank. He and his wife, Kate, built their Wabash Street mansion in 1890. It is an example of eclectic design, though its most distinguishing feature, an oddly roofed turretlike projection on the east façade, has been identified as a Queen Anne device. Attic windows just under the roofline are Italianate. On Joseph's death Kate replaced him on the National Bank board, but the Busick name did not persist in Wabash long past her death, and their home became an apartment house and business space. The home's terraced lawn remains intact, though it is plainly landscaped.[20]

Before leaving consideration of Wabash Street homes, notice should be taken of two others in the area. Doctor James H. Ford, son of the pioneer doctor, James Ford, built a comely frame home at 287 North Wabash. Ford was a highly respected physician locally and worked also as surgeon in chief for the two railroad lines that passed through town. He lectured in other cities on various aspects of medicine, establishing a statewide reputation. It has already been noted that as a member of the School Board of Trustees he pushed for the construction of the 1894 high school. His work with the railroads eventually necessitated his moving to Indianapolis, where he died in 1915. In an 1891 near tragedy he demonstrated that he might have been as absentminded as his father was occasionally thought to be. On his way home one day he inadvertently left his medical case at a drugstore. Realizing his mistake after crossing the railroad tracks on Wabash Street, he quickly retraced his steps, then tripped near the rails and fell—with a leg extended on the track against a slowly moving train that had just deposited passengers at the depot. Hearing his yell, people ran from the depot to help. Ford directed them in their application of first aid, but his foot was mangled and subsequently had to be removed. His home on Wabash Street has been described as "cottage style" and was painted mauve. It is an important addition to the town's domestic architecture not only for its style, but also because it illustrates that the town's prominent citizens did not uniformly aspire to own elaborate and spacious houses.[21]

In the same area of town, just one block from Wabash Street, at 479 North Huntington Street, is a house that John Latchem built, possibly in partnership with A. M. Atkinson. It is a Queen Anne structure with an especially perpendicular appeal: elongated bays, long narrow windows, and steeply pitched roof. At one time it had a wraparound porch that modified the perpendicular appearance of the place. The interior is unusual for the period in that the modestly sized entrance hall contains a welcoming hearth but not the staircase, which is, instead, a utilitarian affair located near the kitchen. Latchem was founder and operator of the Wabash Limestone and Gravel Company, headquartered on Sinclair and Huntington streets with temporary outlets also on East Canal Street. He was a director of the town's first building and loan association, an investor in the Underwood Manufacturing Company, a silent partner in the Ply and Nye marble works, an officer in First National Bank, and president of the Wabash Bridge and Iron Company that built the 1895 bridge over the river. Latchem was married to Amelia Alber, daughter of Phillip Alber, who owned the brewery on North Cass Street. He was a member of the county Democratic committee, attended the Presbyterian church, and was very active in the Masons. The Latchem family name persisted in Wabash into the latter half of the twentieth century.[22]

Another street abloom with domestic masterpieces that illustrated their owners' civic prominence is Sinclair (a.k.a. St. Clair). Here the Cowgill family dominated, two generations eventually building three enormous houses within a block of each other. On the north side of Sinclair, at number 56, halfway between Wabash and Miami streets, Calvin Cowgill, quite likely Wabash's most distinguished and venerated citizen of the nineteenth century, built an Italianate masterwork in the early 1880s. It replaced his earlier house that had stood to the west. The newer building is a brick structure rising on stone foundations. It has three large bays projecting east, south, and west, with a large entrance on the south façade. The roof is unusually complex, and beneath its gutter line was a series of oval cornice windows that were covered over in the twentieth century. Gone also are high, multistaged chimneys. Bowing to 1890s styles, Cowgill added a porch that wrapped around the southeast corner, but this was removed three decades later in order to restore the appearance of the original entrance. The hoods, or eyebrows, over the windows are ornate and heavy looking, though they are fashioned of sheet metal and have withstood the test of time. After Calvin's death in 1903 the house continued to shelter two families of Cowgill relatives and remained in family hands through the 1930s.

Cowgill died in possession of a multitude of honors that he had piled up unstintingly since his arrival in the area in the late 1840s. A fellow lawyer, James Brownlee, whose reminiscences of antebellum Wabash are so valuable, said that Cowgill, Hugh Hanna, John U. Pettit, and Stearns Fisher "were never still where the interests of Wabash were [concerned]." He believed that Cowgill, in particular, was "the best manager and leader in public improvement who ever lived on the Wabash." Although Cowgill practiced law, entered politics, and helped run Camp Wabash during the Civil War, his larger gift to the city was his intense effort to get railroads built through Wabash, first in connection with the east-west Wabash line in 1854 and even more so with the north-south line (later the Big Four) in 1872. Cowgill secured the loans, raised the subscriptions, and pestered corporate and civic officials to complete the projects. He became president of the north-south line. His ascent through political offices was also impressive. He was county treasurer, a state legislator, a U.S. congressman, and a county judge. Eulogies sang his strengths and ignored all weaknesses, as expected. If he were headstrong and opinionated, such possible flaws were translated into virtues: "He was a man who always led; he was never content to be a follower. . . . His opinions were invariably outspoken, and no one remained in doubt as to his attitude on any subject." He was laid to rest "with impressive services, in the presence of a great concourse" of friends and neighbors who were grateful for one "whose whole life had been devoted to the upbuilding of the community."[23]

The elements of Cowgill's funeral were typical of those used at the passing of very prominent citizens. At the Sinclair Street house the crowd of mourners came to pay respects and view the corpse before the service and then overflowed onto street, sidewalk, and lawn. A quartet of women sang as folks milled about. At two o'clock sharp the women sang "Rock of Ages," calling the gathering to worship. Various ministers of the town prayed or eulogized. The quartet sang "Nearer, My God to Thee." Then Cowgill's pastor, Charles Little, delivered the sermon of the day, based on a passage from Ecclesiastes, and pronounced the benediction. Eight official pallbearers plus eight honorary pallbearers accompanied the casket to Falls Cemetery for burial. The names of the sixteen pallbearers included at least eleven of men who belonged to Wabash's professional, business, and civic leadership. Cowgill's passing ended what was probably the single most impressive public career in Wabash in the nineteenth century, and he represented a generation of movers and shakers who were now quickly dying off. Many of them had risen to prominence during the Civil War.[24]

Two other Cowgill homes were located on Sinclair Street in the late nineteenth century but only one survives. Calvin's son, Cary Cowgill, who had followed his father into law and was also a revered community bigwig in his time, built a showplace less than a block east of his parents' home, just across Wabash Street from the Busick house. It was unapologetically a mansion, built in the Queen Anne mode: massive, complicated, ornate, seriously "porched," and displaying a splendid gravitas. It became the scene of elaborate social occasions and was reportedly stuffed with art and artifacts that the younger Cowgills collected on extensive travels. This house fell to the wrecker's ball halfway through the twentieth century and was replaced with a gas station. Meanwhile, Carey's sister, Catherine Cowgill, married a future circuit judge, Harvey B. Shively. The Shivelys built another impressive Queen Anne home on the northeast corner of Sinclair and Miami streets, less than half a block west of her parents' place.[25]

Three other Sinclair Street houses are worthy of mention, one solely for its architectural interest and two because of the community standing of their original owners as well as for their architecture. Noted for its architecture alone is a house at 58 East Sinclair Street, east of where Carey Cowgill had built his mansion. It is a two-story brick house (possibly Adam or eclectic) of uncluttered design, originally with a large, handsome, square cupola on top and a balcony over an attractive front porch. It dates from late in the nineteenth century when it belonged to Joseph and Mary Gries. They were natives of Baden-Baden, Germany, had lived in Wabash since 1861, and were members of Saint Bernard Roman Catholic Church. Although little else of substance is known about the Grieses, the *Plain Dealer* wrote that their dog was decapitated after putting its head on the railroad track and labeled it a clear case of suicide. The house suggests that the Grieses were moderately prosperous folks of elegant taste. Members of the Gries family continued to reside there through much of the twentieth century; the Grieses' son-in-law, Charles D. Bolte, was chief of police for several terms and, afterwards, a bartender. The Wabash County Historical Museum owns a photo of the Gries place taken about 1897: its lot nicely landscaped, surrounded by a wooden fence, and with many members of the Gries household present to have their photograph taken at the home place.[26]

Directly south across the street stands the Ken Crace home at 45 East Sinclair (a property that had belonged to the Gries family for a time). Phillip Alber, the founder of the hugely productive brewery on the northwest side of town, bought the lot in 1848 for ninety dollars, building the house soon afterwards. The house was the site of the wedding of Amelia Alber, Phillip's daughter, to John Latchem, whose Treaty Creek Stone and Lime Company was just to the east of the Alber property (Wilkinson Lumber Company, 2010). The house is unique in Wabash. It is built of brick in a simple version of the Federalist style. Although it is only one story, that story is perched on high foundation walls, as if it belonged on a busy cobblestone street in an Eastern colonial city. The area within the foundation walls may have provided a cool place to store beer, for at one time Alber used the property as a tavern. A beer garden in the back accommodated train passengers who were waiting to embark, or who had just disembarked, across the railroad tracks at the depot. The house's most unique exterior feature is a narrow, double staircase (currently without railings): steps climb the foundation wall from two directions and meet at the central front door.[27]

At the far western end of Sinclair Street, where it ends at Fisher Street, is the former home of John A. Bruner. Bruner came to the area with his family as a child in 1851. His father Levi Bruner was soon a partner in Hanna's spoke and bending factory. As an adult John assumed his father's position in that trade and used the property as the Wabash Baking Company. John's interests broadened with age: he was an early director of the Wabash National Bank, was involved in the creation of the Wabash Screen Door Company, owned a piece of the Wabash Cabinet Company, and served a stint on the city's common council. Bruner was very active in the Methodist church as were others of that family name. He also ranks as a major Wabash "persister" in the sense that throughout the twentieth century and into the twenty-first century his descendants continue to be prominent in Wabash affairs. He had married twice; his first wife was Lucinda Kemp. Their second daughter, Florence, married into the William P. Jones family, founders of South Wabash and prominent in furniture and funeral businesses. The offspring of Bruner's grandson, Edward Kemp Jones, were teachers and journalists who assumed community leadership roles in cultural, historical, musical, and religious causes. Bruner's Italianate home at Sinclair and Fisher streets is a moderately sized, pleasantly proportioned two-story brick with many of its original features intact. However, it is missing both a small balcony over the front door and a side porch. The front porch is modern. The house probably dates from the 1880s.[28]

Nearby, at 86 North Comstock Street, a block west of the Bruner property, stands the outstanding Queen Anne brick house that Charles Haas built, probably the best example of this style in Wabash today. The corner turret is especially grand externally and unusually cozy internally. The house is considered to be a "sister house" of the Bigler home because the interiors are so similar. In contrast, the Bigler house is frame, not brick. Deserving special mention are the staircases in these two homes, which feature heavy wood casings and magnificent walls of art glass at their turnings.

Charles Haas was born in 1859 in the home of his parents, Adam and Eliza Haas, at a corner of Market and Miami streets. At that time Adam, at age sixty, had already been in Wabash twenty-three years. He was one of the many early dry goods merchants in town. Before and during the Civil War he supported the Underground Railroad, though in exactly what capacity is not clear. Failing health forced his retirement from trade when Charles was five years old. Charles was schooled exclusively in Wabash. When he was twenty-two he became a reporter for the *Wabash Courier*, employment that determined his career. Two years later the *Fort Wayne Sentinel* hired him to be its city editor; but he soon returned home to take a similar position with the *Courier*. In 1887 Haas was involved in the merger of the *Courier* with the *Plain Dealer*, extinguishing the former paper's name. He soon became editor of the *Plain Dealer* and after the turn of the century added the position of president of the company to his job description. He was no doubt instrumental in the decision to build a new *Plain Dealer* building in 1895 on the northeast corner of Market and Miami streets, a building that subsequently has been home to many succeeding businesses. Banking was also Haas's field. He was invested in the Wabash National Bank and served on the board of directors of the Farmers and Merchants Bank, eventually becoming its president. Haas's one foray in political office was as a city councilman in the late 1880s. He and his wife, the former Lilla Pyke of Fort Wayne, built their Comstock Street home in the 1890s.[29]

Three blocks northeast of the Haas home—at the triangular corner of Falls Avenue and Fisher Street—is the survivor of two King family mansions that decorated Wabash in the latter years of the nineteenth century. The King brothers, George Norman and his younger sibling Thomas Wellman, built large and lavishly. They were sons of Peter and Elizabeth King who migrated to the Wabash area from Pennsylvania in 1841. The family being of somewhat modest means, the sons began their careers as dry goods clerks and in other entry-level positions, but they soon began investing with their father in larger affairs. Their mounting resources were to come from the King grain mill on East Canal Street, from partnerships in local hardware trade, and, subsequently, from banking. The King name continued to have high recognition in the twentieth century in connection with the King-Hipskind Hardware Company on West Canal Street.

Wellman—the younger brother—built a red-brick Italianate mansion with mansard roof on the northeast corner of Main and Miami streets in 1883. It was splendidly positioned on the side of the bluff to overlook the downtown, with its terraced grounds shored up by a substantial set of parallel brick retaining walls, defining a flourishing flower garden, thick with irises in the spring. This King house survived most of the twentieth century as an apartment building in increasingly derelict condition. Eventually the county destroyed it to make room for courthouse parking, replacing its flower garden terrace with a heap of raw rip-rap stone.

George's home, at Fisher Street and Falls Avenue, survived into the twenty-first century as a funeral home. Most of the succeeding mortician/owners have been responsible custodians of the place. Save for the south side of the building—where the addition of a modern mortuary chapel has destroyed its appearance—many external and internal details have been retained and maintained. The elaborate roof has kept its original, peculiar angularity despite the loss of decorative features. The Italianate house is built with pale yellow external brick walls, set off by ornate wood trim, dramatic windows, and attic dormers. Its main west porch is especially massive and attractive. The surrounding iron fence repeats the same basic design and vertical dimensions as the 1879 courthouse fence. Although slightly more elaborate than the courthouse (and Rodef Shalom) fencing, it was probably manufactured by the same firm.[30]

A couple of loosely documented stories about George's house continue to be repeated in the twenty-first century. One is that George built his home in a lavish style in order to elevate the status of his wife in Wabash society. As a young man George reportedly fell in love with a poor local Irish lass, but his stern father disapproved of the relationship and forbade a marriage. No doubt there was frequently a social disconnect in Wabash and elsewhere between upwardly mobile people and those of less fortunate economic condition. George nonetheless pursued a liaison with the woman, established her in a home in the West Market Street area, and fathered two children with her. When he was independent enough to defy his father, George married his mistress and built the mansion on Falls Avenue, largely in her honor. A variation of this tale has George housing his Irish mistress in a house he built for her next door to his mansion. In one version the woman's name was Moriah Maloney.

Whether these tales are mostly old, flimsy gossip or the detritus of truth, the facts are that George N. King married Maria M. Maloney (Malony) in February 1882. She was born near Dublin in 1847 and arrived in town in 1855 as an eight-year-old. In the 1870 census of the city of Wabash she is listed as "Marrah," twenty-three, a head of household by status and a housekeeper by occupation, with no street address listed. Her five-year-old daughter, Nellie, who later married into the local Snavely family, lived with her. Nellie was born in 1865. A son, George L. King, was born in 1882, the year his parents married. George L.'s 1930 obituary listed Nellie as his sister. In 1870 George N., the father, had been thirty-six years old and—legally at least—still living with his parents. These facts seem to support the idea that the tale was substantially true in the sense that George maintained an address with his parents for a long time as a bachelor, and that Maria apparently had one child—Nellie—out of wedlock. The facts also suggest that the expectation of George L.'s birth in 1882 prompted a marriage that year and also Maria's moving into the King mansion on Falls Avenue, whether the aging Peter, who lived until 1891, approved or not.

The second story is that George and Maria King were good friends of famed authoress Gene Stratton-Porter who sometimes stayed at the King home during visits to Wabash. On one of those visits, while gazing out a bedroom window, Stratton-Porter spotted the local eccentric, Nancy Everly, who was standing on a nearby Falls Avenue corner waving a white flag (as earlier noted), which for her was a sign of salvation for all who walked beneath it. The sighting inspired Stratton-Porter to write her novel, *The White Flag*, in which the character Crazy Becky is based on Everly.[31]

The parallel streets of Hill and Main run more than a mile east and west, a block apart, forming the principal nineteenth-century residential corridor. It was along the future site of these two streets—it will be recalled—that the Frenchman, Augustin Mottin de LaBalme, had marched eastward toward his death at the hands of Little Turtle near Fort Wayne in 1780. Hill Street follows a crest of the bluff for almost its entire length. Main Street, a block south, follows the same level east of Huntington Street and west of Fisher Street but between those two streets—because of topographical variance just there—Main dips to a lower level, halfway down the bluff. Prominent community leaders built major homes along these two residential avenues. Already noted are Warren Bigler's Queen Anne house at Hill and Fisher streets, Josiah and Minerva Daugherty's large brick Federal home near City Park, James Ford's Italianate, and Charles Little's manse near Miami Street.

One door east of the Daugherty house is lumberman William Yarnelle's elegant Colonial Revival, built in 1900. Yarnelle was a Republican, a Presbyterian, and respected as a man of cultured tastes, amiable habits, and superior business instincts. He was born in Ohio. As an adult he worked in Fort Wayne and Nebraska before settling in Wabash. Although he had experience in the dry goods business, in Wabash he became a business manager for the Duck and Pressler lumber company. He married Mildred Duck in 1882, a fact that may have facilitated his rise to a partnership in the firm that eventually bore his name alone, the Yarnelle Lumber Company. Apparently he was an aggressive, progressive merchant, adding coal, paint, sewer pipes, cement, and other construction items to his inventory. Buildings, sheds, and storage yards eventually extended for a thousand feet on ten lots that backed onto the old canal line. By century's end the company was doing a hundred thousand dollars worth of business annually. Not content with a single enterprise, Yarnelle invested in twelve oil and gas wells located at Richvalley, and he was a stockholder in a local telephone company. His house at 614 West Hill remained in the Yarnelle family for most of the twentieth century.[32]

Clarkson Weesner and his wife, Anna, resided in two exemplary, and very different, Queen Anne homes located on Hill and Main streets. From early days Weesner was a rising star in Wabash community affairs. He came to the town as a child in 1844 and was educated locally. As he matured he broadened his academic interests by reading philosophy and studying Darwinian science. Although Anna Weesner was active in both the Methodist Church and the Woman's Christian Temperance Union, her husband was enough of a free thinker to be labeled a "religious liberal." It is possible that he breathed some of the same intellectual air as his fellow citizen and neighbor, Warren Bigler, whose religious views, it will be remembered, were unorthodox and whose interest in the liberal arts and in science were probably ahead of common local standards. Unlike Bigler, however, Weesner had a strong yen for politics. He was deputy county treasurer in the 1860s and clerk of the Wabash Circuit Court in the 1880s. Between service in those two positions he was elected mayor of Wabash in 1876. Although Weesner began his adult career as a teacher, he was admitted to the bar in 1870 and conducted a successful career as an insurance lawyer. Perhaps his major contribution to the community was the two-volume *History of Wabash County*, completed in 1914.

In 1885 the Weesners built a bulky frame Queen Anne home at 313 West Hill Street. The property has survived to the twenty-first century in excellent shape, including a whimsically designed stable at the rear of the house. Although composed of a medley of gables, porches, and balconies, the house has been a local architectural curiosity principally because of a large round window that dramatizes the northeast corner bay. This house is probably the third to sit on the site. Originally the property was four lots in size, rather than one, and may have been heavily wooded. The Presbyterian minister, Reverend James Thomson, built his humble log manse there, "west of town," in the 1840s. In the 1850s John Sivey—a prominent lawyer, a county clerk, and a real estate developer—and his wife Lucinda replaced Thompson's cabin with a charming Gothic revival "cottage" that faced Hill Street. It featured steeply pitched roofs, a sheltered balcony, tall windows, and intricate wood trim. However, in the twenty-first century this house no longer faces north toward Hill Street, but south toward Main Street, number 306, at its junction with Carroll Street. Apparently Weesner divided Sivey's former property into four lots before building his 1885 house and in the process moved the Sivey residence to the southeastern most lot. It has since been restored to an admirable condition by the Loren Watkins family.

Just after the turn of the century the Weesners sold their home on Hill Street in order to move into their second Queen Anne house, at 206 West Main, which they had purchased from William and Mary Talbert. The purchase was partly a trade, in that the Talberts took over the Weesner house on Hill Street. This second Weesner home may date from about 1890. Its design is extraordinary, with unexpected flourishes in the form of bays, porches, turret, and balcony. Since 1924 the house has had a variety of owners.[33]

A half block east of Weesner's Hill Street house stands Harmon and Carolyn Wolf's unusual, monumental stone pile at 261 West Hill. It was built in the mid-1890s, but the builders are unknown and the Wolfs did not live there until just after the turn of the century. Both its style and the stone with which it is built tied the house to its erstwhile neighbor, the 1894 high school, for although it is of basically simple construction, it reflects the Richardsonian/Romanesque elan of that neighbor. Indeed, its stonework may be leftover construction material from the high school project. It has also been described as being eclectic in design because it displays elements of both Queen Anne and Colonial Revival. Few houses in Wabash appear to be so solidly built, which accounts in part for the fact that it appears in the twenty-first century to be as close to its original external presentation as any nineteenth-century building in town.

Wolf was associated with an importing business located on South Wabash Street that specialized in Belgium draft horses. Bred originally for heavy farm work, these horses were admired for their massive size and strength. There was a period from the late nineteenth century into the twentieth century when the Belgium draft-horse craze captivated Wabash County horse fanciers and investors. Wolf and J. D. Conner Jr. (Hugh Hanna's grandson) were among a number of citizens who were intensely interested in perpetuating the breed, increasingly as much for show as for farm work. The result was that Belgium draft horses continued to attract enthusiasts long after tractors had replaced them in agriculture. As noted earlier, in the twentieth century

Conner Jr. was knighted by the Belgium crown for his leadership in draft horse circles. In the twenty-first century the Belgium Draft Horse Association continues its tradition of maintaining headquarters in Wabash.[34]

Directly across the street from the Wolf house, at 256, stands a handsome, understated quasi-Adam style home, in brick, with a broad front porch that was probably a later addition. The house originally belonged to that premier woodworking mogul of Wabash, Thomas F. Payne, who had operated two outlets downtown: his furniture factory south of the canal on Wabash Street and his display building on the southeast corner of Miami and Market streets. His Hill Street home came into being in at least two stages. An 1853 house still stands, set back on the lot, probably as it did originally. The 1875 map of Wabash and the 1901 Sanborn insurance map together suggest that at an undetermined date—possibly before 1875—Payne and his wife, Lucetta, added the neatly executed double-story front that has since identified the house. Only recently have its present owners become aware that two separate structures comprised the one house on their property. The Paynes raised four sons in the house, all but one of whom sought their fortunes in other cities. Thomas retired from his furniture company in 1895 and continued to live at home until his death in 1918, at the age of ninety-three. He had lived in Wabash since 1849 and had been a Methodist all those years.[35]

When Payne's neighbor, Thomas McNamee, died in 1916 the *Plain Dealer* eulogized, "His best epitaph is his name."[36] Indeed, few names carried more weight in late-nineteenth-century Wabash than McNamee. Few homes illustrate more emphatically the prominence and style of successful Wabash Victorians than McNamee's Second Empire/Italianate house (Ted Eilts house). Although three highly desirable McNamee homes survive to the twenty-first century (Thomas Jr.'s at 240 North Cass Street, Henry's at 536 North Wabash Street, and Thomas Sr.'s at 208 West Hill), Thomas Sr.'s is the most evocative of its age. McNamee and his wife, Mary, built it about 1870; more than a century and a quarter later it stands in as close to its original condition as might be hoped. The McNamees were also the first homeowners in Wabash known to have installed indoor plumbing and bath facilities. The building features heavy window eyebrows, pillared porch, a mansard roof, and a squarish entrance tower. Although its present shrouding by mature trees casts a "Charles Addams," haunted-but-beguiling look upon it, the house remains a significant emblem of a gilded age and has been recognized in statewide publications as an important representation of its era. It remains a visual draw for both residents and visitors.

This "moral and commercial leader," McNamee, arrived in Wabash from Ohio at age eleven, already prepared to earn a living in the tanners' trade. A few years later, in 1852, accompanied by his cousin, George Cissna of Wabash, he attended the University of Notre Dame for a year, adding a little polish to what had probably been a lackluster education in early local schools. Back home, he established a tin shop and stove store downtown and then, in 1857, partnered with Madison Whiteside and James McCrea to launch a hardware company. McNamee's partnerships changed over the years, adding such names as George King and John H. Bruner to the mix while Whiteside and McCrea took up other pursuits. After McNamee sold his share, the company name continued as King-Hipskind through much of the following century. In 1877 McNamee joined with King and Joseph Busick to form the Wabash County Bank. At the time of his death, McNamee was president of that bank's successor, the Wabash National Bank, located—as previously noted—in an important building at the foot of the Wabash Street hill. Though not an especially fervid political animal, McNamee was a Republican who served terms on both the county council and the Wabash Common Council. He was known also for his support of the local hospital and for his devotion to his church. His good friend and pastor, Charles Little, may have been privy to the man's flaws and foibles as well, but true to the practice of the age he did not reveal such matters publicly, eulogizing the man as "faithful, true and frank," a "fountain of advice" for associates. He praised McNamee also for his leadership and generosity in the successful construction of the 1880s Presbyterian sanctuary. Like his residence, McNamee is himself an icon of the age. Ambitious, hardworking, nimble in business matters, community-minded, spiritually motivated, and sensitive to tastefulness and style, he exemplifies an ascending benevolent influence among Wabash's nineteenth-century movers and shakers.[37]

William A. and Ellen Elward lived exactly five streets east of Thomas and Mary McNamee at 192 East Hill Street. The external appearance of the Elward home survives largely intact. Although it has known decades as an apartment building, it remains a prominent and distinguished building in that part of Wabash. Its age is uncertain, but it has probably always seemed to be large for its lot, having been built close to the edge of it. The house is a red-brick Italianate with some characteristics of Queen Anne. Its perpendicularity is enhanced by a turret, long windows, and placement close to the sidewalk corner.

Elward was born in Lagro Township in 1838, attended backwoods county schools, and began his adult career teaching in some of those schools. At age twenty-one he hired on as a clerk with a Lagro merchant for a hundred dollars a year, but in short order he found a more promising job as the town's railroad station agent. A decade later he took a similar position at the Wabash station and moved to the county seat, where he served as agent until 1892. Typical of his generation, however, Elward did not stick with a single occupation. About 1870, shortly after moving to Wabash, he joined with pioneer Samuel Steele to start a grain elevator on Sinclair Street, less than a block from his home and probably equally close to his railroad agency office. Steele and Elward eventually added elevators at Lagro and Richvalley to their enterprise. Elward was one of a relatively few prominent Democrats in the Republican stronghold, serving for a time as his party's county chairman. He also ran for county auditor and, later, for mayor of the city, losing both elections. He nonetheless held a seat on the school board for several years. Elward and his wife were members of Saint Bernard Church. Although that parish's records offer little additional information about Elward, his business and public career may have burnished Saint Bernard's rising profile in the community.[38]

Clearly not all so-called movers and shakers in nineteenth-century Wabash left behind a major relic of themselves in the form of a nineteenth-century home of substance, nor did the presence of a fancy house necessarily identify a civic leader. Some personages of standing who built notable homes have already been mentioned in connection with other topics. Doctor John H. DePuy's eclectic brick at 189 North Miami Street has long been a gem inside and out. DePuy's son, Romeo, building next to his father at 77 West Sinclair, created a moderately large Queen Anne house that boasts seven roofline gables, none of which duplicates any of the others in design. Low-profile, less-newsworthy citizens sometimes built lavishly while, conversely, more influential folks might need their homes to be little more than walls, rooms, and roofs on a plot large enough for gardening. Another category includes citizens such as Cary Cowgill, James McCrea, Reuben Lutz,

John U. Pettit, and Will Stitt whose considerable houses have not survived the wreckage of progress, although their names and their careers have been mentioned in other contexts. Lutz's Market Street house, in particular, was a stunning example of Queen Anne style. Judge Alfred Plummer was a man who was rising to prominence as an attorney in the 1890s and who lived in a moderately sized Queen Anne house on North Miami Street, but whose personal influence—as well as the prominence of his offspring at the bar—was greater in the twentieth century. Like Plummer—though a Democratic leader rather than a Republican one—Nelson G. Hunter, as noted earlier, was also achieving name recognition at century's end, though, again, most of his work unfolded in the following decades. Hunter's house on Ferry Street has been replaced by a modern home. It is important to acknowledge, also, that Wabash has scores of other notable nineteenth-century houses—the identities of their successive occupants often uncertain—that continue to house folks safely and comfortably in the twenty-first century.[39]

A prominent citizen whose name is not tied to any premier real estate, but who was as well known and well honored by contemporaries as any was Elijah Hackleman, some of whose contributions to Wabash's story have already been noted. He also happened to be a "persister." Hackleman's line continues to be known in Wabash through the Bent, Shroyer, and Skeans families. Hackleman was a natural historian who loved to write at length of the national, state, and cultural developments that preceded the emergence of northern Indiana from its native past. He was especially interested in the setting of his own education and development in Rush County where he spent his youth, taught school, was admitted to the bar, and served as a justice of the peace before coming to Wabash County in the 1840s. Hackleman's appointment as county surveyor in the early 1850s forced him to move from his 160-acre farm near Ashland (LaFontaine) to Wabash, though he continued to develop his rural spread. He also served eight years as county clerk, was a state senator, seriously considered running for Congress in 1878, and was a perennial pillar of the Christian Church. In 1867 he purchased ground that rose northeast from the crossing of Ferry and Fisher streets in the Ewing Addition and built a relatively modest home. He and his wife, Margaret, raised nine children, two of whom died young and three others of whom were given the unusual names of Leonidas, Constantine, and Pleasant. A stone retaining wall north of Ferry Street on Fisher Street may be one that Hackleman erected to shore up the sloping ground near his house, which is probably no longer extant.[40]

Hackleman made four generous contributions to the study of Wabash history: first, his general histories of pioneer times, noted above; second, his personal diaries that date from 1861 to 1901; third, his scrapbooks in which he pasted news items and personal observations; and fourth, his encouragement of the Old Settlers Association, the records of which contain reminiscences of early Wabash.

Hackleman's diaries are both charming and frustrating. Charming is his somewhat capricious recording of observable, though not always fascinating, natural phenomenon: a sudden temperature change, a thunderstorm, a freeze, a heat wave, an astrological event, an insect infestation, or the depth of street mud. Or, if one would like to know, say, something memorable about the town's celebration of the Fourth in 1878, Hackleman might offer an abbreviated overview: "A very quiet day in Wabash, a promiscuous gathering [at] the fair Grounds."[41] Of course, it might not be clear what he meant by "promiscuous." When a friend and neighbor, Milo Haas, hired workers to build his house in 1889, Hackleman kept a succinct record of its progress, by which it can be deduced that to create a new home in that neighborhood at that time required approximately three months of decent weather. Construction on Haas's place began on August 31 with a public water hookup and ended on November 27 when finishing touches were made. Hackleman's snippets of information here are typical of all his entries: masons start laying stone foundation (September 11); carpenters begin work (October 1); roofing (October 7); flooring (October 10); fencing (October 29); gas-fired stoves dry plaster (November 11); Haas moves in (November 11). Sometimes other Hackleman entries simply repeat current local chitchat, if not gossip, such as his notation of the news that Thomas and Lucetta Payne's son, Frank, had married poet James Whitcomb Riley's sister. Sometimes he simply preserves for later generations small hints of what the mundane side of life might have been like: December 3, 1867, "Confined to bed with piles"; March 16, 1870, "Bought 50 cords of wood from Jonathan Bird"; July 25, 1884, "Finished mending Socks, a Weeks work."[42]

Less charming and more frustrating is the bloodless reporting of events—some emotionally charged—that might normally have deserved some fleshing out but which, instead, leave more questions posed than answered. For example, the destruction in 1889 of the old Wabash Street canal bridge; the death of Warren Pauling, age thirteen, when railroad cars crushed him; a public assault by boys on *Courier* editor, Lee Linn; the Presbyterians' and Methodists' refusal to decorate soldiers' graves because the event was scheduled for the Sabbath; the news that Hackleman's mother's body, which had recently been disinterred in another part of the state, had petrified; the complete extraction of Margaret's teeth; and the early death in 1890 of his son, Pleasant. While many entries in the diary add a soupçon of flavor to the substance of the past, they only whet appetites for what he has omitted. The man was no more forthcoming about his own aches, pains, and approaching exit. For the year Hackleman himself died, 1901, his diary is a total blank except for one notation on the last page: "Finis."[43]

The surviving house in Wabash that may represent the town's nineteenth-century experience better than any other is J. D. Conner's stately Federal at 187 East Main Street. After the Conner family sold it early in the twentieth century the interior was cut into apartments. Subsequently, however, it was owned and occupied by members of a series of prominent families—including the Haldermans, the Hetzners, and the Duffeys—who treated it lovingly so that the exterior continues to appear largely as Conner probably envisioned it in the 1850s: commodious, durable, understated, dignified, and prominently situated on "Conner's Hill" above the downtown. In spite of the fact that the fading twentieth century was not kind to property conditions in that end of Wabash, the Conner house had held its own.

One reason Conner looms large as iconic of his age and place is that he married the proprietor's daughter, Julia Ann Hanna, in 1842. Conner, rather than one of Julia's brothers, became the principle bearer of Hanna's legacy in Wabash, in part because the Hanna sons did not maintain permanent residence in the place, but mostly because Conner's own career had a glow of success that few other citizens could match. Possibly only Calvin Cowgill was a more ascendant personality as the century unfolded. Although Conner could bask in the personal connections he had with the town's founder and with other progressive citizens, in one regard Conner did not emulate the pattern of their success. Many town leaders had done as Hanna had, pursued several interests at once in a style that a later age might call multitasking. No doubt it was a common strategy that took advantage of the needs and opportunities in emerging communities. Hanna had learned it from his brother Samuel: open a store, start a business, support a church, boost education, start another business, buy property, sell property, run for office, push reforms, start another business . . . . ad infinitum in a layered collection of projects and enterprises. Conner, by contrast, seemed focused upon narrower concerns and, in that sense, may have been ahead of his time. In any case his ambitions targeted the practice of the law and its sister vocation, politics. He no doubt invested his money in various ventures, but these investments were not the kind to demand much of his attention. From the moment he hung his shingle near Hanna's Corner in 1840, Conner was on a single-minded, inexorable climb to prominence in law and politics.

Historian Clarkson Weesner wrote that Conner had "that inestimable faculty of being able to grow in power and resources along with his community, and by the time he had been in Wabash ten years, he was recognized as the foremost lawyer of the county bar."[44] In 1856 he won a delegate's seat at the first Republican National Convention, which nominated John C. Frémont for president in Philadelphia. The same year Conner secured a seat in the state legislature. Soon thereafter he worked successfully for the formation of a Republican Party, a major heir of the Whig Party in Indiana. In 1859 he was elected to represent Wabash and Kosciusko counties in the state senate. By 1861 his statewide standing was such that the governor appointed him to the committee that welcomed to Indianapolis the newly elected Abraham Lincoln, who stopped there on his way to his inauguration in Washington, D.C. Lincoln was someone with whom Conner had personal connections through Caleb Smith, soon to be Lincoln's Secretary of the Interior. President Lincoln later offered Conner the post of U.S. District Judge in Nebraska Territory, but Conner declined. Instead he continued to practice law and politics in Wabash, a concentration that led to his election in 1884 as judge of the twenty-seventh judicial district comprising Wabash and Miami counties. He filled this position for six years.[45]

Although raised as a Baptist, Conner had followed his wife into the Presbyterian fold upon their marriage. The most prominent offspring of that union was J. D. Conner Jr., who made his mark in the comparatively esoteric world of Belgium draft horse importation and breeding. As noted earlier, the Hanna/Conner bloodlines were represented among Wabash's business and social lions through much of the twentieth century. Given James D.'s standing in Wabash at the end of the nineteenth century, his family's lineal connection with the town's original proprietor, and the promising future that seemed open to Hanna/Conner offspring, it would not be a great stretch of reason to say that Hanna's Town had effectively morphed into Conner's Town by the time Conner reinterred his father-in-law in 1902.[46]

Sightseers on top of Citizen's imaginary courthouse observation deck, after surveying the public buildings, courts, schools, churches, homes, and other substantial developments that decorated the Wabash acropolis, could not have missed Memorial Hall immediately to the west. Although the hall was a county project rather than a town project, it completed the visual center of Wabash and intensified the soaring profile of the place: a proverbial "city set on a hill that could not be hid." Rising high beyond the tree line and standing at bluff-top sixty feet above the river's flow were the courthouse tower, the high pitched roof and two corner turrets of Memorial Hall, the priapic high school tower, and four handsome church steeples. Behind all these—poking up through tree branches—were the slate peaks of schools and the signature rooflines of dozens of fashionable homes.

Memorial Hall was not dedicated until Thursday, November 2, 1899. It was a day of inclement weather. Folks crowded the interior, where a band played, the lieutenant governor was welcomed, and Reverend Little spoke on behalf of a grateful citizenry. Plans for a memorial of the Civil War had by then been in the works for sixteen years, gaining momentum and complexity as that war's battles receded into the past and veterans aged toward death. Its inception may have occurred in early June 1883, the day Edwin Harter attended a veterans' meeting and proposed starting a fund for a suitable memorial of the local Civil War experience. The *Plain Dealer* promoted the idea and in short order two hundred thirty-four dollars was raised in cash and subscriptions, a sum that would have gone a long way toward the erection of a monument in stone or marble. That the project ballooned into something far more grand and useful may be credited to two other veterans, Captain Alexander Hess, who was serving in the state legislature, and Captain Benjamin Franklin Williams, James Ford's son-in-law, who was the county's auditor. These two were not satisfied with a traditional memorial that might have been little more than an oversized tombstone with veterans' names engraved on it. Weesner later wrote that they wanted a public building that would be "creditable to the city and its people" as well as being a "fitting memorial to Union patriotism."[47]

In 1886 the *Courier* reported that the local chapter of the Grand Army of the Republic was sponsoring an "Art Loan Exhibition," a public display of hundreds of war relics, Native American articles, prehistoric and geological specimens, "Fancy Work," and various antiques, pictures, and objets d'art that citizens would lend for the occasion. There were at least six committees organized—finance, decorations, refreshments, music, donations, and transportation—to create the event, for which scores of prominent town and county residents volunteered their support. Expenses totaled between eight hundred and nine hundred dollars, but ticket receipts were double that amount. About the same time the Indiana legislature authorized the purchase of a site. Hess, Williams, and others began stumping hard to bring the county's commissioners into favorable alignment, a campaign that eventually produced a tax levy of $25,000 and the purchase of lots west of Court Street for ten thousand dollars. Ab Haas's novelty store at the corner of Hill and Court streets and a house farther west were to be razed to make room for the project.

Built of Bedford limestone with three stories of useful space, Memorial Hall was intended to be a venue for community gatherings. The basement level stretched under the entire structure, had a cement floor throughout, and was designed to accommodate veterans' banquets and to provide a place where aging soldiers could gather informally to smoke and reminisce. The middle story, accessible by an exterior stone staircase, housed a huge assembly room. That room, as well as the "Grand Army" room above it, were described as among the "finest apartments of the kind" in the state. The building also housed a museum and the headquarters of the county's historical society. Reportedly, the hall was the second of its kind in the nation. The exterior was (and is in the present day) almost chateaux-like in appearance, a major piece of local architecture, and worthy of its setting. Life-size statues of a soldier and a sailor flanked the front steps. In its early years the corner turrets help up tall flagpoles topped with eagles. In 1902 two Civil War cannon were installed in front of the hall, arriving from Fort Jefferson in the Dry Tortugas of Florida. One cannon was a twenty-four-pounder Flank Defense Howitzer; the other was a thirty-pounder Parrot Rifled Cannon.[48]

In the twenty-first century the county reconfigured the hall's interior, lowering ceilings and cutting up floor space in order to provide an annex of cubicles and offices for court and county business. Commissioners also added a wing to the south. The exterior of that addition is itself a monument to good taste and wise forethought to the degree that it mirrors the original hall, even to the point of having two corner turrets.

Wabash's nineteenth-century acropolis continues to be well served in the twenty-first century by Memorial Hall, by the courthouse, by several churches, and by a splendid array of extant nineteenth-century homes, many in excellent condition. As it always did, the ancient forest—or its successor—keeps the heights robed in green for summer and etches its winter horizon with upward-spreading, barren branches. Although the bluff still offers its natural divide between the old business center and the old residential center of town, one should not suppose that this divide was ever absolute. Since the beginning there have been houses on the east and west extremes of Market and Canal streets, including quite large, expensive homes that once stood where Market and Cass streets cross. Likewise, the northern reaches of town were never purely residential, only dominantly so. The Alber brewery on Cass Street, the Pioneer Hat Factory on Manchester Avenue, and the Treaty Creek Stone and Lime Company flourished there. Small neighborhood shops, though rare, were not unknown. A compact commercial strip toward the south end of Falls Avenue, for example, eventually supported three or four businesses throughout most of the next century.

Although both bluff top and valley suffered urban blight in the succeeding decades of the twentieth century, it is possible to imagine what Hanna's Town was like, there being relics of it everywhere in the form of late-nineteenth-century buildings, downtown and uptown. Quite likely it was a beautiful place, a comfortable place, a progressive place, and a stylish place—populated by folks who for the most part were proud of their town and optimistic about its future. Their leaders were often men and women of fashion, broad learning, multiple talents, vision, and personal spiritual strength. They were ambitious for their community as well as for their own prosperity. As with any human gathering, Wabash was subject to the inevitable dark side: filth, pollution, mud, squabbling, prostitution, philandering, drunkenness, petty crime, major crime, sexism, racism, poverty, materialism, snobbery, and spiritual hypocrisy, to name a few examples. Given that no town of comparable size lacked a comparable dark side, it may be permissible to posit the idea that Wabash citizens, more than most, were privileged to engage in the normal battles between good and evil in an unusually gorgeous and topographically fascinating setting.

The great curiosity about Hanna's Town—the great mystery, still—is the proprietor's imposition of his Original Plat on a piece of ground that had a forty to sixty foot high bluff running through the center of it. On the surface it was idiocy. This seems especially true when one considers how he made no allowances for a gradual, possibly curvilinear, ascent of streets from the bottoms to the tops in order to facilitate traffic. Granted, straight-line grids were thought to be either practical or fashionable. So, in defiance of obvious topographical facts, Hanna let his plat dictate that traffic on such streets as Wabash, Allen, Miami, and Cass would have to ascend steeply as best it could in daring denial of gravity. Huntington Street lies upon the Original Plat as confirmation of such idiocy. No one ever tried to open that street between Market and Main streets; the bluff at that point is simply too intimidating. There may have been contemporaries of the proprietor who thought that Wabash Street hill also should be abandoned, for similar reason. It is possible, of course, that Hanna had simply miscalculated in some way. He might have supposed, for example, that a plat of land the size he had in mind could be laid out on level river bottom, and, then, having discovered during visits to Treaty Ground how often and how deeply the bottomland flooded, decided that a soaring bluff was less trouble than an inundated floodplain.

On the other hand (too-steep streets to the contrary), there could have been genius—perhaps even artistry—in part of Hanna's idiocy. The clue here is Hanna's early selection of a site for the public square. He chose bluff top. A more logical—and traditional—selection might have been the downtown square bounded by Wabash, Market, Miami, and Canal streets. At the time there was nothing practical about his choice of a public square site between Main and Hill streets, unless one wants to accuse Hanna of giving to the county some of the least accessible lots in town. But that accusation does not carry much weight because Hanna chose the bluff top as the locus of his own home. He must have found the high ground desirable.

Probably, then, Hanna had what a lot of Wabash citizens still have, an ill-defined, scarcely articulated love affair with the topography of the place. He chose one of the steepest, most highly situated pieces of ground on his plat to locate its most important building, the county's courthouse. At that point he probably did not care (or realize) that horses would strain to mount Wabash Street hill (as it was then) and that citizens would descend the oozy mud of it in terror. At that point he wanted his town to have an acropolis, a place where the judicial, spiritual, intellectual, and domestic dimensions of life would be encouraged. His placement of cemetery, church lot, school lot, and his own house on high ground supports that idea. He wanted such an area to be differentiated from the commercial, financial, and industrial base. The bluff in the middle of his Original Plat gave Hanna an opportunity to create a slightly different sort of town, one with a distinct agora and a distinct acropolis, even if he had never heard of such terms.

14

Perpendicularity: The Author's Apologia

The twenty-first-century community of Wabash, Indiana, is not Hanna's Town. Hanna's Town is a little world we have lost. It did not disappear all at once. It gradually eroded under the mighty dislocations of the twentieth century, with its many revolutions in transportation, communications, urbanization, globalization, and population shifts. Many such revolutions were inevitably for the general good, bringing, among other blessings, progress in America against evils such as sexism, racism, and hopeless poverty. No one should want to turn the clock back. Nevertheless, it has been instructive, if not inspiring, to study an enclave of folks and their immediate successors who built their town from a huddle of abandoned log cabins near an ancient spring. In just over six decades it had become an attractive, promising, optimistic, and growing community with a bustling agora and a soaring acropolis.

Changes in the rate of population growth after 1900 might have been enough to rob the town of its gusto and communal optimism. During the previous decades nothing had stemmed the tide of new residents. There were reportedly 966 citizens in 1850, the beginning of a steady, quickening increase. During the last decade of the nineteenth century, the town's population jumped from just over 5,000 in 1890 to 8,600 in 1900, an average of 300 new residents each year. Then, in the first decade of the twentieth century, the ascent abruptly stalled. Between 1900 and 1910 the population scarcely moved, creeping forward at a rate of about seven new residents a year. In the same period, neighboring county seats were not stagnant. Peru jumped from 8,400 residents to almost 11,000. Marion increased by 2,000, Huntington by roughly 800. There is no obvious explanation for Wabash's loss of momentum in population growth during this period, unless the economic uncertainties of the 1890s had been more dramatic in their effect locally than had appeared to be true at the time.[1]

The demise of Hanna's Town is especially evident in the draining of vitality from the downtown agora during the course of the twentieth century. Where once—in the 1890s—there had been roughly half a dozen empty storefronts out of eleven dozen storefronts or more, today most buildings there cry out for vital occupancy. Gone, too, are all but a few industrial outlets along the route of the old canal. Industry and commerce fled to the outskirts, mostly far north, leaving the old agora to rusticate.

The flight from downtown was partly a result of the advent of the automobile, which was undoubtedly a blessing until there were too many of them to be parked easily along Wabash's downtown streets. Twentieth-century experiments with parking meters there succeeded only in adding a new irritant to the original irritant. The solution seemed to be: take commerce to the outskirts; pave large parking lots where fields had been; build horizontally because there is plenty of room; build easily disposable structures to facilitate adaptation to the next fashion; build cheaply with featureless concrete block, flat roofs, walls of uninteresting windows, and cookie-cutter design, and do not worry about lasting style or individuality. A corollary to this trend was an attempt to bring older buildings up to twentieth-century standards by covering nineteenth-century brick, stonework, and windows with metal and vinyl. In that regard what had been beautiful to a Hanna, a Conner, a Haas, or a Bigler had become both passé in style and economically unfeasible to maintain.

Folks in the twenty-first century are painfully aware of this state of affairs and seem to be struggling to do something about it. The continuing—indeed, increasing—vitality of the community center that Sanford Honeywell's son gave to Wabash in the 1940s; the newer Ford family theater attached to it; the state-of-the-art county museum; the renovated Charley Creek Inn (formerly the Hotel Indiana and the Red Apple Inn); the new YMCA complex; the proposed renewal of Eagles Theater; City Hall's influence; Marketplace Inc.; the Chamber of Commerce; the Charley Creek Foundation (created by Richard E. Ford in part to spur renewal projects); plus a handful of viable, upscale commercial outlets are providing palpable hope for the old agora. Significantly and symbolically, Hugh Hanna's ancient spring, incorporated now into a lush park, testifies that renewal is possible.

On the heights, meanwhile, strong hints of Hanna's Town remain in streets overarched with shade trees, in private properties—new and old—positioned close together, and in the long sidewalks and long alleys, parallel and at right angles to one another that slice the bluff top into neatly criss-crossed neighborhoods. Yet, many of the nineteenth-century houses there are in shabby condition with ill-tended grounds: witnesses to their owners' economic trials. Too many houses have been abandoned, and many others testify that their owners have not a clue—or a care—about their property's historic or artistic value. There are exceptions, but generally speaking, the acropolis also rusticates, though perhaps more slowly than the agora.

Carried away by the ubiquitous automobile, twentieth-century homeowners and businesses fled to the outskirts and beyond—to the country. Autos made it possible to live miles from the old center of things, giving rise to housing developments, such as Bonbrook, which are beyond easy walking distance of downtown, and to the establishment of large, well-financed county-based schools. As Wabash spread out geographically, it probably lost its critical mass of community identity and loyalty. One might now have cheered on one's school, business, family, or church while making apologetic, even disparaging, remarks about one's town. Small Town, Indiana, in general, has not been a cutting-edge place to live since World War II or before.

Possibly the greatest loss, however, is an immeasurable, spiritual one: a can-do mentality that Hanna's Town had once exuded and that, like all spiritual matters, is not as susceptible to analysis as bricks and mortar. One way it can be measured imperfectly is by taking into account the way so many businessmen seemed to have had a work ethic that propelled them into multiple concerns, both of the moneymaking variety and the community-building variety. As with Hanna, it was not enough to earn a living; one might very well have a passion to earn several "livings," in layered, developing projects while, at the same time, investing time and talent in church work, social reform, and local politics. Town leaders seemed very nimble in this way. Their multitasking work ethic may have created a critical mass of localized vitality. Thus, Hanna's Town was a state of mind as well as a physical place. It seemed not to occur to nineteenth-century community leaders to doubt their ability to transform the place. Many individuals were upwardly mobile and were in close, frequent, and informal communication with others of their kind. It may have seemed unthinkable to them that their community could not make progress, borne forward by everyone's workaday labors.

Probably many such residents—but certainly not all residents—cared rather deeply about good citizenship and community responsibility. That caring inspired some to be prophetic, unafraid to address issues via their personal involvement, or to criticize openly what (or who) fell short, whether it was over a political issue or about a privy vault that had not been cleaned out. To such ends, Wabash has no greater nineteenth-century civic hero than the journalist Naaman Fletcher, who was devout about promoting community improvements. He was not alone. Other Wabash editors and newshounds knew their community intimately and commented candidly on what they knew. Fletcher, however, was the best of the lot, and his premature death was an enormous loss. He must have toured the agora on foot almost daily, dropping into shops, taverns, and businesses—or buttonholing pedestrians—to exchange news or gossip. He was on a first-name basis with politicians, preachers, teachers, bankers, industrialists, and ordinary folks. In print he was the town's chief booster and cheerleader. He was also its prophet: he scolded, cajoled, antagonized, accused, editorialized, and publicized jeremiads about a broad range of issues that pertained to the improvement of Wabash's physical and spiritual well-being. Fletcher and other editors of his ilk did Wabash immense good, promoting education, culture, business, religion, and a sense of humor while excoriating poor leadership, shoddy infrastructure, shady behavior, laziness, and a host of other negatives that might reflect poorly on the town.

The tradition of a prophetic class of professionals, such as editors and clergy, is an aspect of Hanna's Town we have lost. Twenty-first-century Wabash is forced to exist without the public conscience once embodied in newspapers and pulpits. Modern small-town papers have promoted good (usually uncontroversial) causes, but—for understandable economic reasons—they neither lecture, judge, scold, or accuse (save in the most benign language), nor do they seem to articulate a vision for the town. Likewise, modern clergy may wrap their homilies in various moralisms but, like newspapers, they tend to be toothless watchdogs of a town's reputation and progress. To be fair, Fletcher did not have to worry about libel suits, and nineteenth-century preachers may have been better schooled in the Old Testament prophets than later ones were. The earlier preachers and editors were often supportive of similar goals, even though, personally, they might occupy opposite sides of a sacred/secular intellectual divide. There was religious fervor to support almost any reform that Fletcher and his kind espoused, even though Fletcher himself was not religious. Whatever pulpit jargon the clergy may have used, the important preachers wanted to convince parishioners that God commended the creation of a healthy, progressive, and spiritually vibrant town.

On that score Fletcher and the clergy were of a single conviction.

It is unfortunate for places such as twenty-first-century Wabash that American governments—federal, state, and local—have not studied the possibility of adopting versions of Europe's so-called green laws. The initial impetus for green laws in Europe was probably to save country landscapes from becoming overrun by sprawl, but they have proven to be a boon for the towns and villages as well. The laws limit new building outside community corporation lines. With nonporous town and village boundaries largely preserved, businesses and houses do not "bleed" onto nonurban fields and forest. A subsidiary result—that would be so very beneficial for Wabash—is the dramatic rise in the value of town and village property, since that property is where residents must largely live and conduct business. As American tourists know well, a direct result of the green laws is the excellent condition, preservation, and charm of European communities. Few of these communities have more potential as attractive addresses than Wabash.

Nothing and no one specifically is to blame for the loss of Hanna's Town, unless it is a generalized American proclivity to embrace the new, perhaps because it *is* new. There is something admirable and exciting about that proclivity. As W. Somerset Maugham wrote, "We Americans like change. It is at once our weakness and our strength."[2] In 1835 Hanna might have understood emphatically the lure of the new, seeing that he was intent on changing an old forest into a new town and intent, also, on getting as rich as possible in the process. Yet, clearly, it was a *town* he was after, a community of community builders and neighbors, not a spread of loosely related entities, and not the construction of expendable, throwaway homes and businesses. His very first construction—the sturdy brick Hanna's Corner—proves that. Many of the homes his fellow citizens built confirm it. Hanna was probably trying to build for "Tomorrow," but the "Tomorrow" that was the twentieth century largely rejected what he set in motion. The "Tomorrow" that is the twenty-first century may be better equipped to appreciate—without the distraction of sentimentality—what has been lost.

My initial motivation for researching nineteenth-century Wabash was simply to answer for myself a question: "What was my town like in the beginning?" I was not born in Wabash, Indiana. I was born in Iowa but, as the Hoosier humorist Herb Shriner put it, "I came to Indiana as soon as I heard about it," in 1939 at age one year, to the day. I came to Indiana in order to live in Charles Little's commodious manse, a house so expansive that it was not until I was a college student that I completed exploring the whole of it. Like C. S. Lewis's wardrobe, it went on and on. I slept in Little's bed. I explored the dark recesses of his fruit room by the dim light of an electric bulb so ancient it must have lighted his way there, too. I whistled through the tube that he used to call the maid from downstairs to upstairs, or vice versa. The tube was still there for me to use but the maid, alas, had disappeared.

Little, by the way, was still something of a resident of that manse while I was growing up there. When the metal covering over the fireplace opening in my father's vast upstairs study was rattled by wind coming down the chimney, my siblings and I told each other it was Little's ghost we were hearing, a rumor begun by my mother, which I half believed. My recent research has revealed to me that Little was not the portly, pompous-looking gentleman (and ghost) as depicted most often in a twentieth-century photograph. He had once been a skinny, scraggly-bearded (almost hippy-looking) bachelor who liked to play baseball, sing in public, go on picnics, and engage in an endless round of comradely socializing that might have passed for pastoral attention to the flock, his flock being unofficially the whole town. That change in my appreciation of Little—no longer a ghost or an icon but a cheerful social animal—was just the sort of revelation about my adopted hometown I had hoped for and largely found. It was a real, flesh-and-blood town, not one sanitized by sentimentality.

Contrarily, in retrospect I realize that I grew up with a fantastic, almost storybook, vision of the Wabash that preceded my arrival. Living in that manse was part of the cause. My father had been a worthy candidate to fill Little's shoes. He stayed at his post only thirty years, not fifty, as Little had, but in that time he achieved similar standing in town and enjoyed similar respect, or so it seems to me. In any case, I grew increasingly aware that my father was an important man and that my family lived in an unusual house in a special part of town. When I went out to play in the manse yard, it was to play at the base of a tall, slender steeple. When I shot pigeons with my BB gun those pigeons were high above in the belfry of the steeple. In winter I could start sledding already at the top of a hill and coast at seemingly great speed down Miami Street, sometimes all the way to Market Street, forgetting for that brief, swift time the necessity of trudging back up that steep hill. When I was very small my father had sometimes carried me piggy-back up Miami hill because it was so steep that I could not make it on my own. Indeed, even in these latter years of existence I can zip in my car up Wabash Street hill, from

Market to Hill, in less than a minute. But I never do that nowadays without considering that if that hill were ten to twenty feet higher at the Main Street intersection—as it was in the 1850s—my Grand Prix would have a considerably harder time of it.

Across the street from the manse was another steeple—the Christian church's—and a turret on that church's parsonage. If I wandered less than half a block east there rose there the turrets of Memorial Hall and, just beyond, the tallest thing of all, the clock tower of the courthouse, surrounded by rooftop minarets. A block west of the manse was that gothic donjon, the old high school with a tower so slender it seemed incredibly tall and graceful, despite having been built of large rocks. Along this two-block stretch of West Hill Street was a collection of amazing houses: the McNamee mansion, the Spinney place (James Ford's home), the Bechtol house, Harold Wolf's Italianate, Fred Whistler's mansard-roofed duplex, Lena Rhamy's ancient brick cottage, Homer Hipskind's 1860s duplex, and the Plummers' Queen Anne. Some of them had been turned into apartments by the time I knew them, but each of them made a unique presentation; most were huge, all were solid, and three of them, like the manse, brandished a turret or a tower toward the sky. All this was my playground. In short, my childhood unfolded in a little world of perpendicularity, among soaring monuments from the past.

The effect this had on me—in addition to making me feel more important than I had a right to feel—was to plant in my soul the idea that daily I was living, moving, and playing in the shadow of long-gone cultural giants, of people who, in some ways, were more accomplished than contemporary adults. It was like living near Stonehenge or along Hadrian's wall or on the Nile's banks, although, admittedly, less dramatically so. Look at the artifacts Wabash's founders had left behind—beautiful buildings. Seemingly no expense was spared on these buildings; they were ornately wrought, spacious, and impractical things, reaching proudly toward the sky. Who were these people to have created such a place out of the wilderness!?

Later, of course, such questions receded from my consciousness. As I grew, I became enamored of all that happened in my postwar world of the 1940s and 1950s. I loved to drive through Bonbrook to admire the sleek, modern ranch houses, so many with a huge picture window rivaling the neighbor's in size, each such window displaying a large table lamp. For a time I thoroughly admired all that was new, fresh, and stylishly "modern." But during this time my family left the old manse to move into a less expansive, twentieth-century house. As acceptable—and more practical—as our new setting was I could not help finally admitting that it could not hold its own against the old manse in terms of pleasant spaces, elegant dimensions, solid construction, thoughtful details, and a romantic atmosphere. It seemed to me we had moved to a lower plane of existence, that those Wabash citizens who had built in the previous century were, somehow, in some ways, superior beings. I needed to know more about them and more about the town they had created.

Eventually I had one more motivation for studying the origins of Wabash: Hugh Hanna. When I was a student in England (1958–59), my mother sent me some genealogical information about her eighteenth-century ancestors, the Hannas of Ballybay, County Monagham, Ireland, suggesting that I might see if I could find any trace of them. I did, first at Ballybay where many male residents looked like clones of my Iowa uncles. I traced Hannas also further back in time, to Sorbie Tower, their clan fortress in Scotland. Decades later in Fort Wayne, Indiana, there hung on the wall of my pastoral study a crude portrait of James Hanna, a founder of First Presbyterian Church there and the father of Samuel, Joseph, and Hugh Hanna, all of whom descend from the Sorbie and Ballybay Hannas. I doubt if Hugh and I share much DNA, but if I manipulate the genealogical tables just right I can prove that he and I are first cousins—five times removed. Nonetheless, the discovery of such a relationship was enough to rally again my inquisitiveness about the origins of my adopted hometown. Its founder and proprietor is, lo! blood kin. In truth Hugh did not look unlike some of my Iowa uncles.

Notes

Prologue

1. Based on the *Wabash Plain Dealer*, February 12, 20, 1863, October 5, 1865, January 21, 28, 1869, November 21, 1902; *Wabash Weekly Intelligencer*, February 12, 1863. The courthouse cited in this prologue is technically the third courthouse, though only the second one built for that purpose, the second being the one Hanna built in the 1840s and the first being Patrick Duffy's tavern on the northeast corner of Market and Huntington streets where officials gathered to do official business. However, town and county officials likely also met at times in other locations, including the cabins at Treaty Ground.

Chapter 1

1. Mark J. Camp and Graham T. Richardson, *Roadside Geology of Indiana* (Missoula, MT: Mountain Press, 1999), 298; Marion T. Jackson, ed., *The Natural History of Indiana* (Bloomington: Indiana University Press, 1997), 24.

2. Jack Sunderman (geologist), interview with the author, Wabash, IN, October 2006.

3. Camp and Richardson, *Roadside Geology of Indiana*, 1–12, 217–27, 250–58; James H. Madison, *The Indiana Way: A State History* (Bloomington: Indiana University Press; Indianapolis: Indiana Historical Society, 1986), 7–10; Thomas B. Helm, *History of Wabash County, Indiana* (Chicago: John Morris, 1884), 72–76; *Rushville Republican*, December 18, 1896. For J. P. Paul's comments about the Wabash area before white settlement, see J. P. Paul "Diary," Wabash County Historical Museum, Wabash, IN (hereafter cited as WCHM).

4. *Rushville Republican*, December 18, 1896.

5. Ronald L. Woodward (Wabash County Historian), interview with the author, Wabash, IN, March 2006; Elijah Hackleman, *Scrapbook IV*, 80 and *Scrapbook VII*, 50, 51, WCHM; Isaac McCoy, *History of the Baptist Indian Missions* (Washington: William M. Morrison, 1840), 136; Helm, *History of Wabash County*, 103; Clarkson Weesner, *A History of Wabash County, Indiana* (Chicago: Lewis Publishing Company, 1914), 88ff.

6. Madison, *Indiana Way*, 1–6; Weesner, *History of Wabash County*, 10–11.

7. Hackleman, *Scrapbook II*, 173; Weesner, *History of Wabash County*, 55; Helm, *History of Wabash County*, 102.

8. *Wabash Plain Dealer*, July 11, 1896; Nellie Armstrong and Dorothy Riker, eds., *The John Tipton Papers*, 3 vols. (Indianapolis: Indiana Historical Bureau, 1942), 1:546–47.

9. Weesner, *History of Wabash County*, 88–94.

10. Warder Crow, *Indians of Wabash County*, pamphlet (Wabash, IN: Wabash County Historical Museum); Armstrong and Riker, eds., *Tipton Papers*, 1:450; letter to the Art Institute of Chicago, December 10, 1959, Mary C. O'Hair file, WCHM; J. T. Biggerstaff, paper, n.d., Chief Charley file, WCHM; *Wabash Plain Dealer*, October 26, 1977.

11. *Wabash Plain Dealer*, May 10, 1878.

12. Ibid., June 5, 1899; Hackleman, *Scrapbook VII*, 121. Twenty-first century value calculated by Frank R. Stewart, timber broker, Spencer, IN.

13. *Old Settlers Book* (a record of Wabash County settler reunions, Wabash County Historical Museum), 179; R. Carlyle Buley, *The Old Northwest: Pioneer Period, 1815–1840*, 2 vols. (Indianapolis: Indiana Historical Society, 1950), 1:159–67.

14. Mary C. O'Hair, "The Rock and the Hospital," in Crow, *Indians of Wabash County*; *Wabash*

Plain Dealer, December 19, 1896; *Old Settlers Book*, 191.

15. *Old Settlers Book*, 150, 151; Andrew R. L. Cayton, *Frontier Indiana* (Bloomington and Indianapolis: Indiana University Press, 1996), 147; Ronald L. Woodward and Gladys Dove Harvey, *Shadows of Wabash: From Native Americans to Industry* (Wabash, IN, 2005), 9; Hackleman, *Scrapbook IV*, 255–57; Weesner, *History of Wabash County*, 121, 144; Helm, *History of Wabash County*, 105; Hackleman, *Scrapbook III*, 188; *Wabash Plain Dealer*, June 8, 1883; Madison, *Indiana Way*, 24–25.

16. *Old Settlers Book*, 179, 229.

17. Hackleman, *Scrapbook IV*, 257; *Old Settlers Book*, 105.

18. Woodward and Harvey, *Shadows of Wabash*, 5–6; Helm, *History of Wabash County*, 139, 140, 153; *Wabash Courier*, August 8, 1877; *Old Settlers Book*, 105.

19. *Old Settlers Book*, 107, 265; Helm, *History of Wabash County*, 102.

20. *Old Settlers Book*, 154–59, 170, 257, 265; Weesner, *History of Wabash County*, 114; Woodward interview with the author, December 2006; Woodward and Harvey, *Shadows of Wabash*, 92, 93; Hackleman, *Scrapbook II*, 170; *Wabash Courier*, January 6, 1878. An old-timer claimed to have killed a rattlesnake in 1848 that was 45 feet long, 4 feet in diameter, and bearing 387 rattles and 62 tail buttons (*Wabash Weekly Intelligencer*, July 15, 1858).

21. Armstrong and Riker, eds., *John Tipton Papers*, 1:546–47.

22. Helm, *History of Wabash County*, 101.

23. Armstrong and Riker, eds., *John Tipton Papers*, 1:566–67; Weesner, *History of Wabash County*, 75; Mary C. O'Hair, *Paradise Springs: The Treaty Held at Treaty Ground*, pamphlet (Wabash, IN: Wabash County Historical Museum, 1962), 2–3, 5–7. Fearing Wabash County's historical foundation was at stake, O'Hair, WCHM curator, compiled all the data that corroborated the tradition that Wabash, not the "mouth of the mississinaway," was the site of the 1826 treaty. See also O'Hair correspondence, Paradise Spring file, WCHM. *Rushville Republican*, December 18, 1896.

24. Hackleman, *Scrapbook II*, "map" (between pp. 168 and 169); James M. Ray in *Wabash Plain Dealer*, June 21, 1878; Armstrong and Riker, eds., *John Tipton Papers*, 1:574–75, 624; Helm, *History of Wabash County*, 90, 101.

25. Hackleman, *Scrapbook II*, "map"; Ray, *Wabash Plain Dealer*, June 21, 1878, February 21, March 20, April 21, August 28, 1896.

26. Hackleman, *Scrapbook II*, 168ff; *Rushville Republican*, December 18, 1896; Ray, *Wabash Plain Dealer*, June 21, 1878, February 21, March 20, April 21, August 28, 1896.

27. Ray, *Wabash Plain Dealer*, June 21, 1878, February 21, March 20, April 21, August 28, 1896; Wilbur D. Peat, *Portraits and Painters of the Governors of Indiana, 1800–1978* (Indianapolis: Indiana Historical Society and Indianapolis Museum of Art, 1978), 22: Donald Carmony, *Indiana, 1815–1850: The Pioneer Era* (Indianapolis: Indiana Historical Society and Indiana Historical Bureau, 1998), 497–555.

28. *Rushville Republican*, December 18, 1896; Buley, *Old Northwest*, 2:84–85, 110–13, 448–58; Carmony, *Indiana*, 116, 240, 543; "Paradise Spring," WCHM file.

29. Cayton, *Frontier Indiana*, 313, 314.

30. Armstrong and Riker, eds., *John Tipton Papers*, 1:1–22.

31. Cayton, *Frontier Indiana*, 53–54, 145–53, 263; Stewart Rafert, *The Miami Indians of Indiana: A Persistant People, 1654–1994* (Indianapolis: Indiana Historical Society, 1996), 37–38, 48, 76, 103.

32. Armstrong and Riker, eds., *John Tipton Papers*, 1:1–22; Cayton, *Frontier Indiana*, 199–204.

33. Armstrong and Riker, eds., *John Tipton Papers*, 1:13–14.
34. *Wabash Plain Dealer*, June 21, 1878.
35. Ibid.; Armstrong and Riker, eds., *John Tipton Papers*, 1:308n.
36. Armstrong and Riker, eds., *John Tipton Papers*, 1:14.
37. Ibid., 16.
38. Ibid., 576–606, 624, 757, 794, 831; Helm, *History of Wabash County*, 91.
39. McCoy, *History of the Baptist Indian Missions*, 130; Armstrong and Riker, eds., *John Tipton Papers*, 1:596, 2:11; David Burr file, WCHM; Hackleman, *Scrapbook II*, 214.

Chapter 2

1. Mary C. O'Hair, *Paradise Spring: The Treaty Held at Treaty Ground*, pamphlet (Wabash, IN: Wabash County Historical Museum, 1962), 13; *Old Settlers Book*, 389 (a record of Wabash County settler reunions, Wabash County Historical Museum [hereafter cited as WCHM]); Thomas B. Helm, *History of Wabash County, Indiana* (Chicago: John Morris, 1884), 91–93; *Wabash Plain Dealer*, August 31, 1883, June 28, 1899; Elijah Hackleman, *Scrapbook II*, 169–70, *Scrapbook III*, 214, WCHM.
2. Ronald L. Woodward, pamphlet: "David Burr," WCHM files; *Samuel Hanna*, pamphlet (Fort Wayne, IN: Fort Wayne and Allen County Public Library, 1953), 7.
3. Nellie Armstrong and Dorothy Riker, eds., *The John Tipton Papers*, 3 vols. (Indianapolis: Indiana Historical Bureau, 1942), 2:11n, 3:235–36; Ronald Woodward, paper, David Burr file, WCHM; Ronald L. Woodward, comp., *The United States Census, Wabash County, 1840* (Wabash, IN: R. L. Woodward, 1980); Gayle Thornbrough, Dorothy Riker, and Paula Corpuz, eds., *The Diary of Calvin Fletcher*, 9 vols. (Indianapolis: Indiana Historical Society, 1972–83), 1:244n, 261, 262, 299, 379n, 397, 398; Ronald L. Woodward, *Grantor's Book I, 1836–1847 (A–H)* (Wabash, IN: Wabash Carnegie Public Library, 1983), 212; Clarkson Weesner, *A History of Wabash County, Indiana* (Chicago: Lewis Publishing Company, 1914), 73; *Wabash Plain Dealer*, June 28, 1899; Hackleman, *Scrapbook II*, 214.
4. Armstrong and Riker, eds., *John Tipton Papers*, 1:757.
5. Ibid., 761–66; O'Hair, *Paradise Spring*, 9; Helm, *History of Wabash County*, 93; Weesner, *History of Wabash County*, 72, 73.
6. *Wabash Plain Dealer*, July 11, 1879.
7. Weesner, *History of Wabash County*, 73; *Wabash Plain Dealer*, July 11, 1879; *Wabash Republican*, July 14, 1871; Helm, *History of Wabash County*, 109; Hackleman, *Scrapbook IV*, 92–94, *Scrapbook II*, 169; Ronald L. Woodward, ed. and comp., *Life in Wabash County: Annotated Diary of Newton Fowler for the Year 1865* (Wabash, 2006); Ware W. Wimberly, ed., *A One Hundred Twenty-five Year History of the Presbyterian Church of Wabash, Indiana* (Wabash, 1961), 11ff.
8. Paul W. Wehr, *James Hanna*, pamphlet (Fort Wayne, IN: Allen County Public Library, 1971), 1.
9. Armstrong and Riker, eds., *John Tipton Papers*, 1:569–70, 728, 794–98; Wehr, *James Hanna*, 1–3.
10. James A. M. Hanna, *James A. Hanna: Hanna of Castle Sorbie, Scotland, and Descendants* (Ann Arbor, MI: Edward Brothers, 1959), 8–17; Wehr, *James Hanna*, 1–3. The author visited Sorbie Tower in 1959, 1983, and 1992.
11. *Samuel Hanna*, 5, 7, 22; W. G. Wood, *The Life and Character of Hon. Samuel Hanna* (Fort Wayne, IN: T. S. Taylor and Company, 1869), 10; Permanent Collection, Fort Wayne Museum of Art, which includes a painting of the Samuel Hanna family, ca. 1843. Dollar conversion based on standard inflation rate over 175 years. Samuel Hanna Collection, box 118, Allen

County Historical Museum, Fort Wayne, IN; Hugh T. Hanna Papers, box 119, Allen County Historical Museum (hereafter cited as ACHM), includes partial assessments of Samuel Hanna's wealth at his death in 1866.

12. Wood, *Life and Character of Hon. Samuel Hanna*, 40–48; *Samuel Hanna*, 22ff.

13. Wood, *Life and Character of Hon. Samuel Hanna*, 42.

14. *Samuel Hanna*, 22ff; Wood, *Life and Character of Hon. Samuel Hanna*, 48; George R. Mather, *Frontier Faith: The Story of Pioneer Congregations in Fort Wayne, Indiana, 1820–1860* (Fort Wayne, IN: Fort Wayne-Allen County Historical Society, 1992), 27–29; Hanna family boxes, 118, 119, ACHM.

15. Wehr, *James Hanna*, 14; *Wabash Plain Dealer*, June 14, 21, 1866.

16. "Hugh Hanna," file, WCHM; *Samuel Hanna*, 7; Wehr, *James Hanna*, 14.

17. Logan Esarey, *The History of Indiana* (Indianapolis: Hoosier Heritage Press, 1970), 352ff; Donald Carmony, *Indiana, 1815–1850: The Pioneer Era* (Indianapolis, Indiana Historical Society and Indiana Historical Bureau, 1998), 186ff; "Hugh Hanna" file, WCHM.

18. Helm, *History of Wabash County*, 92; "Hugh Hanna" file, WCHM; Carmony, *Indiana*, 462–63; Original Plat file, WCHM; Wabash County Courthouse, Recorder's Office, facsimile of original plat of Wabash, Indiana, 1834.

19. *Wabash Courier*, May 14, 1886; Helm, *History of Wabash County*, 101; Elmer H. Cox, "Day Book," 70, WCHM; "map," box 118, Samuel Hanna Papers, box 118, ACHM; *Old Settlers Book*, 388–89; Helm, *History of Wabash County*, 112; Weesner, *History of Wabash County*, 77, 117.

20. *Wabash Plain Dealer*, September 25, 1896; *Old Settlers Book*, 43, 389; *Wabash Courier*, May 14, 1886; Weesner, *History of Wabash County*, 77, 117; Hugh Hanna file, WCHM; Hacklеman, *Scrapbook IV*, 219; *The Hoosier Packet* 2, no. 7 (July 2003); *Wabash Plain Dealer*, August 6, 1923.

21. *Wabash Weekly Intelligencer*, March 19, 1856.

22. *Old Settlers Book*, 389; R. J. Skinner, *Map of Wabash County, Indiana, 1861*, WCHM; *Illustrated Historical Atlas of Wabash County, Indiana* (Philadelphia: Hosea Paul and Company, 1875), 47; *Historic Architecture of North Wabash Historic District*, pamphlet (Wabash, IN: Wabash Market Place, 2006); Virginia McAlester and Lee McAlester, *A Field Guide to American Homes* (New York: Alfred A. Knopf, 1984), 196–209; "Hanna House," photo files, WCHM; Weesner, *History of Wabash County*, 77; Helm, *History of Wabash County*, 91.

23. "Old Mill Race," abstract, prepared 1903, in the author's files, lists Hanna's heirs and their spouses; *Illustrated Historical Atlas of Wabash County*, 45, 47; Helm, *History of Wabash County*, 216; Hanna Family file, WCHM; Weesner, *History of Wabash County*, 117; *Wabash Plain Dealer*, May 14, 1868; *Wabash Weekly Intelligencer*, April 29, 1858, April 5, 1860, February 12, 1863.

24. *Wabash Weekly Intelligencer*, March 19, 1856. The "well known Grove of Locusts" may have been an early picnic area on Hill Street west of Carroll Street.

25. "Old Mill Race," 4.

26. *Wabash Weekly Gazette*, April 16, 1853.

27. Wabash Circuit Court record, March term, 1849, Hugh Hanna file, WCHM.

28. *Wabash Weekly Gazette*, February 9, 1853.

29. *Wabash Plain Dealer*, June 9, 1860.

30. *Wabash Weekly Gazette*, July 7, August 25, 1852, February 9, 1853, September 30, 1857; *Wabash Plain Dealer*, August 22, 1859, May 19, July 28, 1860, July 25, 28, 1867; *Wabash Weekly Intelligencer*, February 20, 1856, December 15, 29, 1859, August 23, 30, 1860, October 24,

1861, November 27, 1862; Weesner, *History of Wabash County*, 81. Hugh Hanna apparently failed to obtain a mail route from Marion to Warsaw twice a week, via Wabash and Laketon, for which he wanted $1,200 a year. Armstrong and Riker, eds., *John Tipton Papers*, 3:478.

31. *Wabash Plain Dealer*, July 11, 1879; Helm, *History of Wabash County*, 196; Mary C. O'Hair, *Court Houses of Wabash County, Indiana, 1835–1960*, pamphlet (Wabash, IN: Wabash County Historical Museum, 1961); Armstrong and Riker, eds., *John Tipton Papers*, 3:149n; Weesner, *History of Wabash County*, 152ff.

32. Helm, *History of Wabash County*, 106, 109–10; *Old Settlers Book*, 43–44; Armstrong and Riker, eds., *John Tipton Papers*, 3:157–58.

33. Original Plat file, WCHM; *Wabash Plain Dealer*, August 12, 1869; James Ford, MD, "Sanitary Topography: Health as Affected by Laws Governing Local Air Currents (a New Discovery)," in Helm, *History of Wabash County*, 80–87; photo of Wabash Street, 1880, files, WCHM; photo of Wabash, 1866, files, WCHM; U.S. Department of the Interior, *Geological Survey, State of Indiana, Department of Conservation, Wabash Quadrangle* (Indianapolis, 1963).

34. Weesner, *History of Wabash County*, 114; *Wabash Weekly Intelligencer*, February 20, 1856; James Thomson to Milton Badger, April 4, 1840, April 4, 1844, in *Indiana Letters*, L. C. Rudolph, Thomas W. Clayton, and W. W. Wimberly II, eds. (Ann Arbor, MI: University Microfilms International, 1975); Asa Johnson to Charles Little, April 1, 1886, in Wimberly, ed., *One Hundred Twenty-five Year History of the Presbyterian Church of Wabash*, 29–33; W. W. Wimberly II, "Missionary Reforms in Indiana before the Civil War: Education, Temperance, Anti-slavery" (PhD diss., Indiana University, 1977).

35. *Wabash Weekly Intelligencer*, July 23, 1863.

36. Ibid., February 20, 1856, May 17, 1860, July 23, 1863, January 7, September 8, 29, 1864; *Wabash Plain Dealer*, June 16, 1860, December 27, 1866; *Wabash Weekly Gazette*, May 12, 1852.

37. Wehr, *James Hanna*, 14.

38. Hugh Hanna to Samuel Hanna, 1857, box 118, Samuel Hanna Collection, ACHM.

39. East end Lot #191, Original Plat, abstract, prepared 1984, author's files; "Hugh Hanna" file, WCHM; Ronald L. Woodward (county historian), conversation with the author, 2008. Woodward thinks Henry Sayre had negative feelings about Hanna, believing he was arrogant; in 1923 Sayre did remember him as an "aristocrat." *Wabash Plain Dealer*, July 30, 1923.

40. *Wabash Weekly Intelligencer*, April 21, 1859.

41. Ibid., January 7, February 25, 1864.

42. *Wabash Plain Dealer*, April 4, 1867; Weesner, *History of Wabash County*, 125ff.

43. *Wabash Plain Dealer*, April 4, 1867; Weesner, *History of Wabash County*, 139ff.

Chapter 3

1. James H. Madison, *The Indiana Way: A State History* (Bloomington: Indiana University Press; Indianapolis: Indiana Historical Society, 1986), 82; *Wabash Plain Dealer*, July 11, 1879.

2. R. Carlyle Buley, *The Old Northwest: Pioneer Period, 1815–1840*, 2 vols. (Indianapolis: Indiana Historical Society, 1950), 1:460–61.

3. Ibid.; *Old Settlers Book*, 388 (a record of Wabash County settler reunions, Wabash County Historical Museum).

4. "Original Plat of Wabash, with 1834 and 1838 notes" (a facsimile of the original), Recorder's Office, Wabash County Courthouse, Wabash, IN; *Wabash Plain Dealer*, July 23, 30, 1923; Susan Neff, comp., *Ford Family History Collection*, Part 4 (Charley Creek Foundation, 2006);

Wabash Tribune, February 4, 1896.

5. *Wabash Plain Dealer*, July 11, 1879, July 30, 1923; *Wabash Tribune*, February 4, 1896; *Wabash Weekly Gazette*, July 11, 1849; Neff, comp. and ed., *Ford Family History Collection*, Part 4.

6. Buley, *Old Northwest*, 2:148–49n; Clarkson Weesner, *A History of Wabash County, Indiana* (Chicago: Lewis Publishing Company, 1914), 72.

7. *Old Settlers Book*, 106–7; Thomas B. Helm, *History of Wabash County, Indiana* (Chicago: John Morris, 1884), 112.

8. Weesner, *History of Wabash County*, 114; Thomas E. Castaldi, *Wabash & Erie Canal, Notebook III: Wabash and Miami Counties* (Fort Wayne, IN: Parrot Printing, 2004), 71; Elijah Hackleman, *Scrapbook II*, 168–69, Wabash County Historical Museum (hereafter cited as WCHM).

9. "Federal Census of Cass County, Indiana, 1830," collection, Public Library, Peru, IN; Ronald L. Woodward, comp., *The United States Census, Wabash County, 1840* (Wabash, IN: R. L. Woodward, 1980), 1–27.

10. "Federal Census of Cass County"; Woodward, comp., *United States Census, Wabash County, 1840*.

11. *Old Settlers Book*, 109; Helm, *History of Wabash County*, 96, 109–10.

12. *Old Settlers Book*, 108, 132, 179, 191–93, 221, 249, 257; Hackleman, *Scrapbook IV*, 179, *Scrapbook III*, 157; Helm, *History of Wabash County*, 113.

13. Buley, *Old Northwest*, 1:145–48; Weesner, *History of Wabash County*, 77–78; Hackleman, *Scrapbook II*, 168–69; Helm, *History of Wabash County*, 101; *Old Settlers Book*, 106.

14. Weesner, *History of Wabash County*, 77–78, 304; Hackleman, *Scrapbook II*, 169; Helm, *History of Wabash County*, 101; *Old Settlers Book*, 106.

15. *Old Settlers Book*, 243; *Wabash Plain Dealer*, July 28, 1923; Helm, *History of Wabash County*, 101, 112; Hackleman, *Scrapbook II*, 169; "Original Plat of Wabash"

16. *Wabash Plain Dealer*, July 30, 1923; Castaldi, *Wabash & Erie Canal*, 71; Weesner, *History of Wabash County*, 78; *Old Settlers Book*, 114, 195.

17. *Old Settlers Book*, 317, 381; Helm, *History of Wabash County*, 109, 112; *Wabash Plain Dealer*, July 28, 1923.

18. *Wabash Plain Dealer*, January 21, 1896; "William Steele Sr.," file, WCHM; Weesner, *History of Wabash County*, 161; *Old Settlers Book*, 108–13.

19. *Old Settlers Book*, 108, 109, 243, 257; Helm, *History of Wabash County*, 97.

20. *Old Settlers Book*, 114, 195.

21. Nellie Armstrong and Dorothy Riker, eds., *The John Tipton Papers*, 3 vols. (Indianapolis: Indiana Historical Bureau, 1942), 1:364; Buley, *Old Northwest*, 1:245–47; *Old Settlers Book*, 387.

22. Castaldi, *Wabash & Erie Canal*, 47–58, helpfully summarizes several original sources, including state papers relating to the Irish War. William Giffin, *The Irish* (Indianapolis: Indiana Historical Society Press, 2006), 17–27, adds some interesting details. Other histories that deal with the event, sometimes only in passing, include Buley, *Old Northwest*, Logan Esarey, *History of Indiana* (Indianapolis: Hoosier Heritage Press, 1970), and George R. Mather, *Frontier Faith: The Story of the Pioneer Congregations of Fort Wayne, Indiana, 1820–1860* (Fort Wayne, IN: Allen County–Fort Wayne Historical Society, 1992). Susan Lawson Hamilton, *The History of Lagro: The Town—the School— the Community* [Lagro, IN: Lagro High School Alumni Committee, 2000], does not have footnotes but helps fill out the story. See also the Canal Society of Indiana publication *The Hoosier Packet* 4, no. 3 (Spring 1993) and 12, no. 4 (Fall 2001). Any good history of Great Britain will offer background on the European connection to the Irish War.

23. *Hoosier Packet* 12, no. 4 (Fall 2001).

24. Paul Fatout, *Indiana Canals* (West Lafayette, IN: Purdue University Studies, 1972), 58.

25. Ibid., 54, 65–75; *Hoosier Packet* 9, no. 3 (Summer) 1998).

26. Canal Society of Indiana *Newsletter* 9, no. 2 (Spring 1998), 9, no. 4 (Summer 1998), 14, no. 6 (June 2000); *Hoosier Packet* 5, no, 2 (February 2006).

27. Charles R. Poinsatte, *Fort Wayne during the Canal Era, 1828–1855* (Indianapolis: Indiana Historical Bureau, 1969), 61–62.

28. *Indiana Canals* 12, no. 4 (Fall 2001); *Hoosier Packet* 5, no. 8 (August 2006); Poinsatte, *Fort Wayne during the Canal Era,* 61–62. See also Fatout, *Indiana Canals*, 57, for a different calculation of wages, indicating they may have been as high as twenty-two dollars a month.

29. Buley, *Old Northwest*, 1:245–47.

30. Canal Society of Indiana *Newsletter* 15, no. 11 (November 2005).

31. Poinsatte, *Fort Wayne during the Canal Era*, 65; Hamilton, *History of Lagro*, 20–21; Giffin, *Irish*, 20–25; Samuel Newbury to Absalom Peters, November 1, 1836, and James Chute to Peters, July 6, 1833, in *Indiana Letters*, L. C. Rudolph, Thomas W. Clayton, and W. W. Wimberly II, eds. (Ann Arbor, MI: University Microfilms International, 1975).

32. *Indiana Canals* 5, no.2 (Winter 1993); Patricia B. Ebrey, *The Cambridge Illustrated History of China* (Cambridge: Cambridge University Press, 1996), 116; Fatout, *Indiana Canals*, 22–38; Buley, *Old Northwest*, 1:500–503; W. W. Wimberly II, "Missionary Reforms in Indiana before the Civil War: Education, Temperance, Anti-slavery" (PhD diss., Indiana University, 1977), 4–6.

33. Castaldi, *Wabash & Erie Canal*, 74; Hamilton, *History of Lagro*, 35; Canal Society of Indiana *Newsletter* 6, no. 1 (Fall 1994), and 6, no.2 (Winter 1994); "Leola Hockett" file, WCHM.

34. Castaldi, *Wabash & Erie Canal*, 74–76; "Leola Hockett," WCHM; Canal Society of Indiana *Newsletter* 11, no. 12 (December 1997).

35.*Old Settlers Book*, 106–7; Castaldi, *Wabash & Erie Canal*, 74–78; Helm, *History of Wabash County*, 96, 239, 247; Weesner, *History of Wabash County*, 235.

Chapter 4

1. Jesse Williams, "Report of the Chief Engineer," *Documentary Journal*, December 6, 1849, quoted in Thomas E. Castaldi, *Wabash & Erie Canal, Notebook III: Wabash and Miami Counties* (Fort Wayne, IN: Parrot Printing, 2004), 77.

2. Clarkson Weesner, *A History of Wabash County, Indiana* (Chicago: Lewis Publishing Company, 1914), 301.

3. Ronald L. Woodward, comp. *The United States Census, Wabash County, 1840* (Wabash, IN: R. L. Woodward, 1980), 19; Ronald L. Woodward, Helen Bruss, and Linda Robertson, *1850 Census of Wabash County* (Wabash, IN: Wabash Carnegie Public Library, 1983).

4. *Wabash Plain Dealer*, February 5, 1909.

5. "J. D. Conner, Jr." file, Wabash County Historical Museum (hereafter cited as WCHM). *Wabash Courier*, May 14, 1886, includes Conner's entire speech, which, unless otherwise noted, is the source for this section, including quotations.

6. *Wabash Weekly Gazette*, June 27, 1855.

7. Castaldi, *Wabash & Erie Canal*, 84; "Ferry License, 1841" file, WCHM.

8. *Wabash Courier*, May 14, 1886, contains the text of Mackey's speech. *Wabash Plain Dealer*, November 11, 1887, which, unless otherwise noted, is the source for this section, including quotations; author's inspection of Mackey tombstone in Falls Cemetery.

9. *Old Settlers Book*, 192 (a record of Wabash County settler reunions, WCHM); Ronald L.

Woodward and Gladys Dove Harvey, *Shadows of Wabash: From Native Americans to Industry* (Wabash, IN, 2005), 14–15.

10. Mary C. O'Hair, *Court Houses of Wabash County, Indiana, 1835–1960*, pamphlet (Wabash, IN: Wabash County Historical Museum, 1961); *Wabash Courier*, May 14, 1886; Elijah Hackleman, *Scrapbook IV*, 82, WCHM.

11. *Wabash Plain Dealer*, June 11, 1886; *Old Settlers Book*, 214; W. W. Wimberly II, "Missionary Reforms in Indiana before the Civil War: Education, Temperance, Anti-slavery" (PhD diss., Indiana University, 1977), 150–52.

12. Wimberly, "Missionary Reforms in Indiana before the Civil War," 140–50, 162ff; James Thomson to Absalom Peters, January 7, 1843, in *Indiana Letters*, L. C. Rudolph, Thomas W. Clayton, and W. W. Wimberly II, eds. (Ann Arbor, MI: University Microfilms International, 1975).

13. Wimberly, "Missionary Reforms in Indiana before the Civil War," 13ff; Colin Goodykoontz, *Home Missions on the American Frontier* (Caldwell, IA: Caxton Printers, 1939). Rudolph et al., eds., *Indiana Letters*, 149–50, 167, 181–82, 195, 211, 225–26, 240–42, 258–59, 286, 303–5, 330–32, 351–53, 409–11, 471, 512–13, 562–63, provide details on missionary work in Wabash in the 1830s and 1840s and provide sources for this section.

14. Weesner, *History of Wabash County*, 343–53, summarizes the growth of church life in the nineteenth century in Wabash and provides a more general overview than the AHMS letters.

15. Asa Johnson to Milton Badger, May 16, 1839, Rudolph et al., *Indiana Letters*. See also note 13.

16. Johnson to Badger, May 16, 1839, ibid.

17. Johnson to Badger, May 1842, ibid.

18. James Thomson to Milton Badger, April 23, 1840, ibid.

19. Thomson to Badger, January 7, July 3, 1843, April 4, October 10, 1844, ibid.; Ware W. Wimberly, ed., *A One Hundred Twenty-five Year History of the Presbyterian Church of Wabash, Indiana* (Wabash, 1961), 13.

20. Thomson to Badger, November 22, 1844, Rudolph et al., *Indiana Letters*.

21. Thomson to Badger, July 1, 1845, ibid.

22. Thomson to Badger, July 1, 1846, March 16, 1847, ibid.

23. Thomson to Badger, March 16, 1847, ibid.

24. Thomson to Badger, October 30, 1846, ibid.

25. Samuel D. Smith to Milton Badger, March 29, July 14, 1848, ibid.

26. Samuel D. Smith to Charles Hall, October 24, 1848, ibid.

27. Smith to Hall, April 16, July 19, 1849, ibid.

28. Smith to Hall, October 10, 1849, ibid.; Wimberly, ed., *One Hundred Twenty-five Year History of the Presbyterian Church of Wabash*, 12–14.

29. *Wabash Plain Dealer*, September 15, 1882; Elmer Cox, "Day Book," inside front cover, 45–133, WCHM. Except as otherwise noted, this section on Cox is based on his "Day Book."

30. Unless otherwise noted this section, including quotations, is based on Susan Neff, comp. and ed., *Ford Family History*, Part 4 (Charley Creek Foundation, 2006); *Wabash Tribune*, February 4, 1896.

31. Thomas B. Helm, *History of Wabash County, Indiana* (Chicago: John Morris, 1884), 98; Woodward, *United States Census, Wabash County, 1840*; Woodward, et al., *1850 Census of Wabash Count*; Cox, "Day Book"; Wimberly, ed., *One Hundred Twenty-five Year History of the Presbyterian Church of Wabash*, 11–14.

Chapter 5

1. *Wabash Weekly Gazette*, January 21, 1856.
2. Ibid., January 21, 30, 1856.
3. Ibid., January 30, 1856.
4. Ibid.
5. *Wabash Weekly Gazette*, March 21, 1855.
6. Ibid., May 30, 1855.
7. Files, Phi Gamma Delta headquarters, Lexington, KY, provided by William Martin, executive secretary; *Wabash Plain Dealer*, December 29, 1864.
8. *Wabash Weekly Gazette*, May 16, 1855.
9. Files, Phi Gamma Delta.
10. Ibid., Logan Esarey, *The History of Indiana* (Indianapolis: Hoosier Heritage Press, 1970), 2:776–81.
11. Files, Phi Gamma Delta; Richard H. Crowder, "Mystery Surrounding Life of Fiji's Founder Naaman Fletcher Dispelled by Wabash Research," *The Phi Gamma Delta Magazine* (December 1962).
12. *Wabash Weekly Gazette*, June 27, 1855.
13. Clarkson Weesner, *A History of Wabash County, Indiana* (Chicago: Lewis Publishing Company, 1914), 331–33; Thomas B. Helm, *History of Wabash County, Indiana* (Chicago: John Morris, 1884), 233–34; *Wabash Weekly Gazette*, March 21, 1855.
14. Files, Phi Gamma Delta; Weesner, *History of Wabash County*, 331–33; Helm, *History of Wabash County*, 233–34; *Wabash Weekly Gazette*, April 29, 1858; *Wabash Plain Dealer*, February 29, 1872; *Wabash Weekly Intelligencer*, April 29, 1858.
15. *Wabash Weekly Gazette*, February 20, 1849.
16. Ibid., July 11, 1849.
17. Ibid., April 20, July 11, 25, 1849.
18. Ibid., April 25, 1849.
19. Ibid., May 9, 1849.
20. Ibid., April 25, May 9, July 11, August 1, 1849.
21. Ibid., November 11, 1857.
22. Ibid.
23. *Wabash Weekly Gazette*, May 30, 1855.
24. Ibid., May 30, 1855, November 4, 1858, April 21, 1859.
25. Ibid., April 21, 1859.
26. Ibid., June 17, 1858.
27. Ibid.
28. *Wabash Weekly Gazette*, September 29, 1859.
29. Ibid., June 17, July 28, 1858, April 21, September 29, 1859.
30. Ibid., August 15, 1855, October 28, December 23, 1858, March 24, April 21, October 20, 1859.
31. Weesner, *History of Wabash County*, 144; *Wabash Weekly Gazette*, July 29, 1858.
32. *Wabash Weekly Gazette*, February 20, 1849, May 5, 1859.
33. Ibid., May 9, 1855.
34. Ibid., October 20, 1859.
35. Ibid., May 9, 1855.
36. Ibid., March 31, May 5, 1859.

37. Ibid., December 30, 1858.

38. Ibid., May 11, 1853, June 6, July 4, October 24, 1855, June 2, 1858, March 31, April 21, May 5, 1859.

39. Ibid., December 5, 1855, November 4, 1859.

40. Ibid., June 13, 1855.

41. Ibid., April 11, June 13, July 18, August 15, 1855, November 3, 1857.

42. Ibid., November 21, 1855, September 9, 1858.

43. Ibid., September 9, 1858.

44. Ibid., February 6, 1849; Helm, *History of Wabash County*, 143–44; Weesner, *History of Wabash County*, 227–29; R. Carlyle Buley, *The Old Northwest: Pioneer Period, 1815–1840*, 2 vols. (Indianapolis: Indiana Historical Society, 1950), 1:449–64; Esarey, *History of Indiana*, 1:254–60.

45. *Wabash Weekly Gazette*, February 20, 1849.

46. Ibid., February 6, 20, 1849; Ronald L. Woodward and Gladys Dove Harvey, *Shadows of Wabash: From Native Americans to Industry* (Wabash, IN, 2005), 23, 24.

47. *Wabash Weekly Gazette*, January 2, 30, February 6, 20, April 18, 1849, July 1, 1858, January 6, 1859; Woodward and Harvey, *Shadows of Wabash*, 23, 24.

48. *Wabash Weekly Gazette*, March 13, 20, 1849.

49. R. V. Skinner, *Map of Wabash County* (Hamilton, OH: R. V. Skinner, 1861); Helm, *History of Wabash County*, 143–44; Weesner, *History of Wabash County*, 227–29; *Wabash Weekly Gazette*, January 2, February 6, March 13, 20, 1849, January 6, May 5, 1859; *Wabash Weekly Intelligencer*, January 9, May 16, 1856; Woodward and Harvey, *Shadows of Wabash*, 23, 24.

50. *Wabash Weekly Gazette*, March 13, 20, 1849.

51. Helm, *History of Wabash County*, 143–44; Weesner, *History of Wabash County*, 227–28; *Wabash Weekly Gazette*, March 13, 20, 1849, January 9, 1856.

52. *Wabash Weekly Gazette*, March 24, 1859.

53. Ibid., February 17, March 24, April 21, 1859.

Chapter 6

1. Unless otherwise noted, this section on John Hubbard, including quotations, is based on material found in the *Wabash Weekly Intelligencer*, December 19, 1855, and the *Wabash Weekly Gazette*, December 12, 1855. See also "John Hubbard" file, Wabash County Historical Museum, Wabash, IN (hereafter cited as WCHM); *Wabash Weekly Gazette*, March 23, April 4, 18, September 5, December 26, 1855; *Wabash Weekly Intelligencer*, September 5, December 12, 1855; *Wabash Times*, October 31, 1895; Elijah Hackleman, *Scrapbook III*, 190, WCHM; Thomas B. Helm, *History of Wabash County, Indiana* (Chicago: John Morris, 1884), 150–52; Clarkson Weesner, *A History of Wabash County, Indiana* (Chicago: Lewis Publishing Company, 1914), 192–93.

2. "Mary C. O'Hair" and "John Hubbard" files, WCHM.

3. *Marion Chronicle-Tribune*, May 29, 1994.

4. *Wabash Courier*, January 24, 1880; *Marion Chronicle-Tribune*, May 29, 1994.

5. "John Hubbard" file, WCHM; *Wabash Courier*, January 24, 1880.

6. Mrytle Gay to Wabash County Courthouse, undated, and Mary C. O'Hair to Myrtle Gay, "John Hubbard" file.

7. *Wabash Weekly Gazette*, September 8, 22, 1859. These notations apply to the section on Samuel Hadley, including quotations, unless otherwise noted.

8. *Wabash Weekly Gazette*, May 9, 1848, August 18, 1852, March 23, 1855, February 20, 1856, February 17, July 14, 1859; *Wabash Weekly Intelligencer*, February 20, 1856, August 1, 12, December 16, 1858, April 14, 19, 1860.

9. *Wabash Weekly Gazette*, December 16, 1858, covers George Cissna's death, including quotations.

10. Ibid., June 1, 1853.

11. Ibid., September 15, 1852; *Wabash Plain Dealer*, November 17, 1859.

12. *Wabash Weekly Intelligencer*, May 16, 1855.

13. Ibid.; *Wabash Weekly Gazette*, September 15, 1852, June 1, 1853, October 28, 1857; *Wabash Plain Dealer*, November 7, 1859, contains other examples.

14. R. Carlyle Buley, *The Old Northwest: The Pioneer Period, 1815–1840*, 2 vols. (Indianapolis: Indiana Historical Society, 1950), 1:376–79; *Wabash Weekly Intelligencer*, February 10, March 24, 1859; *Wabash Weekly Gazette*, January 26, 1853.

15. *Wabash Weekly Intelligencer*, November 18, 1858.

16. Ibid., July 25, 1855, November 18, 1858; "Overseer of the Poor files, 1855–57," WCHM; *Wabash Weekly Gazette*, June 20, 1849, August 22, 1855.

17. *Wabash Plain Dealer*, March 16, 1865. Unless otherwise noted, this section on James Ford comes from Susan Neff, comp. and ed., *Ford Family History*, Part 4 (Charley Creek Foundation, 2006).

18. Weesner, *History of Wabash County*, 142.

19. *Wabash Weekly Intelligencer*, November 3, 1859.

20. *Wabash Weekly Gazette*, June 13, August 1, 1848.

21. *Wabash Weekly Intelligencer*, July 21, 1864; *Rushville Republican*, January 4, 1872; *Wabash Weekly Gazette*, July 18, 1849.

22. *Wabash Plain Dealer*, April 13, 1865; *Wabash Weekly Gazette*, July 18, 1849, January 12, April 20, May 12, 1853; *Rushville Republican*, January 4, 1872.

23. *Old Settlers Book*, 264 (a record of Wabash county settler reunions, WCHM); *Wabash Plain Dealer*, April 5, 1861.

24. *Wabash Weekly Gazette*, July 18, 1849, January 12, April 20, 1853; *Wabash Weekly Intelligencer*, March 10, 15, May 13, 1860; *Wabash Plain Dealer*, March 10, 1860, April 13, 1865; Ronald L. Woodward and Gladys Dove Harvey, *Shadows of Wabash: From Native Americans to Industry* (Wabash, IN, 2005), 135.

25. *Wabash Weekly Gazette*, May 30, July 11, 18, 1849.

26. *Wabash Republican*, June 15, 1871.

27. *Wabash Weekly Intelligencer*, September 16, 1858, January 13, 1859, May 9, 1861; *Wabash Republican*, March 30, October 5, 1871.

28. W. W. Wimberly II, "Missionary Reforms in Indiana before the Civil War: Education, Temperance, Anti-slavery" (PhD diss., Indiana University, 1977), 176–79; *Wabash Weekly Gazette*, March 2, 1853.

29. Wimberly, "Missionary Reforms in Indiana before the Civil War," 215–24; Logan Esarey, *The History of Indiana* (Indianapolis: Hoosier Heritage Press, 1970), 613–19.

30. *Wabash Argus*, February 24, 1847; "William Johnson" file, WCHM; *Wabash Weekly Gazette*, June 9, 1852; *Wabash Weekly Intelligencer*, May 30, 1855.

31. *Wabash Weekly Gazette*, May 2, June 6, 1855.

32. Ibid., May 2, 30, June 6, 1855; *Wabash Weekly Intelligencer*, June 20, 27, 1855.

33. *Wabash Weekly Gazette*, July 11, 1855.

34. *Wabash Weekly Intelligencer*, July 18, 1855.

35. Ibid., November 14, 1855.

36. Ibid., January 30, 1856.

37. *Wabash Weekly Gazette*, January 30, 1856.

38. Ibid., January 30, 1856, June 9, 1859; Esarey, *History of Indiana*, 613–19.

39. *Wabash Weekly Gazette*, February 13, 1856, June 9, 1859; *Wabash Weekly Intelligencer*, January 30, 1856; Wimberly, "Missionary Reforms in Indiana before the Civil War," 215–24.

40. *Wabash Weekly Intelligencer*, March 12, 1856.

41. *Wabash Weekly Gazette*, November 28, 1855.

42. Ibid., January 30, 1849, November 28, 1855; Esarey, *History of Indiana*, 698–702.

43. Esarey, *History of Indiana*, 702–14; *Wabash Weekly Gazette*, March 21, 1855.

44. *Wabash Weekly Gazette*, July 18, 1855.

45. Ibid., April 28, May 19, 1852, July 25, December 5, 1855; *Wabash Weekly Intelligencer*, June 20, 1855.

46. *Wabash Weekly Intelligencer*, June 11, 1863.

47. Ibid., June 20, 1855, October 21, 28, 1859; "Wabash High School" file, WCHM.

48. *Wabash Courier*, May 14, 1886; "Wabash High School" file.

49. Ibid.; Elijah Hackleman, *Scrapbook III*, 131; *Wabash Weekly Gazette*, September 8, 1859; *Wabash Plain Dealer*, September 1, 1860.

50. *Wabash Plain Dealer*, September 1, 1860.

51. *Wabash Weekly Gazette*, July 14, September 8, 1859.

Chapter 7

1. Except where otherwise noted, this section about Stockton Campbell, including quotations, is based on *Wabash Plain Dealer*, August 10, 24, 1865; Elijah Hackleman, *Scrapbook III*, 200, Wabash County Historical Museum (hereafter cited as WCHM); *Wabash Times*, April 6, 1898. (Additionally, the *Wabash Plain Dealer*, April 29, June 8, 1864, March 9, 1865, contains examples of Campbell's war correspondence.)

2. Clarkson Weesner, *A History of Wabash County, Indiana* (Chicago: Lewis Publishing Company, 1914), 261; Thomas B. Helm, *History of Wabash County, Indiana* (Chicago: John Morris, 1884), 207–9; "J. D. Connor Jr." file, WCHM; William C. Davis, *Rebels and Yankees: The Fighting Men of the Civil War* (London: Salawander Books, 2001), 153–67.

3. *Wabash Plain Dealer*, May 4, 1883.

4. Weesner, *History of Wabash County*, 262; *Wabash Courier*, November 20, 1885; Elijah Hackleman, Diary, 1861, WCHM; *Old Settler's Book*, 221–22.

5. *Wabash Courier*, November 20, 1885; *Wabash Plain Dealer*, April 19, 1861; *Wabash Weekly Intelligencer*, April 25, 1861.

6. Ronald L. Woodward and Gladys Dove Harvey, *Shadows of Wabash: From Native Americans to Industry* (Wabash, IN, 2005), 19; *Wabash Weekly Intelligencer*, April 25, 1861.

7. *Wabash Weekly Intelligencer*, April 25, 1861.

8. Susan Neff, comp. and ed., *Ford Family History*, Part 4 (Charley Creek Foundation, 2006).

9. Ibid.

10. Ibid.; Weesner, *History of Wabash County*, 263–65; *Wabash Plain Dealer*, August 2, 1861.

11. Neff, comp. and ed., *Ford Family History*, Part 4; Weesner, *History of Wabash County*, 263–65; *Wabash Plain Dealer*, August 2, 1861; Bruce Catton, *The Centennial History of the Civil War*, 3 vols. (New York: Doubleday and Company, 1961–65), 1:409. Other accounts of battles

in which Wabash men fought can be found in William L. Shea and Earl J. Hess, *Pea Ridge: Civil War Campaign in the West* (Chapel Hill: University of North Carolina Press, 1992); Shelby Foote, *The Civil War: A Narrative*, 3 vols. (New York: Random House, [1958–74]); Neil Kagan and Stephen G. Hyslop, *Eyewitness to the Civil War* (Washington, D.C.: National Geographic, 2007).

12. Weesner, *History of Wabash County*, 268–69; Foote, *Civil War*, 1:282–91; Kagan and Hyslop, *Eyewitness to the Civil War*, 109. Newspapers of the day are full of vignettes about military experiences. See, for example, *Wabash Weekly Intelligencer*, September 25, October 9, 1862.

13. *Wabash Plain Dealer*, January 25, 1866; *Wabash Weekly Intelligencer*, January 1, October 22, November 19, 1863; Weesner, *History of Wabash County*, 268–85; Helm, *History of Wabash County*, 198–200; Foote, *Civil War*, 3:108–11. See also *Wabash Plain Dealer*, October 12, 19, 1883, regarding articles on Fort Pillow.

14. *Wabash Plain Dealer*, May 10, 1861.

15. Weesner, *History of Wabash County*, 267–68; *Wabash Weekly Intelligencer*, March 17, 1864.

16. Weesner, *History of Wabash County*, 272–74; *Wabash Weekly Intelligencer*, September 1, 1864.

17. Weesner, *History of Wabash County*, 276–78, 471–73ff, 521; Woodward and Harvey, *Shadows of Wabash*, 42–44; *Wabash Weekly Intelligencer*, August 6, 1863, May 26, 1864; *Wabash Plain Dealer*, May 10, 24, November 29, 1861, March 22, 1866. Interestingly, Polk and James Ford had public words in print through the *Wabash Plain Dealer* in November 1861. Polk wrote that military physicians were "not worth a cuss" and that Ford, far from doing his duty, was overly familiar with brandy, had crowded patients into small quarters unnecessarily, and was prescribing medicine irresponsibly. Ford wrote to object to Polk's charges, citing his own illnesses and the unsubstantiated nature of Polk's charges.

18. *Wabash Weekly Intelligencer*, August 14, 1862; Logan Esarey, *The History of Indiana* (Indianapolis: Hoosier Heritage Press, 1970), 776–93.

19. *Wabash Weekly Intelligencer*, August 14, 1862.

20. *Wabash Plain Dealer*, January 4, 1861, March 14, 1867; *Wabash Weekly Intelligencer*, October 9, 1862; Esarey, *History of Indiana*, 776–93.

21. Mary Blair Immel, "Dismissed Union Officer Delivers Fourth of July Speech in 1863," *The Hoosier Genealogist: Connections*, vol. 46, no. 1 (2006): 4; Esarey, *History of Indiana*, 776–91.

22. All of the quotes in this section come from the *Wabash Weekly Intelligencer*, May 1, 7, 1863, May 14, 1864.

23. Immel, "Dismissed Union Officer Delivers Fourth of July Speech in 1863," 4–7; Esarey, *History of Indiana*, 776–92; *Wabash Weekly Intelligencer*, May 14, 1863.

24. *Wabash Weekly Intelligencer*, May 1, 1862, May 14, October 22, 1863; *Wabash Plain Dealer*, August 8, 1859, February 4, 1860, December 1, 1893; William S. Stitt, "The Diary of Will S. Stitt, Journal for 1863," WCHM; "Archibald Stitt" file, WCHM. Mrs. Stitt's obituary said nothing about her home-front war efforts.

25. *Wabash Weekly Intelligencer*, May 1, 1862, February 4, March 3, 1864.

26. Ibid., May 15, 1862.

27. Ibid., May 2, 1861, May 1, November 27, 1862, December 10, 1863, December 15, 1864.

28. Ibid., May 2, 1861, April 17, 1862, November 19, December 3, 1863.

29. Ibid., May 7, December 17, 1863, January 7, February 4, March 10, August 4, 11, 25, September 22, October 6, 1864; *Wabash Plain Dealer*, July 22, 1864, January 5, 12, February 28, 1865.

30. *Wabash Weekly Intelligencer*, November 15, 1860, September 8, 1864.

31. Ibid., March 21, 1861.

32. *Wabash Plain Dealer*, June 28, 1861.

33. "Wabash Union School" photo file, WCHM. An abstract for the east end of lot 191, East Sinclair Street, owned by Kenneth Crace (2010), indicates that the house was probably built in mid-century. Wabash Marketplace Inc., *Historic Architecture of the West Wabash Historic District* (Muncie, IN: Ball State University, Center for Historical Preservation et al., 2006); Virginia and Lee McAlester, *A Field Guide to American Houses* (New York: Alfred A. Knopf, 1984); *Wabash Weekly Gazette*, April 24, May 5, 1859; *Wabash Weekly Intelligencer*, April 24, 1859; *Wabash Plain Dealer*, June 28, 1861.

34. Weesner, *History of Wabash County*, 183; *Wabash Plain Dealer*, June 28, 1861; *Wabash Weekly Intelligencer*, November 11, 1858, February 25, 1864; *Wabash Weekly Gazette*, November 11, 1857, October 16, 1862. See also the *Wabash Weekly Intelligencer*, October 30, December 11, 1862, for the report of forty to fifty employees at the slaughterhouse.

35. References to merchandise, goods, and services are extremely numerous in local newspapers, both in advertisements and in reportorial comments. The following are examples used in this paragraph: *Wabash Weekly Gazette*, July 11, 1855, May 12, June 30, September 1, 1859; *Wabash Weekly Intelligencer*, December 26, 1855, June 10, November 11, 1858, April 21, September 1, November 10, 1859, July 3, 1862, February 25, 1864; *Wabash Plain Dealer*, October 3, 10, 1859.

36. Helm, *History of Wabash County*, 131–34; *Wabash Plain Dealer*, September 1, 1860; *Wabash Weekly Intelligencer*, January 12, 26, February 2, 1860, June 12, 1862.

37. *Wabash Plain Dealer*, September 1, 1860, February 20, 1863, May 19, August 31, 1865, January 21, 1869; *Wabash Weekly Intelligencer*, January 26, February 2, 1860, June 12, September 11, 1862, February 12, 1863.

38. *Wabash Plain Dealer*, August 31, 1865; *Wabash Weekly Intelligencer*, April 24, 1862.

39. *Wabash Weekly Intelligencer*, February 6, 1862.

40. Ibid., January 29, 1863.

41. Ibid., May 21, 1863; *Wabash Plain Dealer*, June 30, 1860.

42. *Wabash Plain Dealer*, June 30, 1860, November 1, 1861; *Wabash Weekly Intelligencer*, April 19, June 27, 1861.

43. *Wabash Weekly Intelligencer*, August 18, 1861, May 22, June 5, 26, 1862, May 21, June 11, November 5, 1863. Although the early town ordinances have been lost in their original state, due to fire or other mishap, they were often reported at the time in fairly complete form by the local papers.

44. *Wabash Weekly Intelligencer*, May 21, 1863. See chapter 12 for information about the railroad "cut."

45. Neff, comp. and ed., *History of the Ford Family*, Part 4; *Wabash Plain Dealer*, April 13, 1865, September 7, 1910.

46. Weesner, *History of Wabash County*, 158–59; Elijah Hackleman, *Scrapbook IV*, 127; *Wabash Courier*, July 24, 1880; Hackleman, "Diary," April 30, 1865.

47. *Wabash Plain Dealer*, January 25, February 1, 1866.

Chapter 8

1. Unless otherwise noted, information in this section related to the 1866 Moore photograph, including quotations, is based on the *Wabash Times*, January 17, 1897. See also the *Wabash Weekly Intelligencer*, March 31, 1864; Elijah Hackleman, *Scrapbook VII*, 53ff, Wabash

County Historical Museum (hereafter cited as WCHM); "Jewish Congregation" file, WCHM; Ronald L. Woodward, Helen Bruss, and Linda Robertson, *1850 Census of Wabash County*, Wabash County Public Library.

2. *Wabash Plain Dealer*, August 20, 1868, February 11, 1869.

3. *Wabash Weekly Intelligencer*, June 9, 1864; Elijah Hackleman, *Scrapbook II*, 149–64; Ware W. Wimberly, ed., *A One Hundred Twenty-five Year History of the Presbyterian Church of Wabash, Indiana* (Wabash, 1961), 24ff; "St. Matthew's Church Bell" file, WCHM; *Wabash Plain Dealer*, April 13, 1968.

4. *Wabash Plain Dealer*, August 20, 1868.

5. *Wabash Times*, January 17, 1897.

6. *Wabash Plain Dealer*, May 9, 1867.

7. *Wabash Weekly Gazette*, January 9, 1856. Examples of Wabash fires may be found in ibid., October 10, 1849, March 9, 1853, January 2, 1856; *Wabash Weekly Intelligencer*, October 31, 1855, January 16, 1856, June 10, 1858.

8. *Wabash Weekly Gazette*, October 10, 1849; *Wabash Weekly Intelligencer*, March 28, 1861.

9. *Wabash Weekly Intelligencer*, March 28, 1861; *Wabash Plain Dealer*, March 29, 1861.

10. *Wabash Weekly Intelligencer*, March 28, 1861; *Wabash Plain Dealer*, March 29, 1861.

11. *Wabash Weekly Intelligencer*, March 28, 1861.

12. Thomas B. Helm, *History of Wabash County, Indiana* (Chicago: John Morris, 1884), 240; Clarkson Weesner, *A History of Wabash County, Indiana* (Chicago: Lewis Publishing Company, 1914), 307; *Wabash Plain Dealer*, April 27, 1883; *Wabash Republican*, April 21, May 26, 1870; *Wabash Weekly Gazette*, October 31, 1855. See note 9 for examples of town fires.

13. Except where otherwise noted, the story of the 1870 fire, including quotations, comes from the *Wabash Republican*, April 21, 1870.

14. Elijah Hackleman, Diary, April 14, 1870, WCHM; Mary C. O'Hair: Courthouses of Wabash County file, WCHM; *Wabash Courier*, July 14, 1880.

15. Elijah Hackleman, *Scrapbook IV*, 127; Hackleman Diary, April 14, 1870; O'Hair: Courthouses of Wabash County file.

16. O'Hair: Courthouses of Wabash County file, 5–7; *Wabash Republican*, April 21, 1870.

17. *Wabash Plain Dealer*, November 15, 1866.

18. *Wabash Weekly Intelligencer*, May 22, 1862; *Wabash Plain Dealer*, April 11, 1872.

19. *Wabash Weekly Intelligencer*, November 6, 1862.

20. *Wabash Plain Dealer*, December 26, 1867; *Wabash Weekly Intelligencer*, February 26, 1863.

21. *Wabash Plain Dealer*, January 18, 1866, December 26, 1867, November 26, 1868; *Wabash Weekly Intelligencer*, November 28, 1861.

22. *Marion Chronicle-Tribune*, September 9, 1990; "Josiah Daugherty" file, WCHM.

23. *Wabash Plain Dealer*, November 28, 1861, August 8, December 26, 1867, November 26, 1868; Ronald L. Woodward, *Watching Wabash Grow: Businesses of 1881* (Wabash, IN: Ronald L. Woodward, 2004), 18–19; *Wabash Weekly Intelligencer*, June 17, 1858.

24. *Wabash Plain Dealer*, August 8, 1867; Woodward, *Watching Wabash Grow*, 41–43; *Biographical Memoirs of Wabash County, Indiana* (Chicago: B. F. Bowen, 1901), 219ff, 303–5, 552ff, 616.

25. Woodward, *Watching Wabash Grow*; *Wabash Plain Dealer*, January 16, February 13, 1868; "The Department of Statistics and Geology of the State of Indiana, 1879" file, WCHM; "Woodworking Industry (Wabash), 1870" file, WCHM.

26. *Wabash Weekly Intelligencer*, June 17, 1859, June 7, 1860; *Wabash Plain Dealer*, April 6, 1865, February 5, April 4, July 25, August 5, 1867, January 16, February 13, June 8, 1868; "Woodworking Industry (Wabash), 1870" file; "The Department of Statistics and Geology of the State of Indiana, 1879" file, WCHM; Woodward, *Watching Wabash Grow*, 41–43.

27. *Wabash Plain Dealer*, April 6, 1865, April 4, July 25, August 1, 1867, January 16, February 13, June 18, 1868, January 10, 1879, May 9, 1890, offer examples of industrial and business growth. Woodward, *Watching Wabash Grow*, 62; "The Department of Statistics and Geology of the State of Indiana, 1879" file; "Woodworking Industry (Wabash), 1870" file; *Wabash Weekly Intelligencer*, June 17, 1858.

28. *Wabash Plain Dealer*, April 6, 1865, April 4, May 16, July 25, August 1, 1867, February 20, June 18, October 15, November 5, 1868, February 25, 1869.

29. Ibid., February 20, 1868.

30. *Wabash Weekly Intelligencer*, June 28, 1860, August 4, 1864; *Wabash Republican*, November 2, 1871, January 4, 1872; *Wabash Plain Dealer*, February 25, 1864, April 6, November 19, 1865, May 16, July 25, August 5, 1867, October 15, 1868.

31. *Wabash Republican*, May 19, August 3, October 12, November 2, December 21, 1871; *Wabash Plain Dealer*, July 25, 1872.

32. *Wabash Republican*, May 19, 1870, June 15, November 23, 1871; *Wabash Plain Dealer*, July 25, 1872.

33. *Wabash Republican*, July 6, August 3, December 21, 1871; *Wabash Plain Dealer*, April 5, 1878; Ronald L. Woodward (Wabash County Historian), conversation with the author, March 2006.

34. *Wabash Republican*, January 5, November 9, 1871; *Wabash Plain Dealer*, February 29, March 14, 21, 28, May 16, December 5, 12, 1872.

35. Helm, *History of Wabash County*, 218–19; Weesner, *History of Wabash County*, 301ff.

36. *Wabash Plain Dealer*, March 15, 1866.

37. Ibid.

38. Ibid.; "Mayors of Wabash" file, WCHM.

39. *Wabash Weekly Intelligencer*, October 4, 1860; *Wabash Plain Dealer*, September 29, 1860.

40. *Wabash Plain Dealer*, October 27, 1860, June 13, 1872; *Wabash Weekly Intelligencer*, January 19, 1860; Weesner, *History of Wabash County*, 141ff; *Wabash Weekly Gazette*, August 11, 1859.

41. *Wabash Weekly Intelligencer*, October 13, 1864.

42. Ibid., November 8, 1860, October 15, 1863; *Wabash Plain Dealer*, July 28, August 11, 1860.

43. *Wabash Weekly Intelligencer*, November 8, 15, 1860; *Wabash Plain Dealer*, May 19, 1860.

44. *Biographical Memoirs of Wabash County*, 266ff, 314ff, 317ff, 324; "Mayors of Wabash" file; *Wabash Plain Dealer*, July 12, 1878.

45. *Wabash Plain Dealer*, January 21, March 17, 1896, May 3, 2004.

46. Common Council Records, 1865–76, Wabash City Hall; *Wabash Republican*, May 18, July 20, 1871; Ronald L. Woodward, comp., "Journal of the Rock City Hook and Ladder Company" (Wabash, IN: R. L. Woodward, 1981).

47. Wimberly, ed., *One Hundred Twenty-five Year History of the Presbyterian Church of Wabash, Indiana*, 24–25.

Chapter 9

1. Unless otherwise noted, the section on the New-Barth wedding, including quotations, is based on the *Wabash Plain Dealer*, September 23, 1880, and Elijah Hackleman, Diary, October 10, 1899, Wabash County Historical Museum (hereafter cited as WCHM). Absalom Haas had built the Opera House in 1871.

2. *Wabash Courier*, February 5, 1881.

3. *Wabash Plain Dealer*, July 29, 1887; Ronald L. Woodward, "The Wabash Jewish Experience" (Produced for the Indiana Jewish Historical Society, n.d.).

4. Unless otherwise noted, this section on Wabash Jews is based on Woodward, "Wabash Jewish Experience."

5. W. William Wimberly II, *The Jewish Experience in Indiana before the Civil War: An Introduction* (Fort Wayne: Indiana Jewish Historical Society, 1976); Howard Morley Sachar, *The Course of Modern Jewish History* (New York: Delta, 1963), 165–80.

6. Wimberly, *Jewish Experience in Indiana before the Civil War*, 1–21.

7. Ibid., 2.

8. Ibid., 7–14; Joseph Levine, *From Peddlers to Merchants* (Fort Wayne: Indiana Jewish Historical Society, 1979).

9. "Rodef Shalom" file, WCHM.

10. *Wabash Plain Dealer*, November 25, 1887.

11. Wabash Roundtable program, 1880–81, including membership list, Wabash Carnegie Public Library archives, Wabash, IN; Levine, *From Peddlers to Merchants*; *Wabash Plain Dealer*, July 9, 1868, March 3, 1882.

12. Bea Porter, "Historic Houses of Wabash" file, WCHM.

13. "Eugenia Honeywell" file, WCHM; Martha Biggerstaff Jones, conversations with the author, 2004–5, and her Honeywell House video about its history and collections.

14. Leewell H. Carpenter, *Lest We Forget: The Story of the Wabash Christian Church from Its Founding to the Present* (Wabash, IN: Published by the church, 1976); *Wabash Plain Dealer*, January 12, 1871, July 27, 1883; *Wabash Republican*, January 5, 12, 1871; Elijah Hackleman, "Christian Church Record No. 3, 1842–1909," WCHM; Thomas B. Helm, *History of Wabash County, Indiana* (Chicago: John Morris, 1884), 220–25; Clarkson Weesner, *A History of Wabash County, Indiana* (Chicago: Lewis Publishing Company, 1914), 343–66; author's tour of the sanctuary, 2006.

15. Edward D. Cochley and Gladys D. Harvey, *History of the First United Methodist Church, 1837–2000* (Wabash, IN: Printed by the church, 2000); *Wabash Plain Dealer*, June 10, 1869; *Wabash Republican*, January 5, 1871.

16. *Wabash Plain Dealer*, November 7, 1867, October 8, 1868, March 25, April 15, June 10, October 21, 1869, January 9, 1923; "St. John's AME" file, WCHM; "Friends Church" file, WCHM. The first St. Bernard's building is located (2010) in the 400 block of West Maple Street. See also Weesner, *History of Wabash County*, 343–66.

17. *Wabash Weekly Intelligencer*, August 20, 1863, January 14, 1864; *Wabash Plain Dealer*, November 26, 1868, January 8, 28, February 25, December 2, 1869, May 18, 1883.

18. *Wabash Plain Dealer*, January 14, 1869, April 26, 1878; J. C. Furnas, *The Americans: A Social History of the United States, 1587–1914* (New York: G. P. Putnam's Sons, 1969), 736ff; "WCTU" files, WCHM.

19. Ware W. Wimberly, ed., *A One Hundred Twenty-five Year History of the Presbyterian Church of Wabash, Indiana*, (Wabash, 1961), 16; *Wabash Plain Dealer*, March 1, 1866.

20. *Wabash Plain Dealer*, March 5, 22, 1866, May 27, 1869, June 8, 1871.

21. Ibid., March 1, 5, 22, April 5, 1866, May 27, 1869, June 8, 1871, June 7, 1878.

22. Ibid., June 7, 1878; First Presbyterian Church of Wabash, *Session Records*, 1836–70, 1864–97, church archives. Sackett was clerk of the session (church board) for a number of years.

23. *Wabash Plain Dealer*, July 1, 1864, August 7, 1868, February 11, September 2, 1869, September 23, 1880; *Wabash Gazette*, May 26, June 2, 9, 1859; Hackleman, *Scrapbooks III*, 343ff.

24. *Wabash Plain Dealer*, November 1, 1861, July 1, 1864, October 4, 1880.

25. Ibid., November 1, 1861.

26. Ibid., May 10, 1866, September 19, 1867, January 13, 1870, October 4, 1880; *Wabash Republican*, January 4, 1872. In the *Republican*, November 9, 1871, a journalist was disapproving of the "very unseemly" conduct of "certain misses" in the rear pew of the Methodist church. There was also journalistic disgust registered about spitting tobacco juice in church on Sundays. *Wabash Plain Dealer*, February 10, 1870; *Wabash Republican*, November 9, 1871.

27. This section on A. S. Reid and Thad Butler, including quotations, is based on the *Wabash Republican*, February 9, 16, 1871.

28. Cochley and Harvey, *History of the First United Methodist Church*; "Baptist," "Christian," "Friends," "Methodist," "Presbyterian," "Rodef Shalom," "St. Bernard's Catholic" files, WCHM.

29. *Wabash Plain Dealer*, September 8, 1860, February 18, 1869, October 25, 1878, October 2, 11, 1880, August 17, 24, September 28, 1883, September 28, 1888; "St. John's AME Church" files, WCHM; *Wabash Republican*, August 4, 1870, March 30, July 13, October 26, 1871, January 4, February 10, 1872; Ronald L. Woodward (county historian), conversation with the author, 2008; "St. John's A.M.E. Church" file, WCHM.

30. Weesner, *History of Wabash County*, 343ff; *Wabash Plain Dealer*, November 28, 1872, February 7, 1910; Cochley and Harvey, *History of the First United Methodist Church*.

31. Unless otherwise noted, this section about L. L. Carpenter is based on the *Wabash Plain Dealer*, February 14, 1910; L. H. Carpenter, *The Tall Sycamore of the Wabash* (Wabash, IN: Leewell H. Carpenter, 1971); Elijah Hackleman, *Scrapbook III*, 199.

32. Carpenter, *The Tall Sycamore of the Wabash*, 113; *Wabash Plain Dealer*, July 18, 1898; Hackleman, *Scrapbook III*, 199.

33. Unless otherwise noted, this section on Charles Little is based on Wimberly, ed., *One Hundred Twenty-five Year History of the Presbyterian Church of Wabash*; "Charles Little" file, WCHM; *Wabash Plain Dealer*, September 19, November 7, 1890; author's conversations with Martha Biggerstaff Jones, 2003–4.

34. *Wabash Plain Dealer*, October 3, 31, 1872; W. W. Wimberly II, "Missionary Reforms in Indiana before the Civil War: Education, Temperance, Anti-slavery" (PhD diss., Indiana University, 1977), covers the work of the American Home Missionary Society in Indiana and the causes it espoused. L. C. Rudolph et al., *Indiana Letters: Abstracts of Letters from Missionaries on the Indiana Frontier to the American Home Missionary Society, 1824–1893*, 3 vols. (Ann Arbor: University Microfilm International, ca. 1981) has dozens of entries related to Henry Little, Charles's uncle.

35. Photograph collection, archives, WCHM; "Charles Little" file, WCHM; *Wabash Plain Dealer*, November 2, 1883, June 6, 1890, July 28, 1896. In his later years Little was described as "a large man with a grey moustache and imperial." *Wabash Plain Dealer*, September 19, 1890.

36. *Wabash Plain Dealer*, October 19, 1899.

37. Ibid., September 23, 1880, September 21, 1883. The structure cost $22,000.

38. Photograph collection, archives, WCHM; *Wabash Plain Dealer*, September 21, November 2, 9, 23, 1883. The following sources indicate that renovations occurred after 1900: *Wabash Plain* Dealer, December 23, 1904, January 6, 1905.

39. *Wabash, Indiana, 1896* (New York: Sanford Insurance Map and Publishing Co., 1896). The author grew up in this building, which accounts for his somewhat lengthy description of the place. See also chapter 14.

Chapter 10

1. Except where otherwise noted, this section on the Biglers, including quotations, comes from the *Wabash Plain Dealer*, September 29, 1930, June 20, 1939; "Herbert Bigler" file, Wabash County Historical Museum (hereafter cited as WCHM); Wabash High School *Alumni Directory, 1872–1934* (1935), 6. Pete and Susie Jones, conversation with the author, autumn 2007; "The Bigler Collection of Letters," held by Pete and Susie Jones. In addition, Judy Cheatham of the Shelbyville County Library's genealogical department confirms that Carrie Bigler was a close relative of the well-known Hoosier author, Charles Major, but believes that evidence conflicts about whether she was his sister or his cousin. She is listed as a cousin in her *Shelbyville Democrat* obituary. Although an 1870 census lists her as living in the same household as Charles, there is no indication that she is the daughter of Stephen Major, the head of the household and Charles's father; she could have been living in her uncle's home.

2. Linda Robertson, *History of the Library* (Wabash, IN: Wabash Carnegie Public Library, 1981).

3. *Wabash Plain Dealer*, May 17, 1873; "William Winton" file, WCHM.

4. Unless otherwise noted, this section on the Winton trial, including quotations, is based on Presbyterian Church of Wabash, "Records of Session, 1858–59," pp. 12-25, Archives, The Presbyterian Church of Wabash.

5. This story of the buggy ride by two young men is an example of family lore; it is based on a verbal report to the author by Howard R. Temple, who received it from his father, Rex Temple, who was purportedly the young friend invited to ride in the buggy. There is no written documentation of the story.

6. Unless otherwise noted, this section on the Madame Lum Hong story, including quotations, comes from Elijah Hackleman, Diary, July 20, 1896, WCHM; *Wabash Plain Dealer*, July 24, 1896, February 24, 1905, December 24, 1909; *Wabash County Directory 1894* (Lima, OH: Trusler and Parmenter, 1894); "Lum Hong" file, WCHM; George and Rita Dingledy, *St. Bernard's Roman Catholic Church Records, 1871–1986*, vols. 1 and 2 (Wabash, IN: George and Rita Dingledy, 1989).

7. *Wabash Plain Dealer*, July 20, 1883.

8. *Wabash Republican*, July 6, 1871.

9. *Wabash Plain Dealer*, June 1, 1883.

10. Ibid.

11. Ibid., August 3, 1883.

12. Ibid., March 8, 1878.

13. Ibid., May 18, 1883.

14. Ibid., January 24, 31, 1890.

15. Ibid., February 7, May 4, July 27, December 7, 1883, May 26, 1896.

16. Ibid., April 27, 1883.

17. Ibid., April 27, May 4, 1883.

18. *Wabash Republican*, February 2, 1871.

19. *Wabash Plain Dealer*, May 11, 1883.

20. *Wabash Republican*, October 5, 1871; *Wabash Weekly Intelligencer*, October 3, 1861.

21. *Wabash Plain Dealer*, August 29, 1872, June 7, October 7, 1878, September 11, October 5, 1880, June 1, 1883, July 22, 1904; Elijah Hackleman, *Scrapbook III*, 193, WCHM.

22. *Wabash Plain Dealer*, May 4, 11, 1883, August 3, 1884, July 22, 1904; *Wabash Courier*, June 1, 1878.

23. *Wabash Plain Dealer*, May 11, 18, December 7, 1883.

24. Ibid., March 9, 1883.

25. *Wabash Weekly Intelligencer*, April 26, 1860.

26. Hackleman Diary, January 12, 1881; *Wabash Weekly Intelligencer*, March 3, 1864; *Wabash Plain Dealer*, June 9, 1880, May 19, 1896.

27. *Wabash Plain Dealer*, June 8, 15, 1883.

28. Ibid., June 22, 1883, April 24, June 2, 1896; *Wabash Republican*, June 15, 1871.

29. *Wabash Plain Dealer*, November 21, 1872.

30. Ibid., May 15, 1896. See *Wabash Weekly Intelligencer*, September 1, 1864, for another example.

31. *Wabash Plain Dealer*, June 21, 1864.

32. Ibid., July 13, 1883; Ronald L. Woodward and Gladys Dove Harvey, *Shadows of Wabash: From Native Americans to Industry* (Wabash, IN, 2005), 47. The *Wabash Plain Dealer* of January 15, 1892, records a woman thrown from a buggy and impaled on the courthouse fence. She survived.

33. *Wabash Plain Dealer*, April 14, 1893, July 7, 1908; "Nancy Everly" file, WCHM; Gene Stratton-Porter, *The White Flag* (New York: Doubleday, Page and Company, 1923).

34. *Wabash Weekly Intelligencer*, February 3, 1859.

35. The remainder of this section, including quotations, on the Orphan's Home comes from the *Wabash Plain Dealer*, May 31, 1889, May 30, 1890, February 7, May 1, June 9, October 9, 1896; Woodward and Harvey, *Shadows of Wabash*, 34–35; "Orphan's Home" file, WCHM.

Chapter 11

1. *Wabash Republican*, May 18, 1871.

2. *Wabash Plain Dealer*, January 21, 1896.

3. Ibid., March 24, 1896.

4. Ibid., March 17, 1882, February 14, March 24, 1896.

5. Ronald L. Woodward and Gladys Dove Harvey, *Shadows of Wabash: From Native Americans to Industry* (Wabash, IN, 2005), 111; *Wabash Plain Dealer*, October 31, December 5, 26, 1859, January 2, 1860; *Wabash Weekly Intelligencer*, November 10, 1859.

6. *Wabash Weekly Gazette*, June 13, 1855; *Wabash Weekly Intelligencer*, July 11, 1855.

7. *Wabash Plain Dealer*, June 22, 1883; Clarkson Weesner, *A History of Wabash County, Indiana* (Chicago: Lewis Publishing Company, 1914), 182–83; "Fairs" file, Wabash County Historical Museum (hereafter cited as WCHM); "Leda Hochet" file, WCHM; *Marion Tribune-Chronicle*, July 27, 1986; *Wabash Weekly Intelligencer*, July 12, 1860; *Wabash Republican*, September 28, 1871.

8. Weesner, *History of Wabash County*, 182–83; *Marion Chronicle-Tribune*, July 27, 1986; "Leola Hockett" file; *Wabash Weekly Intelligencer*, October 7, 1858, June 21, July 12, 1860,

October 1, 1863; *Wabash Plain Dealer*, October 11, 1861, July 11, 1872, June 12, July 7, 1896; *Wabash Republican*, September 28, 1871; *Wabash Weekly Gazette*, October 7, 28, 1857, September 8, 1859; Elijah Hackleman, Diary, July 4, 1889, WCHM; *Old Settlers Book* (a record of Wabash county settlers reunions and meetings at annual fairs, WCHM); *Marion Tribune Chronicle*, July 27, 1986.

9. *Wabash Weekly Gazette*, July 11, 1855, May 5, 1859; *Wabash Republican*, February 15, 1872; *Wabash Plain Dealer*, October 10, 1859; *Wabash Weekly Intelligencer*, June 27, 1855, February 10, 1858.

10. *Wabash Weekly Intelligencer*, March 24, 1859, January 12, March 1, 22, 1860, February 11, 1864; *Wabash Plain Dealer*, December 21, 1860, October 26, 1883, March 14, 1890; *Wabash Weekly Gazette*, January 2, 9, 1849; *Old Settlers Book*, 248.

11. *Wabash Plain Dealer*, January 23, 1860, March 3, 1896.

12. Ibid., August 12, 1864, July 27, 1883; *Wabash Weekly Gazette*, August 4, 1859; *Wabash Weekly Intelligencer*, August 29, September 26, 1855.

13. *Wabash Weekly Intelligencer*, June 6, 1855, May 21, 1863; *Wabash Weekly Gazette*, June 13, 1855.

14. *Wabash Plain Dealer*, February 29, March 7, 1872.

15. Ibid., July 26, 1878, April 21, 24, June 5, September 1, 1896; *Wabash Courier*, June 1, 1878.

16. *Wabash Republican*, April 27, 1871.

17. *Wabash Plain Dealer*, July 25, 1867, July 12, 1870, May 11, July 6, 27, 1883, February 14, 21, 28, 1890, September 7, 1910; *Wabash Republican*, April 27, 1871.

18. "Wabash Athletic Association" file, WCHM; Woodward and Harvey, *Shadows of Wabash*, 120. WCHM also holds in its archives copies of *Diaries of Calvin Stephen Hutchins*, a founder of the Wabash Athletic Association.

19. *Wabash Plain Dealer*, March 16, 1883, January 21, August 4, 15, 21, September 22, 1896; Woodward and Harvey, *Shadows of Wabash*, 112; *Wabash Republican*, March 23, May 25, 1871.

20. *Wabash Plain Dealer*, June 8, 1883.

21. Hackleman Diary, January 5–9, 1895.

22. *Wabash Plain Dealer*, November 21, 1859.

23. Ibid., May 10, 1866, October 26, 1883, February 1, 1884, April 21, June 26, 1896; *Wabash Intelligencer*, March 9, 1860; Hackleman Diary, January 19, 1887.

24. Hackleman Diary, May 19–25, 1867.

25. Ibid., July 13, October 2, 7, 1871, October 2, 1872, July 4, 1878, July 31, 1887; *Wabash Gazette*, July 28, 1859; *Wabash Plain Dealer*, June 21, 1861, July 13, 1883.

26. Hackleman Diary, December 31, 1863.

27. *Wabash Intelligencer*, January 7, 1864.

28. Ibid., February 6, 1856; *Wabash Gazette*, December 26, 1855.

29. *Wabash Gazette*, November 15, 1855, November 11, 1857.

30. Ibid., May 30, 1858.

31. *Wabash Intelligencer*, June 17, 1858.

32. Ibid., December 30, 1858.

33. Ibid., June 17, 1858, May 26, 1859, January 1, 1863; author's conversation with local historian, Pete Jones, 2008; *Wabash Plain Dealer*, April 14, 1860.

34. Hackleman Diary, June 2, 1883; *Wabash Plain Dealer*, February 9, 1883.

35. *Wabash Plain Dealer*, September 21, 1883, March 27, April 3, 1896; *Wabash*

Intelligencer, December 1, 1859.

36. *Wabash Gazette*, February 8, 1848; *Wabash Intelligencer*, October 14, November 11, 1858, February 10, November 10, 1859.

37. This section on the Round Table is based on "Round Table" files held by the Wabash Carnegie Public Library (hereafter cited as WCPL), including a collection of programs, minutes, and various undated papers; and on the *Wabash Plain Dealer*, January 17, 1890, February 21, March 13, 1896, June 5, 1900.

38. This section on the public library is based on the "Round Table" files, including a copy of a letter from Mrs. C. E. Cowgill to Andrew Carnegie; "Constitution, Women's Library Association"; and WCPL file, WCHM.

Chapter 12

1. *Wabash Plain Dealer*, January 6, 1870. Except as otherwise noted, this section on the 1879 courthouse, including quotations, is based on Mary C. O'Hair, *Courthouses of Wabash County* (Wabash County Historical Museum, 1960); "Leola Hockett" and "Wabash County Courthouse" files, Wabash County Historical Museum (hereafter cited as WCHM); Wabash County, *Records of the County Commissioners*, especially Book J, 1876–79, pp. 517–55 Wabash County Courthouse.

2. Clarkson Weesner, *A History of Wabash County, Indiana* (Chicago: Lewis Publishing Company, 1914), 159.

3. Martha Biggerstaff Jones formed an opinion about eastern European influence after seeing a building in that part of the world that strongly resembled the 1879 courthouse.

4. *Wabash Plain Dealer*, August 23, 1878.

5. *Wabash Courier*, May 18, 1878; *Wabash Plain Dealer*, March 15, 1878. A perch is 5.5 yards in length or 24.75 cubic feet of stone.

6. *Wabash Plain Dealer*, January 31, 1879.

7. The author took measurements of the fence at the cemetery, February 2008.

8. *Wabash Plain Dealer*, November 22, 1878, May 11, 1883.

9. Ibid., May 10, 1878.

10. Weesner, *History of Wabash County*, 160–61.

11. Ibid., 161–62.

12. *Wabash Plain Dealer*, November 1, 1880. This section on the Brush lights is also based on the Wabash Common Council "Records," 1880, which are located at the Wabash City Hall.

13. *Wabash Plain Dealer*, September 7, 1910.

14. Ibid., July 4, 1976; "Wabash County Courthouse" file, WCHM.

15. L. H. Carpenter, *The Tall Sycamore of the Wabash* (Wabash, IN: Leewell H. Carpenter, 1971), 123.

16. *Wabash Plain Dealer*, January 6, 9, 26, March 16, November 2, 9, 1883.

17. Ibid., April 13, 1883.

18. Ibid., July 4, 1976; "Wabash County Courthouse" file, WCHM. Courthouse Brush lights were replaced with incandescent lights in 1888. Elijah Hackleman, Diary, June 13, 1888, WCHM.

19. Elijah Hackleman, *Scrapbook III*, 218–22, WCHM; *Wabash Plain Dealer*, March 29, 1878; Weesner, *History of Wabash County*, 300–4.

20. H. Paul, *Atlas of Wabash County, Indiana* (Philadelphia: Hosea Paul and Company, 1875).

21. J. W. Shea, *Map of the City of Wabash* (Philadelphia: Hosea Paul and Company, 1888).

22. Robert Woods, *Map of Wabash, Indiana, 1891*, WCHM; "Wabash Maps" file, ibid.

23. Unless otherwise noted, the section on South Wabash (South Side), including quotations, is based on Ronald L. Woodward, *From South Wabash to South Side: 113 Years of Progress* (Wabash: R. L. Woodward, 2007); Howard Williams, "The Wabash Female Seminary" (master's thesis, Indiana University, 1932); Mrs. Robert Abernathy, Mrs. Walter Schuckard, Harold Burkholder, Irene Hoffmart, eds. and publishers, "The South Side: A Thriving Community on the South Banks of the Wabash," 1954, "South Wabash" file, WCHM.

24. *Wabash Weekly Intelligencer*, August 16, 1860.

25. *Wabash Plain Dealer*, August 1, 1867, August 13, 1868, March 18, July 4, 8, 1869; *Wabash Republican*, September 7, October 5, 1871.

26. *Wabash Plain Dealer*, October 24, 1890.

27. Ibid., May 26, 1896.

28. Weesner, *History of Wabash County*, 201, 278, 293, 304–5, 346, 356; *Wabash Plain Dealer*, December 31, 1880, November 22, 1927, September 27, 2006; *Wabash Courier*, December 11, 1880, January 1, 1881; Jack Francis (who owns the Smith home, 2010), conversation with the author; Pete Jones, conversation with the author, 2010.

29. Weesner, *History of Wabash County*, 309–11; Hackleman Diary, March 14, 26, April 2, 16, 30, 1887; Richard L. Bird, conversations with the author, 2008. Bird grew up in the Blount house; he and the author toured the house in 2008.

30. The name "Tin Cup" has been passed down by word of mouth; a printed source for this information has eluded the author.

31. Unless otherwise noted, the section on the Big Four shops fire is based on the *Wabash Plain Dealer*, October 24, 26, 1894.

32. Sanborn maps, 1896; *Wabash Plain Dealer*, January 14, February 21, March 24, April 21, August 28, September 22, 1896; Hackleman, *Scrapbook VII*, 46; Hackleman Diary, October 21, 1896.

33. Sanborn maps, 1887, 1893; "Wabash Street Bridge" file, WCHM; George Courtright, "Wabash Street Bridge" (paper, August 3, 1961), ibid; *Wabash Plain Dealer*, March 27, 1896.

34. Photograph collection, including the Frank DePuy collection, WCHM. The DePuy collection includes many informal, high-quality late-nineteenth-century photographs of citizens, buildings, and streets. *Wabash Plain Dealer*, September 28, 1880, February 14, March 24, 1896; Sanborn maps, 1887, 1893, 1896.

35. *Wabash Plain Dealer*, March 21, 1890.

36. Unless otherwise noted, this section on industry is based on the Sanborn maps, 1887, 1893, 1896, 1901; *Wabash Plain Dealer*, March 27, 1878, February 4, March 29, October 16, 30, 1896; Woodward, *Watching Wabash Grow: Businesses in 1881* (Wabash, IN: Ronald L. Woodward, 2004).

37. *Wabash Plain Dealer*, May 17, 1878; April 20, 1883.

38. Ibid., March 20, 27, April 28, September 11, 1896; "Board of Trade," "Diamond Paper Mill (aka Diamond Match Company)" files, WCHM.

39. *Wabash Courier*, May 18, 1878; Mary C. O'Hair, "Courthouses of Wabash County" file, WCHM; "Woodworking Industry, Wabash, Department of Statistics and Geology, State of Indiana" file, 1879, WCHM.

40. The types and locations of downtown businesses of the period are made plain on the Sanborn maps; the 1896 and 1901 maps are especially pertinent to this section.

41. *Wabash Plain Dealer*, April 20, June 29, August 24, 1883, October 31, November 28, 1890, September 12, 25, October 30, 1896.

42. Sanborn maps, "Wabash," 1887, 1893, 1896, 1901. See also the *Wabash Plain Dealer*, February 21, March 6, 1896, for conditions of the canal. The Sanborn maps do not help settle an age-old question about the existence and purpose of downtown subterranean, man-made caverns, a topic, which, in the twenty-first century, continues to be discussed, if not argued over, among local cognoscenti. Whatever the full truth may be, it is manifest that beneath some (possibly many) downtown sidewalks there exist excavated spaces or "vaults" that have, or had, both doors and sizable windows opening into the basements of commercial buildings along Canal and Wabash streets and possibly along others. Referred to popularly as "tunnels," these spaces are often constructed of rough limestone blocks of an early era. Spaces range in width from approximately two and a half to seven feet and rise in height from basement floor level to the sidewalk. Through most of the twentieth century downtown sidewalks were punctuated with railed-in openings with downward steps that led to commercial basements. In some places artificial basement lighting shining into these spaces through doors and windows was augmented by natural lighting that radiated down through sidewalk openings. Sometimes sidewalk manhole covers that had been studded with lenses of clear glass were used; one of these covers still exists (2010) at the southwest corner of Wabash and Canal streets, casting considerable illumination into the vault beneath. A feature of these spaces in the twenty-first century is the fact that they are not tunnel-like at all because they are segmented—blocked—by impenetrable walls constructed roughly at property lines. These segmented spaces are typically referred to as "vaults."

An oft-repeated theory is that uninterrupted "tunnels" had once incorporated the later "vaults" and radiated into the business district from the main canal dock on the southwest corner of Wabash and Canal streets, where the old Bradley building (Francis building, 2010) stands. Tunnels would have penetrated north on Wabash Street, west on Canal Street, and possibly farther. Carts or trams pushed by men, or even pulled by donkeys, carried cargo from the dock to basement storage areas, both avoiding weather in the process and completing deliveries without the necessity of carting cargo up to street level from the canal and then back down stairs to basements.

A few observations support this idea. One is that the same barriers that presently divide the "tunnels" into separated "vaults" sometimes appear to be of later construction than the "tunnel" walls themselves. Second, an objection that few of the buildings that would have been served by these spaces date from the canal era is answered by a supposition that, in some cases, original (canal era) foundations were incorporated into later structures. Third, the presence of surprisingly large windows opening from basements into the "tunnels" suggests that merchants had a desire to lighten the darkness of the "tunnels" with artificial light from their basements.

Some civic leaders tend to support the reality of "tunnels," though no definite proof has been offered and, to date, no ancient blueprints (of Hanna's Corner, for example) have surfaced to lend credibility to the "tunnels" theory. Neither has any other written material (old newspapers, diaries, business papers, canal-related data) surfaced to support it. On the other side of the issue, in addition to a lack of hard evidence, is the testimony of Richard L. Bird, a third-generation Wabash abstractor and previous owner of one of the Victorian-era buildings on Wabash Street, who has told the author that he has no knowledge of any abstract passing through his company's hands that would substantiate the presence of a "tunnel" on the properties in question.

The author has inspected a few of the spaces in question and has consulted with the following persons on the "tunnel" v. "vault" debate: Kent Henderson, Richard L. Bird, Thomas Kelch,

Jack Francis, Ronald L. Woodward, Pete Jones, Thomas Castaldi, Brian Haupert, and Heather Allen.

43. Weesner, *History of Wabash County*, 306ff; author's tour of the building, 2008.

44. *Wabash Plain Dealer*, May 11, 18, 1883; Weesner, *History of Wabash County*, 306ff.

45. Wabash Common Council Records, 1881–85; *Wabash Plain Dealer*, September 21, 1883, February 4, March 27, 31, April 24, May 1, 12, 19, 1896, May 19, 1909. A few newspaper examples of the council's regular concerns can be found in *Wabash Plain Dealer*, June 8, 15, 1883, February 1, 1884, June 13, November 14, 1890, May 5, 25, June 15, 26, 1896; Hackleman Diary, June 8, 1900. It is generally believed that the football ticket office on the Wabash High School campus (2010) is constructed of recycled bricks from Wabash streets.

46. *Wabash Courier*, May 25, 1878.

47. *Wabash Plain Dealer*, May 9, 12, 1890; "Mayors of Wabash" file, WCHM.

48. *Wabash Plain Dealer*, November 16, 1888.

49. James H. Madison, *The Indiana Way: A State History* (Bloomington: Indiana University Press; Indianapolis: Indiana Historical Society, 1986), 210–11; *Wabash Plain Dealer*, November 9, 1888, August 8, 1890.

50. *Wabash Plain Dealer*, February 7, September 5, 1890, February 5, April 21, May 1, 8, November 3, 1896, November 6, 2006.

51. Ibid., January 3, 1890, March 24, July 14, August 11, September 11, 1896.

52. Weesner, *History of Wabash County*, 285–86. Except where otherwise noted, this section on the Spanish-American War, including quotations, comes from material found in Ronald L. Woodward, *Wabash County and the Spanish-American War* (Wabash, IN: R. L. Woodward, 2008), sections 1 and 2.

53. Unless otherwise noted, this section on Rose Kidd Beere comes from Woodward, *Wabash County and the Spanish-American War*, section 3; *The Colorado Magazine of History* 26, no. 3 (July 1949): 161–65.

54. "Masonic Lodge" file, WCHM; "Hanna Lodge #61, Masonic Order" file, WCHM.

Chapter 13.

1. Except where otherwise noted, this section on the Wabash schools is based on Wabash City Schools Records, 1887–97; *Wabash Times*, October 28, 1897; *Mirror*, 1897 (Wabash yearbook), 4, 7–9, 65–67, 83–87; Wabash Common Council Records, 1890–96; "Wabash Schools" file, Wabash County Historical Museum (hereafter cited as WCHM); "Wabash Schools at Work, 1946," compiled by the Wabash School Corporation; Gladys Dove Harvey and Martha Biggerstaff Jones, *A History of Wabash High School*; Ronald L. Woodward, "Centennial 2000" (paper, n.d.), WCHM; H. Paul, "Map of Wabash," in *Historical Atlas of Wabash County, Indiana* (Philadelphia: Hosea Paul and Company, 1875), 47; Sanborn insurance maps of Wabash for 1883, 1887, 1896, and 1901. Although the author believed his choice of the term "acropolis" to describe the bluff top of Wabash was original with him, he has discovered that Steve Jones, correspondent for the *Marion Courier-Times*, used the term when writing about the courthouse for the June 23, 1985, edition of that paper.

2. Clarkson Weesner, *A History of Wabash County, Indiana* (Chicago: Lewis Publishing Company, 1914), 187–88; Ronald L. Woodward, comp., *The 1870 Census of Wabash County, Indiana*, compiled from the U.S. government census records, Wabash Carnegie Public Library (hereafter cited as WCPL); Trusler and Parmeter, *Wabash County Directory, 1894* (Lima, OH, 1894); Helen M. Bruss, comp., "1880 Census of Wabash County," WCPL.

3. *Wabash Plain Dealer*, March 20, 24, 27, 1896.

4. Ibid., March 14, 1890; *Mirror*, 8.

5. Robert and Laurie Kiefaber, Bill Stouffer, and possibly other citizens own pieces of decorative stonework from the high school, including grotesques.

6. Unless otherwise noted, this section on Adelaide Steele Baylor, including quotations, is based on Ronald L. Woodward and Gladys Dove Harvey, *Shadows of Wabash: From Native Americans to Industry* (Wabash, IN, 2005), 116; *Wabash Plain Dealer*, March 14, 1911, May 15, 1922, May 27, 1959; "Adelaide Steele Baylor" file, WCHM.

7. *Wabash Plain Dealer*, February 4, 1896; *Mirror*, 66–67.

8. Weesner, *History of Wabash County*, 182–86; "Maps of Wabash" file, 1888 map and Woods's 1891 map, WCHM; Ronald L. Woodward (county historian), conversation with the author, 2006.

9. *Wabash Plain Dealer*, October 26, 1977. Ronald L. Woodward's "Index to Falls Cemetery," WCHM, reproduces an original designation of "colored" interments.

10. *Wabash Plain Dealer*, March 22, 1878, March 23, September 21, 1883, March 28, June 20, 1890, May 1, 1896; Weesner, *History of Wabash County*, 241–43.

11. Unless otherwise noted, this section on domestic architecture is based on Virginia and Lee McAlester, *A Field Guide to American Houses* (New York: Alfred A. Knopf, 1984); Wabash Marketplace Inc., *Historic Architecture of Wabash* (Wabash Marketplace, 2006); author's visual inspection of the properties covered.

12. *Wabash Plain Dealer*, October 16, 1899.

13. Mary Ellen Gadski, "History of the Atkinson, Hess and Ford House" (compiled for Richard E. Ford, 1987–88); "A. M. Atkinson" file, including extracts from the *Wabash Plain Dealer*, June 1, 1883, through September 5, 1893; *Wabash Plain Dealer*, September 7, 1883, October 16, 1899.

14. *Wabash Plain Dealer*, July 8, 1887.

15. Ibid., April 27, July 13, 1883.

16. *Biographical Sketches of Wabash County, Indiana* (Chicago: B. F. Bowen, 1901), 414–18; Priscilla Walter Jasen, conversation with the author, 2008. Jasen's husband is the CEO of the B. Walter Company.

17. This section on W. P. Jones, including quotations, is based on *Biographical Sketches of Wabash County*, 552–54; *Wabash Plain Dealer*, October 16, 1899; Stephen Jones, "Sketch of W. P. Jones," 2008; Pete Jones, conversations with the author, 2008.

18. *Biographical Sketches of Wabash County*, 610–11; Kent Henderson, conversation with the author. Henderson owns the Sharpe house.

19. *Wabash Plain Dealer*, March 12, 1897, October 16, 1899, April 20, 1977.

20. Ibid., May 5, 1896, March 12, 26, 1897.

21. Susan Neff, Comp. and ed., *Ford Family History Collection,* Part 8 (Charley Creek Foundation, 2006).

22. Weesner, *History of Wabash County*, 533–35; Heather Allen (WCHM archivist), conversations with the author. Allen owns the Latchem house.

23. *Wabash Plain Dealer*, February 12, 1903.

24. "Our Heritage Houses" photo file, WCHM, and in *Wabash Plain Dealer*, September 22, 1967. See also *Wabash Plain Dealer*, June 21, 28, 1878, April 7, 1882, February 12, 1903.

25. *Wabash Times*, Board of Trade Edition, 1897; *Wabash Plain Dealer*, September 17, 1909; *Wabash Times*, March 24, 1899; "Our Heritage Houses" file, WCHM.

26. *Wabash Plain Dealer*, March 15, 1878; *Wabash Times*, March 24, 1899; "Our Heritage Houses" photo file.

27. Abstract, Lot 191, Original Plat, Wabash, Indiana, August 24, 1848; Kenneth Crace (the house's owner), conversation with the author, 2006.

28. *Wabash Plain Dealer*, October 10, 1927; Peter Jones conversation with the author, 2007. Jones is the grandson of Edward Kemp Jones.

29. Robert and Laurie Kiefaber, conversation with the author, 2006. The Kiefabers own the house and have been publicly recognized for their restoration work on it. "Charles S. Haas" file, WCHM; Weesner, *History of Wabash County*, 473–75.

30. "Our Heritage Houses" photo files; Weesner, *History of Wabash County*, 566–67, 588–89; *Biographical Sketches of Wabash County*, 304–6; *Wabash Plain Dealer*, February 9, 1897, July 16, 1949.

31. The undocumented tales about Mrs. George King and Gene Stratton-Porter come to the author from county historian Ronald L. Woodward and from Wabash attorney Joseph Eddingfield, whose father once owned the King mansion. Other sources include the *Wabash Times*, June 4, 1917; *Wabash Free Trader*, October 24, 1873; Marriage Records, Wabash County, 1835–81, WCPL; and Ronald L. Woodward, *The 1870 Census* (Wabash, IN: WCPL, 1982).

32. *Biographical Sketches of Wabash County*, 304–6.

33. Ibid., 284–88; *Wabash Times*, April 7, 1924.

34. "Wabash Importing Company" file, "How It All Began," WCHM; "Belgium Draft Horse Association of America" file, WCHM.

35. Paul, *Historical Atlas of Wabash County*, 43; Sanborn insurance maps, 1896, 1901; *Wabash Times*, May 27, 1918; Linda Gable, conversation with the author. William and Linda Gable own the house.

36. Unless otherwise noted, this section on Thomas McNamee, including quotations, is based on the *Wabash Plain Dealer*, June 1, 1916. Information about the house comes from sources cited in note 11.

37. *Biographical Sketches of Wabash County*, 240–42; Weesner, *History of Wabash County*, 573; "Thomas McNamee" file, WCHM.

38. *Wabash Times*, August 21, 1920; Weesner, *History of Wabash County*, 668–70.

39. Reuben Lutz's large Queen Anne house that was located on the southeast corner of Cass and Market streets was an especially lavish example of that style; a photograph of it appears in the *Wabash Times*, Board of Trade edition, 1897; *Wabash Plain Dealer*, February 21, 1927, September 23, 1935.

40. *Wabash Plain Dealer*, January 18, 1901; Elijah Hackleman, Diary, May 22, August 25, November 25, 1865, November 25, 1867, WCHM; Elijah Hackleman, *Scrapbook III*, 153–55, WCHM; *Wabash County History* (1976), 313.

41. Hackleman Diary, July 4, 1878.

42. Ibid., March 16, 1870, August 31, September 11, October 1, 7, 10, 29, November 12, 27, 30, 1889, December 6, 1893.

43. Ibid., January 31, 1861, December 16, 1862, May 30, 1869, August 4, 1884, March 11, 1889, November 24, 1890, December 2, 1892, March 13, December 2, 1893, last page (n.d.), 1901; *Wabash Plain Dealer*, January 18, 1901.

44. Weesner, *History of Wabash County*, 493–95.

45. *Biographical Sketches of Wabash County*, 332–36; Weesner, *History of Wabash County*, 493–95.

46. Weesner, *History of Wabash County*, 493–95; "J. D. Conner" file, WCHM.

47. *Wabash Plain Dealer*, June 1, 1883, November 3, 1899; Weesner, *History of Wabash County*, 281–82.

48. *Wabash Courier*, July 2, 1886; Weesner, *History of Wabash County*, 281–82; "Memorial Hall" file, letter to the mayor of Wabash, May 31, 1984, regarding the Memorial Hall cannon, WCHM; *Marion Courier-Tribune*, January 18, 1897.

Chapter 14

1. Logan Esarey, *The History of Indiana* (Indianapolis: Hoosier Heritage Press, 1970), 979–80.
2. W. Somerset Maugham, *The Razor's Edge* (Middlesex, UK: Penguin Books, 1944), 10.

Index

Page numbers in italics refer to illustrations